To Hear Only Thunder Again

STUDIES IN MODERN AMERICAN HISTORY

Series Editor: Allan J. Lichtman, American University

This series will publish works that make an original contribution to historical knowledge through new evidence, methods, and ideas. It will cover the period from the mid-nineteenth century to the present and range broadly across fields of study. We especially invite manuscripts and proposals that integrate archival research with interdisciplinary methods.

Social Change and the Empowerment of the Poor: Poverty Representation in Milwaukee's Community Action Programs, by Mark Edward Braun

The Origins of the Southern Strategy: Two-Party Competition in South Carolina, by Bruce H. Kalk

To Hear Only Thunder Again: America's World War II Veterans Come Home, by Mark D. Van Ells

To Hear Only Thunder Again

America's World War II Veterans Come Home

Mark D. Van Ells

LEXINGTON BOOKS
Lanham • Boulder • New York • Oxford

LEXINGTON BOOKS

Published in the United States of America
by Lexington Books
4720 Boston Way, Lanham, Maryland 20706

12 Hid's Copse Road
Cumnor Hill, Oxford OX2 9JJ, England

British Library Cataloguing in Publication Information Available

Library of Congress Cataloging-in-Publication Data

Van Ells, Mark D. (Mark David), 1962–
    To hear only thunder again: America's World War II veterans come
home / Mark D. Van Ells.
        p.   cm.—(Modern American history)
    Based on the author's thesis (doctoral—University of Wisconsin-Madison).
    Includes bibliographical references and index.
    ISBN 0-7391-0243-5 (alk. paper)—ISBN 0-7391-0244-3 (pbk.: alk. paper)
    1. Reconstruction (1939–1951)—Wisconsin.   2. World War, 1939–1945—
Veterans—Wisconsin.   3. Veterans—Legal status, laws, etc.—United States.
4. Wisconsin—History—20th century.   I. Title.   II. Modern American
history (Lanham, Md.).

D828.W6 V36 2001
305.9'069709775—dc21   00-054600

Printed in the United States of America

♾™ The paper used in this publication meets the minimum requirements of American
National Standard for Information Sciences—Permanence of Paper for Printed Library
Materials, ANSI/NISO Z39.48–1992.

Contents

Preface

At the conclusion of his book *Brave Men*, journalist Ernie Pyle—the celebrated spokesman of the American World War II soldier—described an eerie moment he experienced during his travels through northern France with American troops in the summer of 1944:

> Last night we had a violent electrical storm around our countryside. The storm was half over before we realized that the flashes and crashings around us were not artillery but plain old-fashioned thunder and lightning. It will be odd to hear only thunder again. You must remember that such little things as that are in our souls, and will take time.

As American forces drove toward Germany that summer, Pyle told his readers that with World War II drawing to a close "thousands of our men will soon be returning home to you," and warned that those who served and fought in the conflict would require a period of readjustment to civilian life. "They have been gone a long time and they have seen and done and felt things you cannot know," he told America. "They have changed. They will have to learn how to adjust themselves to peace."[1] Pyle was eventually killed in combat in the Pacific at the tail end of the war. Although the great spokesman for the American GI did not survive the war, sixteen million American veterans of World War II did return to civilian life. Their return home is one of the most significant yet neglected stories in American history.

World War II was by far the most important military conflict in twentieth-century American history, and second only to the Civil War in terms of the number of casualties. More Americans donned a uniform during World War II than in any other conflict. According to the U.S. Veterans' Administration (VA), living participants of World War II numbered 16,051,000 when the government declared an official end to the conflict on July 25, 1947. The figure represents more than 10 percent of the American population in 1940.[2] Nearly all of America's World War II soldiers[3] were men, though 350,000 women also served in the conflict. Most were of European descent, though African Americans composed one in eight U.S. troops, and Native Americans, Asian Americans, and other minority groups contributed significant numbers to the ranks. Of all American soldiers in World War II, most were draftees and fully 73 percent saw service overseas. The vast majority of U.S. troops in World War II did not experience the terrors of mortal combat. One historian has estimated that "fewer than one million, and probably no more than 800,000, took part in any extended combat."[4]

A thorough and lively historical literature exists on the lives of American soldiers in World War II,[5] but what happened to GI Joe and GI Jane once they left the armed services? Surprisingly few scholars have examined the question in any detail. Military historians have traditionally been concerned with the campaigns, strategies, and tactics of the war. Social and cultural historians of the military have focused on the minute details of the soldiers' lives—their attitudes, clothing, even their sex lives—but once the troops are discharged from the service the military historian tends to dismiss them as well. In a 1997 essay on the possibilities for further scholarship on World War II, historian Gerhart Weinberg listed numerous fields for future inquiry, such as the potential for research in the now-open Soviet archives and the role of intelligence in the conduct of the war, but he failed to mention veterans' affairs. At the same time, historians in other disciplines seldom consider veterans as actors in the postwar world. The historiography of postwar America has been focused primarily on the issues such as communism and anticommunism, the origins and development of the Cold War, and the fight for civil rights. All of the above-mentioned subjects are vitally important and clearly warrant the attention they receive. Nevertheless, it does seem that sixteen million veterans have slipped between the cracks of the historian's standard disciplinary categories. Could it be that these men and women simply took off their uniforms and put the war behind them, and that the experience of war and readjustment had little impact on their lives or on American society generally?[6]

What follows is an effort to explore the process of veteran readjustment to civilian life in the United States following the Second World War. It has two primary goals. First, it will discuss the various problems veterans faced in returning to civilian society. Men and women who are inducted into the armed forces undergo an intensive indoctrination into the peculiar world of military service. The military, according to historian John Keegan, is "a world apart, an ancient world, which exists parallel to the everyday world, but does not belong to it."[7] Those initiated into this "world apart" during the war were faced with a reacculturation back into the "everyday world" once the war was over. Soldiers who had learned to work and fight as a team, for example, returned home to face competition in a society that emphasized individual achievement. Having been removed from civilian society for months and years, veterans were often at a disadvantage in that competition. Those who returned physically or mentally scarred by war would forever face difficulties fitting back into society. Ultimately, readjustment to civilian life was an individual journey. No two veterans shared exactly the same problems, experiences, and emotions upon returning home. However, this work will attempt to highlight those readjustment issues most commonly encountered by America's World War II veterans.

The second goal of this work is to discuss the political response to the turbulence in the lives of returning veterans. As was the case after previous wars, American government after World War II took steps to assist veterans in their return to civilian life. After all, it is government that employs or conscripts young men and women into service and then uses them to further its goals and policies. What makes the case of the World War II veteran so worthy of further study is the comprehensive nature of the programs that emerged. After World War II, veterans' programs covered a wider range of readjustment issues than ever before and unlike past wars included meaningful assistance to both disabled and nondisabled veterans. As a result, veterans' programs following World War II were remarkably effective in assisting soldiers in becoming civilians again.

Key to the development and maintenance of such a broad range of programs was overwhelming public support. Never before—or since—had Americans taken such a keen interest in veterans' affairs. As this study suggests, there were several reasons for such immense public interest in the veteran. First, the sheer size of the World War II veteran population demanded that the nation face the issue squarely. One out of every ten Americans returned home from military service, but the question of veteran readjustment affected more than just those who served. Veterans who returned unemployed, mentally ill, or otherwise mal-adjusted to civilian life affected all of those around them. The parents, siblings, and spouses of returning veterans also had to deal with the readjustment issue. Indeed, because so many Americans had gone to war, the so-called "veteran problem" after World War II affected virtually every family in the United States. For Americans in the 1940s, veteran readjustment was not an abstraction, but an immediate and personal issue they confronted each and every day.

Another factor motivating support for veterans' affairs, and one nearly for-gotten about in later years, was the potential threat veterans posed to the social and political order. Historically, readjusting soldiers to civilian life had always been a difficult task. In particular, the traumas of the post-World War I period and the Great Depression strongly influenced discussions of veterans after World War II. In Europe, veterans played a significant role in the rise of fascism, which led directly to the outbreak of the World War II. In the United States, veterans suffering through the ravages of the Great Depression marched on Washington in 1932 to demand an early payment of a promised bonus payment. The Bonus March, as the episode became known, ended only after army troops forcibly removed the ex-soldiers from their encampment. When World War II concluded, America would experience the greatest influx of veterans in its history. A comprehensive program of benefits for returning soldiers, Americans believed and hoped, would not only reward veterans for their sacrifices but also protect the fabric of society itself.

Ultimately, readjustment programs were products of the political process, and public support for veterans' programs translated into political action. A complex set of factors, interests, and motivations influenced the scope and con-text of veterans' programs in the 1940s. There was, of course, a genuine desire on the part of many lawmakers to alleviate the problems veterans faced and demonstrate to them the gratitude of the nation for their wartime efforts and sac-rifices. In many cases politicians and interest groups simply tried to capitalize on the public interest in veterans' affairs to further their own political agendas. Vet-erans' organizations played a crucial role in shaping policy toward World War II veterans. In part, the activities of these associations were calculated to increase their own membership and political influence. However, underlying the outlook of veterans' groups were their own personal experiences with veteran readjustment. In particular, veterans of World War I, who had lived through the turbulent interwar years, pushed forward their own veterans' affairs agenda out of a sincere desire to ensure that World War II veterans did not suffer as they had.

In short, this study will explore the interplay between the readjustment problems faced by returning World War II veterans and the political response to them. It will discuss the strengths of the veterans' programs following World War II, as well as assess their weaknesses and limitations. Much of the work will focus on the political process and debate surrounding the creation of the World War II veterans' programs. At the same time, this study will also elucidate the personal experiences of individual veterans that stimulated the creation of those programs in the first place. It will utilize memoirs, oral histories, and other accounts ex-soldiers have generated in order to present a veteran's eye view of the readjustment problem. As Dixon Wecter wrote in his classic 1944 study of the American veterans' experience, *When Johnny Comes Marching Home*: "Always behind the routine of demobilization stands a man."[8] In examining veterans' programs after World War II, this study will respect Wecter's wise observation.

This work will also focus on one particular state: Wisconsin. The study of veterans' affairs at the state level has several advantages. First, it allows a more detailed look at veteran readjustment at the grass roots, and provides a better appreciation of the impact of veterans' policies on ordinary Americans, their families, and their communities. It also facilitates the study of state and local programs for veterans, which provides a basis for comparison with federal programs, allows for an exploration of alternative ways of tackling veterans' issues, and presents the full range of benefits available. Wisconsin's population was large and diverse enough to offer a fair cross section of American society in the 1940s: urban and rural, rich and poor, minority and white. The population of the Badger State in the 1940 census stood at 3,137,587. According to the VA, Wisconsin contributed 332,200 troops to the World War II military effort, of whom 8,410 were killed. As was the case nationally, most of Wisconsin's World War II soldiers and sailors were white males, but the diversity of the state was also reflected in its veteran population. By 1960, 5,546 veterans classified by the Census Bureau as "non-white" lived in the Badger State. Of Wisconsin's veterans, roughly 9,300 were women.[9]

Politically, Wisconsin provides a particularly interesting study. The Wisconsin political tradition is an unusual one, but one that has had an important impact on national politics. Home of the progressive crusader Robert M. LaFollette, Wisconsin played a key role in the political reform movements of the early twentieth century. Though the age of progressivism had passed by the time of World War II, its spirit lived on in the Badger State. Indeed, Wisconsin has gained a reputation for being on the cutting edge of social policy throughout the century. Among the many issues Wisconsin lawmakers addressed was that of veterans. After World War II, Wisconsin formulated what it believed to be a sweeping program of state veterans' benefits to supplement those of the federal government. How representative Wisconsin's veterans' programs were as compared to other states is not known; almost no scholarship whatsoever exists about veterans' affairs on the state level. But given Wisconsin's activist political history, the Badger State offers a lively and informative point of departure from which to begin an exploration of veterans' affairs beyond the federal government.

Because of the complexity of the veteran readjustment problem, this work is by necessity interdisciplinary in nature. The work is composed of six topical chapters, arranged so as to follow a typical veteran through his or her readjustment process. An introductory essay discusses the history of veterans before World War II, a troubled past that greatly shaped debate over veterans' affairs in the 1940s. Chapter 1 outlines the development of federal, state, and local services available to veterans, as well as the rationale and political pressures behind them. Chapter 2 explores social and cultural readjustments to civilian life, including discussions of such topics as the veteran's emotional state, family and marriage, and the attraction of veterans' organizations. Chapter 3 examines the medical readjustments many veterans faced, ranging from physical disabilities to psychological problems. Chapter 4 focuses on educational benefits for veterans, and the veteran's influence on colleges and universities. Chapter 5 discusses the establishment of the veteran back into the nation's workforce and economic life. Chapter 6 explores housing programs for returning veterans, which contributed significantly to the suburbanization of America. Generally speaking, this study will explore the process of veteran readjustment between 1945 and 1950. "Although the consequences of any big war spread in circles to infinity," wrote Dixon Wecter, "for the common soldier the first five years are probably the hardest."[10] However, readjusting to civilian life can be a lifelong process for many veterans. In order to follow the veteran through each of the above-mentioned readjustment steps, this study will occasionally discuss their experiences beyond 1950.

Ernie Pyle noted that World War II was changing those who served and fought in it. This study explores the ways in which those young men and women were changed back into civilians. The thunders of war—the roar of gunfire, vehicle engines, and artillery—would reverberate through the lives of veterans for years after the conclusion of international hostilities. Thanks to a thoughtful and generous package of readjustment benefits, that thunder would gradually roll off into the distance for the majority of America's World War II veterans.

Notes

1. Ernie Pyle, *Brave Men* (New York: Henry Holt, 1944), 320.

2. U.S. Department of Commerce, *Historical Statistics of the United States: Colonial Times to 1970* (Washington, D.C.: GPO, 1975), 1140; U.S. Veterans' Administration, *Administrator of Veterans' Affairs Annual Report*, 1947 ed. (Washington, D.C.: GPO, 1948), 1.

3. Generally speaking, this work will use the term "soldier" to describe all of those who served in the American armed forces during World War II, including the army, army air forces, marines, and navy. However, service-specific terminology (i.e., sailor, marine, etc.) will be used when referring to specific individuals or branches of service.

4. Gerald F. Linderman, *The World within War: America's Combat Experience in World War II* (New York: Free Press, 1997), 1.

5. For an introduction to the history of America's World War II military personnel, see Stephen E. Ambrose, *Citizen Soldiers: The U.S. Army from the Normandy Beaches to the Bulge to the Surrender of Germany, June 7, 1944—May 7, 1945* (New York: Simon and Schuster, 1997); Eric Bergerud, *Touched with Fire: The Land War in the South Pacific* (New York: Viking, 1996); Henry Berry, *Semper Fi, Mac: Living Memories of the U.S. Marines in World War II* (New York: Arbor House, 1982); John Ellis, *The Sharp End: The Fighting Man in World War II* (New York: Scribner, 1980); Edwin P. Hoyt, *The GI's War: The Story of American Soldiers in Europe in World War II* (New York: McGraw-Hill, 1988); Lee Kennett, *GI: The American Soldier in World War II* (New York: Warner Books, 1987); Linderman, *The World within War*; and Samuel Stouffer, et. al., *The American Soldier*, 2 vols. (Princeton, N.J.: Princeton University Press, 1949). For more on the role of African Americans, see Bernard C. Nalty, *Strength for the Fight: A History of Black Americans in the Military* (New York: Free Press, 1986) and Neil A. Wynn, *The Afro-American and the Second World War*, rev. ed. (New York: Holmes and Meier, 1993). For more on Native Americans, see Alison R. Bernstein, *American Indians and World War II: Toward a New Era in Indian Affairs* (Norman: University of Oklahoma Press, 1991). For more on American women's participation in the military, see D'Ann Campbell, *Women at War with America: Private Lives in a Patriotic Era* (Cambridge, Mass.: Harvard University Press, 1984) and Susan M. Hartmann, *The Home Front and Beyond: American Women in the 1940s* (Boston: Twayne, 1982).

6. Gerhart Weinberg, "World War II Scholarship: Now and in the Future," *Journal of Military History* 61 (1997): 335-346.

7. John Keegan, *A History of Warfare* (New York: Knopf, 1994), xvi.

8. Dixon Wecter, *When Johnny Comes Marching Home* (New York: Houghton Mifflin, 1944), 7.

9. Wisconsin Legislative Reference Bureau, *Wisconsin Blue Book*, 1962 ed. (Madison: Legislative Reference Bureau, 1962), 255-258; William F. Thompson, *The History of Wisconsin*, vol. 4, *Continuity and Change, 1940-1965* (Madison: State Historical Society of Wisconsin, 1988), 28-103, 323; U.S. Veterans' Administration, *Veterans in the State of Wisconsin, 1960* (Washington, D.C.: GPO, 1963), 5.

10. Wecter, *When Johnny Comes Marching Home*, 6.

Acknowledgments

At the risk of omitting names, I would like to acknowledge the contributions of the many people who have helped to shape this work and make it possible. This study is based on my 1999 doctoral dissertation at the University of Wisconsin-Madison. First and foremost, I would like to thank my adviser, Professor John M. Cooper Jr. for working with me. Professor Cooper provided me with generous amounts of advice, criticism, encouragement, and guidance. He also allowed me the freedom to shape the work in my own way. I could not have asked for a more pleasurable research experience, and I know that I am a much better scholar for having worked under him. I would also like to thank the other members of my dissertation committee for their insight and challenging commentary: Professors John B. Sharpless, Stanley K. Schultz, Gordon Baldwin, and Harold Cook.

This book has been shaped and influenced by many others. The University of Wisconsin-Madison was an especially fruitful place to study. In addition to my dissertation committee, I would also like to thank Professors Edward M. Coffman, Stanley I. Kutler, and Alfred W. McCoy for their interest in my research. Professor Coffman, in particular, has long encouraged me to think seriously about the war veteran, and his work on the American soldier—always written with a wonderful sense of humanity—has been an inspiration and a model for me. I presented the first chapter of this work at a 1998 dissertator seminar in political history funded by the Mellon Foundation and conducted by Professors Cooper and Thomas J. Archdeacon, who along with my fellow students provided thoughtful commentary on the work in progress. My colleagues at the City University of New York and the University of Wisconsin-Platteville were also encouraging, supportive, and filled with suggestions. In particular, I must single out Professor Thomas B. Lundeen at Platteville for his guidance in my research into Wisconsin history, and David Blanchar at CUNY who gave me helpful suggestions on medical history. My research involved several disciplines, and I also sought advice from experts in specific fields. Help with legal terminology and technicalities came from my brother Brian D. Van Ells, as well as my friends Edward M. Coffman Jr. and Charles Crueger. Dr. Jerry L. Halverson, another long-time friend, assisted me in my dabbling into the world of medicine by helping me locate sources and providing me with advice on terminology. Dr. Robert P. Hartwig of the Insurance Information Institute in New York City took time out his busy schedule to share with me his insights on post-

World War II economic matters. I have incorporated the wisdom of these scholars into the work to the best of my ability. Any remaining misconceptions are entirely my own.

The sources of this study came from many libraries and archives, and in all cases I found information professionals willing and able to assist me. The library systems of the University of Wisconsin-Madison, the University of Wisconsin-Platteville, and the City University of New York were invaluable. The staff at the State Historical Society of Wisconsin was exceptionally helpful—in particular Harold Miller and his assistants in the archives. The Wisconsin Legislative Reference Bureau in Madison was a tremendous resource, and I would like to thank the staff there for helping me wade through the countless government documents and news clippings in its collections. Joe Wojtowicz at the Wisconsin Law Library and Eric Lent at the Wisconsin National Guard Museum (subsequently absorbed by the Wisconsin Department of Veterans' Affairs) provided me with assistance in using those facilities. Public libraries are an underappreciated resource in America today. In addition to academic libraries, I was often able to find rare and useful works in the public library systems of Madison, Wisconsin, and in Westchester County, New York. Larry Danielson of the Wisconsin Department of the Veterans of Foreign Wars and Sister Jean Richter of the Edgewood College archives went above and beyond the call of duty in sending me information I should have unearthed myself.

My research has been greatly shaped by my experiences at the Wisconsin Veterans' Museum, an agency of the Wisconsin Department of Veterans' Affairs, where I worked for nine years in part-time and full-time capacities. While serving as the archivist at that institution I was able to collect a broad range of veteran-related materials and talk with veterans of many different wars and learn from their experiences. I would like to thank the museum's director, Dr. Richard H. Zeitlin, for affording me those opportunities. In addition, Dr. Zeitlin also provided thoughtful commentary on my manuscript. Especially valuable to this work was the Wisconsin Veterans' Oral History Project, which I was privileged to administer between 1994 and 1997. I received interview suggestions from many different sources, but those of three museum volunteers were especially important: Drs. James Angevine, Charles Larkin, and James McIntosh. I would also like to thank William F. Brewster, Michael E. Telzrow, and James Dittberner, one-time colleagues of mine at the museum, for their help with the oral history project. Once I left the museum, Richard W. Harrison and his staff allowed me the use of interviews conducted after my departure. Most of all, I am greatly indebted to all of the veterans who agreed to share their experiences.

Portions of chapter 1 are derived from a history of Wisconsin's County Veterans' Service Officers, which I completed in 1995. I would like to thank the Wisconsin CVSO Association, and association president Dave Thomas in particular, for allowing me to borrow liberally from that work. In my years at the Wisconsin Veterans Museum I found the CVSOs supportive of our efforts to preserve the Badger State's veterans' history and I learned much about the operations and nature of veterans' affairs agencies from my dealings with these men and women. I would especially like to thank William Stiefvater in Manitowoc County and Tom Taber in Grant County for working with me.

Finally, I would like to thank my family for tolerating me while I have been researching and writing these past years. My wife Paula completed her dissertation several years before I did, and understood well the challenges before me. Her professional advice and editing skills, as well as her personal support, were invaluable. This work is dedicated to Paula, as well as my daughters Annika (who is very much interested in the "olden days") and Sarah, born August 9, 1999—the day I defended my dissertation.

Introduction

The "Veteran Problem" in History

Warfare is one of mankind's oldest activities, and perhaps its most tragic one. Although the American men and women who fought in World War II returned victorious from the greatest conflict in all of human history, countless war veterans had experienced the transition from military to civilian life for millennia before them. A multitude of books has been written about war, but the scholarship on veterans is fragmentary at best. Most veterans have left few if any records about the joys they felt, the disappointments they met, or the problems they faced. The governments that employed these veterans have left somewhat more clues, but even these usually only hint at the problem of reintegrating veterans back into the civilian world. The work of those few scholars who have examined the world of the ex-soldier suggests that veterans have experienced similar problems throughout recorded history. In short, the "veteran problem" is as old as war itself, but not nearly as well understood.

In examining the history of veterans, several themes emerge. First, veterans frequently suffer war-related health problems. Whether from battle wound or disease, whether their scars are physical or psychological, health problems often follow the veteran into civilian life, and many never fully recover from their war experiences. Second, veterans have historically faced economic difficulties. Soldiers are separated from the civilian economy while under arms, but during wartime a nation's economy often changes dramatically. As a result, returning veterans face economic competition for which they are often unprepared or ill trained. Economic obstacles to readjustment has often led ex-soldiers into lives of poverty and crime. Finally, veterans have long been associated with the potential for social and political disorder. Veterans often return feeling angry, disillusioned, and disconnected from the rest of society. Though nations depend on armies in times of war, in peacetime the existence in civilian society of disgruntled warriors knowledgeable about organization and discipline has often instilled fear into the minds of nonveterans. The possibility that veterans might use their military expertise to impose their will on society has traditionally disturbed both citizen and ruler alike. As Americans in the 1940s looked at the history of veterans' affairs, they saw a troubled past and worked assiduously to ensure that such problems would not plague the nation in the years after World War II.

The Veteran in Western Civilization

For most veterans in the ancient world, the glory of their martial exploits or the plunder they extracted from the enemy was probably the only form of readjustment benefits they received. However, some early civilizations understood that war could have a tremendous impact on those who fight, and took into account the postwar needs of the soldiers they employed. Ancient Greek literature hints at the readjustment problems veterans faced, for example. As psychiatrist Jonathan Shay has shown in his work *Achilles in Vietnam*, Homer's classic tales reveal that the ancient Greeks understood the psychological impact of war on combat soldiers. In *The Iliad*, Shays points out that Achilles the warrior exhibits many of the same emotional reactions to combat during the Trojan Wars that the Vietnam War veterans he treated in the Boston area had manifested thousands of years later—the emotional bonds among soldiers, the rush of emotion and energy in combat, resentment toward superiors. In *The Odyssey*, the hero Odysseus returns home after years of war and wanderings only to find that numerous suitors had beset his wife Penelope. Odysseus must kill the suitors and then fight their vengeful relatives before the gods impose a final peace. Most veterans of war in ancient Greece could not count on divine intervention to guarantee a smooth readjustment to civilian life, however. The Greek city-states made few provisions for returning soldiers. Destitute veterans, like others in ancient Greece, were eligible for meager relief payments.[1]

Veterans of the Roman legions benefited from some rather thoughtful government programs. From the earliest days of the professional Roman army, its retirees were granted cash bonuses upon their discharge, the amount of which depended on rank. Rome also provided veterans with land and resettled them in colonies. The first veterans' colonies were located in Italy, but over time these settlements were founded on the frontiers of the empire. In fact, some scholars have argued that veterans' communities were key elements in Romanizing many conquered territories. The cities of Narbonne, Arles, Béziers, Orange, and Fréjus in southern France, for example, were originally veterans' settlements that were possibly founded by Julius Caesar himself. Emperor Augustus claimed to have resettled nearly 300,000 ex-soldiers in Italy, France, and Spain in the years following the battle of Actium in 31 BC. The policy not only placed experienced fighters on the borders of the empire, but also kept potential agitators away from Rome. (In fact, the empire had been plagued by several soldier revolts.) Ex-legionnaires even formed veterans' associations. Evidence suggests that such societies existed in the Rhineland of present-day Germany as early as the Julio-Claudian period, indicating the formation of a distinct group consciousness among former Roman soldiers. Despite readjustment benefits, scholarship suggests that the Roman veteran probably had a lower standard of living than his nonveteran counterpart, although veterans in the provinces were economically better off than those in Italy.[2]

The rise of the European nation-state after 1500 necessitated the development of sizeable standing armies, which in turn led to the development of an exserviceman class. In the five centuries between the Renaissance and World War I, the armies of Europe engaged each other in several series of long, bloody wars.

Like their predecessors in the ancient world, many European veterans experienced difficulties integrating themselves back into society. Upon discharge, soldiers usually received any back pay owed to them, perhaps a small cash payment to see them home, and little else.

Prior to the sixteenth century, European states made only modest and largely ineffective efforts to assist former soldiers. Traditionally, monasteries cared for aged and disabled veterans. However, both parties disliked the arrangement; veterans resisted the pious ways of the priests, while clergymen complained about the profane ways of ex-soldiers. The close quarters of camp life frequently spread contagious diseases, such as typhus, tuberculosis, or various strains of influenza. Disease could plague a veteran for the rest of his life, and veterans could also spread disease to the rest of society upon returning home. Social dislocation hindered the veteran's integration back into the economy, and those who could not find work frequently resorted to begging. Some localities provided local veterans with a "beggar's license" exempting them from vagrancy laws, while others drove them from their midst. In some cases, bands of dislocated veterans roamed the countryside in search of sustenance and plunder. Returning soldiers often faced social stigmatization upon their return. As historian Henry Webb has pointed out, for example, rogue veterans were a frequent theme in Elizabethan literature in England. Maladjusted veterans posed obvious problems for European societies. Indigent veterans only added to the growing ranks of Europe's poor, while criminal bands posed a threat to law and order. Military officials often complained that the sorry plight of veterans hindered recruiting efforts.[3]

By the end of the sixteenth century, European nations had begun to develop more comprehensive solutions to the problem of veteran readjustment. Improvements occurred in three primary areas. The first was the creation of veterans' homes. As armies grew larger and wars more destructive, the monastery system of care for disabled veterans grew obsolete. The Dutch wars for independence spurred the creation of the first homes for ex-soldiers. Spain founded a military hospital in Mechelen, Belgium, in 1585. Primarily a surgical hospital, the facility also provided long-term care for permanently disabled soldiers. By the early seventeenth century the numbers of maimed soldiers had grown so large that Spain established a home solely for disabled veterans at Hal, Belgium. French efforts to create a home for veterans also date to the turn of the seventeenth century, but it was not until King Louis XIV founded the Hôtel Royal des Invalides in 1674 that France succeeded. Located in the heart of Paris, the Hôtel des Invalides became Europe's premier home for ex-soldiers. The facility was open to both disabled and retired veterans. Officials divided the residents into three categories based on rank, required the wearing of military uniforms, and imposed strict discipline. The facility had a capacity of 3,000, but the actual number of residents was often much higher. England also struggled to create an institution for its veterans. In 1692, King Charles II founded the Royal Chelsea Hospital near London on the grounds of a failed college. Other nations soon created facilities similar to the Hôtel des Invalides and Royal Chelsea Hospital. During the eighteenth century, Prussia, Russia,

Portugal, and Sweden all founded veterans' homes. In one decade, the 1720s, Austria founded no fewer than three homes for ex-soldiers.[4]

The early veterans' homes of Europe undoubtedly kept many off the streets and away from criminal activity. However, the facilities only had a modest impact on the overall problem of veteran readjustment. Officials usually devoted only meager resources to the homes, resulting oftentimes in veteran suffering. "A most unhealthy stench" was said to emanate from the Prussian soldiers' home in Berlin, for example, where conditions were so austere that residents reportedly had to work outside the facility in order to keep from starving. Many homes accommodated only small numbers of veterans. Because demand for care far exceeded available space, the homes were subject to overcrowding. Royal Chelsea Hospital rarely housed more than 500 veterans, for example, while the Prussian home in Berlin accommodated just 600. To alleviate the congestion, France created *compagnies détachées d'invalides* in 1690. The companies were composed of relatively healthy veterans who were tasked to perform guard duties at military posts. The policy not only alleviated veterans' suffering, but it also freed up regular soldiers to fight. By the end of the Seven Years War in 1763, France had employed more than 150 companies, involving nearly 15,000 veterans. "Invalid" companies grew in popularity throughout Europe. Great Britain created the Invalide Home Defence Companies in 1708, for example, while in Prussia veteran companies played an important role in home defense during the Napoleonic Wars.[5]

Pensions were another method of meeting the needs of discharged soldiers and sailors. Prior to the sixteenth century many veterans, especially high-ranking officers, appeared on royal pension lists. However, such payments were based more on patronage and connections than actual readjustment needs. But as the ranks of ex-soldiers grew, some nations created standardized pension programs for veterans. The foundation of the English system was the Acte for the Reliefe of Souldiours, passed by Parliament in its 1592-93 session. The statute entitled veterans disabled in the war with Spain then occurring to pension payments based on rank and degree of injury, with a ceiling set by law. England also offered pensions based merely on service. A 1698 royal warrant, for example, provided British-born officers with a pension of halfpay. In addition, England also created a system of Royal Chelsea Hospital "out-pensioners," allowing veterans who could not be accommodated at the crowded facility to obtain relief yet remain at home. On the eve of World War I, British veterans could receive pensions based on disability or service, on a permanent or temporary basis, at widely varying rates. By the eighteenth century, numerous other nations had developed pension systems. Places as small as the German free city of Hamburg, for example, deducted a small amount from a soldier's pay for the relief of retired soldiers. The French pension system did not emerge until the Seven Years War. Beginning in 1762, French military retirees were eligible for pensions based on rank and years of service. Two years later, disabled soldiers could receive a *pension d'invalide* to ease the crowding at the Hôtel des Invalides, similar to the British out-pensioner system. The French pension system of the Ancien Régime, which in its basic form weathered the French Revolution and the Napoleonic Wars, was widely regarded as Europe's most comprehensive and effective.[6]

The pension systems affected many more veterans than did the homes, but this method also had its shortcomings. Standardized pension systems did not stop the gross inequalities in pension payments. In Frederick the Great's Prussia, for example, a general officer might receive a pension of 1,000 thalers annually, while an enlisted man might collect one or two thalers a month. In 1789, half of France's estimated 24,000 pensioned veterans accounted for just 24 percent of pension expenditures, whereas the 590 largest disbursements accounted for nearly 30 percent. Pensions frequently failed to keep veterans above the poverty line. Because Parliament in 1711 had not appropriated pension monies, Chelsea Hospital outpensioners were "lying in the streets," according to one of the facility's governors, "in a starving and perishing condition, severall [sic] of them not having the wherewithall to cover their nakedness, their wounds yet uncured." Even in France, local pension administrators reported to Paris that veterans could not survive on their pensions alone and depended on work or family support to supplement their incomes. Some veterans in need of assistance received no pensions at all. In Great Britain between 1861 and 1898, for example, only 65.9 percent of disabled veterans and 37.9 percent of all discharged soldiers received any kind of pension payment.[7]

The third area of veterans' service development involved the reemployment of veterans after discharge. European governments developed several techniques to help veterans find work and integrate themselves into the civilian economy. The British Parliament's 1713 Act to Enable Officers and Soldiers to Exercise Trades, for example, exempted veterans previously employed in a particular trade from apprenticeship regulations in that occupation. More commonly, states provided veterans with preferential treatment for government jobs. Prussia, for example, set aside work in the kingdom's tobacco monopoly and postal system for veterans. Russia employed veterans in government positions such as guards, couriers, fire fighters, and clerks. By the nineteenth century, military service had become a gateway to civil service positions in many countries, particularly France and Germany. But the reemployment programs, like those for veterans' homes and pensions, suffered important shortcomings. For one, they often involved small numbers of veterans. In Great Britain between 1876 and 1891, for example, veterans filled only 220 of 4,700 lower civil service positions. Second, the programs sometimes suffered from limited vision. By the nineteenth century, some reformers saw the opportunity for the military to offer technical training with civilian applications. In 1862 and again in 1871, British parliamentary committees suggested the development of military technical training programs. But citing their cost and the departure from a soldier's "legitimate duties," the military ignored the proposals.[8]

The emerging network of programs for veterans met only a portion of the returning soldier's needs and concerns. Many readjustment problems went unaddressed. As early as the seventeenth century, for example, Spanish military doctors in the Netherlands noted a psychological condition in some combat soldiers that they called *el mal de corazón* (heart sickness) or *estar roto* (to be broken), which rendered the soldiers unable to perform their duties. Puzzled by the condition, the doctors simply discharged the men from the service. Alcohol abuse also plagued European armies. One historian, for example, has argued that an "alcoholic culture" pervaded the British army during the eighteenth century. Many soldiers left the service addicted to the substance. Social attitudes toward veterans had changed rather little; the veterans still aroused fear in the civilian population. As historian Jean-Pierre Bois has pointed out, for example, the public in eighteenth-century France continued to associate veterans with crime and vagabondage, despite the fact that only 1.75 percent of documented mendicants in that country between 1769 and 1789 were veterans. While veterans inspired fear in the civilian world, in the military they were sometimes viewed with contempt. In eighteenth-century Prussia, retired soldiers were often the subject of ridicule among those still on duty. His carriage beset by begging veterans, Frederick the Great reportedly told his assistants to "drive the scum away."[9]

To handle readjustment problems that governments left unaddressed, veterans began to organize among themselves, particularly after 1789. The French Revolution, with its principle of citizen participation in government affairs, sparked the formation of Europe's first veterans' pressure groups. French veterans at the Hôtel des Invalides, unhappy with the more conservative directory and its veterans' policy, became involved in the Neo-Jacobin movement of the late 1790s. The directory transferred the activists out of Paris before a strong veterans' movement could emerge. In Greece, veterans of that country's war for independence against Turkey organized to influence the writing of a new constitution in the 1840s. Among the activists were veterans of Bulgarian, Serbian, and other Balkan origins, who had fought for Greece and whose ethnic brethren were still fighting Turkish rule. Veterans also organized to address bread-and-butter concerns. In 1900, about a dozen private societies assisted veterans in Britain in finding employment, among them the Army and Navy Pensioners' and Time-Expired Men's Society, the National Association for the Employment of Reserve and Discharged Soldiers, and the Corps of Commissioners, the latter of which focused specifically on disabled veterans. Such societies may have been responsible for more than 3,000 veterans being hired by British railway and police forces. Some veterans' organizations grew quite large. In Germany, several different veterans' groups merged in 1900 to form the Kyffhäuser Bund, Germany's first national veterans' association. On the eve of World War I, veterans' organizations in Germany may have involved as many as three million former soldiers.[10]

The veterans' homes, pensions, and reemployment programs that had evolved in Europe by the dawn of the twentieth century were clearly an improvement over the monastery system and begging licenses of the Renaissance period. "A brighter place in civilian society [for veterans] had been secured," wrote French historian Jean-Pierre Bois, "the army no longer engendered poverty."[11] Though the "veteran problem" was far from solved, the basic outline of veterans' assistance in Western civilization was complete by the eve of World War I, but had not yet been combined into an effective package.

The Veteran in American History

The problem of veteran readjustment to civilian life in the United States is as old as American civilization itself. Veterans' affairs in America followed the same pattern as in Europe.[12] With colonists fighting wars against nearby Native Americans as well as participating in the American extensions of larger European disputes, war greatly affected colonial Americans. Legislation for disabled veterans was among the earliest enactments of the colonial governments. The Plymouth colony, for example, passed a pension law for veterans as early as 1636. Virginia enacted a disabled soldier pension in 1644. Rhode Island had perhaps the most comprehensive pension legislation of all the American colonies. Under the colony's 1718 pension law, soldiers disabled while in service were entitled to have their wounds cared for out of the colonial treasury and receive a pension to keep them out of poverty. In addition, the families of those killed in battle were also entitled to pensions. In most cases, veterans had to have been wounded, and their disabilities had to keep them from making an adequate living, in order to qualify for pension payments.[13]

The soldiers who fought in the Continental Army during the American Revolution faced a number of problems readjusting to civilian life—difficulties that have traditionally bedeviled ex-soldiers. As in countless wars before, thousands returned home suffering from physical wounds or the lingering effects of disease. The unstable nature of the postwar American economy made it particularly difficult for veterans to find a niche in the civilian world. Some soldiers had served in the army for as many as eight years, and having been away from their farms or workbenches for such long periods of time only complicated their economic readjustment further. The returning Continentals also faced difficulties peculiar to the milieu of revolutionary America. Many citizens viewed veterans with particular suspicion, fearing they might spread camp "vices and immoralities," such as drinking and gambling, among the general public—a great danger among a people who tended to see moral virtue as crucial to the survival of the American republic. In a nation instilled with a fear of a "standing army," many citizens feared that the regimentation of military life might promote "militarism" among the war veterans, and thus pose yet another threat to the tenuous new republic. Though independence had been won through war, the men who fought that war were frequently the objects of fear and contempt when they came home.[14]

The United States government was responsive to the needs of the veterans; indeed, ex-soldiers were among the first concerns of the Continental Congress. As early as August 1776, Congress passed a pension law for soldiers disabled while in service. Congress also authorized "bounty land warrants" for veterans, entitling them to plots of land on designated areas of the frontier. Ex-soldiers who chose not to settle in frontier regions could sell their certificates for cash. State governments, following colonial precedents, also passed pension laws for veterans. But the new nation's shaky economic foundation severely hindered the maintenance of established programs and the creation of new ones. For example, Congress was forced to reduce disability pensions to $5 for enlisted men and no more than half pay for officers. Efforts to create a service pension for officers along the same lines as Great Britain also proved difficult. Because the officer ranks in the Continental Army were growing depleted late in the war, Congress voted officers halfpay for life in 1780. Once the war was over, however, officer pensions outraged many civilians. Critics charged that the pensions would allow officers to live lives of "luxury and splendor" on the backs of the ordinary taxpayer. At any rate, Congress had difficulty finding the money to pay for pensions. The Commutation Act of 1783 reduced the officers' pensions to the equivalent of five years pay in the form of government certificates, but the inflationary postwar economy made the certificates nearly worthless.[15]

The chaotic status of readjustment assistance caused both anger and confusion among the returning Continentals. Veteran unrest occasionally resulted in outbreaks of violence, or threats of it. In 1783, Philadelphia witnessed a soldier mutiny that briefly forced the Continental Congress to withdraw from the city. In the Continental Army's camp at Newburgh, New York, that same year, officers unhappy with the lack of congressional support for officer pensions hinted at a coup d'état, but Gen. George Washington managed to quell the crisis. The discontent of the officers at Newburgh led to a more concrete result—formation of the Society of the Cincinnati, a fraternal association of former army officers. The Cincinnati seemed to many Americans little more than an elitist clique that disdained the democratic tendencies of the postrevolutionary era, and further raised public misgivings about the role of veterans in a republican society. Several years later, violence broke out in western Massachusetts among economically pressed farmer-veterans. Many farmers returned from the war to find themselves deeply in debt after years away from home, but creditors in Boston nevertheless insisted on timely payments of the money owed. By 1786, farmer-veterans attempted to close local courthouses in order to gain relief from their debt. In January 1787, a band of farmers led by Daniel Shays, a former Continental Army officer, attempted to seize the arsenal at Springfield. Boston militiamen soon quelled "Shays' Rebellion," as the unrest in Massachusetts became known, but the violence only further reinforced the fear that veterans might threaten liberty and order in the new republic.[16]

Meaningful veteran pensions did not come until the prosperous and confident "Era of Good Feelings" following the War of 1812. In 1818, Congress approved a service pension for Continental Army veterans who were in "in reduced [economic] circumstances." Veterans of the War of 1812, the various Indian wars on the frontier, and the Mexican War of 1846-48, eventually received disability pensions similar to those provided Revolutionary War veterans. Land grants also remained an important benefit for veterans in the early years of the republic. In fact, many veterans used land warrants to help settle areas of Wisconsin before and after statehood in 1848, especially around Green Bay and Mineral Point. Taking advantage of the pension and land grant programs presented numerous problems, however. Frequent changes in benefit laws could be confusing to veterans. Poverty often forced veterans to sell their land warrant certificates, highly sought after by land speculators, at a much reduced value.[17]

The Civil War that erupted in 1861 was by far the bloodiest and most traumatic event in American history. In all, more than 600,000 Americans died in the conflict—roughly 2 percent of the entire 1860 population. Estimates of the number of nonfatal casualties range as high as 400,000 in the Union states alone. The Civil War spawned numerous pieces of legislation for that conflict's veterans. On July 14, 1862, Congress passed what became known as the "general law system" of pensions. Under the act, all soldiers and sailors who suffered disabilities due to their military service would receive a federal pension, the amount of which depended on rank. The law also included the mothers, widows, and orphans of the soldiers killed or those of deceased disabled veterans. Congress designed the system so that veterans of subsequent wars would be covered as well. Two days later, Congress agreed to provide free prosthetic devices to Union veterans who had lost limbs. In 1865, the federal government established the National Asylum for Disabled Volunteer Soldiers, later renamed the National Home for Disabled Volunteer Soldiers. Civil War veterans received preference for federal government jobs as well. State governments also made provisions for Civil War veterans. In 1866, Wisconsin lawmakers passed two bills that protected veterans from state seizures of land due to failure to pay taxes while in the service. Legislation in 1867 authorized towns to raise money for needy veterans, assisted the poor with certain service-connected medical expenses, and exempted disabled veterans from poll taxes and peddler license fees.[18]

Never before had the nation addressed the problem of veteran readjustment so promptly or so thoroughly. Nevertheless, legislation for Civil War veterans fell far short of meeting the needs of many veterans. Most legislation did little or nothing for the nondisabled veteran in finding his place in the civilian economy. Rapid demobilization of the Union Army flooded the labor market, and many veterans experienced troubles finding adequate jobs. Some soldiers returned addicted to morphine and other painkilling drugs used in field hospitals. Indeed, drug addiction in late nineteenth-century America was sometimes referred to as the "soldier's disease." During the war, military physicians noted a mental condition among combat soldiers known variously as "nostalgia," "irritable heart," or "sunstroke," characterized by social withdrawal and homesickness. Upon returning home, many veterans continued to exhibit symptoms of psychological stress, including sleeplessness, depression, guilt, and paranoia. Such men often proved to be a burden on family members, and many eventually landed in local jails or in mental asylums. Confederate veterans faced a particularly difficult situation. They returned to a defeated land devastated by years of modern warfare. Back pay, bonuses, and land warrants promised by the Confederate government were worthless. As soldiers in a rebel army, they received nothing in the way of federal assistance. Although considered heroes of the "lost cause" among most Southern whites, these veterans could count on little concrete readjustment assistance from their poor and politically embattled state governments.[19]

As in the past, veterans organized after the Civil War, and the veterans' associations played important roles in turbulent politics of Reconstruction. In the South, a group of Confederate veterans organized a social club they called the Ku

Klux Klan, which evolved into a secretive terrorist organization designed to intimidate African Americans and white Republicans in the postwar South. Fearing that politicians after the war would lose the victory they had won on the battlefield, many former Union soldiers agitated for a harsh Reconstruction program to transform the South and ensure that the war they had fought would not be repeated. In Illinois in 1866, political involvement among Union veterans led to the formation of the Grand Army of the Republic (GAR), the most important veterans' association among former Union soldiers. The GAR was open to all honorably discharged Union veterans. In its early years, the GAR was a highly partisan extension of the Republican Party which urged Union veterans to "vote the way you shot" and oppose Democratic efforts for a moderate Reconstruction program. After 1870, the GAR evolved into more of a fraternal society for Union veterans, in some ways akin to the Freemasons, the Odd Fellows, the Knights of Pythias, and other such societies that then dotted the American social landscape. Growing to more than 400,000 members by 1890, the GAR was the largest veterans' organization the United States had yet seen, and the first of the modern American veterans' organizations.[20]

The GAR took a keen interest in the social and economic well-being of Union veterans. Every local GAR post was required to maintain a "relief fund" to assist indigent veterans in their community. Grand Army men and their families who found themselves in need might find that the local post helped them cover medical expenses, find temporary work, or defray the costs of a respectable funeral. Such charitable efforts conformed to the social ideology of the Victorian period, which stressed personal freedom and independence. However, the GAR also became notorious for its political lobbying to expand the scope of government pensions for veterans. The Civil War veterans did not view pensions as charity. Rather, the veterans saw themselves as the "saviors" of the Union, and believed the government had an obligation to repay a "debt of gratitude" to them. During the 1880s and 1890s, the GAR became a powerful voice for increased Union veteran pensions in Washington. The GAR's crowning achievement was the Dependent Pension Act of 1890, which provided payments to Union veterans and their dependents for disabilities incurred both during and after military service. The national soldiers' home system had also been expanded during the late nineteenth century. By 1900, nearly 100,000 Union veterans lived in federal veterans' homes across the country.[21]

GAR political efforts for veterans' relief also extended to the states. The year 1887 proved to be a particularly fruitful year for the Wisconsin Grand Army. One of the Wisconsin GAR's top priorities was care of poor veterans at the local level. On April 2, 1887, the state legislature passed an act that required counties to levy taxes to help support indigent Union veterans and the poverty-stricken dependents of the deceased, so that "no honorably discharged soldier, sailor or marine [would] be sent to a poorhouse." The fund was disbursed by Soldiers' and Sailors' Relief Commissions, which were appointed by local county judges. Six days later, the legislature approved a bill that required local governments to ensure that poor veterans received a "decent and respectable" burial at government expense. Within two weeks, Wisconsin legislators authorized the creation of the Grand Army Home in Waupaca County (near the present-day village of King), later known as the Wisconsin Veterans' Home, to care for disabled and aging Union veterans. GAR efforts in other states resulted in similar programs across the country.[22]

At a time when Americans looked with disdain and suspicion at government welfare benefits, Union veterans of the Civil War had managed to build an extensive welfare network using the moral force of their wartime service and their strength in numbers. As a measure of the GAR's political power and effectiveness, veterans' pensions in 1893 accounted for more than 40 percent of all federal government spending. However, the growth of the veterans' welfare state alarmed many. In an age noted for its political corruption, veterans' benefits seemed to some one of its most odious components. For a fee, a lawyer known as a "pension agent" (often a veteran himself) assisted veterans in making claims. Although many pension agents were undoubtedly honorable persons interested in helping their clients, others were not, and pension agents soon gained a reputation for chicanery and corruption. Note, for example, the particularly scathing characterization of pension agents in historian William H. Glasson's introduction to his 1918 study of veterans' pensions:

> As is usual . . . when money is to be paid out to numerous individuals in the community, a class of people fastened themselves as parasites on the beneficiaries. The pension agent appeared early on the scene. Under the pretense of assisting prospective pensioners, he soon reached a stage where he absorbed a large part of the benefit of the country's generosity. He was in very truth a blood-sucker on the pensioner, although posing as his friend. When his evil activities were attacked by disinterested citizens, he stirred up the prejudices of those he was fleecing by imposing on their credulity and leading them to believe that their interests and his were the same. . . . The public treasury became, in the minds of many, a proper source of loot.

In devising benefit programs for veterans of subsequent wars, the abuses—real and imagined—in the development of Civil War pensions would loom large in the minds of policy makers and citizens alike.[23]

Reform in veterans' services would have to wait until well into the twentieth century, however. Added to existing federal and state veterans' programs were the soldiers of the Spanish-American War (1898), the Philippine-American War (1899-1902), and other turn-of-the-century imperialistic ventures. By 1916, more than 28,000 veterans and family members of the Spanish-American War era received federal pensions under the general law system enacted during the Civil War. In Wisconsin, the law governing the Soldiers' and Sailors' Relief Commissions was altered so that impoverished veterans of any conflict could obtain relief from those bodies. In 1911, veterans of all wars became eligible for residence at the Grand Army Home. But as with previous legislation, many Spanish-American War veterans found readjustment problems inadequately addressed. In particular, many of these men returned home with malaria and other tropical diseases that eluded treatment with existing medical knowledge. To lobby for benefits and join together socially, the new veterans formed their own societies, the two most important of which were the United Spanish War Veterans (USWV), founded in 1904, and the Veterans of Foreign Wars (VFW), formed in 1914. The VFW was the first major American veterans' organization to accept ex-soldiers from more than one conflict, but members had to have served overseas.[24]

World War I and Its Aftermath

The bullet of an assassin in Sarajevo in June 1914 sparked a powder keg of tensions in Europe that led to World War I. The so-called "war to end all wars" was the most fierce and bloody the world had yet seen. War waged between the Central Powers (Germany, Austria-Hungary, and Turkey) and the Allies (France, Great Britain, Italy, and Russia) for four years, and as it dragged on year after year mass armies emerged. In all, belligerent nations mobilized more than seventy million men. Particularly gruesome were the trenches of the western front in France. Soldiers in opposing trenches led charge after futile charge against the enemy. Machine guns and pulverizing artillery led to a mechanized form of killing and an unprecedented death toll. Widespread use of chemical weapons, which could burn or asphyxiate their victims to death, added further to the horror of the trenches. By the time the war ended on November 11, 1918, nearly ten million combatants had been killed, and about twice that number had been wounded or suffered disease.

Once the war was over, sixty million veterans returned home worldwide. No war had ever penetrated so deeply into European societies. In France, 79 percent of men aged fifteen to forty-nine saw military service. In Germany, the figure was 80 percent. Germany mobilized 13.2 million men, more than any other nation. Germany also had more men killed than did any other nation—more than two million in all. France mobilized nearly 8 million men, and lost 1.3 million. During the war, 13.2 percent of Frenchmen between the ages of fifteen and forty-nine died in the war. In Serbia, 22.6 percent of men in that age range died, and that nation lost roughly 5 percent of its total population in the war. The toll was especially hard on those born in the 1890s, who were in their late teens and early twenties at the time of the war. In Germany, roughly 35 percent of men born between 1892 and 1895 died in the war.[25]

After the war, the returning veterans faced the same basic problems that veterans had historically encountered, but the scale of the "veteran problem" was vastly increased. The medical problems facing the veterans and their governments, for example, were unprecedented in the history of warfare. In Germany alone 4.3 million wounded veterans returned home. Countless ex-soldiers suffered long-term ill health from diseases acquired in the military. Perhaps most characteristic of World War I was the psychological toll of the war on the minds of its combatants. The mass mechanical slaughter on the western front vastly increased incidents of combat-induced mental breakdowns among soldiers. At the time of World War I, modern psychology and psychiatry were in their infancy, and the notion of a subconscious was not yet widely accepted. Before World War I, cases of men breaking down in combat were believed to be the result of a soldier's moral and character flaws, or perhaps an organic problem of the victim's brain. But in World War I even the best soldiers broke down and physicians sought new answers. Believing initially that exploding artillery shells caused chemical changes in the brain, combat-related mental breakdowns were labeled "shell shock." Though physicians soon concluded that this was not the case, they still could not agree on why so many soldiers continued to suffer from combat-related mental problems. Traditional notions of morality and character persisted, and in many cases mentally disturbed veterans were not recognized as combat casualties and received little if any readjustment assistance after the war.[26]

As the conflict raged, political leaders in virtually all combatant nations had given little thought to the "veteran problem," and when the war finally ended the veterans endured much suffering in integrating themselves back into civilian society as a result. Under strong public pressure, governments demobilized their armies as quickly as possible. Releasing the men from service during a time of postwar economic crisis led to a massive unemployment problem, however. In Great Britain, for example, 300,000 veterans received unemployment "donations" in March 1919. World War I veterans overwhelmed existing facilities for ex-servicemen. Pension systems for veterans proved woefully inadequate, given the scale of suffering the war caused. In Italy, the government made virtually no provisions for the reintegration of ordinary veterans, and in fact reneged on a promise of free land for that nation's ex-soldiers. What readjustment provisions governments did make were undermined by economic and political turbulence. Germany devised perhaps the most comprehensive system of pensions for disabled veterans, but the inflationary postwar economy made them largely ineffective.

The mass armies of World War I led to mass veterans' organizations after the war. In France, such groups involved roughly 3.5 million of the nation's 6.6 million *anciens combattants* during the 1920s and 1930s. Typically, ex-soldiers joined such organizations for the purposes of camaraderie, memorialization of the war dead, and as a political interest group to further the needs of veterans. Most of the major organizations to emerge from the war, like the British Legion (organized in 1921) or the *Union fédérale des associations françaises d'anciens combattants et victimes de la guerre* (UF), eschewed partisan politics. That is not to say that veterans' groups did not play a role in European politics, however. Large groups such as the British Legion and the UF, taking the cue from the Grand Army of the Republic in the United States, were important pressure groups pushing European governments to enact, improve, and maintain government readjustment programs for veterans.[27]

However, in the turbulent aftermath of World War I veterans gained a reputation for political radicalism. While some ex-soldiers became involved in communism and other left-wing radical movements, veterans were most commonly associated with agitation from the extreme right. It has been argued that the values of the military, such as duty, obedience, nationalism, were inculcated into a generation of European men and contributed to the development of fascism in the interwar period. Although only a minority of veterans participated in the early fascist organizations, that minority was often vocal and visible. Rightist veterans were important in the February 1934 demonstrations in Paris that brought down the Daladier government, for example. Veterans also played a role in early British fascism.[28]

In Italy and Germany, where the central governments were especially weak, right-wing veterans played key roles in their downfall. Veterans were prominent in Benito Mussolini's black-shirted *fascio di combattimento*, which marched on Rome in 1922 and established the first fascist dictatorship. In Germany, the Weimar Republic established after the war was wildly unpopular with that nation's ex-soldiers. Veterans were angered not only by the republic's failure to build a memorial to the nation's war dead, but many also believed that it was responsible for the supposed *dolchstoss* (stab in the back) that—as they saw it—forced an undefeated German army to surrender. In the political chaos that followed the war in Germany, numerous right-wing paramilitary groups, often dominated by veterans, battled leftists in the streets for years. The largest of such groups was the *Stahlhelm* (Steel Helmet), which at one point numbered an estimated 400,000 members. Veterans were also prominent in the National Socialist German Worker's Party (NSDAP), or Nazi Party, led by Adolf Hitler, a former corporal in the German army. Hitler and the Nazis exhibited a tendency toward violence and a disdain for democratic political institutions. In 1923, the Nazis attempted to take over the Bavarian government by force in the famed "Beer Hall Putsch." While in prison for his coup attempt, Hitler wrote his political manifesto *Mein Kampf*, outlining the racist, militaristic, and nationalistic Nazi worldview. Hitler was soon released from prison, and by 1933 had gained control of the German national government and extinguished the hated Weimar Republic. The activities of militaristic, right-wing veterans in Italy and Germany led to the crises that sparked World War II, and heightened traditional fears about veterans posing a potential threat to the social and political order.[29]

The situation in the United States was much the same as in Europe. Between 1914 and 1917, the United States watched in horror as Europe seemed to commit suicide. As a rising world power, the United States was not immune to the European calamity. American economic ties to the Allies, and Germany's attempts to cut them through submarine warfare, eventually dragged the United States into the conflagration. On April 6, 1917, Congress declared war on Germany, and by the end of the year Americans were in combat on the western front in France. The war eventually involved nearly five million Americans under arms, with two million soldiers overseas in Europe, both numbers without parallel in American history. More than 116,000 Americans died and more than 200,000 were wounded in the nineteen months between the declaration of war and the armistice of November 1918—meager by European standards, but second only to the Civil War in American history up to that time.[30]

In preparing for World War I veterans, President Woodrow Wilson and his progressive policy makers in Washington sought to avoid the corruption and expense surrounding the GAR and pensions for Civil War veterans. Rather than placing World War I veterans under the existing general law pension system, the federal government devised a whole new plan for veterans' affairs, the cornerstone of which was the War Risk Insurance Act of 1917. This act provided participating soldiers with up to $10,000 in life insurance, which could be converted to cover the veterans in civilian life as well. Veterans could also receive disability pensions under the new law, but the disability had to have been incurred in the line of duty, not as the result of misconduct, and decrease the veteran's economic earning capabilities. Disabled veterans could receive job training through the Federal Board of Vocational Education. The federal government also began a hospital construction program for veterans under the Public Health Service. In 1919 Congress appropriated more than $9 million, with a later allotment of $18.6 million, for veterans' hospitals and rehabilitation.[31]

Despite good intentions, President Wilson's plan was a failure. Like European nations, the American government did little about unemployment for able-bodied veterans. America also demobilized quickly during an economic recession, sending veterans from the inspection line to the bread line in a relatively brief period of time. Rapid demobilization left the government flooded with veterans' claims and unable to process them effectively. Strict interpretation of "service-connection" denied pensions to many veterans who had contracted diseases like tuberculosis while in service, or who suffered from psychiatric disorders. Veterans found that running from agency to agency was confusing and difficult. In 1921, Wilson's successor, Warren G. Harding, combined most veterans' programs into one agency, the Veterans' Bureau, and liberalized program eligibility, but federal programs remained largely ineffective. The new Veterans' Bureau was still unable to handle the thousands of claims it received, and corruption exacerbated its problems. The bureau's director, Charles Forbes, was one of the most corrupt appointees in the scandal-ridden Harding administration. Forbes diverted millions of dollars from the bureau into his own pockets and those of his friends—money meant to assist the returning veterans.[32]

Veterans' groups pressed the federal government for better readjustment aid. The most important organization of World War I veterans in the United States was the American Legion, founded by doughboys in Paris in 1919. Having been the men who fought President Wilson's war to make the world "safe for democracy," the Legionnaires saw themselves as the guardians of American patriotism and exhibited a strong crusading spirit. They championed what they called a "100 percent Americanism," though the organization failed to define exactly what that meant. The Legion gained fame in its early years for its zealous anticommunist campaigns, but its main successes came in pressuring lawmakers for better veterans' benefits. Like the GAR decades before, Legionnaires saw themselves as the saviors of the nation and believed that it should reward the veterans with generous benefits to assist their readjustment back into civilian life. But unlike the GAR, the American Legion was a national organization (as opposed to the sectional nature of the GAR), with a membership fluctuating in the 1920s and 1930s between 600,000 and one million. Legionnaires built strong organizations in every state and territory. Although the American Legion was the most powerful veterans' organization of the time, it was not the only one. World War I veterans also founded the Disabled American Veterans (DAV) in 1920 and ex-doughboys soon dominated the Veterans of Foreign Wars. The DAV and the VFW also pressured lawmakers for action on veterans' matters.[33]

The American Legion, VFW, and DAV were successful in bettering the readjustment benefits for veterans. The organized veterans pressed for a "bonus," a cash payment to all veterans to compensate them for economic opportunities lost while in service. Congress passed several such measures, only to have them meet presidential vetoes. In 1924 Congress overrode President Calvin Coolidge's veto and passed into law the Adjusted Compensation Act, also known as the "Bonus Bill." Veterans would receive cash payments based on the length and type of service, but not payable until 1945. Congress also passed the World War Veterans' Act in 1924, which reorganized the Veterans' Bureau, codified existing veterans' legislation, and further extended eligibility for benefits to include pensions and hospitalization rights for non-service-connected disabilities. During the 1920s, three federal agencies managed most veterans' programs: the Veterans' Bureau, the Bureau of Pensions, and the National Home for Disabled Volunteer Soldiers. The American Legion lobbied for the consolidation of agencies handling veterans' affairs, a goal largely realized in 1930 with the creation of the Veterans' Administration.

Many state governments devised their own veteran readjustment programs. Lawmakers in Wisconsin adopted some particularly innovative programs. In contrast to the contentious bonus debate in Washington, legislators in Madison in 1919 provided Wisconsin's World War I veterans with a choice of two bonuses. Veterans could apply for a lump-sum cash payment, the amount of which was fixed at $10 per month of service but not lower than $50 total. Veterans could instead opt for an educational bonus, which provided up to $1,080 for schooling. The educational bonus addressed the problem of vocational dislocation for the nondisabled ignored by federal officials. In 1919, the state legislature also appropriated $500,000 to aid sick, wounded, and disabled veterans during convalescence periods, and established the Wisconsin Memorial Hospital near Madison to care for veterans with mental disorders. The convalescence aid and the hospital were financed by the state's general fund, but the bonus payments came from special taxes authorized by a September 1919 referendum. The Soldiers' Rehabilitation Board, a new agency that fell under the state's adjutant general, disbursed the bonus payments. State legislators also made World War I veterans eligible for many existing facilities and programs, including admission to the Grand Army Home.[34]

Although Americans, unlike Europeans, enjoyed great economic prosperity during the middle and late 1920s, the Great Depression that struck in 1929 brought severe economic hardship to America. Claims filed with the Veterans' Administration increased as the depression grew worse. A movement developed among veterans for an early payment of the federal bonus authorized in 1924. In 1932, disgruntled veterans organized a "Bonus Army" to camp out in Washington until lawmakers approved the early bonus payment. Congress rejected an early payment, however, and President Herbert Hoover ordered General Douglas MacArthur to remove the veterans from their encampment on the Anacostia Flats. Cavalry, tanks, and troops with machine guns appeared in the streets of Washington. Federal troops burned down the veterans' camp and forcibly broke up the Bonus Army. The 1932

Bonus March raised the specter of a violent revolution in a depression-desperate America. Coming during the age of Hitler and Mussolini, the Bonus March reinforced in the minds of many the suggestion that angry veterans could be a threat to the social and political order as well as a drain on the treasury.[35]

In March 1933, the Great Depression brought Franklin D. Roosevelt to the presidency and his New Deal political program to combat economic hard times. Although the New Deal increased government spending in many areas, veterans' affairs was not one of them. In fact, Roosevelt decreased spending on veterans significantly to pay for his New Deal programs. His primary target was the pension system. The president scrapped the existing pensions for World War I and Spanish-American War veterans and instituted a new one with tightened eligibility requirements that virtually eliminated pensions for non-service-connected disabilities. Roosevelt also opposed the early payment of the bonus, but Congress overrode his veto in 1936. In all, President Roosevelt decreased veterans' spending from $705 million in 1932 to $551 million by 1936. Roosevelt had won a rare victory over the American Legion and other veterans' groups, but the battle embittered relations between FDR and the veterans for years to come.[36]

Conclusion

As Americans in the 1940s anticipated the return of sixteen million veterans following World War II, the historical record suggested to them that the transition could be rocky at best, and potentially devastating to American society and the republic itself. The past loomed large in the minds of many Americans during World War II. In particular, the sorry state of veterans' affairs after World War I would have a great, haunting impact on Americans as they prepared to receive veterans of World War II. The turbulent memories of Mussolini and Hitler, Bonus Marchers, impoverished veterans—still fresh in the minds of millions of Americans—suggested to them that with the cessation of hostilities, a period of conflict and crisis might continue for some time to come.

Americans during World War II undoubtedly longed for an end to the war and the return of their loved ones. However, intertwined with that desire was a hint of apprehension. Would disgruntled veterans roam the streets of America? Would ex-servicemen turn to political action—even militarism and dictatorship—to achieve their goals? For Americans in the 1940s, these were not abstract or exaggerated questions, and it was with such questions in mind that American citizens, as well as their elected representatives charged with the welfare of the nation, anticipated the return of the largest generation of veterans in all of American history.

18   Introduction

Notes

1. Jonathan Shay, *Achilles in Vietnam: Combat Trauma and the Undoing of Character* (New York: Scribner, 1994); A. F. Sisson, *History of Veterans' Pensions and Related Benefits* (Washington, D.C.: American University, 1946), 1; Martha Edwards, "Philoctetes in Historical Context," in *Disabled Veterans in History*, ed. David A. Gerber (Ann Arbor: University of Michigan Press, 2000), 64.
2. Charles Ebel, "Southern Gaul in the Triumviral Period: A Critical Stage in Romanization," *American Journal of Philology* 109 (1988): 572-590; Yann Le Bohec, *The Imperial Roman Army* (New York: Hippocrene, 1994), 223-225; Hagith Sivan, "On Foederati, Hospitalis, and the Settlement of the Goths in A.D. 418," *American Journal of Philology* 108 (1987): 759-772; G. R. Watson, *The Roman Soldier* (London: Thames and Hudson, 1969), 133-154.
3. André Corvisier, *Armies and Societies in Europe, 1494-1789* (Bloomington: University of Indiana Press, 1979), 82-86; Jean-Pierre Bois, *Les anciens soldats dans la société française au XVIIIe siècle* (Paris: Economica, 1990), 25-38; Henry J. Webb, *Elizabethan Military Science: The Books and the Practice* (Madison: University of Wisconsin Press, 1965), 171-176.
4. Geoffrey Parker, *The Army of Flanders and the Spanish Road, 1567-1659: The Logistics of Spanish Victory and Defeat in the Low Countries' Wars* (London: Cambridge University Press, 1972), 168; Lucienne Van Meerbeeck, "L'Hôpital Royale de l'Armée espagnole à Malines en l'an 1637," *Handelingen van de Koninklijke Kring voor Oudheidekunde, Letteren en Kunst van Mechelen* 54 (1950): 81-125; Bois, *Les anciens soldats*, 38-72; Isser Woloch, *The French Veteran from the Revolution to the Restoration* (Chapel Hill: University of North Carolina Press, 1979), 3-76; C. T. G. Dean, *The Royal Chelsea Hospital* (London: Hutchinson, 1950), 15-43; Corvisier, *Armies and Societies*, 86; Elise Kimerling Wirtschafter, "Social Misfits: Veterans and Soldiers' Families in Servile Russia," *Journal of Military History* 59 (1995): 219-221.
5. Christopher Duffy, *The Army of Frederick the Great* (London: David and Charles, 1974), 60-62; Bois, *Les anciens soldats*, 38-72, 205-262; Woloch, *French Veteran*, 3-76; R. E. Scouller, *The Armies of Queen Anne* (London: Oxford University Press, 1966), 328-329; William O. Shanahan, *Prussian Military Reforms, 1786-1813* (New York: Columbia University Press, 1945), 161-162, 169-170.
6. Alan Ramsay Skelley, *The Victorian Army at Home: The Recruitment and Terms and Conditions of the British Regular, 1859-1899* (Montreal: McGill-Queens University Press, 1977), 205-216; Scouller, *Armies of Queen Anne*, 326-328; Joachim Ehlers, *Die Wehrverfassung der Stadt Hamburg im 17. und 18. Jahrhundert* (Boppard am Rhein: Harald Boldt Verlag, 1966), 70-78; Bois, *Les anciens soldats*, 73-106; Woloch, *French Veteran*, 6-17, 96-109, 295-299.
7. Duffy, *Army of Frederick*, 41, 60-61; Woloch, *French Veteran*, 13; Bois, *Les anciens soldats*, 285-287; Scouller, *Armies of Queen Anne*, 334; Skelley, *Victorian Army at Home*, 209.
8. Scouller, *Armies of Queen Anne*, 325-326; Duffy, *Army of Frederick*, 41, 60-62; Shanahan, *Prussian Military Reforms*, 32, 70; Wirtschafter, "Social Misfits," 223-224; Skelley, *Victorian Army at Home*, 98-101, 214. Russia, with a vast abundance of uncultivated land, also employed a program to resettle veterans on vacant government lands. See Wirtschafter, "Social Misfits," 226-227.
9. Parker, *Armies of Flanders*, 169; Paul E. Kopperman, "'The Cheapest Pay': Alcohol Abuse in the Eighteenth-Century British Army," *Journal of Military History* 60

(1996): 445-470; Bois, *Les anciens soldats*, 282-292; Duffy, *Army of Frederick*, 41-42, 60-62.

10. Woloch, *French Veterans*, 172-191; V. Trajkov and S. Papadopolous, "La société Thraco-Bulgare en Grèce durant les années 40 du XIXe siècle," *Balkan Studies* 25 (1984): 573-582; Skelley, *Victorian Army at Home*, 214-216; James M. Diehl, *Thanks of the Fatherland: German Veterans After the Second World War* (Chapel Hill: University of North Carolina Press, 1993), 6-7.

11. Bois, *Les anciens soldats*, 291.

12. The best survey of the American veterans' experience remains Dixon Wecter's *When Johnny Comes Marching Home*. See also Richard Severo and Lewis Milford, *The Wages of War: When American Soldiers Came Home—From Valley Forge to Vietnam* (New York: Simon and Schuster, 1989).

13. William H. Glasson, *History of Military Pension Legislation in the United States* (New York: Arno Press, 1968), 12-14; William H. Glasson, *Federal Military Pensions in the United States* (New York: Oxford University Press, 1918), 1-19.

14. Wecter, *When Johnny Comes Marching Home*, 21-100, Severo and Milford, *Wages of War*, 19-80. For an excellent discussion of the war and society, see Charles Royster, *A Revolutionary People at War: The Continental Army and American Character, 1775-1783* (New York: Norton, 1979).

15. Glasson, *History of Military Pension Legislation*, 14-24; Glasson, *Federal Military Pensions*, 19-53.

16. Severo and Milford, *Wages of War*, 51-63; Wecter, *When Johnny Comes Marching Home*, 73-81. For history of the Society of the Cincinnati, see Minor Myers Jr., *Liberty without Anarchy: A History of the Society of the Cincinnati* (Charlottesville: University of Virginia Press, 1983). For more on Shays' Rebellion, see Robert A. Gross, *In Debt to Shays: The Bicentennial of an Agrarian Rebellion* (Charlottesville: University of Virginia Press, 1993).

17. Glasson, *History of Military Pension Legislation*, 25-69; Glasson, *Federal Military Pensions*, 54-122; John P. Resch, *Suffering Soldiers: Revolutionary War Veterans, Moral Sentiment, and Political Culture in the Early Republic* (Amherst: University of Massachusetts Press, 1999); Constance B. Schulz, "Revolutionary War Pension Applications: An Overview," in *Our Family, Our Town: Essays of Family and Local History Sources in the National Archives*, ed. Timothy Walch (Washington, D.C.: National Archives, 1987); James W. Oberly, *Sixty Million Acres: American Veterans and Public Lands before the Civil War* (Kent, Ohio: Kent State University Press, 1990).

18. Glasson, *History of Military Pension Legislation*, 70-87; Glasson, *Federal Military Pensions*, 143-167; Wisconsin Legislative Reference Bureau, *A Thumbnail History of Wisconsin Veterans' Legislation* (Madison: Legislative Reference Bureau, 1988), 1-2. For more on the development of the National Home, see Patrick J. Kelly, *Creating a National Home: Building the Veterans' Welfare State, 1860-1900* (Cambridge, Mass.: Harvard University Press, 1997).

19. Severo and Milford, *Wages of War*, 119-186; Wecter, *When Johnny Comes Marching Home*, 101-244. For discussion of the war's effects on American society, see Maris Vinovskis, "Have Social Historians Lost the Civil War?: Some Preliminary Demographic Speculations," in *Toward a Social History of the American Civil War: Exploratory Essays*, ed. Maris Vinovskis (New York: Cambridge University Press, 1990), 1-30. For more on "nostalgia," see Eric T. Dean Jr., *Shook over Hell: Post-Traumatic Stress, Vietnam, and the Civil War* (Cambridge, Mass.: Harvard University Press, 1997).

20. For more on the origins of the Ku Klux Klan, see Wyn Craig Wade, *The Fiery Cross: The Ku Klux Klan in America* (London: Simon and Schuster, 1987), 31-118. For

more on the GAR, see Stuart McConnell, *Glorious Contentment: The Grand Army of the Republic, 1865-1900* (Chapel Hill: University of North Carolina Press, 1992) and Mary R. Dearing, *Veterans in Politics: The Story of the GAR* (Westport, Conn.: Greenwood Press, 1974). For Wisconsin perspective on national events, see Richard H. Zeitlin and Mark D. Van Ells, "Politics, Community, Education: A Brief History of Veterans' Organizations in Wisconsin and America," *Wisconsin Academy Review* 40 (1994): 4-5.

　　21. Dearing, *Veterans in Politics*, 308-351; McConnell, *Glorious Contentment*, 125-165. For veterans' pensions in the overall context of the development of the American welfare state, see Theda Skocpol, *Protecting Soldiers and Mothers: The Political Origins of Social Policy in the United States* (Cambridge, Mass.: Harvard University Press, 1992).

　　22. McConnell, *Glorious Contentment*, 138-153; Hosea Rood, *History of the Wisconsin Veterans' Home, 1886-1926* (Madison, Wis.: Democrat Press, 1926), 13-30. While Confederate veterans did not receive federal pensions, southern state governments passed pension laws and established homes for their Civil War veterans. For more, see R. B. Rosenburg, *Living Monuments: Confederate Soldiers' Homes in the New South* (Chapel Hill: University of North Carolina Press, 1993).

　　23. Vinovskis, "Have Social Historians Lost the Civil War?" 21-28; Glasson, *Federal Military Pensions*, vii-viii.

　　24. Glasson, *Federal Military Pensions*, 145; Legislative Reference Bureau, *Thumbnail History*, 1; Severo and Milford, *Wages of War*, 187-228. For more on the Veterans of Foreign Wars, see Bill Bottoms, *The VFW: An Illustrated History of the Veterans of Foreign Wars of the United States* (Rockville, Md.: Woodbine House, 1991).

　　25. Casualty figures vary. For an international comparison of World War I casualties, see Boris Urlanis, *Bilanz der Krieges: Die Menschenverluste Europas vom 17. Jahrhundert bis zur Gegenwart* (Berlin: Deutscher Verlag der Wissenschaft, 1965), 127-160, 267-273, 336-359. For an excellent English-language discussion of Germany in particular, see Robert Weldon Whalen, *Bitter Wounds: German Victims of the Great War, 1914-1939* (Ithaca, N.Y.: Cornell University Press, 1984), 37-48.

　　26. For a survey of the condition of veterans in postwar Europe (as well as the United States), see Stephen R. Ward, ed., *The War Generation: Veterans of the First World War* (Port Washington, N.Y.: Kennikat Press, 1975). For more on psychological problems in the context of the time, see Ted Bogacz, "War Neuroses and Cultural Change in England, 1914-1922: The Work of the War Office Committee of Enquiry into 'Shell Shock,'" *Journal of Contemporary History* 24 (1989): 227-256.

　　27. For an overview, see Ward, *War Generation*. For Great Britain, see Graham Wootton, *The Politics of Influence: British Ex-servicemen, Cabinet Decisions, and Cultural Change, 1917-1957* (London: Routledge & Kegan Paul, 1963). For France, see Antoine Prost, *Les anciens combattants et la société française, 1914-1939* (Paris: Fondation Nationale des Sciences Politiques, 1977). Prost's landmark study is available in abbreviated form in English as *In the Wake of War: "Les Anciens Combattants" and French Society* (New York: Berg, 1992).

　　28. Ward, *War Generation*, 3-9; Rene Remand, "Les anciens combattants et la politique," *Revue française de science politique* V (1955): 267-290; Richard Bessel and David Englander, "Up from the Trenches: Some Recent Writing on the Soldiers of the Great War," *European Studies Review* 11 (1981): 387-395. For an overview of fascism and its development, see Stanley Payne, *Fascism: Definition and Comparison* (Madison: University of Wisconsin Press, 1980).

29. For more on Italy, see Philip Morgan, *Italian Fascism, 1919-1945* (New York: St. Martin, 1995). For Germany, see A. J. Nicholls, *Weimar and the Rise of Hitler* (New York: St. Martin, 1991).

30. The best account of American involvement in World War I remains Edward M. Coffman, *The War to End All Wars: The American Military Experience in World War I* (New York: Oxford University Press, 1968). For American casualty statistics, see Leonard P. Ayres, *The War with Germany: A Statistical Summary* (Washington, D.C.: GPO, 1919).

31. Glasson, *Federal Military Pensions*, 283-295; William Pyrle Dillingham, *Federal Aid to Veterans, 1917-1941* (Gainesville: University of Florida Press, 1952), 25-72.

32. Severo and Milford, *Wages of War*, 229-280; Wecter, *When Johnny Comes Marching Home*, 370-405; Glasson, *Federal Military Pensions*, 283-295; Dillingham, *Federal Aid to Veterans*, 25-72.

33. For more on the American Legion, see William Pencak, *For God and Country: The American Legion, 1919-1941* (Boston: Northeastern University Press, 1989) and Thomas A. Rumer, *The American Legion: An Official History, 1919-1989* (New York: M. Evans, 1990). For more on the Wisconsin Department of the American Legion, see George E. Sweet, *The Wisconsin American Legion: A History, 1919-1992* (Milwaukee: Wisconsin American Legion Press, 1992). No comprehensive history of the DAV exists. For the Wisconsin context, see Zeitlin and Van Ells, "Politics, Community, Education," 6-7.

34. Legislative Reference Bureau, *Thumbnail History*, 3-5.

35. The best account of the Bonus March remains Roger Daniels, *The Bonus March: An Episode of the Great Depression* (Westport, Conn.: Greenwood Press, 1971).

36. Dillingham, *Federal Aid to Veterans*, 73-82.

Chapter One

"The Art We Must Perfect":
Government Planning for
World War II Veterans

In his 1944 book *The Veteran Comes Back,* Columbia University social worker Willard Waller called veterans "our gravest social problem." According to Waller, veterans often returned home from war angry and embittered about the sacrifices the nation had demanded of them, and he warned America that veterans might lash out at society. *"The veteran is, and always has been,"* the author claimed, *"a problematic element in society, an unfortunate, misused, and pitiable man, and, like others whom society has mistreated, a threat to existing institutions"* [italics in original]. America would soon be faced with the largest veteran influx in its history. "We must somehow find a way to win them back," Waller warned. But how? "What the times demand is a new art," he argued:

> the art of rehabilitation. We know how to turn the civilian into a soldier. History has taught us that all too well; tradition has given us marvelously adequate techniques. But we do not know how to turn the soldier into a civilian again. This is the art that we must perfect if we are to ever solve the problem of the veteran in our society.

During World War II, the American political system, at the federal, state, and local levels, searched for new ways to handle an old problem—the returning war veteran.[1]

The desire to aid World War II veterans led to intense political battles at all levels of government during the 1940s. The size of the World War II veteran population demanded that lawmakers take some kind of action on veterans' readjustment benefits. Fueling the drive for new veterans' programs were painful memories of past postwar periods. Although lawmakers at all levels of government spoke of generosity toward returning ex-soldiers, they were sometimes motivated as much by fear of veterans and their potential impact on society. References to episodes like the Bonus March, the rise of fascism in Europe, and the economic suffering of the Great Depression peppered discussions of postwar planning. With sixteen million veterans about to come home, lawmakers hoped a generous package of benefits would help head off veteran agitation in the post-World War II period. The American Legion, a politically potent organization of World War I veterans, played a key role in shaping policy toward veterans. To be sure, the Legion, which in 1942 voted to include World War II veterans in its ranks, hoped that political advocacy for veterans would bring recruits and expanded political power. However, Legionnaires also hoped to avoid a repetition of the turbulent and traumatic readjustment they had experienced just decades before.

Washington's Plans for Veterans

As the segment of government that wages war, maintains armies, and conscripts soldiers, the federal government assumed the primary role in readjusting veterans to civilian life. Washington in the 1940s saw an unprecedented outpouring of laws related to veterans. The most important piece of veterans' legislation produced during the 1940s was the Serviceman's Readjustment Act of 1944, better known as the GI Bill of Rights.[2] This law included not only the famed educational provisions, but also loan programs and unemployment insurance, and included nearly all World War II veterans.

Planning for the return of World War II veterans began even before Pearl Harbor. The Selective Service Act of 1940, America's first peacetime conscription law, sparked fierce debate in Congress regarding America's policy toward the European conflict and the potential for "militarism" infecting American society. It also included a provision for the reemployment of those young men drafted into military service. Section 8 of the law stipulated that draftees, under certain conditions, would be allowed to reclaim their jobs once their military obligation had ended. However, the provision contained numerous loopholes for employers. For example, employers were not obligated to rehire a draftee if "changed circumstances" had made his position obsolete. Such loopholes drew fire from critics of the measure. For example, Senator Burton K. Wheeler, Democrat of Montana, charged that many of the bill's proponents "do not hesitate to promise blindly that this clause will guarantee conscripts the return of their jobs." Nevertheless, Section 8 signaled a change in policy toward veterans fostered by the experience of World War I and the massive veteran unemployment problem created by hasty demobilization. It also marked the beginning of the effort to rectify past mistakes and broaden the scope of veterans' readjustment benefits.[3]

After American entry into the war, federal discussion of the veteran problem began under the auspices of the National Resources Planning Board (NRPB), headed by the president's uncle, Frederick A. Delano. Barely six months after Pearl Harbor, Delano suggested to Roosevelt "a small planning committee" within the NRPB to discuss postwar reconversion, including the role of veterans in the national economy. The president agreed to the formation of the committee, but only on the condition that its work be kept unpublicized and "off the record," so as not to distract the government and the public from the task of winning the war. The resulting Conference on Postwar Readjustment of Civilian and Military Personnel, better known as the "Postwar Manpower Conference" (PMC), became a kind of clearinghouse of ideas and information on the problem of veteran readjustment.[4]

The conference examined and discussed a wide range of programs and ideas—some tested, some not—in reestablishing veterans in civilian life. One topic of considerable discussion was Wisconsin's 1919 educational bonus for World War I veterans, which had provided veterans up to $1,080 for educational attainment. The conferees also studied the Canadian government's planning for that nation's World War II veterans, which included programs ranging from unemployment insurance to education to resettlement of veterans on farms. Indeed, PMC members in 1943 traveled to Canada to discuss ideas with Canadian veterans' officials. The conference's final report, issued in June 1943, contained ninety-six proposals, many of which related to veteran readjustment. One recommendation, for example, called for discharged veterans to receive a "furlough," a lump sum cash payment to tide them over until they could find work. Taking a page from the Canadian plan, the PMC report also called for an unemployment insurance program for veterans. The final report emphasized education for veterans rather strongly. It suggested a two-part education plan. Under the proposal, all veterans would be entitled to one year of schooling or training. After that, a select group of veterans, who had distinguished themselves in the first year, would be eligible for an additional three years of education. In each case, the government would pay tuition, as well as provide for books and living expenses. Such a plan would not only provide America with trained and educated workers, the PMC argued, but would also keep many veterans off the unemployment rolls while they were in school. Many of the PMC's recommendations represented a departure from previous veteran programs—most notably, they advocated assistance to the nondisabled for education and employment assistance. Once again, federal policy makers were broadening the scope of veterans' benefits.

The PMC was not the only body in the executive branch to explore ideas for veterans' policies. In typical Rooseveltian fashion, the president put others on the task of studying veteran readjustment. In November 1942, he announced the extension of draft eligibility from twenty-one to eighteen years of age. To soften the blow of this action, he also announced that he was creating a committee to study the problem of the veteran whose education had been interrupted by the war. The committee, led by Brig. Gen. Frederick H. Osborn, submitted its final report on July 30, 1943. The committee's conclusions were rather similar to those reached by the PMC with regard to education and the veteran. The committee recommended one year of college or technical education for veterans who had served honorably for at least six months. Those student-veterans who showed particular talents might receive an additional two years of training at government expense.

Although Roosevelt kept his postwar planning initiatives largely under wraps, by the middle of 1943 public discussion of veterans' affairs increased. After a year and a half of war, many veterans had already returned home, most of whom were afflicted with physical or mental disabilities. In addition, the tide of war had shifted rather decisively toward the Allies, and Americans began to anticipate the postwar years. Roosevelt's first public statements on the question of veterans came during a "fireside chat" on July 28, 1943. In his remarks, the president underlined the seriousness of the veteran readjustment issue by invoking the memories of the early 1920s and the Great Depression. "Our gallant men and women in the armed services," he said, "must not be demobilized into an environment of inflation and unemployment, to a place on the breadline or the corner selling apples." Recalling the confusion of the World War I demobilization, Roosevelt insisted that "we must, this time, have plans ready—instead of waiting to do a hasty, inefficient, and ill-considered job at the last moment." The president outlined his basic agenda for veterans, including "mustering out pay" for discharged veterans, an unemployment insurance program, and federal educational programs for veterans. He promised that specific proposals would come "in a few weeks."

Executive action took months rather than weeks, but Roosevelt proposed several pieces of veteran-related legislation during the latter half of 1943, based on the findings of the PMC and the Osborn report. On October 27, the president called for an educational program for honorably discharged veterans. The program would provide at least one year of study at government expense to qualified veterans who had served at least six months, and a select group would receive up to three years of schooling. Such a program, he argued, would not only provide America with a more educated workforce, but student-veterans would also stay off the unemployment rolls for several years, easing any possible postwar unemployment problem. The program, Roosevelt added, might cost upwards of $1 billion. In November, Roosevelt proposed legislation for mustering out pay for veterans, providing $300 to discharged veterans in three monthly installments. The president reiterated his desire not to repeat the post-World War I experience. "We must have plans and legislation ready for our returning veterans instead of waiting until the last moment," he declared.

Roosevelt and the executive branch had clearly been leading the way in preparation for postwar veterans' readjustment, but they were not alone in their concern for the veteran in the postwar period. Congressmen and veterans' groups had also been working on postwar problems. Organized veterans' groups such as the Disabled American Veterans, the Veterans of Foreign Wars, and especially the large and powerful American Legion, had long had friends in Congress. As veterans returned and victory seemed ever more likely, Congress—particularly the president's political opponents—grew increasingly vocal on veterans' issues. During the war years, the fortunes of the Democrats and the New Deal seemed to be on the wane. Anti-New Dealers in Congress saw an opportunity to criticize Roosevelt and curry favor with a potentially large voting block of voter-veterans.

With regard to the veteran education proposal, critics charged that Roosevelt was spending too much money. The reaction in Wisconsin was typical of that in Washington and in other parts of the nation. Some saw the proposal as a wasteful perpetuation of the New Deal. Speaking before the Wisconsin legislature, Gilman Stordock, adjutant of the Wisconsin Department of the American Legion, characterized the plan as a "scheme to perpetuate the brain trusters in office or a way of creating a new bureaucracy in Washington," and warned that "the federal government might want to provide textbooks filled with propaganda." Education for veterans was a worthy idea, in Stordock's view, but one best handled at the state and local level—not by New Dealers in Washington. Others viewed the president's education proposal more positively. The *Milwaukee Journal* considered the effort worthy but found the price tag alarming, and warned that "we will not want to repeat the mistake made after the last war in thinking that mere uncontrolled grants of money represent true generosity. This time we will want to give real help, not just money." The *Menomonee Falls News* called the billion dollar price tag "modest." "It is one of the supreme ironies of our time," the *News* argued, "that men who show no hesitancy whatever in dumping billions into educating our youth for the highly refined skills of modern warfare are horrified at the prospect of spending a modest amount toward aiding these same young men and women [to] make something worthwhile of their lives" once the war was over.[5]

The mustering out pay proposal also generated a firestorm of controversy. In this instance, FDR was criticized for spending too little. Soon after debate over mustering out pay began, the American Legion entered the fray. On November 29, American Legion national commander Warren H. Atherton appeared before the House Veterans' Affairs Committee with 1,536 accounts—collected from local American Legion posts across the nation—of World War II veterans who had returned home without being able to obtain adequate readjustment assistance. Typical of the stories Atherton told was that of "Bill Smith." A grenade at Guadalcanal had left Bill partially paralyzed. After six months in military hospitals, "they sent Bill home paralyzed, and penniless." His army pay, on which his mother survived, had vanished with his discharge. Bill had to wait four months before the Veterans' Administration would act on his disability claim. Atherton told many other stories of callous officials, red tape, and an overworked staff at Veterans' Administration facilities—all of which kept veterans from getting what help there was available to them. "Even a convict who is discharged from prison is given more money and a suit of clothes," Atherton told the Congressmen, but "the veteran, when he is discharged from the hospital or separation center, is given neither." The government was simply dumping discharged veterans back into the communities, Atherton claimed, in particular disabled veterans—heroes who had to depend on charity and welfare to survive. Atherton called on Congress to increase the proposed $300 in mustering out pay to $500.[6]

The American Legion found a valuable ally in the Hearst newspaper chain. William Randolph Hearst, a pioneer in sensationalistic journalism and a vehement Roosevelt opponent, used the veteran issue to bludgeon the president and the New Deal. Hearst newspapers across America—including the *Milwaukee Sentinel* in Wisconsin—ran a series of articles beginning in late 1943 urging action on mustering out pay and other veterans' issues. "The vague and spacious promises of President Roosevelt and the unformed plans of Congress for assistance to veterans . . . all rest on the assumption that there is plenty of time," a

Hearst commentary stated in December 1943, but "THE POST-WAR PERIOD HAS ALREADY ARRIVED FOR MORE THAN SIX HUNDRED THOUSAND VETERANS." The Hearst articles often described the postwar years in sensationalistic terms that recalled the 1920s and 1930s:

> We must have no repetition of the shabby chapter of ingratitude written in the government's treatment of veterans of World War I. We must have no jobless, pitiful heroes selling apples or poppies on the streets; no homeless veterans huddling under viaducts, no ragged, trusting bonus army marching hopefully on Washington to be driven out by fire and bullets, as if they were enemies of the land they saved.

Hearst lay the blame for the plight of veterans squarely at the president's feet. "But for all the fine promises of the New Deal administration," one Hearst editorial complained, "the discharged soldier in this war is being NEGLECTED and virtually ABANDONED." "TODAY'S heroes must not be treated as tomorrow's hoboes," read one editorial urging Congress to take action on veterans' affairs.[7]

In Congress, many of Roosevelt's political opponents—largely silent on the issue before the president's fireside chat of July 1943—now lambasted him for his apparent lack of attention to veterans' affairs. Congressman William Lemke, Republican of North Dakota, criticized Roosevelt's mustering out pay proposal as a "sop tossed to the service man to keep him quiet," and proposed an even more generous payment to veterans, including a full year of military pay to discharged veterans. Committees battled each other for jurisdiction over veteran-related matters. A spate of veterans' bills appeared in Congress. The *Milwaukee Journal* estimated that as of December 10, at least 232 veteran-related bills and resolutions were before Congress. The *Journal* feared that heated partisan rhetoric over veterans' affairs might endanger an effective program for veteran readjustment. The *Journal* criticized those in Congress who "believe that they can win votes . . . if they can establish a record of having demanded the ultimate in cash and privileges for the returning veteran and his family." The *Journal* characterized these politicians as "small caliber and short range leaders," and warned its readers to "guard against the politicians and those who, by immoderate campaigns and unwise proposals, want to help themselves more than the defenders of the nation."[8]

The mustering out bill became law in February 1944. Slowly, the president had been gaining enactment of the recommendations of the PMC and the Osborn report into law. Roosevelt had proposed far reaching programs for veterans—programs that had already surpassed in scope those provided to veterans of past wars. But Roosevelt's program had been enacted piecemeal. It was the American Legion that originated the idea of an "omnibus" bill for veterans. In November 1943, the Legion assembled a committee to study the needs of World War II veterans. The Legionnaires consulted with officials from the armed services and the Veterans' Administration, as well as leaders in the fields of business, labor, and education, about postwar issues. After just five weeks, the Legion committee wrote a model bill encompassing its findings. In particular, former commander Harry W. Colmery was said to have written the bill in a hotel room in Washington on hotel stationary in just two days. Once drafted, the new bill needed a name. After reading the draft bill, Jack Cejnar, the American Legion's acting public relations director, reportedly exclaimed that it was a "bill of rights for GI Joe and GI Jane." The name stuck, though shortened to the "GI Bill of Rights." "The name was something close to genius," the American Legion later bragged. "It was short, punchy, easily grasped. It told the whole story—and it became a fighting slogan from coast to coast."[9]

The original American Legion draft contained several proposals, many of which were already being discussed in Washington; others were new. Like President Roosevelt, the Legionnaires were greatly concerned with employment. For those veterans who could not find work, the American Legion proposed federal unemployment benefits to veterans of up to $25 a week for one year. The Legionnaires also addressed education. The original American Legion proposal followed the president's own plan rather closely—honorably discharged veterans whose education had been interrupted would receive one full year of college or vocational training, with a select group of students eligible for additional federal aid. But the Legion's plan went beyond reemployment and education. For example, it called for low-interest loans to veterans for homes, businesses, or farms. The Legion draft included revised procedures for discharge reviews and claims. Finally, the Legionnaires' proposal called for the further consolidation of most federal veterans' programs under the Veterans' Administration, instead of dividing veteran-related functions among several different branches of federal government.

The American Legion proposal proved exceedingly popular in Congress. When Congress reconvened in January 1944, Representative John Rankin, Democrat of Mississippi, chairman of the World War Veterans' Legislation Committee, sponsored the proposal in the House. In the Senate, the proposal found a sponsor in Joel Bennett Clark, Democrat of Missouri, chairman of the Senate's Subcommittee on Veterans' Legislation. In the Senate, the American Legion proposal saw relatively smooth sailing. Clark's committee made some minor modifications to the proposal, but kept its general outlines intact. The most notable revision the committee made combined the American Legion's education proposals with those of the president's plan, and indeed expanded eligibility to all veterans discharged under other than dishonorable conditions, not just those whose education and training had been interrupted by the war. In March 1944, the Senate passed the omnibus veterans bill 50-0, and sent it on to the House.

The GI Bill proved to be more controversial in the House, where it came under the jurisdiction of Rankin. A frankly racist southern white Democrat, Rankin expressed a generally favorable attitude toward the GI Bill, though he voiced concerns about its social implications. He saw the bill's educational provisions, for example, as creating an overeducated, undertrained society. Reminiscent of Gilman Stordock's remarks before the Wisconsin legislature in 1943, Rankin also expressed reservations about sending large numbers of veterans to the environment of the college campus. "I would rather send my child to the red school house than the red school teacher," he once quipped. Rankin also worried about the bill's provision for unemployment benefits. "We have 50,000 Negroes in the service from our state," he complained, "and in my opinion . . . the vast majority of them would remain unemployed for at least a year, and a good many white men would do the same." The House version of the GI Bill scaled down many of the provisions in the Senate version. It cut back the period of unemployment benefits from fifty-two to twenty-six weeks, and restricted the educational provisions to only those veterans whose schooling had been interrupted by the war.

The GI Bill then went to a conference committee to hammer out the differences between the House and Senate versions. The conference was deadlocked. Breaking the logjam fell upon the shoulders of Representative John Gibson, Democrat of Georgia. Gibson originally backed Rankin's House bill. During the conference, Gibson returned to Georgia due to illness, and gave Rankin the authority to cast his vote by proxy. However, Gibson changed his mind while back home in Georgia and decided to back the Senate version. Rankin refused to cast Gibson's vote in favor of the Senate version. Without Gibson's vote, the conference would remain deadlocked, and the conference committee had scheduled a final vote on the GI Bill on June 10. At this point, the American Legion swung into action. Legionnaires scoured Georgia in search of Representative Gibson. Once located, the Legion arranged to have him flown to Washington to cast the deciding vote. The Senate version had won out. On June 12, the Senate passed the conference version of the GI Bill, and the House also passed it the following day. On June 22, President Roosevelt signed the Serviceman's Readjustment Act, better known as the GI Bill of Rights, into law.

The final bill was a combination of Roosevelt's plans and the American Legion's proposals. Perhaps the most important section of the GI Bill was Title II, regarding education. Veterans with more than six months of service were eligible for one year of education at government expense, with additional years of training available to those who completed the first year successfully. In addition to covering tuition, student-veterans would also received money for books and living expenses. Under the 1944 bill, veterans over age twenty-five had to prove their education had been interrupted to qualify. Veterans had to attend institutions accredited by the state in which they operated, but this still gave veterans and incredibly wide range of educational and training opportunities from which to choose. Veterans under the GI Bill could attend both public and private institutions, as well as vocational and technical schools, and could even take correspondence courses at government expense (see chapter 4 of this book).

But the GI Bill was more than an educational program, and other portions of the law would also have a great impact on America. In addition to sending veterans to a college, university, or other such school, Title II also made provisions for veterans to receive "on-the-job training" with employers (see chapter

5). Title III provided qualified veterans with loan guarantees up to $2,000 for homes, farms, or businesses. Loans were not to exceed 4 percent interest (see chapters 5 and 6). Title V contained provisions for unemployment compensation. Those veterans who could not find work were eligible for unemployment compensation for fifty-two weeks at the rate of $20 a month (see chapter 5). The GI Bill was the most far-reaching program for veteran readjustment in American history. The law addressed postwar problems that had traditionally vexed returning veterans, included the nondisabled, and did so in a generous manner. The law would, in later years, revolutionize American higher education and contribute mightily to the suburbanization of America. The GI Bill might well rank as one of the most important pieces of social legislation the federal government has ever enacted.

Legislation affecting veterans did not stop with the GI Bill. Indeed, the volume of federal veterans' legislation produced during the war was staggering. Between the passage of the Selective Service Act in September 1940 and the end of the war in 1945, the federal government enacted 187 laws affecting veterans. By July 1948 that total had risen to 462.[10] In an effort to provide new leadership in veterans' affairs, President Harry S. Truman brought Gen. Omar Bradley to Washington to become VA administrator in 1945. Bradley served two years before returning to the army, and was replaced by Carl R. Gray Jr., a railroad executive and also a former general. But the revolutionary aspect of this body of laws was not its size but its substance. The legislation of the 1940s not only continued and refined policies formulated after previous wars, but expanded into areas long considered outside the government's ability to influence or its moral obligation to the veterans—namely, unemployment compensation and education. The desire to avoid the mistakes of the past, combined with the immense scope and scale of the American military mobilization for World War II, led to an unprecedented outpouring of federal veteran-related legislation during the 1940s.

Wisconsin's Plans for Veterans

Though the primary responsibility for veteran readjustment rested with the federal government, veterans' affairs greatly concerned state and local governments in the 1940s as well. State governments had long enacted legislation for benefits, both out of gratitude to the veterans and fear of them. Should the federal government fail in its responsibility to readjust veterans adequately, it fell upon state and local governments to care for the ex-soldiers. As Washington struggled with the question of the returning veterans, so did legislators in state capitals, including the Wisconsin State Legislature in Madison. Events on Madison's Capitol Square proceeded roughly along the same lines as at the federal level. In Wisconsin, public demand for veterans' programs and fear of the veteran played key roles in formulating a generous policy toward veterans. The memories of World War I and the Great Depression haunted Madison's lawmakers as well. The

American Legion also played a key role at the state level. Indeed, organized
veterans in Wisconsin seem to have had even more influence over state policies
toward veterans than they did in Washington.

At the outbreak of World War II, Wisconsin was a political anomaly among
the states of the union. Republicans dominated all branches of state government
during the 1940s. The Democratic Party, by contrast, was virtually moribund.
During the 1940s, Wisconsin's second strongest party was the Progressive Party,
a loose coalition dedicated to the principles and memory of Robert M. LaFollette and dominated by his two sons, U.S. Senator Robert M. LaFollette Jr. and
former governor Philip F. LaFollette. The 1940s saw the end of the Progressive
Party in Wisconsin; older ex-Progressives returned to the Republican fold while
younger members revitalized the Democratic Party in the Badger State. Overseeing the state's confusing politics during most of the war years was Republican Governor Walter S. Goodland, an octogenarian newspaper owner from
Racine. Goodland was elected lieutenant governor in 1938 and reelected in
1942. The winner of the 1942 gubernatorial contest, Progressive Orland S.
Loomis, died before taking office, making Goodland the acting governor.
Known as the "tough old codger" for his pragmatic and independent style,
Goodland proved very popular among voters, who returned him to office in
1944 and 1946. Born during the Civil War, Goodland led the Badger State
through World War II.[11]

Postwar planning was one of Goodland's top priorities. In his first address
to the state legislature as governor, Goodland devoted considerable time to the
subject. "For the first time since the Civil War," he began, "a new incumbent is
called upon to become Chief Executive of Wisconsin during War Time." The
gravity of the war apparently weighed heavily on Goodland's mind, leaving him to
characterize his predicament as being "more grave and frightening than [that] . . .
facing any of my predecessors." Among the most important of his duties, as
Goodland saw it, was to prepare for the war's end. "We hear some people say that
it is folly to talk about postwar plans before we have won the war," he said, "but . . .
we have learned from bitter experience that the time to plan for peace is while we
are at war." Goodland indicated that the readjustment of veterans was a major part
of the postwar plan. Wisconsin's men and women in uniform, the governor
asserted,

> are entitled not only to the best that we can give them, but to our constant and
> persistent efforts now in preparing for their future social and economic welfare. . . .
> The very least we can do is to try and equalize, as best we can, their sacrifices as
> compared to ours when peace comes and they return home. . . . It is our duty to see
> that the state is prepared to do this in full measure.[12]

The governor translated his words into action. His first move with regard to
veterans was to earmark funds derived from a 60 percent surtax on 1942 state
incomes for veterans' programs. Initially, the legislature hoped to refund the
money to the taxpayers, but Governor Goodland pressured the Republican

steering committee in the Republican-dominated legislature to go along with him. "Transition from war to peace causes disturbances," the governor warned the legislature, disturbances that could be "severe and depressing, causing hardships no less than the wars which bring them on." Planning for the transition to peace had to be undertaken immediately, the governor claimed. "Whether it be done in a statesmanlike way with care and thoughtful foresight, or in a shiftless manner of letting the next Legislature provide, is for you to decide." Public reaction to the governor's designation of money for the problem of veterans' rehabilitation was generally positive. The *Wisconsin State Journal* characterized the move as a "worthwhile . . . initial step toward meeting a major problem of postwar planning." The initial $5 million of surtax funds approved by the legislature in March 1943 established the Veterans' Postwar Rehabilitation Trust Fund, and marked the beginning of Wisconsin's World War II veterans' programs.[13]

Goodland was not alone in his call for action on veterans' issues. Organized veterans, in particular the American Legion, played a key role in the shaping of veterans' policies in the Badger State. At its 1942 convention in August, the Wisconsin Department of the American Legion adopted a resolution calling for a state commission to devise a readjustment program for World War II veterans. To this end, the Legion backed an assembly bill introduced in February 1943 to establish a joint legislative committee on postwar issues. Legislators held many hearings on the bill, but by late spring had taken no action. Frustrated, Wisconsin's American Legion leaders applied political pressure on state lawmakers. A May circular letter to state and local Legionnaires sounded the legislative call to arms. "Because of certain legislation now before the Legislature in Madison, it is necessary for everyone who receives this bulletin to ACT PROMPTLY," the letter began. Leaders asked all posts and auxiliary units to send letters and telegrams to the governor and their legislators urging them to pass the bill establishing the postwar planning committee. Immediate action was crucial, claimed American Legion state commander Val W. Ove, because the legislature was about to adjourn. "The strength of more than 38,280 Legionnaires in Wisconsin must be made known," read the circular, "and must be known NOW." Letters did indeed start to flow into the offices of political leaders, and legislators formed the desired committee, headed by Milwaukee Republican State Senator Milton T. Murray.[14]

Debate then ensued over how to spend the trust fund money authorized for World War II veterans. Assemblyman Charles E. Collar, Republican of Milwaukee, introduced a proposal, in consultation with the American Legion, which would essentially recreate Wisconsin's program of bonuses for World War I veterans for those of World War II. However, momentum built behind a plan devised by Governor Goodland, and sponsored in the state senate by Majority Leader John W. Byrnes, Republican of Green Bay. The governor's plan called for creation of a new Veterans' Recognition Board for World War II veterans, composed of the governor, state adjutant general, and five others who were experts in medicine, agriculture, vocational education, and industry, as well as a representative of the organized veterans' community. Rather than specifically

authorizing bonuses for veterans as was the case after World War I, the new
board would have greater leeway in determining how best to use the money
earmarked for World War II veteran rehabilitation.[15]

The governor's plan met with skepticism from leaders of the American Legion and the Wisconsin Veterans' Council, a legislatively oriented coalition of
state veterans' groups dominated by the American Legion. The veterans argued
that the existing Soldiers' Rehabilitation Board, created to handle veterans' affairs after World War I, was the logical agency to handle those of World War II
veterans, and thus the creation of the Veterans' Recognition Board was unneces-
sary. The veterans' groups also objected to the composition of the proposed
board "because on it there would only be one veteran. Think about it. Just one
veteran on a Veterans Board to administer veterans benefits." A board dominated by veterans, claimed the American Legion, would insulate it from partisan
politics and keep the interests of the ex-serviceman the top priority. "We believe
. . . that only favorites of the political party in power are ever nominated for any
appointment," the veterans argued. The American Legion and the Wisconsin
Veterans' Council backed an amendment to the bill to bring World War II veterans under the Soldiers' Rehabilitation Board and alter the composition of this
board to increase the influence of veterans. According to this proposal, the board
would be composed of representatives of the state's four largest veterans'
groups—the American Legion, Veterans of Foreign Wars, Disabled American
Veterans, and the United Spanish War Veterans—as well as two persons appointed by the governor. The Wisconsin Veterans' Council told state legislators:

> Veterans benefits should be administered by veterans themselves who are qualified
> and capable to handle such matters. No agency charged with the administration
> should be subjected to any kind of pressure, or interference, either political or
> otherwise. We cannot afford to play politics when the lives and the welfare of the
> defenders of our Nation and their dependents are involved.

With a veteran majority, "neither the functions of the board, nor any of its employees, would be subject to the whims of any Governor, and political party or
any other state agency. We insist that the affairs of veterans be administered
without respect to political considerations—and absolutely divorced from politics in every way."[16]

Goodland met with representatives of the veterans' groups to hammer out
the final details of the measure. The two parties agreed on many key principles
that they wrote into the law and that would guide and shape veterans' affairs in
Wisconsin for years thereafter. Each agreed that the board would be a policy-
making entity, employ a director to coordinate federal and state agencies assisting veterans, and dispense trust fund money to qualified veterans. Each agreed
that veterans' welfare was primarily a federal responsibility, and that state assistance was to be used only in cases in which federal aid was insufficient or not
forthcoming. Legionnaires eventually acceded to creation of the Veterans' Recognition Board, but a dispute remained concerning its composition. The Ameri-

can Legion and Wisconsin Veterans' Council continued to insist on a board on which veterans held a majority of seats.[17]

The final bill, signed by Governor Goodland in June, was a combination of both plans. The bill created the Veterans' Recognition Board to tend to the needs of returning World War II veterans. To qualify for assistance, a veteran had to have entered the service from Wisconsin or have resided in the state five years thereafter. The board would employ a director, who would authorize payments of trust fund money for any reason, so long as such payments would alleviate "want and distress" on the part of the veterans and their families. The board was composed of the governor, the state adjutant general, and five persons appointed by the governor and confirmed by the senate. Precisely why the Legion acceded to the governor's plan so compliantly is not known, but an informal agreement to appoint veterans to the board appears to have been made. Three of Goodland's five appointees to the new board were active in the American Legion. In the remaining two appointments, Goodland sought to avoid political partisanship. One nominee was Janesville attorney and prominent Republican William H. Dougherty. Initially, the other was State Senator Fred Risser of Madison, floor leader of the Progressives. A ruling by the state's attorney general, which stated that the senator could not hold two state positions concurrently, doomed Risser's nomination. To replace him, Goodland nominated John E. Joyce, a Democrat and Wisconsin state commander of the Veterans of Foreign Wars. In all, four of Goodland's five initial appointees to the Veterans' Recognition Board were veterans, three of whom were American Legion members.[18]

The first meeting of the Veterans' Recognition Board took place in July 1943, and the search for a director began almost immediately. In all, the board interviewed eighteen men before selecting Lt. Col. Leo B. Levenick of Madison in October. Born in Blue Earth, Minnesota, in 1893, Levenick attended the University of Wisconsin until he enlisted in the army during World War I. He served in France with the 32nd Infantry Division, which contained National Guard units from Wisconsin and Michigan, and during the war he rose in rank from private to sergeant major. After the war Levenick worked for the Soldiers' Rehabilitation Board before taking a job with the state banking commission in 1933. He remained in the National Guard, and upon the mobilization of the 32nd Division in 1940, went back on active duty. He became inspector general for American troops in Northern Ireland and attained the rank of lieutenant colonel until poor health forced him to leave the service.[19]

The bill creating the Veterans' Recognition Board also authorized the creation of advisory committees to provide board members with expert advice on various aspects of veteran readjustment. The first committee consisted of representatives from private service organizations involved in Wisconsin's veterans' affairs. The committee included delegates from the state's four largest veterans' associations as well as the Red Cross. The board sought to include a World War II veteran on the committee, but it was not until 1944 that the board selected Sgt. Theodore Jones, a disabled World War II veteran from Lake Mills. In August 1944 the board created a medical advisory committee composed of a psychiatrist, an orthopedic surgeon, a general practitioner, and later (after pressure from the state dental society) a dentist. In January 1944 the board formed an agricultural advisory committee composed of farmers and agriculture academicians. After the passage of the GI Bill in June 1944, the board established an educational advisory committee.[20]

"Our door is open and we are open for business," Levenick announced in November 1943, but his statement was premature. The Veterans' Recognition Board still had numerous policy issues to work out. By November, Levenick had "made the proper contacts with other agencies" on behalf of the veterans, but had yet to dispense a penny of the rehabilitation trust fund to Wisconsin's returning servicemen and women. The speed with which the recognition board was operating drew criticism. "If the Wisconsin veterans' rehabilitation program is ever to operate in the way the soldiers have a right to expect," complained the *Appleton Post-Crescent*, "the board should not be obliged to 'contact other agencies' but should be allowed and required to act on its own account, promptly and effectively." The *Post-Crescent* noted that numerous agencies already existed to counsel veterans.[21]

Money began to flow from the trust fund to the veterans by the end of the year, but many organizational issues remained outstanding. Because the law establishing the Veterans' Recognition Board was so vague, board members and veterans alike were confused as to the benefits the new agency could distribute. For example, the board initially decided to place a limit of $250 on disbursements. This amount, claimed chairman Dougherty, "should cover every type of emergency." However, one of the first cases before the board involved a request by a Marquette University medical student for $294 to cover emergency expenses. The board approved the amount. Another issue was state residency. A Racine veteran applied to the board for expenses related to his studies at the University of Colorado. The veteran had been discharged due to an asthmatic condition, and he claimed that continuing school in Colorado's more arid climate would be better for his condition. The board decided that it would not issue aid to Wisconsin veterans in other states when needed facilities existed in the Badger State.[22]

The method of dispensing trust fund money also had to be worked out. Board members questioned whether they had the authority to provide loans as well as grants. Initially, the board asked veterans to repay the amount provided to them if repayment did not entail any "undue hardship." Such a policy would, the board believed, provide even more money for veterans in need. However, some veterans complained that the board's part loan, part grant policy was unfair. Further thought and investigation revealed still other problems with creating a lending system. For one, under existing law repaid funds reverted to the state's general fund, not the veterans' trust fund, making the plan to use repaid loans for other veterans unworkable. Levenick also expressed concerns about the difficulties involved in collecting loans. As a result, in March 1944 the board voted to cancel all the loans it had made and consider them grants.[23]

Confusion remained over the extent of the recognition board's powers, a situation that sometimes led to bitter disputes. In May 1944, controversy erupted over educational grants and their impact on the trust fund. Two board members, Joyce and Col. John F. Mullen, argued that education fell outside of the board's powers of "rehabilitation" as traditionally conceived, and thus the board had no authority to provide such grants. Joyce and Mullen feared that the numerous requests for educational assistance were leaving the trust fund dangerously depleted. "You can't grant $1,000 or so to the boys who are already back," argued Joyce, "and not pay any attention to the boys who are yet to come back. They are entitled to some of this money, too." Chairman Dougherty favored a more liberal approach to educational grants. "I'm not interested in how far this money will go," he responded. "The legislature will have to replace this fund when it is used up, or the public will have to tell the veterans that they are not interested in them." He further stated that "I think we have the power to help a returned veteran go to school," and argued that "getting these boys back to their normal way of life—that's rehabilitation." "If this board hasn't got the right to help a veteran go to school," Colonel Levenick joined in, "we have been violating the law right along."[24]

Joyce and Mullen persuaded the board to seek the opinion of the state's attorney general regarding its authority to provide educational grants. The decision outraged Dougherty, not only because he opposed efforts to curtail grant amounts, but also because of the negative publicity it might generate for the board and its efforts. In a letter to Governor Goodland, he argued that the decision to seek a legal opinion "resulted in giving our work a lot of rotten publicity. It gives the press and the public a right to believe that the Board doesn't know what it is doing, nor what it has a right to do." The dispute, widely reported in the press, "came just at a time when . . . our work was beginning to be understood around the state." Dougherty's appeal to the governor produced the desired results. Pressure from Goodland led Joyce and Mullen to withdraw their proposal for a legal opinion at the next board meeting.[25]

The Veterans' Recognition Board slowly began to dispense needed aid to Wisconsin's World War II veterans, but it did so in a rather conservative manner. By the end of 1943 a total of 213 claims had been filed with the board, and through June 1944 the total had risen to more than 800. Of the 839 claims filed as of June 22, the board approved payments in only 129 of them, with a value totaling $8,364.19. Nearly half of the 129 awards involved medical care. Eighteen of the 129 were considered "dependency" grants for veterans or veterans' families in economic trouble. Though educational grants accounted for only twenty-two awards, such grants accounted for nearly 40 percent of cash disbursements. By early 1945, educational grants began to outpace medical awards both in number of cases and of dollars granted to veterans. By the end of March 1945, Levenick had dispensed 359 educational grants totaling more than $20,000. By the end of July the total of educational grants was worth just over $26,000. Medical grants had reached a total of $23,000 by July 1945, just slightly outpacing dependency grants, which had risen precipitously that year and totaled $22,000 by the end of July. On the eve of Japan's surrender, the Veterans' Recognition Board had processed 3,113 aid applications and had disbursed just $77,744.34 to Wisconsin veterans of World War II. Concern about depleting the fund, and dispute about what constituted "rehabilitation," would continue to plague the effectiveness of the new agency into the postwar period.[26]

In November 1943, Veterans' Recognition Board director Levenick told the recognition board that in his experience, "a splendid spirit of cooperation exist[ed]" between the federal, state, local, and private organizations serving Wisconsin's veterans. Cooperation was vital, since numerous agencies handled veterans' affairs. Though it finally relented in its opposition to the Veterans' Recognition Board, the American Legion continued to press for a consolidation of state agencies handling veterans' affairs. The lack of veterans on the Veterans' Recognition Board as first proposed had united the state's organized veterans. However, the question of consolidation divided them. The American Legion continued to press for its own version of a postwar veteran program. Other veterans' groups, most notably the Veterans of Foreign Wars and the Disabled American Veterans, saw the American Legion's actions as a grab for power, as did many legislators and citizens.[27]

The Legion's legislative committee renewed discussion of consolidation in October 1943. The Wisconsin American Legion's plan called for the merger of all state agencies handling veterans' programs, including the Wisconsin Veterans' Home, the Soldiers' Rehabilitation Board, and the Veterans' Recognition Board into a central "Department of Veterans' Affairs." The newly formed Veterans' Recognition Board, according to the Legionnaires' plan, would be the overseeing, policy-making board for the new department. For the most part, agencies would function as they had, and funds raised for specific programs would not be consolidated. Legion leaders introduced their proposal to the state legislature's joint committee on postwar issues on October 28. By mid-December, the committee reported out a bill that largely conformed to the American Legion plan.[28]

The consolidation plan met with initial approval from many quarters. "The Wisconsin department of the American Legion is led by practical and intelligent men," wrote *Green Bay Press-Gazette* political columnist John Wyngaard upon learning of the Legion's proposal. "Public money . . . and effort will not reach their best and fullest until such integration is achieved." He also noted that Governor Goodland had gone on record as favoring consolidation. "As far as can be seen right now," wrote Wyngaard, "there is no reason why the legislature should not act upon the request."[29]

But opposition to the bill emerged. The *Wisconsin State Journal*, for example, characterized the measure as "disquieting." It pointed out that the Veterans' Recognition Board was "slowly but surely swinging into action," and claimed that immediate action on veterans' affairs was not necessary. Committee hearings on the bill revealed more anxiety. Wisconsin's adjutant general, Alvin A. Kuechenmeister (under whom fell responsibility for the Wisconsin Veterans' Home and most World War I veteran programs), called consolidation "an error," arguing that since the federal government usually dealt with his agency in handling certain matters, consolidation would actually increase red tape for veterans. The Wisconsin Taxpayers Alliance feared that the creation of a new agency and new benefit programs would increase taxes. The State Employees Association feared that some workers might lose their seniority in an agency reshuffling. Even the governor began to signal some doubts. Through a spokesman, Goodland told the committee that while he still favored consolidation, too many amendments were being added to the bill. In particular, the governor believed that a bonus provision tacked onto it—at the urging of the American Legion—was "premature." With federal plans for veterans beginning to take shape, Goodland told the legislators that "you will be better prepared by next January, after Congress has acted, to know what to do."[30]

Concern over unchecked American Legion political influence was also growing. In a January 1944 radio address, William T. Evjue, publisher of Madison's *Capital Times*, charged that "the Legion hierarchy, whether national or state, has used the Legion as a pressure group to continually grab more power for itself" and "promote their own reactionary political and economic views." The American Legion's harshest critic in the state legislature was Progressive Senator Fred Risser of Madison. Risser complained that he had received communications from every American Legion post in Dane County (in which his district was located) pressuring him to vote in favor of the measure. "It's been a long time since this body was subjected to an undercover pressure campaign like that connected with this bill," he complained. Consolidation, claimed Risser, had been "forced [on the legislature] by outsiders to take action on a matter which could wait until next January."[31]

Despite these words of warning, the bill's proponents remained confident of victory. The legislature voted overwhelmingly for the consolidation bill, complete with bonus provision, in late January 1944. It sailed through the state senate without a dissenting vote, and passed the assembly with only two votes against. The American Legion even went so far as to arrange to photograph a mock bill-signing ceremony with Governor Goodland for the next edition of the state Legion newspaper. When the measure reached the governor's desk, final approval seemed assured. The legislature adjourned confident that Goodland would sign the bill. To the surprise of most observers, Goodland killed the measure with a pocket veto at the end of the session. Explaining his action, the governor reiterated his belief in the principle of consolidation, but called the 1944 bill an "untimely" one which would "impair rather than improve" state veterans' services. He outlined two primary concerns. First, he sided with those who argued that such state action would be premature before the federal government acted. However, Goodland's primary reason for the veto was his belief that implementing the bill would actually hinder services to the increasing numbers of World War II veterans returning to the Badger State. He stated that the Veterans' Recognition Board was serving World War II veterans adequately, and that no emergency yet existed. Further, Goodland claimed that the board was already overwhelmed with work. "To foist on the board at this time the administration of certain other services concerned with veterans of prior wars," he claimed, "is, in my judgment, not conducive to the best interests of the veterans of World War II."[32]

In reaching his decision, Goodland claimed to have consulted with numerous experts in veterans' affairs, though he refused to name specific persons. However, the governor seems to have been influenced by two main groups. One was the adjutant general's office, a source of open resistance to the bill. After the veto Goodland received many letters from officials in the adjutant general's office supporting his decision. "The chances for [the] neglect and relegation [of World War I veterans] to secondary importance in the great rush of new responsibilities are great indeed," warned Brig. Gen. Ralph M. Immell in a letter to the governor. Dr. William F. Lorenz, Wisconsin National Guard state surgeon and a nationally respected psychiatrist on the University of Wisconsin medical school faculty, told the governor that the differences in ages and needs between World War I and World War II veterans justified the decision to keep these veterans apart. "I wish to register with you my conviction that all veterans have been served best by your action," he concluded. Veterans' groups other than the American Legion, fearing the growth of Legion power and influence, also opposed consolidation. Publicly, the Veterans of Foreign Wars, the state's second largest veterans' group, took no position on consolidation, but privately the organization opposed it. After the veto, John Joyce, VFW state commander (and member of the Veterans' Recognition Board) wrote the governor that "[We] do not care to air our feelings publicly, [but] want to thank you and want you to know that we back your action one hundred per cent."[33]

The veto surprised backers of the bill, and created a firestorm of angry denunciations. State senator Milton Murray, chairman of the legislature's joint committee on postwar issues, said that the veto had left him "completely astounded." In a letter to Goodland, the senator "demanded" that the governor call a special session to reconsider consolidation, arguing that "the legislature would not have adjourned had not the governor told me he would sign the bill." Goodland refused to call the session, arguing that the next legislative session would begin in just a few months, and stated that "we can better save the money of a special session . . . to fulfill our obligations to the veterans as they return." Relations between the governor and the American Legion became especially bitter. American Legion state commander James R. Durfee publicly maintained that the governor had assured him that he would sign the bill. Goodland apologized for any misunderstanding, but assured Durfee that he had promised no such thing. Durfee was cautious in his public statements, but his words in private were apparently quite sharp. "Many stories have been reaching me as to your attitude toward the pocket veto," Goodland wrote Durfee, "[but] I have lived long enough to discount such reports nearly 100 percent." Nevertheless, even the "tough old codger" was wounded in the fray. "There is so much here that is selfish and petty that sometimes I almost lose faith in humanity," Goodland wrote Dr. Lorenz, "but I guess that is part of the game and one must not let that get him down."[34]

Public reaction to the pocket veto was mixed. While the *Milwaukee Journal* characterized the veto as "capricious," most of the state's major newspapers backed Goodland. Madison's *Capital Times* called the move "courageous." "The Legion bureaucracy has been trying to run over the capitol itself and has been using its power to get control of more influence and more jobs," the newspaper claimed, and believed the governor deserved "high praise" for "putting the interests of the veterans and the welfare of good government ahead of political expediency." The *Appleton Post-Crescent* called consolidation a "half-hearted and inconclusive enactment that would have served only to deceive and confuse." One Madison Legionnaire, in a letter to the governor, suggested that the American Legion leadership did not necessarily represent the views of the organization's "rank and file," and described the situation this way:

> It is not the purpose of this writer to express any opinion here . . . but I believe I am correct in the opinion that the general public regards the controversy with a jaundiced eye and will soon echo the rollicking Mercutio's dying Philippic to his lovelorn cousin if the finery of both houses continues to be cleansed in public.[35]

The Wisconsin American Legion resumed its quest for consolidation when the legislature reconvened in January 1945. The 1945 consolidation proposal was largely a rehashing of the earlier attempt, but with a few key differences. The congressional passage of the GI Bill of Rights in June 1944 addressed one of Goodland's major concerns about state consolidation—the uncertainty about federal action on veterans' affairs. That hurdle apparently overcome, the Legionnaires attempted to address the second—the workload on the Veterans' Recognition Board. The new proposal called for a new "Board of Veterans' Affairs" to become the policy-making body of the new agency. The Veterans' Recognition Board and the Soldiers' Rehabilitation Board would remain in operation and serve their respective constituencies, but fall under the new supervising board. The Legion also adopted a more conciliatory tone, at one point admitting that "perhaps there was" merit in waiting for federal action before proceeding with state action. Unlike in the 1943-44 fight, the Legion also sought the cooperation of the state's other major veterans' groups. For example, Legionnaires brought the subject before a January 1945 meeting of the Wisconsin Veterans' Council. "We are open to suggestion," James Durfee told the council, "as to which particular phraseology should be used in this bill."[36]

Even with the passage of the GI Bill in Washington, consolidation continued to spark controversy in Wisconsin. "Wisconsin has adequate machinery for administering the state's functions in the future for the welfare of its men and women in the armed forces" the *Wisconsin State Journal* declared. The Madison newspaper suggested that the federal government had not yet completed "placing its veterans' affairs in final administrative form." "Conceivably," the newspaper argued, consolidation might be wise in the future, but "the time is not ripe." Veterans themselves remained divided on the issue. The meeting of the

Wisconsin Veterans' Council in January 1945 provided one example of this sentiment. The Veterans of Foreign Wars representative, Paul Lappley, told the Legionnaires that while his organization had not spoken against consolidation publicly, the VFW was "satisfied with the situation as it was." M. C. Alexander, representing the Disabled American Veterans, asked pointedly: "What fault is there to find with the existing situation?"[37]

Most important, Governor Goodland continued to caution against moving too quickly toward consolidation. Goodland now claimed to have received letters from Wisconsin service personnel suggesting that further action on state veterans' programs be deferred until World War II veterans returned home "in order that they may participate in its making." Goodland's position won praise in many quarters. "On a matter which is so important to them," argued the *Green Bay Press-Gazette*, "the [World War II] veterans obviously have a right to speak." The American Legion viewed these statements of caution as detrimental to the welfare of veterans. "Comrades," Durfee told the Wisconsin Veterans' Council,

> I think that every one of us can see the essential fallacy in [the governor's] position. That is exactly what the Congress of the United States, in effect, did in 1917-1918. They didn't wait, but they proceeded to enact a hodge podge of legislation and then finally the veterans organizations of America . . . took charge, but during the interval of time thousands of veterans suffered hardships that were the result of unintelligent administration.

World War II veterans could alter the veterans' service system as necessary once they came home, the Legion contended, but immediate action was needed to avoid repeating the experience of World War I.[38]

During the summer of 1945, with the Germans defeated and the Japanese in retreat, the American Legion finally won its battle for consolidation. In August, the legislature passed another consolidation measure, and once again Governor Goodland refused to sign it. However, because the legislature remained in session, the unsigned bill became law under the Wisconsin constitution. The consolidation measure enacted in 1945 strongly resembled the 1943 proposal. The new Wisconsin Department of Veterans' Affairs (WDVA) consolidated the state's disparate veterans' service agencies under one central authority, including the Wisconsin Veterans' Home near Waupaca. The Veterans' Recognition Board was renamed the "Board of Veterans' Affairs," with Levenick as director. The board then assumed control of the new agency. Even the advisory committees of the Veterans' Recognition Board remained. The Soldiers' Rehabilitation Board that administered the trust fund for World War I veterans was abolished; the WDVA now administered World War I veterans' programs as well.[39]

As the trickle of returning veterans prior to 1945 turned into a flood thereafter, the new WDVA grew. Starting out in 1943 as "a Director and a stenographer," as the 1946 *Blue Book* described it rather modestly, by 1946 the WDVA had grown to "60 employees [who] process 500 claims a month in the struggle to meet the mounting needs of a third of a million former service men and women of Wisconsin." By June 1947 the WDVA had grown to 237 employees, working mainly in the State Capitol in Madison and at the Wisconsin Veterans' Home in central Wisconsin. In 1947, Director Levenick died, and was replaced by Gordon Huesby, a WDVA accountant. Governor Goodland also passed away that year. Republican Lieutenant Governor Oscar Rennebohm became acting governor, and was elected to his own terms in 1948 and 1950. Not only did the WDVA continue to distribute trust fund money to veterans in emergency situations, but, like the federal government, Wisconsin's lawmakers also created many new programs for the Badger State's more than 300,000 World War II veterans. Between 1940 and 1949, the Wisconsin state legislature passed no fewer than 134 bills or resolutions affecting the state's veterans.[40]

Veterans' Service at the Grass Roots

"While much of the work of rehabilitating veterans can be accomplished by Federal and State agencies," wrote social worker Willard Waller, "its most important phases can be carried on only by local communities." Ultimately, the veteran would return to a particular city, village, or county. Should the veteran be somehow maladjusted, the problem would likely be first manifested by landing in a local jail, appearing on a local relief roll, or being admitted to a local hospital—all at local expense. "In short," Waller wrote, "the real work of rehabilitation must be done in the local community."[41] Across the nation, county and municipal governments undertook considerable efforts to reintegrate the veterans back into their home communities. In Wisconsin, local efforts focused on acquainting veterans with their rights and benefits under federal and state programs. Such a strategy was aimed at preventing returned veterans from landing on local welfare roles, while at the same time bringing federal and state dollars into the community.

Key to veteran outreach at the local level in Wisconsin was the County Veterans' Service Officer (CVSO). Wisconsin's system of CVSOs, probably the first in the nation, evolved from the "service officer" positions each of Wisconsin's 370 American Legion posts was supposed to maintain. The American Legion post service officer was charged with counseling local veterans about their benefit rights and options, and assisting them in filing claims with the federal or state governments. Post service officers at the time were responsible to the Wisconsin American Legion's departmental service officer, James F. Burns, who maintained his headquarters in Milwaukee. The American Legion service system functioned well during the 1920s, but with the onset of the Great Depression the post service officers found themselves overwhelmed with claims. At the same time, the Soldiers' and Sailor's Relief Commissions in each of Wisconsin's seventy-one counties saw expenditures for indigent veterans rise precipitously after 1929. During the depths of the depression, Wisconsin Legionnaires pressured county governments to hire their own veterans' service officers, arguing that ex-servicemen properly counseled about their benefits would keep most of them off relief and bring federal dollars into the county. Fond du Lac County was the first to hire its own CVSO in 1931. Several nearby counties soon followed suit.

Legionnaires also lobbied state lawmakers in Madison to make the position of veterans' service officer mandatory in every county, a campaign that was partially successful. In May 1935, the state legislature authorized counties to hire a CVSO. The new law stipulated that the CVSO be a war veteran, whose duties would be to "advise with all veterans of wars, residents of the county . . . relative to any complaint made or problem submitted by them to render him such assistance as, in his opinion, he may render." However, the legislature only established standards for the position and did not require county governments to maintain one. Thereafter, Legionnaires lobbied county governments to create veterans' service offices. By the time of America's entry into World War II in December 1941, fifty-nine of Wisconsin's seventy-one counties had hired a CVSO. In addition to counseling veterans, the CVSOs also wrote columns in local newspapers, spoke on local radio broadcasts, and worked closely with local veterans' groups to contact veterans and identify those in need of assistance. To coordinate their efforts, exchange information, and protect their interests politically, the service officers in 1936 formed a statewide organization, the County Veterans' Service Officers' Association of Wisconsin. Before World War II, all the Badger State's service officers were World War I veterans, and most were also active in the American Legion and other veterans' groups.[42]

In Wisconsin, the CVSO was usually the first local official a returning World War II veteran encountered. By November 1943, the Barron County service officer had recorded 138 discharges of local World War II veterans. That same month, the Brown County service officer reported that his office handled four or five World War II cases a day. In the few counties that had not yet hired a service officer, local Legionnaires stepped up efforts to establish the position in their localities. In November 1943, for example, Legionnaires successfully pressed the Dunn County board of supervisors to employ a CVSO. In Kenosha County, the county service officer resulted from an even broader community movement. Not only did local veterans' groups support the hiring of a service officer, but the county board also received communications from organizations such as the Kenosha Manufacturers' Association and the Factory Superintendents' League favoring the proposal. In a March editorial, the Kenosha News also came out in favor of creating the position. Noting how Kenosha was one of the few counties not to have a CVSO, the editorial claimed that counties with functioning service officers "have found that it is not only of benefit to the veteran," but to the population as a whole, by bringing state and federal dollars into the county and "preventing [veterans'] cases from becoming serious community problems." Faced with such widespread backing, the Kenosha County board created the position in May 1944.[43]

By the fall of 1943 the CVSO Association had developed its vision of the postwar service officer. The organization proposed to make the position of service officer mandatory in every county, to have the CVSOs designated the official contact representatives of the proposed state veterans' agency, and for counties to receive state subsidies for service operations. In November, two service officers explained their position before the special legislative committee on veteran rehabilitation. The CVSOs cited their experience as veterans and knowledge of veterans' affairs. "We're in a better position to handle [veterans]," claimed George K. Nitz of Brown County, because "we know these people and we know their problems. Let's not chase the veterans around, but help them in their own communities." Justifying the need for a state veterans' service subsidy to counties, Nitz argued that "a good officer can save . . . money by bringing in more federal money for eligible veterans." The CVSO Association found many allies in county government circles. By the end of 1943 the Wisconsin County Boards Association came out in favor of the CVSO proposal. In January 1944 the Milwaukee County Board passed a resolution asking the legislature to make the CVSOs the "field representatives" of the proposed new state veterans' agency.[44]

But in the bitter 1943-44 debate over consolidation, the CVSOs became another casualty. Combining the state's existing veterans' service agencies was proving to be difficult enough. Adding an army of county service officers to the state payroll was a step many legislators were apparently unwilling to take. The committee's original consolidation bill of December 1943 excluded the CVSOs, and an assembly amendment to make the CVSOs "appointed representatives of the [new] state department" went down to defeat by a vote of 49-25. The vote outraged those who supported the CVSO proposal. The *Green Bay Press-Gazette* claimed that the legislature had "cut its cloth too short." "It is difficult to imagine what could have motivated lawmakers in refusing to accept the patently sensible suggestion," the *Press-Gazette* continued, "but it did so, and presumably the veterans' recognition board is going to continue sitting in the capitol while wounded veterans in Wisconsin cities seek out their relief directors for meal tickets and room rent." To reassure the CVSOs that they would not be "squeezed out" of the new veterans' service system, several state officials attended the CVSO Association's 1944 winter meeting in Green Bay. State senate majority leader John Byrnes told the service officers that due to their proximity to returning veterans, they were the "logical" persons to administer assistance to them. Leo Levenick, director of the Veterans' Recognition Board, pledged to the CVSOs that his agency would "never sanction a field force" since it would interfere with the existing CVSO system and delay assistance to veterans. The remarks mollified the service officers and those who supported them. The *Appleton Post-Crescent* characterized the remarks as "reassuring to many persons who have been compelled to wonder . . . just how the agency quartered in the capitol could be of any real assistance to the new war veterans."[45]

The CVSOs in 1945 resurrected their previous proposal for inclusion into the state service system, but once again the legislature excluded them. However, separate legislation fulfilled most of the CVSO Association's main objectives. Chapter 550, Laws of 1945, abolished the Soldiers' and Sailors' Relief Commissions and made the position of County Veterans' Service Officer mandatory in

every Wisconsin county. The new WDVA—true to Levenick's promise of
1944—did not employ local contact representatives of its own, making the
CVSOs the de facto field agents of the new agency. In addition, state law required veterans to file claims for most state veterans' benefits through a CVSO,
making them an indispensable component of the Badger State's veterans' program. Thus, service officers' activism had essentially produced victory. Law
now required every county in Wisconsin to employ a service officer, and the
CVSOs became in practice the field representatives of the state veterans'
agency. Only one of the CVSOs' wartime goals as stated in the fall of 1943—
state subsidies for county veterans' service operations—had not been enacted by
the end of the war.[46]

The federal government had also given thought to returning the veteran to
his or her home community. The federal presence at the local level, including
those concerned with veterans' affairs, was actually quite substantial. For example, in Wisconsin during World War II there were 154 Selective Service boards,
with each county having at least one and Milwaukee County having more than
thirty. Because the 1940 Selective Service Act protected the veteran's right to
return to his prewar job, each Selective Service board was required to designate
a reemployment committee to assist local veterans in retrieving their old jobs or
finding new ones. Wisconsin also had twenty-five branches of the United States
Employment Service (USES), an agency created in 1933 as a combination fed-
eral-state operation to match workers with jobs, which had been placed under
sole federal jurisdiction during the war. Included in the USES system was the
Veterans' Employment Service, which catered specifically to ex-military personnel. Finally, the Veterans' Administration operated a regional office at
Wood, just west of Milwaukee, and managed three VA hospitals in Wisconsin
(at Milwaukee, Madison, and Waukesha) with one under construction at Tomah.
The VA also employed numerous field representatives who worked out of the
VA centers in Milwaukee and Minneapolis, Minnesota, blanketing the state.
Local VA, USES, and Selective Service branches worked independently of each
other, however. There was no single federal office a veteran could walk into and
inquire about all of his or her benefits.

The Retraining and Reemployment Administration (RRA), created in 1944,
attempted to bring local representatives of all three of these agencies together
and establish "veterans' information centers" in cities and towns across the
United States. Under the RAA General Order Number 1, promulgated on May
17, 1944, officials from each of these federal agencies were to form state and
local veterans' service committees. The Wisconsin state committee was organized in June 1944, chaired by William E. O'Brien, state director of the War
Manpower Commission (under which USES fell); Maj. Paul Froemming, manager of the Milwaukee VA regional office; and Col. John F. Mullen, director of
selective service in Wisconsin. Local committees were formed in subsequent
months. The committees were then tasked with establishing local information
centers for veterans. All USES, Selective Service, and VA offices in the state
would be designated as information centers. In addition, the RRA pledged to

work with existing state and local governments, as well as local charities and veterans' groups, to establish additional centers.[47]

After surveying the situation in Wisconsin, the veterans' service committee was optimistic. "The twenty-five USES offices are geographically distributed at advantageous points throughout the state," O'Brien noted in a letter to Washington, in areas where the bulk of the state's population lived. He also noted a spirit of cooperation among all involved federal agencies. The Wisconsin RRA committee also noted that local groups and agencies were already involved with veterans' service. "It has been the policy of the state committee that when an organization . . . is functioning efficiently," O'Brien wrote to Washington, "we do not try to disturb the community organizational setup by the establishment of a second committee." The RRA committee saw its role in Wisconsin as one of coordination. "Considering the cooperative relationship established with the governor and/or state agencies in developing the program," the committee believed, "it was the opinion that Wisconsin had a correlated program at the present time and that the only necessary new development might be to intensify the action in some territories where the program might be weak." In particular, O'Brien noted that the state's CVSOs were "cooperating." Indeed, federal observers in the Badger State came to see the CVSOs as crucial to the RRA goal of veterans' outreach. "The County Veterans Service Office will be the permanent 'center' set-up in Wisconsin," one VA field representative had concluded by 1946.[48]

However, the RRA did not depend entirely on existing federal facilities and those of the CVSOs, and participated in the development of additional information centers with community groups and local governments. In Madison, for example, the Community Union and the Madison War Chest (two charitable organizations) funded that city's Veterans' Information Headquarters, which also involved local veterans' organizations, civic groups, and local government agencies, as well as the federal agencies involved in the RRA program. The Madison center established an office in downtown Madison and reached out to veterans in several ways: mailing a "welcome home" booklet to returning veterans, publishing a weekly "question box" in a local newspaper, and conspicuously displaying banners around the city. In Waukesha, a similar center made "a personal call . . . on each returning veteran," provided local veterans with a "pocket card" helping to locate their facility, and passed out literature regarding a wide range of topics, including employment, loans, and education. The local CVSO was sometimes crucial in the creation of these community information centers for veterans. As VA field representative Valentine Hoffman observed, in some cases "the service officer has been the man who has brought all of the people together to work with each other and mesh their various activities together so as to render the best possible service."[49]

However, other CVSOs saw the federal involvement in local veterans' service as an intrusion and a threat. Service officers in smaller counties, Hoffman reported, resented the federal presence because many of them feared that "there was not enough work for both" county and federal counseling services. Resentment also came from larger counties, where ill feeling was "due to a desire to get all the work and build up their offices," according to Hoffman. In fact, considerable antagonism soon developed between the CVSOs and the RRA information centers in some areas. "The only person concerned with veterans' affairs not very enthusiastic" about the Madison center, Hoffman told Washington, "was the [local] County Service Officer who feels that nothing much is accomplished by the center." Hoffman noted, however, that the local CVSO, Rudolph Scheibel, also "has the respect of a large part of the community and must be played with rather than bucked." Another federal official touring the state noted "some rivalry" existed between the CVSO and the information center in Milwaukee as well. Valentine Hoffman attended a CVSO conference in 1946 and received numerous complaints from the county officers. "In addition to surface dissatisfaction," he noted, "much bad feeling existed underneath; this seemed to stem from the service officers' belief that that" federal counseling of veterans would "put them out of business."[50]

As veterans returned in large numbers after 1945, it became clear that the community centers organized under RRA auspices did not attract as many veterans as hoped. Despite optimistic predictions about traffic, RRA reports made frequent mention of low visitation. "The infrequency of veteran traffic to the centers is a matter which should be directed to the attention of the sponsors," noted a June 1945 survey of the state's centers, for example. "There is the feeling prevalent in Wisconsin," reported state RRA committee secretary William H. Siemering, "that Information Centers established thus far have not had the traffic that was previously expected of them." Valentine Hoffman believed that the attitude of Colonel Mullen of the state committee was at least partially responsible for lack of business. According to Hoffman, Mullen carried considerable weight in Wisconsin's veterans' affairs community, serving not only on the Wisconsin RRA committee, but also on WDVA's Board of Veterans' Affairs. In addition, he was also involved with the state's CVSO Association. Hoffman quoted Mullen as stating that Wisconsinites "didn't take to" the idea of the RRA information centers "due to the fact that what we had given them was working so well." Hoffman suggested that the powerful Colonel Mullen simply failed to put his weight behind RRA efforts to create veterans' information centers, hindering their effectiveness in Wisconsin.[51]

By contrast, CVSOs saw a sharp rise in workload during and immediately after the war, with a decline stabilizing well above prewar levels. In Manitowoc County, for example, the service officer interviewed on average 2,700 veterans a year between 1940 and 1942. World War II increased those figures dramatically. Between 1943 and 1945 the number of interviews increased from 2,874 to 3,848, and in 1946 skyrocketed to 11,339. Thereafter, the number of interviews declined. In 1947 the number of interviews fell to 9,154, and between 1948 and 1950 averaged 4,500 annually, 67 percent above the first three years of the decade. The estimated monetary value of benefits in that county showed a similar pattern. Averaging $29,000 annually between 1940 and 1942, the numbers rose precipitously, to $62,910 in 1943 to $379,596 in 1944. In 1945 the monetary value peaked at $1,073,974 before falling. Between 1948 and 1950, the Manitowoc CVSO estimated that his office brought on average $206,000 state and federal dollars into the county each year, a six-fold increase from the 1940-42 average. Some CVSOs reported continuous increases throughout the decade. The Sauk County service officer reported an increase of 106 percent in the monetary value of benefits between 1942 and 1946, but after that continued to report increases, the 1950 total being more than 200 percent higher than that of 1942.[52]

Though veterans flooded CVSO offices after the war, federal officials were concerned about the kind of advice they were getting there. The quality of CVSO work, in the observation of these officials, varied considerably. While some CVSOs made a favorable impression on federal observers, others did not. In Brown County, read one report, "the director is an ex-Legion service officer and that background is reflected in the office. The cases heard showed a conspicuous lack of friendliness and smoothness on the part of the counselors." They also believed that many CVSOs were not very well informed about federal programs, and believed the RRA program could increase their knowledge and improve the CVSOs' counseling of veterans. "RRA is unknown to these officials," observed the report from Fond du Lac County. "They can use all the information we can feed them." VA field representative D. D. Stonehocker suggested bombarding the CVSOs—as well as the county boards that employed them—with RRA publications. "I think we can 'educate' them to the point where they will accept a wider viewpoint toward their jobs," he claimed. Valentine Hoffman concurred. "I believe RRA can achieve all of its local goals by educating the county service officers," he reported to Washington.[53]

As workloads increased and veterans' service grew more complicated, the CVSOs themselves recognized the need to improve their operations. The CVSO Association—in cooperation with the University of Wisconsin in Madison—established its own annual training program known as the University Institute, or "short course." The first short course took place at the University of Wisconsin campus on May 26-29, 1947. The participants divided into five workshops of practical interest to the CVSO: legal affairs, office management, publicity interviewing and counseling, and insurance. Each workshop drew up recommendations and wrote reports to help their fellow CVSOs deal more effectively with veterans. The legal affairs workshop, for example, made five recommendations focusing on legal procedures about mentally disabled veterans; the publicity committee made several suggestions regarding outreach and the media. The office management committee made no fewer than eighteen recommendations, ranging from the sorting of mail to graves registration procedures. The interviewing and counseling workshop drew up a three-page guide to help CVSOs glean as much as possible from a personal interview with a veteran.[54]

Capturing the essence of the University Institute was a speech given by Taylor County service officer Oscar N. Markus regarding office management. In describing his philosophies on how a veterans' service office should be managed, Markus expressed the basic philosophy behind the purpose of the CVSOs:

offering the most effective yet sensitive treatment for veterans and their concerns. Markus began by exhorting his fellow CVSOs to "keep the faith" with their comrades lost in war and their fellow veterans in need. No matter what is done," he explained,

> to assist veterans in becoming re-established in society, rehabilitation will be a failure unless the County Veterans Service Officer recognizes and meets his responsibility. The veteran cannot eat citations or medals, and the only way to enable him to eat properly, to work properly, to repair his disabilities, and to put him back into a useful place in our social system is by being prepared to secure for him the maximum benefits he is entitled to under existing . . . laws.

The county veterans' service office, Markus claimed, was the "only effective existing . . . instrument" available in Wisconsin to help ex-servicemen properly. Markus broadly defined the term "office" as more than just "the space [one] might occupy," but also one's "mental attitude," which he believed was "perhaps the most important part." If a CVSO "makes a conscientious effort to understand and analyze the individual veteran's problem," Markus concluded, "not only to assist the veteran temporarily, but for the veteran's permanent rehabilitation . . . [and] will at all times cooperate with existing agencies, ever remembering that he is the employee of the veteran, we will be keeping the faith."[55]

Because of the success of the first University Institute, such meetings became annual events, held each spring on the university campus. Succeeding short courses grew in size and scope, and remained an important medium for the CVSOs to exchange and disseminate vital information about veterans' service with other experts and among their own ranks. The 1948 institute, for example, saw the number of workshops expanded to eight, and included new topics such as correspondence, psychology, and public speaking. At the 1949 institute, sixty persons registered, representing fifty-two counties. The workshops by that year had become even more specialized. A representative from the Allis-Chalmers Manufacturing Company presented a session on interviewing and counseling, and two doctors gave lectures on psychiatry.[56]

The war expanded and strengthened the CVSO system in Wisconsin. Due to this already existing veterans' service system, the RRA program of veterans' outreach was of little consequence in Wisconsin. Nationally, the RRA was also largely ineffective, but for other reasons. While the RRA plans for information centers were ambitious and well intended, in Washington the program faced crippling infighting and rivalry. Each of the agencies involved with the RRA guarded its prerogatives jealously, and found working together difficult. Indeed, the agencies could not even decide upon the scope of their operations. Some wanted an aggressive program and the creation of offices that processed benefit claims as well as distributed information, while others suggested letting state and local governments take the lead. The defederalization of USES in late 1946, under pressure from Republicans who wanted to end wartime controls and agencies as quickly as possible, crippled a key component of the national RRA program. The RRA was abolished in June 1947.[57]

Conclusion

In his call for a "new art" of veterans' rehabilitation, Willard Waller recalled America's past efforts to aid the ex-serviceman. "The history of our policy toward the returned soldier," he wrote, "is in fact so discouraging that one may well wonder whether we shall ever combine intelligence and humanity in the treatment of the men we send to fight for us." Throughout American history, Waller pointed out, "we have spent many billions on veterans' claims, and most of it has been wasted. We have never spent enough at the right time, or spent it on the right persons." As the end of World War II approached, America could not afford to make the same mistakes again. Sixteen million disillusioned and angry veterans, Waller warned, could have a devastating impact on the American way of life. A thoughtful and thorough package of readjustment benefits for veterans, he implied, might well be crucial to the survival of the nation.[58]

Waller was not alone in his concern that America develop an effective program of readjustment for veterans after World War II. The thunder of past wars echoed loudly through the halls of American government as well. Grateful to the men and women who won the war, fearful of their impact on society, and mindful of past failures in veterans' programs, lawmakers at the federal, state, and local levels of government devised a remarkably comprehensive system of programs and benefits to help returning GIs work their way back into the social fabric of America as smoothly as possible. It was not a centralized system, but rather a collection of uncoordinated, overlapping, and sometimes competing programs. Veterans' activists Charles Hurd and Charles Bolté described the situation this way:

> It's a little as if General Patton and General Keyes and Colonel Snooks and Lieutenant Brown and Bill Mauldin's Willie and Joe had set off to capture Berlin without having General Eisenhower to coordinate their actions—and without any radio intercommunication among their separate commands.[59]

Never before had America done so much for its veterans, but would it be enough? As the veterans began coming home, the nation looked hopefully toward the future, but also held its breath to see whether the program of veterans' rehabilitation it had enacted would work.

Notes

1. Willard Waller, *The Veteran Comes Back* (New York: Dryden Press, 1944), 15.

2. Quality works on the history of veterans are rare, but one subject historians have explored in some detail is the GI Bill of Rights. The best work on the subject remains Keith Olson, *The GI Bill, the Veterans, and the Colleges* (Lexington: University Press of Kentucky, 1974), which focuses on its educational components. One recent work, *When Dreams Come True: The GI Bill and the Making of Modern America* (Washington, D.C.: Brassey's, 1996), by journalist Michael J. Bennett, is informative but of uneven quality and ideologically slanted to minimize the role of the Roosevelt administration. Milton Greenberg, *The GI Bill: The Law That Changed America* (New York: Lickle, 1997) is a brief and popular yet informative work covering all aspects of the law. Theodore R. Mosch, *The GI Bill: A Breakthrough in Educational and Social Policy in the United States* (Hicksville, N.Y.: Exposition Press, 1975) covers the World War II GI Bill as well as subsequent laws for Korean and Vietnam War veterans. In examining the development of federal veterans' programs during World War II, see Davis R. B. Ross, *Preparing for Ulysses: Politics and Veterans during World War II* (New York: Columbia University Press, 1969), an exhaustive and indispensable guide through the tangle of laws, lawmakers, and interest groups that produced the GI Bill and other pieces of legislation for ex-soldiers. For overall context of postwar reconversion, see Jack Stokes Ballard, *The Shock of Peace: Economic and Military Demobilization after World War II* (Washington, D.C.: University Press of America, 1983). Unless otherwise noted, descriptions of the GI Bill and its origins have been based on these works.

3. *Congressional Record*, 76th Cong., 2d sess., 1940, 86, pt. 17:10236.

4. For more on government planning at the federal level, see Otis L. Graham Jr., *Toward a Planned Society: From Roosevelt to Nixon* (New York: Oxford University Press, 1976).

5. *Chicago Tribune*, 29 October 1943; *Milwaukee Journal*, 30 October 1943; *Menomonee Falls News*, 11 November 1943.

6. R. B. Pitkin, *How the First GI Bill Was Written* (Indianapolis, Ind.: American Legion Press, 1969).

7. *Milwaukee Sentinel*, 9 December 1943, 10 December 1943, 14 December 1943, 17 December 1943.

8. *Milwaukee Journal*, 10 December 1943, 17 December 1943.

9. Pitkin, *How the First GI Bill Was Written*.

10. U.S. House Committee on Veterans' Affairs, *Laws Relating to Veterans and Their Dependents Enacted on and after September 16, 1940*, 80th Cong., 2d sess., 1948, Committee Print 357.

11. For more on Wisconsin's political milieu during and after World War II, see Thompson, *Continuity and Change*, 467-527.

12. Walter S. Goodland, acting governor of Wisconsin, "The First Message to the Wisconsin Legislature," 14 January 1943, *Executive Report on State Finances and Messages of Acting Governor Walter S. Goodland* (Madison: State of Wisconsin, 1943), 22.

13. Goodland to Members of the Wisconsin Legislature, 17 February 1943, Correspondence file, Papers of Warren P. Knowles, State Historical Society of Wisconsin Archives, Madison, Wis. (cited hereafter as Knowles Papers); *Wisconsin State Journal*, 16 December 1942, 11 June 1943; *Capital Times*, 25 March 1943.

14. Val W. Ove, department commander, to all post, county, district commanders, department officers, 7 May 1943, Records of the American Legion, Department of Wis-

consin, State Historical Society of Wisconsin Archives, Madison, Wis. (cited hereafter as ALP).

15. Rehabilitation for World War II, Radio Address by Assemblyman Charles E. Collar over WHA, 18 February 1943, Knowles Papers; *Capital Times*, 25 March 1943, 7 May 1943.

16. Memorandum on Substitute Amendment 2-S, 4 June 1943, ALP; Wisconsin Veterans' Council to Wisconsin State Senators, 7 June 1943, ALP.

17. *Capital Times*, 10 June 1943; *Wisconsin State Journal*, 11 June 1943.

18. Wisconsin Veterans' Recognition Board, *Attention Returning Veterans (and Families of Veterans)* (Madison: Veterans' Recognition Board, 1943).

19. Veterans' Recognition Board minutes, 30 July 1943, 18 August 1943, 14 October 1943, Records of the Wisconsin Department of Veterans' Affairs, State Government Records, State Historical Society of Wisconsin Archives, Madison, Wis. (cited hereafter as WDVA); Roy L. Brecke to C. A. Dawson, 2 August 1943, Records of the Governor: Walter S. Goodland, State Government Records, State Historical Society of Wisconsin Archives, Madison, Wis. (cited hereafter as Goodland Papers); *Capital Times*, 15 October 1943; *Milwaukee Journal*, 15 October 1943.

20. Veterans' Recognition Board minutes, 14 October 1943, 17 January 1944, 11 August 1944, WDVA.

21. *Milwaukee Journal*, 2 November 1943; *Appleton Post-Crescent*, 8 November 1943.

22. Veterans' Recognition Board minutes, 19 November 1943, 17 December 1943, 17 January 1944, WDVA.

23. Veterans' Recognition Board minutes, 19 November 1943, 11 February 1944, 17 March 1944, WDVA.

24. Veterans' Recognition Board minutes, 26 May 1944; *Wisconsin State Journal*, 27 May 1944, WDVA.

25. Veterans' Recognition Board minutes, 26 May 1944, 23 June 1944, WDVA; Dougherty to Goodland, 7 June 1944, Goodland Papers.

26. Veterans' Recognition Board minutes, 23 June 1944, 9 March 1945, 13 April 1945, 3 August 1945, WDVA.

27. Veterans' Recognition Board minutes, 19 November 1943, WDVA.

28. Minutes of the Special Department Legislative Committee, 14 October 1943, in American Legion file, Goodland Papers; *Milwaukee Journal*, 25 October 1943; *Green Bay Press-Gazette*, 29 October 1943; *Badger Legionnaire*, November 1943; *Capital Times*, 16 December 1943; *Wisconsin State Journal*, 16 December 1943.

29. *Milwaukee Journal*, 25 October 1943; *Green Bay Press-Gazette*, 29 October 1943; *Appleton Post-Crescent*, 8 November 1943.

30. *Wisconsin State Journal*, 11 January 1944; *Capital Times*, 19 January 1944; *La Crosse Tribune and Leader Press*, 19 January 1944.

31. *Capital Times*, 22 January 1944, 24 January 1944; *Milwaukee Journal*, 23 January 1944; *Watertown Times*, 22 January 1944.

32. *Milwaukee Journal*, 18 February 1944; *Wisconsin State Journal*, 18 February 1944, 19 February 1944; *Superior Telegram*, 21 February 1944; *Milwaukee Sentinel*, 22 February 1944; *Oshkosh Northwestern*, 25 February 1944; *Green Bay Press-Gazette*, 26 February 1944.

33. *Milwaukee Journal*, 19 January 1944; Immell to Goodland, 3 March 1944, Goodland Papers; Lorenz to Goodland, 19 February 1944, Goodland Papers; Lorenz to Goodland, 2 March 1944, Goodland Papers; Joyce to Goodland, 23 February 1944, Goodland Papers.

34. Murray to Goodland, 21 February 1944, Goodland Papers; Goodland to Murray, 26 February 1944, Goodland Papers; Goodland to Lorenz, 21 February 1944, Papers of William F. Lorenz, State Historical Society of Wisconsin Archives, Madison, Wis.

35. *Milwaukee Journal*, 19 February 1944; *Wisconsin State Journal*, 23 February 1944; *Capital Times*, 20 February 1944; *Appleton Post-Crescent*, 21 February 1944, 22 February 1944; Walter Bernd to Goodland, 2 March 1944, Goodland Papers.

36. *Capital Times*, 4 January 1945; *Wisconsin State Journal*, 4 January 1945; Wisconsin Veterans' Council meeting minutes, 26 January 1945, ALP.

37. Wisconsin Veterans' Council meeting minutes, 26 January 1945, ALP; *Wisconsin State Journal*, 21 January 1945.

38. *Green Bay Press-Gazette*, 19 January 1945; *Wisconsin State Journal*, 21 January 1945; Wisconsin Veterans' Council meeting minutes, 26 January 1945, ALP.

39. *Wisconsin State Journal*, 24 August 1945.

40. Wisconsin Legislative Reference Bureau, *Wisconsin Blue Book*, 1946 ed. (Madison: Legislative Reference Bureau, 1946), 142; *Blue Book*, 1948 ed., 401; Howard F. Ohm, ed., *Summary of Action of the Regular Session of the Wisconsin Legislature on Some of the More Important Questions Coming before It* (Madison: State of Wisconsin, 1941-49).

41. Waller, *The Veteran Comes Back*, 270.

42. For more on the origins and development of the CVSO, see Mark D. Van Ells, *Serving Those Who Served: A History of Wisconsin's County Veterans' Service Officers* (Manitowoc, Wis.: County Veterans' Service Officers Association of Wisconsin, 1995).

43. Barron County, Wisconsin, Board of Supervisors, *Proceedings*, 10 November 1943; *Wisconsin Counties*, November 1943; Dunn County, Wisconsin, Board of Supervisors, *Proceedings*, 15 November 1943, 17 November 1944; *Dunn County News*, 22 December 1943; Kenosha County, Wisconsin, Board of Supervisors, *Proceedings*, 18 January 1944, 1 March 1944, 18 May 1944, 7 June 1944; *Kenosha News*, 3 March 1944.

44. CVSO Association meeting minutes, 1 October 1943, Minute Book I, Records of the County Veterans' Service Officers' Association of Wisconsin, Wisconsin Veterans' Museum Research Center, Madison, Wis. (cited hereafter as CVSO); *Wisconsin Counties*, November 1943, January 1944.

45. *Wisconsin State Journal*, 23 January 1944; *Sheboygan Press*, 24 January 1944; CVSO Association meeting minutes, 31 January-1 February 1944, CVSO; *Green Bay Press-Gazette*, 26 January 1944; *Appleton Post-Crescent*, 5 February 1944; *Manitowoc Herald-Times*, 2 February 1944.

46. *Milwaukee Journal*, 18 February 1944; *Milwaukee Sentinel*, 22 February 1944; *Wisconsin Counties*, October 1944.

47. O'Brien to Hines, 19 July 1944, Wisconsin files, index to local veterans' information and service centers series, Records of the Retraining and Reemployment Administration, Record Group 244, National Archives, Washington, D.C. (cited hereafter as RG 244). For more on the creation of the RRA, see Davis, *Preparing for Ulysses*, 131-134.

48. O'Brien to Hines, 19 July 1944; O'Brien to Hines, 2 January 1945, RG 244; Minutes of the meeting of the Wisconsin State Veterans' Committee, 19 April 1945, RG 244; Stonehocker to Chief, Field Service Branch, 5 April 1946, RG 244.

49. Articles of organization, Veterans' Information Headquarters (Madison, Wis.), n.d. [c. 1945], RG 244; Hoffman to Chief, Field Service Branch, 18 June 1946, RG 244; Hoffman to Salyers, 28 October 1946, RG 244; Jeffries to Bailey, 9 February 1945, RG 244.

50. Hoffman to Chief, Field Service Branch, 18 June 1946, RG 244; Jeffries to Bailey, 9 February 1945, RG 244; Hoffman to Salyers, 27 October 1947, RG 244; Hoffman to Salyers, 28 October 1946, RG 244.

51. Survey and appraisal of veterans' information centers in Wisconsin, June 1945, RG 244; Siemering to Bailey, 18 August 1945, RG 244; Hoffman to Chief, Field Service Branch, 6 June 1946, RG 244.

52. Manitowoc County, Wisconsin, Board of Supervisors, *Proceedings*, 1940-50; Sauk County, Wisconsin, Board of Supervisors, *Proceedings*, 1942-50.

53. Survey of Wisconsin county service offices, March 1946, RG 244; Stonehocker to Chief, Field Service Branch, 5 April 1946, RG 244; Hoffman to Salyers, 27 October 1946, RG 244.

54. CVSO Association executive committee meeting minutes, 12 March 1947, CVSO; CVSO Association meeting minutes, 26-28 May 1947, which include institute workshop committee reports, CVSO.

55. Oscar N. Markus, "Principles of Office Management," included in institute workshop committee reports, CVSO Association meeting minutes, 28 May 1947, CVSO.

56. CVSO Association executive committee meeting minutes, 6 February 1948, CVSO; Program for Special Short Course, University Institute Report, 22 June 1949, CVSO.

57. Davis, *Preparing for Ulysses*, 141-147, 234-237.

58. Waller, *The Veteran Comes Back*, 14-15.

59. Charles Hurd and Charles Bolté, "How We Planned for the Veterans' Return," in *While You Were Gone: A Report on Wartime Life in the United States*, ed. Jack Goodman (New York: Simon and Schuster, 1946), 536.

Chapter Two

"I Think I Was a Little Futsed Up": Personal Readjustments

Morton Thompson, journalist and World War II veteran, provided advice to ex-GIs about how to survive their first days back in the civilian world. "Many of the habits you had in service will follow you into Civilian life," he told them. When encountering a line, he reminded veterans, "it is not necessary to gallop promptly to the end of [it]." If one needed a place to stay for the night, Thompson told them check into a hotel and not "enter the nearest house, throw the occupants out the window, and take over the premises." Should one "feel calls of nature," he advised veterans, "do not grab a shovel and a piece of paper and run for the nearest garden." Perhaps most important of all, he reminded veterans that they were now free men and women. "Just the mere facts that you can come and go as you please, get up and go to bed when you please, that you're the only one in that country who rates giving you orders," he wrote, "you can't explain to a Civilian why such things are miracles." Thompson made light of a problem many veterans of World War II faced upon their return to civilian life: altering the attitudes and activities of their daily lives from the military to the civilian world. The problem of veteran readjustment involved not only "macro" issues such as education, employment, and housing, but also the mundane aspects of everyday life.[1]

Thompson was just one of many writers to address the many personal readjustments the veterans had to make. American popular culture was inundated with discussion of the veteran's personal problems. Scores of self-help books provided veterans and their family members with guidance on navigating their way through the postwar world. Advice came from many quarters: academicians, mental health professionals, social workers, and veterans themselves. Even Hollywood got into the act, most notably with the film *The Best Years of Our Lives*, winner of the Academy Award for best picture in 1946.[2] Popular discussion of the "veteran problem" provides an unusually revealing glimpse into personal readjustments of veterans after World War II. Advice books covered issues that were intensely personal and difficult to document. Sexual matters, for example, often elude even the most frank of postwar reminiscences. These works also suggested strategies for coping with the turbulence in the veterans' lives, advice that often betrayed anxieties about gender relations in the wake of the war. Generally speaking, the veteran's personal readjustment problems were not long in duration—usually about six months to a year after discharge. However, personal matters posed the first and most immediate issues the veteran faced in their readjustment process. If not adequately addressed, personal problems could produce obstacles to the veteran's ultimate reintegration back into the civilian world.

"Nervous Out of the Service"

Returning home often evoked powerful emotions in the returning soldier. Army veteran and ex-prisoner of war J. J. Kuhn, for example, wrote that he returned to his home in Milwaukee "with tears in my eyes" as "the cab pulled into our driveway." Soldiers were relieved to have survived the war and were anxious to see family and friends again. However, many veterans were also surprised to feel less positive emotions upon returning home. Some experienced feelings of disillusion and bitterness, or felt strangely out of place among civilians. Some returned restless and anxious. In some cases, ex-servicemen even exhibited physical manifestations of emotional problems. Veterans sometimes described this emotional state as being "nervous out of the service." Not all veterans experienced all of these feelings, but most probably felt one or more of them. Indeed, many were probably unaware or unclear about their state of mind upon their initial return home. As Milwaukee native John W. "Jack" Dunn, a paratrooper with the 82nd Airborne Division, recalled after the war: "I think I was a little futsed up. I didn't require any psychiatric care, but—as I look back on it, I think I had a few problems."[3]

Disillusion was a common emotion for returning veterans, sources of which varied. For many, disillusion stemmed from idealized perceptions and unrealistic expectations of returning home. During the war, soldiers often imagined civilian life as a kind of paradise where all of their immediate problems would be solved. "Being out of the armed services stood for happiness and peace," claimed advice writers Dorothy Baruch and Lee Edward Travis. "Suddenly, a page would turn and a new life would begin." The majority of men and women in the armed services were anxious to doff their uniforms and return home as quickly as possible. Few discharged soldiers envisioned a troubled first few months out of the military, but after having built up unreasonably high expectations about the postwar years many found the realities of civilian life disappointing. Advice writers asked veterans to anticipate feelings of disillusion. Morton Thompson told his fellow veterans quite candidly: "Don't come home thinking that because you've taken part in a world battle against two of the biggest diseases that threatened liberty and peace and happiness in the world, that . . . the world is now perfect." "Disillusion is the inevitable aftermath of war," wrote Herbert I. Kupper, a New York psychiatrist who worked with veterans. "It is rare that all the human ideals, the dreams and fantasies, for which we allegedly fight, can reach fulfillment."[4]

Returning veterans were often chagrined to see the numerous changes that had occurred to their hometowns. "All 'home' values assume fabulous heights in the young imagination played upon by distance, time, hardship, and danger," warned Herbert Kupper. Advice writers told veterans that they might feel as though their hometown was now alien territory. "Home may seem to you like a foreign land you've never seen," claimed the authors of *Psychology for the Returning Serviceman*, "the people in it practically strangers." Morton Thompson asked his fellow veterans to view these changes in a humorous way: "Try to imagine you're in some foreign country and trying to get along with the natives and their customs," he advised. In fact, some veterans described the sensation of returning to a strange and different land. "The first thing we heard as we . . . caught sight of the Golden Gate Bridge [was] radio advertising," recalled Milwaukee native Sidney Podell, a bomber navigator in the 20th Air Force. "That was a culture shock," according to Podell, which he likened to "walking into a freezer." "Listening to that radio advertising for funerals and cars and sales," he remembered, "it was another world." Eugene Eckstam, a navy physician from Monroe, Wisconsin, spent more than a year in a remote area of Mindanao in the Philippines. Once back in Wisconsin, Eckstam found automobile rides one of the most "dramatic" personal readjustments he had to make. "Out there on jungle roads [you would drive] twenty-five or thirty miles per hour, and all of a sudden you're hurtling down the road fifty or sixty miles per hour and it was terrifying. I just begged drivers to slow down." Manitowoc native Guy Kelnhofer, a marine captured on Wake Island and incarcerated more than four years in Japanese prison camps, stared in wonderment at a man mowing his lawn. "The lawn cutting," his wife later wrote of the incident, "such an ordinary and peaceful activity, struck my husband as an utterly bizarre behavior."[5]

Veterans found that the people they left behind had changed as well. Parents had aged, for example. Army veteran Jack Plano greeted his mother and father at the train station in his hometown of Merrill, Wisconsin. "They both looked good, but of course somewhat older," he wrote of the encounter. "The most apparent change," he remembered, "was that their grayish hair had, for both of them, changed to a glowing white." "My mother had white hair when I came back," recalled Milwaukee army veteran Jack Chase, "and she wasn't real gray when I left." "I opened the door, walked in, and there were my parents," recalled Madison army veteran Richard Meland of his homecoming. "I'd been gone a couple of years, and they looked twenty years older. I suppose I did, too." Veterans also found that their siblings had changed. Donald Mercier of Eau Claire remembered that when he returned home he met his "mother, father, and this tall guy standing there waiting for me. I said hello to my mother and dad, and started to walk away. The tall guy says, 'Aren't you going to say hello to me?' It was my little brother and I hadn't recognized him."[6]

The war years had changed those who served as well. Many soldiers left home in their teenage years, not having traveled far from their home cities, villages, or farms. These young men and women had matured after years in the military, and the experiences of travel and combat seasoned them further and expanded their horizons. Many returned home to see their homes in a new light as a result. One such army veteran was Robert Peters, who while in Europe had visited London, Paris, and Heidelberg (among other places), and then returned to his parents' farm in the remote Wisconsin north woods near Eagle River. Coming home, his world seemed somehow different. Peters noted, for example, how "the forests appeared far more cut-over and stunted than I remembered." He also looked differently at the house in which he grew up. "The garage had lost one side and the roof had collapsed," he wrote. "The main house, built of logs, seemed much more decrepit than I remembered, and smaller. Though it stood a story and a half high, it seemed possible to grab the metal stovepipe flanged to the tar-paper roof." He made particular note of the family outhouse, "wide enough inside for two crude seats carved from apple-box wood; a sloping roof fell off to the back to make removals of snow easy, and a nail secured a dated Sears Roebuck catalog for wiping yourself. Nothing better symbolized our poverty than the outhouse." He later wrote that "to see how this primitive life had changed was disquieting. My family scrabbled almost as much as the poor Germans made destitute by the war." Home may have changed, but so had the young veteran's perspective.[7]

To many returned soldiers, civilian life seemed remarkably dull and uninteresting. "Things seemed pretty tame to me, with all the excitement I went through" recalled Madison native John Gill, an army medic wounded in the Normandy campaign. "It was almost like I missed it." Some even found civilian life oddly disturbing. "Under combat conditions . . . you never knew what was going to happen," explained Eugene Eckstam, "and now here everything was so free and easy and that didn't sit too well." Those returning to small towns seemed to have a particularly difficult time. Navy veteran Harvey Fehling returned to the village of Horicon, a community where, he lamented, they "rolled the sidewalks up at 8 p.m." Delores Hendersin, who returned from the WACs to teach school in the village of Eleva in rural western Wisconsin, remembered that "it was a little hard to come back to a small town, a small school, and a routine." In particular, Hendersin enjoyed dancing during the war and was disappointed to learn that there was no dance hall in Eleva. Self-help authors assured veterans and their family members that such feelings were normal. Advice writers Alexander Dumas and Grace Keen, for example, asked their readers to imagine the perspective of a young veteran "from a simple, unpretentious home . . . who has never been farther afield than his own state capital. . . . Will it be surprising if he returns from three or four years of adventure and action to find things at home dull and monotonous, to find the dance that pleased him before the war now trivial and boring?" The first to arrive home probably felt the greatest degree of initial alienation from civilian life. "If you are among the first to be mustered out of service," commented World War I veteran Maxwell Droke in his advice book to the veterans of World War II, "you will be impressed and distressed by the absence of many of your contemporaries." "There weren't many guys around who were in my class because they were all in service," remembered John Gill of his return to Madison before the end of the war, "so I bummed around with some of the guys in high school . . . that lived in my neighborhood."[8]

Another source of disillusion for the veteran was having to think and act for oneself. Herbert Kupper his informed readers that the military had placed their loved ones in a state of childlike dependency:

> Like a child, he is awakened at the hour when he must get up in the morning, he is provided with clothes to wear, he is given specific chores to do, he is shown just how to make his bed, he eats what is set before him, he is told where he may go to look for entertainment, and how late he may stay up at night—all this and more. Does it all have a familiar ring in the ears of parents?

Upon discharge, the veterans now had to make many decisions on their own, a task some found daunting. "It's not easy getting out of the service," according to WAC veteran Gladys Day of Racine, "because when you're in the service you have a great deal of security. . . . All of a sudden it's like being thrown out into the world, and you have to fend for yourself." Another WAC veteran, Lorraine M. "Connie" Allord of Madison, likened her discharge to being "let out of a cage. . . . Your life was so structured by the military that when you got out you didn't quite know how to act. You were kind of waiting for orders, then you realized there weren't any." Some veterans "will find this sudden release from regimentation difficult," Dumas and Keen told their readers, an observation many veterans found to be true. In leaving the familiar, structured environment of the military for the unfamiliar civilian world, veterans sometimes felt adrift in postwar America—no longer part of the military but not yet quite a civilian. "Really, you're just floating around," ex-marine Robert Botts of Madison recalled, "like a leaf on a pond with the wind blowing. You didn't know what you wanted to do, and you really weren't trained to do anything." Advice writers indicated that such feelings were normal, but that they had to be confronted. "Every independent action, from adding up his income taxes to choosing a career, may seem endless and painful," wrote Dumas and Keen. Some veterans, they suggested, might "lean on family and friends, as he has on his sergeants, lieutenants, and captains." Such a person, they wrote, "will have to be encouraged to stand on his own two feet once more."[9]

Disillusioned with the civilian world they had dreamed about for years, many veterans soon began to look fondly upon their days in the armed services. "There are moments when you are overwhelmed with the most unexplainable feelings," wrote Maxwell Droke. "Let's put those feelings into words—and without delay: *You are homesick for military life!*" Returning veterans found that the amenities of military life were gone forever. "Hundreds of young men in hundreds of towns stand on street corners expecting to hitchhike as they have in their army days," wrote Baruch and Travis, "only to find that there aren't any more free rides. Hundreds more discover that there are no more free shows, no more free lunches, no more free candy bars or cigarettes." Soldiers often enjoyed the respect and admiration of civilians during the war, but those often feelings evaporated with the cessation of hostilities. "When you step out of that uniform," Droke told veterans, "you will leave something behind—something you will never experience again in the civilian world. I don't know what to call it; there just isn't any name. Adulation? Regard? Reverence? None of these quite fit." Not only was the glamour of the uniform gone, but veterans also found that accomplishments important in the military world often meant little to civilians. Milo Flaten, an infantryman from Madison who fought from Normandy to the Elbe in the 29th Infantry Division, stopped into a restaurant on his way from Fort Sheridan to his parents' home in the Milwaukee suburb of Shorewood. "I walked in there and said, 'I'll have a beer,'" he recalled, "and [the bartender] asked me for my ID card because I wasn't twenty-one." Being unable to buy a beer shocked the young veteran. "I thought, 'Here I am, a hero with all these ribbons sewn on my uniform and he won't give me a beer?'" "Frequently I became depressed in my new freedom," wrote Eugene Peterson of Milwaukee, a veteran of the 3rd Marine Division, "and for brief moments found myself envying the guys who had stayed in service."[10]

One group particularly disillusioned with its postwar reception was women veterans. While in the military, many women gained a sense of their own self-worth and understanding of their abilities. Before the war "you want to get married, you want to have children, this sort of thing," recalled WAC veteran Priscilla Hargraves of Milton, Wisconsin, "and then you get into the service and think there's more to living than just getting married and having a family." Annette Howards of Milwaukee noted that after several years in the marines, "I became a person who always sat in the back of the bus to somebody who moved up to the front." Military service, she noted, "made me realize I am real self-sufficient, that I can take care of myself, that I can make my own decisions." But after the war, women veterans found that society expected them to resume more traditional roles. "When we did get out of the service," Connie Allord recalled, "it was the attitude that now you can go back to your kitchens where you belong." "For awhile after I got married my husband took over," remembered Annette Howards, "[we] fell into those old roles of husband and wife where the husband's the head of the household, or the husband takes care of everything. And suddenly I'm back to that old role of being submissive." Many women carried lingering resentment into postwar period. "I don't think we'll ever, ever really get past that entirely," claimed Connie Allord.[11]

Since women comprised less than 2 percent of the American military in World War II, women veterans were only a minor concern to the authors of self-help literature for veterans. A few acknowledged that some women suffered readjustment problems. Baruch and Travis, for example, noted the case of a woman who had been poorly treated in a VA hospital: "They don't believe there is really anything wrong with you," the woman veteran complained, "unless the problem was pregnancy, syphilis, or 'you're a psycho." Morton Thompson often had high praise for women comrades: "A lot of Wac [sic] and WAVE and SPAR and lady Marines have done plenty to earn respect," he wrote. However, women's readjustment issues make only scattered appearances in self-help literature for veterans, and were never handled in any systematic way. "Nobody looks for any special large-scale problems of adjustment so far as the females in the armed forces are concerned," claimed Thompson, since "women just naturally adjust better than men."[12]

In addition to a sense of disillusion, many veterans returned filled with feelings of bitterness. "The majority of servicemen have fought the war because it had to be fought," wrote Dumas and Keen, but "this does not mean that they did not resent deeply the need for doing it." One source of bitterness was a sense of regret for time and opportunities lost as a result of military service. Former paratrooper Jack Dunn, for example, expressed the sentiment that he sometimes felt "cheated" out of two years of his life. "I feel the same way today as I did then," recalled Madison army veteran Raymond Malmquist more than fifty years after the war—that military service "took four and a half years out of my life, productive years." Many veterans felt that they had borne an unfair burden in winning the war. While soldiers had been drafted, sent overseas, and often placed in harm's way for little pay, civilian workers back home saw wages increase dramatically. Maxwell Droke summed up the perspective of many veterans this way: "He contrasts his fifty dollars a month with the fifty dollars a week that his 4-F cousin in Milwaukee is dragging down, to say nothing of overtime; and the comparison makes him pretty peeved." Not all veterans held such views. "There was much talk about us young people having wasted the best years of our lives," wrote Eugene Petersen. "I tried to explain I did not feel that way. I helped defend my country from the German and Japanese military threats, but believed I had also aided less fortunate peoples to obtain the blessings of democracy."[13]

Nevertheless, civilians frequently became the targets of veteran bitterness. Soldiers "have heard or read stories," explained Dumas and Keen, "of huge crowds gambling away hundreds of thousands of dollars at the racetracks, tales of booming business in gay nightclubs, reports of jam-packed department stores and tremendous stocks sold out at fabulous prices at Christmastime." Army surveys indicated that many soldiers believed certain segments of society had taken advantage of the war for their own personal gain. Soldiers frequently identified groups such as businessmen, Jews, and African Americans, but were particularly critical of labor unions, which had staged several strikes during the war. Fully 41 percent of soldiers surveyed believed that labor leaders were "not doing nearly as much as they could" to win the war. Returning veterans often believed that civilians did not understand or appreciate the sacrifices they made, and found civilian complaining about wartime sacrifices particularly galling. "I got madder than the dickens at my mother," Madison army veteran Gerald Wilkie remembered:

> She started telling me all about her hardship and not being able to get the sugar
> she wanted in order to do the canning, at which time I promptly told her about

having to use gasoline to wash out your clothes and get anything clean . . . and telling her that as far as I was concerned, I didn't care if she had an ounce of sugar the entire time I was gone. Gee, that was terrible!

Eugene Eckstam found "depressing and disgusting" the sometimes "callused" attitudes of civilians. "I felt almost like I [wanted] to get out a tommy gun" and "cause a ruckus to make them duck for cover and make them have a little idea of what we went through." Though he "bore no resentment for those who had not served, nor envied them the fruits of their wartime labor," Eugene Peterson explained that he was nevertheless "dismayed that the idealistic objectives of our national efforts had somehow escaped them."[14]

Morton Thompson asked his fellow veterans to appreciate the sacrifices made by those on the home front. "If [civilians] need to be they can be pretty tough," he assured his readers. "They have proven it in the course of this war. Don't forget that every time you lost a buddy they lost a son or a brother or a husband or a wife." Advice writers warned that veterans might make certain segments of society convenient targets for their anger. "When we are hit and knocked down," Baruch and Travis told veterans, "we naturally want to lift ourselves up again." But they admonished returning soldiers not to "scapegoat" vulnerable segments of society such as Catholics, African Americans, and Jews, since it "defeats the very principles for which we fought." Thompson also attempted to head off such feelings among fellow veterans, reminding them, for example, that "a Red" was someone "you rushed to shake hands with over in Germany." In fact, the majority of veterans believed that civilians had made important contributions to victory. A 1943 army survey indicated that 78 percent of soldiers believed that a majority of civilians were "trying to do everything they possible can" to win the war, and 54 percent thought that most civilians were "taking the war seriously enough." Veterans often resented the heavy burdens military service had placed on them, but most also understood that civilians had made important contributions to the victory as well.[15]

Animosities stemming from wartime experiences also lingered on into the postwar world. Bitterness toward the Germans and Japanese, for example, sometimes followed veterans into civilian life. Glen Meisner of Franksville, Wisconsin, a veteran of the Pacific war, returned with lingering hatred of the Japanese. He recalled the horrors of war he had witnessed in the Philippines. "I'll never forget this town called Trinidad," he recalled. "All the children were blind. The Japs poked their eyes out." In another nearby town, Meisner remembered that "there were kids, not more than three years old, walking around on their ankles" because the Japanese had broken their feet. "When you've seen things like that," he argued, "it's pretty hard to forgive [th]em. . . . To me, a Jap is a Jap." George Nieweem, an army x-ray technician from La Crosse, recalled that about half of the patients he had seen were Filipinos, "many of them twelve or thirteen years old," brutalized by the Japanese. "It was awful receiving droves of kids like that," he recalled. "I don't think I can ever forgive the Japs for the way they conducted the war. They hit below the belt." Lester Doro, army veteran from Appleton, had lingering hostility toward the Germans. The veteran claimed that he had "a few choice words" for relatives whom he characterized as "German sympathizers." "If they had been where I was and saw," Doro insisted, "they'd have a different opinion."[16]

Even after discharge, the military could still elicit bitter feelings from veterans. One theme that veterans complained about for years after the war was waste. At the conclusion of hostilities, the military destroyed tons of equipment. Madison native Charles Bradley was shocked to see the army destroy perfectly good materiel as he was leaving the Aleutian Islands. His bitter feelings began when he asked to keep a small camp stove. The request was denied, but Bradley then watched as a soldier threw it into a trash can. Shortly thereafter, he witnessed a pile of unused sleeping bags being burned. "The acrid scent of scorched goose down harmonized well with my rising fury," he recalled. "All over Adak," he later wrote,

> base fires were burning up the leftovers from the campaign, much of it still in unopened cartons. Out in Kuluk Bay heavier unburnables such as weapons and machine parts were pushed overboard to decorate the bottom of that fiord. One of my 10th Mountain gang told me he had watched unopened cartons of the little camp stoves being loaded on a barge to be dumped out in the bay.

Bradley found the burning of a lumberyard the most egregious offense. "I thought of the Aleuts," he recalled, who "would have cherished the supply and used it well." Bradley was not alone in his feelings. Soon after returning to his native Oshkosh, bomber pilot Frank Stoll was asked to speak about the war to students at Oshkosh State Teachers College. Stoll told the students that "the main thing about the war" was "waste," and recounted numerous incidents. On the ship back home, for example, the navy "took away all the army blankets, threw those overboard, and gave us navy ones." He also recalled seeing airplanes "worth God knows how much being bulldozed into the ocean." For a generation having grown up during the Great Depression, witnessing such apparently pointless waste and destruction was shocking and embittering. For men and women who referred to themselves as "GI" (government issue), such destruction may have had an even more personal meaning to them.[17]

While self-help writers assured veterans that their disillusion and bitterness were normal, they instructed them to, as Baruch and Travis wrote: "FACE IT." "We must look squarely at the way we feel," they told veterans. "We must admit that we do hold bitterness, resentment—even hatred—inside of us." Dumas and Keen informed readers that veterans had to put the past behind them. "Feeling sorry for himself won't put spilled milk back in the bottle," they wrote. "His regrets and recriminations . . . are just wasting time. He has returned to the civilian world and he must live in it, so the sooner he accepts its ways . . . the better off he will be." How else could veterans cope with their feelings? Morton Thompson suggested that they use the same technique that got them through tough spots while in the service: "bitching." Thompson told veterans that, if used properly, this skill would be useful in civilian life too. "Well directed . . . bitching will help more to nail down and make secure what you fought for than all the sweet smiles, patient resignation, and tolerant acceptance the anxious ones hope you can muster." He even suggested that "some very nifty reforms" might arise out of angry young GIs' complaints:

> Keep your bitterness. Use it to advantage. There is great, there is enormous, there is incalculable good in it. You have learned to fight as a team. Keep fighting that way. That's something Civilians know little or nothing about. That is something you can teach them, a dowry you will bring to them out of the war.

Baruch and Travis made a similar suggestion. "Letting out our anger need not be wrong or destructive," they told their readers. "It's how we use our anger that counts."[18]

The ways in which veterans might use their anger greatly concerned many civilians, however. Fears that disgruntled veterans might pose a threat to the political and social order have long followed wars. In the 1940s, memories of the tumultuous post-World War I years were still fresh in the minds of millions of Americans, including episodes like Bonus March and veteran involvement with the rise of fascism in Europe (see introduction). Concern that veterans might promote militarism and threaten the republican form of government were not uncommon after World War II. Herbert Kupper, for example, reminded his readers that "the service man . . . has left the 'totalitarian' state for the 'democratic' one." Social worker Willard Waller was particularly alarmed about the potential threat veterans posed to society. "The veteran is politically dangerous because he has a great deal of hatred to work off," he wrote. "By making him a soldier we have cultivated his sadistic-aggressive impulses, taught him to fight and kill without mercy, and then done him a series of injustices—should we then be surprised if he then fights back?" Waller warned that the disgruntled veteran was "the ready tool of the demagogue," and wondered openly: "Will the veteran of World War II turn into Storm Troopers who will destroy democracy?" Waller believed it was certainly possible. "American veterans could never behave like German veterans," he wrote:

> They could never become Storm Troopers, never be the hired bullies, thugs, and assassins of a stupid counterrevolution. Or could they? Armies . . . are strangely alike, and there are striking similarities in the behavior of army-made men, of veterans, in all times and places. Perhaps if the American veterans of World War II return to a society similar to that of Germany of 1918-1932 they too will raise up . . . a Hitler.[19]

Whatever fears civilians might have had about veterans, militarism, and political stability, it was clear that the returning serviceman did not have revolution on his mind. "I wanted to get as far away from the military as possible," recalled Madison army veteran Raymond Malmquist of his return to America. "Now my life was once more my own," wrote Eugene Petersen, "and the future was in my hands. I could do what I wanted, live where I wanted, spit at a colonel if I wanted. The shackles of military life with its artificial and undemocratic hierarchy would never frustrate me again." A 1943 army survey asked soldiers their opinion about whether or not soldiers "should take over the country and run it" after the war. Forty-one percent—the most common response by far—described themselves as being "strongly against it." Another 27 percent responded that "it doesn't seem like a good idea." Only 6 percent described themselves as being "strongly in favor of it." Although the returning soldiers did not find civilian world the paradise they had hoped, they very much preferred it to the military one they had just left.[20]

In addition to feelings of disillusion and bitterness, being "nervous out of the service" was manifested in other ways. Restlessness was another common personal readjustment problem. Many returning soldiers had trouble finding ways to relax after the war. Akira Toki, a veteran of the famed Japanese-American 442nd Regimental Combat Team, recalled that he was "was pacing the floor [and] smoking" for a time after returning to his hometown of Madison. Often such restlessness was manifested in carousing. While many veterans gathered and celebrated their homecoming in taverns (see below), restlessness led some to pursue the nightlife to extremes. Army infantry officer Roth Schleck recalled that he was "pretty wild" in his first months back home. "You just didn't care or nothing could affect you," he explained. "You were a free spirit. I think I drank quite a bit and you just flew around like a lost chicken." "I went on a three month binge," recalled Lester Doro, "booze and women. I had one hell of a time." Hulbert Pinkerton, an army air force veteran from Madison, recalled that he had engaged in excessive drinking and "some wild life" after the war, and attributed it to the fact that "I probably wasn't all that settled down yet. Probably disturbed by all the sights to some extent."[21]

In some cases, restlessness turned into wanderlust. Many veterans moved far from their original hometowns after the war. Oftentimes such migrations occurred for economic reasons, but in many cases the desire to move to another place emanated from the ex-serviceman's inability to settle down. Paul Van Ells, a marine corps cook in the Pacific, hitchhiked with a friend after the war from his home near Manitowoc because he "wanted to see the country." They went south to Florida where his friend "got homesick" and returned to Wisconsin, but Van Ells made his way up the Atlantic seaboard to New England where he eventually settled. While Van Ells went from Wisconsin to New England, army veteran Joseph Taber did the opposite. A native of New Bedford, Massachusetts, Taber "didn't want to go back to the east coast" after the war, explaining that "people change" and that the region had grown too "congested." He also enjoyed the people of the Midwest, whom he described as "a lot more friendly and open" than folks in New Bedford. He married a woman from Chicago and took a job with Walgreens drugstores. When Walgreens wanted him to transfer to Connecticut, Taber left his job and bought a small general store in Cuba City, Wisconsin. Many of Wisconsin's prodigal sons and daughters returned to the Badger State once their restlessness had worn off. The war "made me tired of being in Milwaukee," recalled coast guard veteran Marjorie Boxill, "so after that time I always took jobs out of the state." Boxill took civil service positions closing military bases in the Caribbean before eventually returning to Wisconsin.[22]

Not all veterans who wished to hit the road did so. After the war, ex-bomber pilot and former POW Paul Fergot of Oshkosh discussed with his wife the possibility of moving to Alaska and opening a music store. The couple decided the idea was just a "pipe dream," and Fergot followed a more conventional path and studied engineering at the University of Wisconsin. Herman Owen, a veteran of the New Guinea campaign in the army's 32nd Infantry Division, also thought that "maybe" he "should go to Alaska," but instead took a job with the Barron County Veterans' Service Office. Ex-fighter pilot D. C. Pressentin of Madison enrolled at the University of Wisconsin after the war, but considered moving to South America. "I had an opportunity to go to Brazil to teach fighter pilots how to fly," he explained. "I thought, 'Well, why not?' And I had a hell of a time settling down and studying after you lived the life I lived for a couple of years." Though his wife was "100 percent anything I wanted to do," Pressentin could not decide what to do. After deciding he would take the Brazil job, he changed his mind and decided to "stay here and finish school." It should be noted that not all veterans experienced a sense of wanderlust. Marine corps veteran Roger Scovill of Madison spoke for many veterans when he stated emphatically that he had "seen all of the world I wanted to" during the war. In fact, a 1947 study indicated that 85 percent of World War II veterans still lived in their home states.[23]

Family members were often puzzled about the restlessness of their veterans. Milwaukee navy veteran Richard Scheller noted that "my mother and father were a little disappointed that I didn't 'settle down' that summer. And I didn't." Italo Bensoni, an army combat veteran from Hurley, Wisconsin, ended his restless streak only after a stern lecture from his mother. "My mother . . . told me, 'It's time to settle down now,' and she bawled the hell out of me, and I thought she was right. So I just settled down." Suggestions from self-help books on how to handle veteran restlessness depended on gender. Male veterans were urged to take action to solve the problem. Baruch and Travis told veterans that they should channel their energy into a hobby. "A man makes his own adventures," they wrote. "He creates them when he knows what he's after." Women family members were asked to play a passive, supportive role. Dumas and Keen assured their readers that restlessness would pass. "Let him walk off his restlessness in the wind and rain," they advised, "and when he returns welcome him back naturally and casually."[24]

The maelstrom of conflicting, unexpected emotions, advice writers warned, might also lead veterans to become distant and moody. Sometimes veterans experienced physical symptoms of emotional wounds, such as headaches, shortness of breath, stomachaches, weight loss, inability to concentrate, or even "the jitters." "My head just started going," recalled Joseph Taber upon meeting his new wife's family. "I had to get away from there, and go where everything was quiet." He "went and laid down in bed," he recalled, adding, "I don't know what would have happened had I stayed there." In some cases, veterans were known to have gone on verbally abusive tirades, or even outbursts of physical violence. Merchant mariner Donald Fellows remembered one violent outburst he witnessed as a student at the University of Wisconsin after the war. He recalled a blinded classmate who "used to beat his Seeing Eye dog with a chain, [but] nobody would stop him because he was a war veteran. You could tell he was taking out his frustration about being blinded. That poor dog would just howl." Former paratrooper Jack Dunn spoke for thousands of veterans when he noted that "I think I might have been a difficult person to get along with at that time." Self-help writers assured veterans that these behaviors were normal and conquerable. Baruch and Travis, for example, stated that such complaints were not "imaginary," and that "an emotional problem . . . does not indicate that a person [is] crazy or feeble-minded." "No matter what sort of . . . emotion underlies the aches and jitters," they wrote, the "road toward cure lies in facing and meeting the emotional difficulty."[25]

For veterans unable to conquer their emotional problems themselves, advice writers usually suggested a visit to a mental health professional. "There is a point in the fighting man's adjustment to civilian life where members of the family must recognize their limitations," psychiatrist Herbert Kupper told his readers. If a veteran shows no signs of improvement after about three to six months, Kupper believed, "we must assume that he requires outside help." Mental health professionals were not the only self-help authors urging veterans to seek psychological attention if they needed it. A psychologist, Baruch and Travis assured veterans, "will be best able to facilitate facing, meeting, and getting rid of what is troubling the person underneath." Advice writers devoted considerable time trying to dispel traditional notions about psychologists and those who used their services. Morton Thompson called the psychiatrist a "magnificent weapon" in league with penicillin and sulfa drugs, but bemoaned the fact that "it's a disgrace to use it." He equated going to see a psychiatrist with visiting any other doctor. "It's like appendicitis," he told skeptical veterans. "You don't know why you've got pains, you go see a doctor, he knows where to look, he looks, finds it's your appendix, he opens you up, takes it out, he sews you up again. It's that simple."[26]

Personal Relationships

"Your transition to civilian life," Maxwell Droke told veterans, "might . . . be a good deal easier if it were not for two things: your family and your friends." If veterans were surprised to feel like strangers in their hometowns, they were even more surprised to feel like strangers in their own homes. Many veterans returned from war to wives or husbands. Others had become romantically involved before or during the war, and longed to marry in the postwar world. Younger veterans typically returned to the homes of their parents rather than their own households. The return of veterans from war caused great stress in families all across the United States. Fitting themselves back into a network of family and friends was another personal challenge the veterans often faced upon returning home. Youth counselor Grace Sloan Overton claimed that the threat World War II posed to the American family was *"the most desperately serious one the American family has ever faced"* [italics in original] and was "the central problem which faces the American nation."[27]

Self-help writers spent considerable time advising veterans and their family members on questions regarding marriage and romantic relationships. Authors warned that after long periods of separation, the veteran's relations with his spouse or sweetheart might be rough for a while after the homecoming. According to sex therapist Howard Kitching, separation "threatened marriage at its very roots," an observation that applied to unmarried couples as well. "When separation occurs it creates new problems," wrote Kitching, "and out of those problems further problems still. The situation is like a snowball rolling down a hillside. It starts out being as big as a baseball and may end up being as big as a house." Most advice writers stated that after long periods of separation and growing as individuals, couples would have to get to know each other again. "Reunion, after a long separation such as war occasions, is very like getting married again," Kitching told his readers. Once again, unrealistic visions of home life led to disappointment after the war. "The pangs of disillusionment at discovering that home life is different from what he expected assail the returned husband as keenly as they do the unmarried man," wrote Yale psychiatrist George K. Pratt. "No major human activity disintegrates families like war," claimed Grace Sloan Overton.[28]

The war provided young Americans with many new opportunities for coupling, but also created conditions decidedly unfriendly to the creation of stable relationships that might lead to marriage. A common story of wartime romance was that of Gaylord Nelson, an army officer from Clear Lake in northwestern Wisconsin who would later become Wisconsin's governor and U.S. senator. At Fort Indiantown Gap in Pennsylvania, Nelson met a young army nurse from Virginia named Carrie Lee Dotson. Nelson, who commanded a company of African American soldiers, was sent to Okinawa, but by chance so was Dotson. Reunited on the island, their romance blossomed and by 1946 Nelson had given Dotson "a little silver band that one of his soldiers made—took quarters and pounded them into rings." Nelson returned to Wisconsin to pursue a career in politics, and Dotson left her home in Virginia to join him. The couple was married in November 1947. However, equally common was the story of Madison army veteran Joseph Connors. Upon joining the army, Connors left behind a young woman whom he had been dating since high school. But as Connors was fighting in the Pacific, his girlfriend started seeing someone else. "I couldn't blame her," he later reflected. "Here she's all by herself. She doesn't live with her family; she was living with her sister when I left. Then her sister got married, and she's all by herself." Connors received his infamous "Dear John" letter shortly before being wounded in the drive toward Manila. "I get the letter on the 7th, get hit on the 9th, and I'm going home on the 10th," he recalled. The young soldier's story may be poignant, but it was hardly an isolated case; countless GIs received such letters during and immediately after the war. Annette Schubert of New York City "had an understanding" with a young man back home, but during the war she fell in love with a fellow marine, Bernard Howards of Milwaukee, whom she agreed to marry. "I had to write [my old boyfriend] a 'Dear John' letter," she recalled, but noted: "I don't think he suffered too much because he got married right after the war."[29]

Young Americans flocked to the altar during and immediately after World War II. The reasons why young men and women married with such eagerness were numerous. Many believed marriage would provide a sense of permanence to their relationships in a time of great flux and instability. Marriage also legitimized sexual relations. Young men, often facing the very real prospect of death in combat, were especially anxious to enjoy the pleasures of a marriage and a sexual relationship at least once in their lives. According to Grace Sloan Overton, young American women also feared what she called an "impending husband shortage" that "has very naturally resulted in a feeling of desperation on the part of many." For the unmarried veteran, marriage was often one of his or her top priorities upon returning home. After years of war, travel, and life-threatening experiences, veterans often saw marriage as a way to settle down and put the war years behind them. "It was only logical and inevitable that [after the war] cupid would enter the picture," wrote ex-POW Asbury Nix of Stevens Point, Wisconsin, and he "decided that it was time for me to settle down and take a wife." Jack Plano of Merrill, Wisconsin, felt similarly. "No wife or girlfriend awaited my return," he wrote, "but I'll take care of that in due time, I remember thinking on the train" home. For those veterans who had sweethearts waiting for them, marriage often followed soon after the veteran's return. Madison army veteran Robert Esser, for example, described himself as having "walked off the gangplank and right up the aisle." In 1939, the marriage rate in the United States stood at 10.7 per 1,000 persons. By 1942, the rate had risen to 13.2, and peaked at 16.4 in 1946 before declining. In Wisconsin, the marriage rate climbed from 7.5 per 1,000 persons in 1940 to a peak of 12.3 in 1946.[30]

However, in the rush to marry, many young Americans often made unfortunate and ill-considered decisions. "With the glamour of the uniform gone,"

warned Dumas and Keen, "they may find each other less attractive as life partners than they thought when they were under the unnatural excitement of war."
Kitching went so far as to label many wartime marriages nothing more than
"pleasant fictions" and "legalized temporary sexual liaisons." In fact, many war
marriages failed. Delores Hendersin, a WAC from La Crosse, married a fellow
soldier at Luke Field in Arizona during the war. The army then sent her husband
to the Pacific, while Hendersin returned to Wisconsin and found work teaching.
Separated, the couple gradually drifted apart. As her husband's discharge approached, he wrote to his wife and informed her that he would "send for" her
soon. "That finished it," Hendersin recalled, "because nobody sends for me." A
tragic wartime marriage also shook the family of Dr. William F. Lorenz, noted
University of Wisconsin psychiatrist and chief surgeon of the Wisconsin National Guard. In May 1942, a relative of Dr. Lorenz left the United States for
combat duty in the southwestern Pacific—just months after he had been married
and his new wife had become pregnant. While her husband was away, the young
woman apparently began drinking heavily, consorting with other men, and ne-
glecting the newborn child—including an incident in which she left the infant in
an automobile while she patronized a tavern. In 1944, the woman suddenly left
Wisconsin and eventually landed in Los Angeles, where police found her living
with another man in an apartment described as being "littered with whiskey bottles, pop bottles, and dirty, filthy surroundings generally." The family shielded
the young soldier from the situation as long as it could, but in August 1944 Dr.
Lorenz arranged to have the young man returned from the Pacific to divorce his
wife.[31]

As the marriage rate rose during the 1940s, so did the divorce rate. In 1939,
the divorce rate in the United States was 1.9 per 1,000 persons. It rose throughout the war years, and peaked in 1946 at 4.3—more than twice the prewar figure.
Wisconsin had a divorce rate lower than did the nation as a whole, but the same
pattern emerged. From a rate of 1.1 in 1940, the divorce rate in the Badger State
rose to 2.6 in 1946. In an age when divorce carried significant social stigmatization, self-help writers urged veterans and their families to hold out hope even for
the most rocky of wartime marriages. While acknowledging that "a fair proportion of such war marriages may prove unworkable," Dumas and Keen stated that
if the couple tried hard enough such a marriage might work. "They must both
have time to evaluate their relationship, to develop mutual understanding, toler-
ance, cooperation, and compromise." Nevertheless, many young veterans began
their postwar lives with the disgrace and humiliation of a failed marriage and a
divorce.[32]

Writers provided newlyweds with copious advice on how to handle marital
stress and tension. Whether in an existing marriage, a new one, or merely in
courtship, the veteran's romantic readjustment would be greatly aided, most
writers suggested, if women assumed a submissive role in household affairs.
Male veterans "need a period of being undisputed captains of their own souls,"
wrote Dumas and Keen. Writers frequently urged women not to "nag" their hus-

bands about household affairs. "If a woman finds herself inclined to . . . put the state of the house above the comfort of the family," Dumas and Keen advised:

> She will do well to make a change in herself. She must learn to get satisfaction from creating order anew each day out of the chaos [her family might] leave behind. And if this does not satisfy her passion for neatness, she can work it off in sidelines—like the wife who kept lovebirds and took out her reforming instincts on them instead of her husband. Their dexterity in slinging birdseed over the deep-piled carpet proved a good match for this passion in her.

Herbert Kupper echoed this theme, telling women that they had their own postwar readjustments to make. "Initially," he wrote, "there must be few demands on the man." He suggested that women use their "intuition" and "feminine charm" to make the man feel as if he were in charge. As an example, he told the story of a couple married ten years. Upon the man's return from war, the wife "scolded" as she had before, but now he grew angry. "Her old devices of 'getting around' him did not work," wrote Kupper, but "since she was persistent, and feminine," he wrote, "she intuitively felt that just as he had changed, so must she. . . . Being a clever wife, *she* adjusted." The popular culture message to young veterans and their spouses was clear: the reestablishment of the the traditional gender order would provide further reassurance in the uneasy postwar world.[33]

Veteran readjustment literature focused heavily on sexual relations. For the young men and women in uniform during World War II, the war years were often a sexual awakening. Young soldiers were not only freed from parental constraints during the prime of their sexual lives, but social standards about sex were also loosened in the emergency atmosphere of wartime. In addition, many men and women entered the military already married and experienced an interruption to their normal sex lives. "Sex," wrote Baruch and Travis, "often becomes the highest and most immediate goal to go after when the serviceman who has been away returns home. Whether he is married or not, invariably the first thing he wants to do is seek out a sex partner and have himself a 'perfect time.'" "There is always the release of the sex impulse under the masquerade of war," claimed Grace Sloan Overton. "What is more natural than that they find themselves with exaggerated mating desires?" According to Howard Kitching, "a happy sex life is absolutely essential if a marriage is to develop . . . into something that endures [and] grows in strength in spite of all obstacles." Judging from the readjustment advice literature, sex was often one of the veteran's major disappointments.[34]

The sources of sexual problems varied greatly. For some, relative sexual promiscuity during the war apparently had an impact on their postwar sex lives. The war years presented numerous opportunities for young men and women to engage in sexual activity. Many young couples dated in the traditional fashion, but many others engaged in illicit or questionable sexual activities as well. Prostitution often flourished wherever large numbers of troops were gathered, for example. Overseas, large cities such as London or Paris were notorious among

GIs for prostitution, but even in remote areas soldiers and sailors could often find such accommodations. "On the edge of town," wrote Charles Bradley of his arrival in Kodiak, Alaska, in 1944, "there was a long, silent, widely spaced line of males leading to the door of a small home. Every few minutes the line would move forward one notch." In the Philippines, navy physician Eugene Eckstam recalled how prostitution flourished even in the remote villages of Mindanao in the Philippines where he was stationed. In addition, Eckstam noted that many men—enlisted men and officers alike—had acquired "emergency wives" in nearby villages for small sums of money. Upon returning home, wartime promiscuity was often manifested in feelings of guilt. "Many have wandered widely over the face of the globe and have let fancy rest where it would," lamented Baruch and Travis. But "when a man has a series of casual experiences," they continued, "he feels guilty, he feels tense." Conversely, many GIs expressed anxieties about the faithfulness of the spouse or sweetheart they had left behind. "'What's she been doing all these months?'" Baruch and Travis quoted one veteran as saying. "'Maybe she's like all the rest of the girls we've been having. . . . Such thoughts drive you crazy.'" Even for those who abstained from sexual activity, the often bawdy atmosphere of barracks life or a shore leave might lead to increased sexual anxieties. "He has heard a lot of sex talk," wrote Baruch and Travis of the young GI.[35]

Self-help literature acknowledged that sexual problems could manifest themselves in any number of ways. Several writers covered a topic of apparent concern to many men: premature ejaculation. Morton Thompson told the story of a young submariner who rushed off on his first liberty in months:

The next morning he was sitting on the end of the same dock, looking pensive. "What's the matter, son?" asked the three-striper. "Nothing, sir!," murmured the boot. He turned his face to the three-striper, his brow creased in bewilderment. "But ain't it funny, sir—how far behind a fellow can get on his women—and how quick he can catch up!"

Baruch and Travis noted the same concern. "He has dreamed and waited and dreamed and waited; and then, when the moment comes, he is so keyed up and so eager to prove himself that the very reverse may occur." Thompson assured his fellow veterans that "it's a big continent, and they haven't run out of she Civilians for years and years and there's more than enough to go around. Take it easy. At least first take off your skis." Several authors addressed anxieties about masturbation. Though he characterized it as an "incomplete and immature form of sexual activity," Kitching told veterans that masturbation was "harmless unless practised to great excess." Veterans "may kid themselves that it's not harmful," according to Baruch and Travis, "and yet funny old horror stories . . . are apt to creep into the mind." They told veterans that "good scientific evidence" proved that masturbation did not cause insanity or "take away from potency."[36]

More serious sexual problems sometimes plagued the sex lives of veterans. Another frequently discussed topic was impotence. Kitching told veterans that "bridegroom's impotence," caused by "fear, embarrassment, and overanxiety," was common, but it was a problem that "usually passes in a few days or weeks unless more hidden and long-standing causes make it continue." Self-help authors identified other sources of impotence. Baruch and Travis, for example, told veterans that "guilt and tension" could "interfere with potency." Another problem writers discussed was promiscuity, which several advice writers also linked to a crisis of self-confidence. A "hidden fear of impotency," according to Baruch and Travis, "may spur him to prove his potency," but it would not "leave him peacefully satisfied." Self-help books identified still other sexual difficulties. The authors of *Psychology for the Returning Serviceman* reminded men that "you are behind the times if you expect your wife to be only the passive recipient of your attentions. It is now quite widely known that women are people too. And the frequency and urgency of her desires may be quite different than yours." A woman's lack of interest in sex, writers tended to agree, tended to result from a lack of male awareness of a woman's sexual needs. Kitching reminded the anxious male veteran to engage in foreplay. "Only when the wife is ready," he told them, "should the next stage of intercourse . . . take place." Advice writers assured the veteran that sexual problems did not make him any less of a man. "When things go wrong in a man's sex life," wrote Baruch and Travis, "he needs to know that the major issue is not one of loss in virility. . . . It is rather a problem in forming a good, solid, and loving personal relationship." Should sexual problems continue for a period of months or even years, writers agreed, expert advice should be sought.[37]

The subject of homosexuality is one that appeared infrequently in readjustment advice literature. Gays, according to the 1940s popular stereotype, were supposed to be effeminate men too weak to control their own "perverse" sexual desires—the ultimate symbol of male weakness. Baruch and Travis touch upon the subject only briefly, stating that "perhaps [a man] gives up women altogether and turns to homosexuality as a way out" of his sexual problems. Kupper was one of the few advice writers to discuss the subject in any detail. "It is an 'open' secret," he wrote, "that homosexuality is one of the prevalent wartime problems." While he acknowledged that "many outright homosexuals got into the military [despite] strict regulations to the contrary," Kupper sought to reassure the wives and lovers of veterans that their inability to perform sexually was not the result of having become homosexual in the military. While all men have a "feminine" side, "the vast majority of men never become homosexual," he wrote, and insisted that "homosexuality is never produced in the service."[38]

Although the military may not have "produced" homosexuality, many young men and women did indeed discover their own homosexual desires as a result of military service. Gay men and women in uniform experienced the same sexual awakening as did heterosexuals, and were presented with the same basic opportunities. Indeed, as historian Allan Bérubé has pointed out, the war "placed a whole generation of gay men and women in gender-segregated bases where they could find each other, form cliques, and discover the gay life in the cities." Robert Peters of Eagle River, Wisconsin, was one such soldier for whom World War II was a gay sexual awakening. Peters found himself exposed to much sexual activity while in the army in Europe, including advances from several men. Although he initially denied his own attraction to other men, over the course of the war he found that men were in fact the objects of his favorite sexual fantasies. Peters continued to be conflicted sexually upon returning home to Eagle River. "Some of my restlessness was sexual," he wrote. "I was a strapping youth now isolated, with no possibility of a liaison with either gender." Peters wrote that after the war he had a recurring dream in which "a series of females served me," but "when I dreamed of love as tenderness, males were always the object." Officially, the armed services forbade homosexuals from military service, and discharged at least 9,000 servicemen and women for homosexual acts or proclivities with a general discharge (known as a "blue discharge" or a "blue buzzer" for the color of the paper on which it was printed). For gays and lesbians, World War II was a time of both tragedy and opportunity. Several scholars have credited the war with launching the modern gay and lesbian movement.[39]

Advice writers assured male veterans that their sexual problems were probably temporary. Morton Thompson urged men to proceed slowly: "A man who's been hungry for a long time doesn't put forty pounds on his starved ribs the first hearty meal he eats," he insisted. "It takes days of feeding." Baruch and Travis urged veterans to discuss their feelings with their partners "frankly and openly," though they warned them that when discussing their wartime sexual behavior, "confession . . . may be good for the soul but bad for the wife." Kitching discussed the problem of confessing wartime infidelities in some detail. "We are told that confession is good for the soul," he wrote, but asked: "Confession to whom?" Kitching leaned against confession to spouses in most cases, and posed the following scenario:

> Suppose a man has really tried to be faithful, but has perhaps on one or two occasions, after a party or celebration, slipped up. It has, if you like, been a lapse of morals and self-control. There is no question of his having been emotionally attached to his partner in the act or of her to him. If he is a genuine person, sincerely wanting to make his marriage a good one and his family happy, it is difficult to see what useful purpose would be served by telling his wife on his return, or vice versa if the situations are reversed.

Feelings of guilt "may be regarded as punishment," he claimed, and a deterrent from straying again. If, on the other hand, one had become emotionally attached to another, "there can be no question of ignoring it or of not being honest with the original partner."[40]

In the postwar sexual readjustment, women were once again asked to subordinate their expectations to the man's. Kupper told his readers that in sexual matters "she must submerge her feelings and drives" because the veteran "must be understood as a man who is attempting to regain the tenuous strings of an adequate sexual existence." He suggested that women behave as if in early courtship, where "a young girl will flatter a man, accede to most of his desires, and conform to his masculine notion of motherhood." With a woman too aggressive, he warned, the veteran "may fail in satisfying these demands and become utterly incapable." Thompson described what he believed to be the most desirable way to rekindle a sexual relationship. "The wife keeps her peace," he wrote. "Anything he wants to do, she wants to do; he's the guy with the initiative, she's the warm, quick responder."[41]

Despite whatever sexual difficulties the returning veterans may have had, postwar America saw a sharp increase in the birthrate. During the Great Depression, the birthrate in the United States dropped dramatically. During the 1920s, it averaged 25 births per 1,000 persons, but dropped to just 19.2 during the 1930s. "Almost everyone today knows that the birthrate before the war was disturbingly low," wrote Howard Kitching, "and that with the advent of normal conditions it will undoubtedly fall again, and that unless something is done the future of the race may be seriously imperiled." Kitching's prediction proved to be decidedly inaccurate. Instead, the birthrate continued to rise after the war. For the 1940s, the rate averaged 22.6 births per 1,000 persons, and peaked in 1947 with a rate of 26.6. Though far above the 1930s figure, the birthrate of the 1940s was still below that of the 1920s. Nevertheless, the postwar baby boom had begun.[42]

Children were an integral part of many returning veterans' personal lives. While many veterans began their families after the war, others went away to war with young ones left behind. For those veterans returning to children, advice writers also warned of stress in this area. As difficult as years of separation were for adults, for children they often represented a lifetime. Indeed, many children would not remember their soldier-parent at all. Self-help writers warned that children might initially view their fathers as strangers and resent their arrival into the household. Children might revert to temper tantrums and bed-wetting to protest "the stranger's" presence. In fact, many veterans returned home to find less than welcoming receptions from their infants and toddlers. Upon meeting his son for the first time, Charles Bradley found that Charles Jr. did not recognize him. On the drive home, the boy would not sit in the veteran's lap. "Charlie's verbal vocabulary was not great yet but he was exceptionally eloquent in body language." Indeed, the boy insisted that Bradley was not "Daddy" at all, an assertion the father found puzzling. However, upon arriving home the identity of "Daddy" was made clear:

> Indicating that we were to follow, he climbed the stairs rapidly on all fours and crawled to the bathroom, pulled himself upright on the leg of the wash basin and said, "uuh-uuh" to get our undivided attention. Then he pointed to Maynie's folding alarm clock and said, "Daddy." He was right. For the last two years Maynie had pointed toward a photograph mounted in the clock and said "Daddy." He had learned it well and could even say it.

Albert Giese, navy veteran from Nekoosa, Wisconsin, received a similar welcome from his young son. "His mother worked real hard with pictures," he recalled, but when Giese came home the toddler "took one look at me and went
and hid. He'd peek out." George Pratt warned veterans that rekindling relationships with children would require "a dint of patience, understanding, and . . .
vigorous effort."[43]

Self-help books warned mothers about the way that the fathers might resent
the child. A veteran's wife "may proudly plant a two-year-old child on [his] lap,
fully expecting him to be overjoyed by the product of his paternity," warned
Dumas and Keen, "to find instead that he behaves as if his collar were choking
him." While in service the veteran idealized both wife and child but, "probably
has not . . . fit his two dreams together and reconcile[d] the conflict between
them." The behavior of young children could sometimes enrage the already-tense
returning veteran. "I used to have a phonograph collection before the war," recalled Madison army veteran Joseph Tauchen, but "when I came back from the
service I was lucky if I had twenty left. My wife would let him play with the dog-
gone things, and he broke them." Jean Lechnir of Prairie du Chien, Wisconsin,
remembered that her husband, Ray, "couldn't stand the kids [fighting]," after he
came home from the army. Their squabbling "made him very nervous—very,
very nervous." Advice writers again suggested that the problems would naturally
subside. "As he becomes more adequate to fatherhood again," Kupper assured,
"love and tenderness for his children become more obvious."[44]

Many veterans were young and unmarried, and returned not to wives and
children but to their parents' homes. After years of living as adults while in
service, veterans often returned to find their parents still treated them like children. "My mother was convinced that the army had tried to starve me," recalled
Jack Plano, "so she embarked on a campaign to fatten me up"—a campaign
which worked "all to well," as he recalled. "The only trouble readjusting was
living at home," remembered Madison's Robert Clampitt, who served in the 88th
Infantry Division in Italy. "Your parents think you're still twelve years old," he
claimed, "no matter where you've been or what you've done." In particular,
Clampitt recalled that his parents wanted him to come home before midnight. "I
said, 'Well, I don't come home until at least an hour after the taverns close.'"
Just as separation led some married couples to drift apart, it also affected many
parent-child relationships. Eugene Petersen returned to his family's home in
Milwaukee, but felt estranged from them. "I realized that other than a blood relationship I had nothing in common with these people," he remembered. "Perhaps I did not understand them and certainly they did not understand me."[45]

Advice literature reminded parents that their children had grown up. "He
may have grown ten years in two," Kupper told them. Writers also reassured
parents that a young person's desire for independence was natural. Like spouses,
parents were asked not to make too many demands on the returned veteran.
Baruch and Travis warned, for example, that traditional parental authority might

remind their "returning hero" of military life and stimulate resentment or perhaps outbursts. "Armed forces' regulations," they told parents, "and regulations that had been imposed earlier in the home [are] readily lumped together with their overlapping qualities of unwelcome discipline, of demands for orderliness, for subservience, for obedience and keeping to rules and regulations." Mothers were told not to be "oversolicitous" or to "baby" their returning sons. A father, Kupper advised, could "best meet the situation by treating his son as an equal and a friend." Fathers could still attempt to guide their sons, Kupper said, but since veterans would resent authority, he must "not too obviously seek to help him." Veterans, in turn, were reassured that their parents were not ogres, but had simply fallen back on former modes of behavior. Baruch and Travis told the story of a veteran who, when his parents tried to tell him what to do, nodded politely and did whatever he wanted to do anyway.[46]

Whether veterans returned to spouses or parents, former soldiers often found that everyday behaviors picked up in the military were not suited to civilian life. One such hangover from military life was the use of profanity. Soldiers have long been associated with foul language. Military profanity in World War II "concentrated almost exclusively on a dozen words," observed advice writer and World War II veteran Benjamin Bowker, "including damn, hell, God, Christ, bastard, bitch, and the blunt ugly monosyllables denoting the sex act, defecation, urination, and the physical organs involved." Returning veterans found such language often followed them into civilian life. "You're used to a different vocabulary," explained ex-bombardier John Scocos of Fond du Lac. "It just naturally comes after you've been gone three or four years." "I used the four-letter word too frequently," Beloit army veteran Lloyd Page admitted (without specifying the word in question). "One time I used it in front of my mother," Page recalled, "and I thought she was going to have a heart attack right there." Such language was also unwelcome in most workplaces. John Wozniak of Stevens Point felt compelled to warn his employer that he "might start using language people had been accustomed to in service." John Winner, army veteran of Madison, noted that upon returning to law school he had to "clean up [his] language a little bit," but that it was not too difficult. Self-help writers reassured readers that veterans would not speak this way for long. "Experience with hundred of veterans," Bowker wrote, "indicates that most of them dropped their camp language as fast as they had picked it up."[47]

Veterans often returned home having acquired other habits often considered undesirable in most American households—at least for young men and women in their twenties. Many returned from the military smoking cigarettes, for example. Driving to his home from the train station in Eagle River, Robert Peters lit a cigarette, an ordinary act that surprised his mother. "Everybody in the army smokes," Peters felt compelled to explain. "The Red Cross used to give us free Camels with our doughnuts." "Almost the first question my Dad asked," recalled Jack Plano, "was: 'Did you start smoking while you were overseas?' Knowing how strongly he had always warned me about not taking up that 'nasty habit,' I didn't have the heart to come right out and tell him that I had." Drinking habits formed in the military also followed many veterans into civilian life. Bruce Willett of Eau Claire grew up in a conservative Methodist environment in which drinking was forbidden. He remembered that after the war his brother was "appalled" at his newly acquired penchant for drinking beer. He also recalled that "the first time I was home, I poured my milk by tipping my glass," as one would pour beer to reduce the amount of foam. Marine corps flight surgeon William Luetke of Ontario, Wisconsin, recalled that "my dad looked at me one morning, and . . . I was smoking, hung over, and he said, 'God, you've really gone to hell, haven't you?' I had at the time."[48]

Both veterans and family members expressed great concern over how to discuss the experience of war. "It is quite natural," Baruch and Travis informed veterans, "and quite to be expected, that those who are close will want to know about the experiences that their men have lived through." In fact, many veterans returned home only to be blitzed with questions from curious friends and family members. "Everybody was all questions," remarked WAC veteran Juanita Wilkie after her return to Madison. Gifford Coleman of Rice Lake, Wisconsin, recalled that after coming home from service with the 32nd Infantry Division in the Pacific that he had to "answer a lot of questions" from relatives. Eugene Petersen returned to Milwaukee only to find that "for the next two days" he was "paraded before many aunts and uncles" who questioned him about the war. Americans had been absorbed by the war for four years, and when it was over they wanted to know more about the role their friends and family members had played in winning it. Many veterans were quite willing to talk about military life, the people they had met, and the exotic places to which they had traveled. World War II had been the most exciting episode in their lives.[49]

Many others, however, were reluctant to discuss their war experiences. Many veterans were simply were taciturn by nature, or modest men and women who did not want to appear braggarts. As Eugene Petersen explained to his inquisitors, "most of military life was pretty boring." However, there were other reasons for the silence of veterans. Many were sensitive about being made a spectacle. "I disappointed the old man because as soon as I got home I took off my uniform and never wore it again," recalled Frank Stoll. "He wanted to show me off." "I came home in the morning," remembered marine veteran Clayton Chipman of Milwaukee, "and my mother prepared lunch for all the relatives who came over, and I was edgy, eating in that small kitchen, after eating in mess hall and outside for two years. You come back here and you're sitting in a small kitchen with a bunch of people piled in. You just couldn't get used to it." Perhaps no Wisconsin veteran felt more like a curiosity than did John Bradley of Antigo. A navy corpsman, Bradley had gone ashore with the marines at Iwo Jima in 1945. In the midst of the battle, Bradley had been one of six men to raise the American flag on Mount Suribachi, an episode immortalized in a Pulitzer Prize-winning photograph. One of only three flagraisers to survive the battle, Bradley and the others were whisked from combat and sent on a nationwide savings bond tour, which included meeting the president and attending a massive rally in Times Square in New York City. Later, the flag raising was featured in the 1949 film *The Sands of Iwo Jima* (in which the survivors performed small roles), and the photograph became the basis of the Marine Corps Memorial outside Washington. Bradley was widely hailed as a "hero," but the veteran apparently believed that his actions did not warrant the attention he received. He consistently refused press interviews, and even resisted discussion of the war with his children, despite their intense interest. When Bradley's son James asked his mother why the veteran did not speak about the war, she once replied: "Your father feels the real heroes were the men who died on Iwo Jima."[50]

Combat veterans like John Bradley had a particularly difficult time discussing the war. Talking about combat could revive horrible memories the veterans longed to forget. For veterans who returned still suffering from the psychological trauma of combat, war-related questions could stimulate feelings of guilt and depression, or vivid dreams and flashbacks (see chapter 3). Finding language that would convey their experiences accurately also vexed the combat veteran. As Bradley's son later surmised, "the totality of [the war] was simply too painful for words."[51] Veterans usually had no desire to inflict their own searing war memories on friends and family. Silence was a way to protect them from the horrors of war. When veterans did discuss the fighting, the response they received was often one of shock or disbelief. "It was difficult to tell anyone what it was like unless they had been there," reflected army combat veteran James Underkoffler of Portage, Wisconsin. As a result, he "never talked to anyone at great length" about the war after coming home. Though his family was interested in his military experiences, "they sensed I'd rather not talk about it" and refrained from asking questions. John Bradley's silence about the war, according to his son James, lasted "for decades—an entire generation." In his forty-seven-year marriage, he spoke of the war with his wife only once, "for seven or eight disinterested minutes." Bradley continued to turn down interview requests. The veteran had instructed his children to tell callers that he was fishing in Canada, but, as his son noted, "my father never went fishing in Canada. Often, as we gave this excuse, he was sitting across the table from us." When asked why he refused to talk about the war, "the best he could do was to give a barely perceptible shake of his head as if he were dealing with a common inconvenience like hay fever or nearsightedness. It was his personal affliction." It was not until after Bradley's death in 1994 that his family learned that he had been awarded the Navy Cross— the navy's second highest decoration.[52]

Baruch and Travis suggested that veterans attempt to change the subject if they did not feel like talking about the war, but told them that talking to close friends and family members would help them come to terms with their experiences. "A man has to talk," they wrote, "but he must talk at his own speed, in his own time, and according to his own volition." Writers urged family members to proceed cautiously in asking questions about the war. Herbert Kupper, for example, suggested that families not call a family reunion which would "expose him to the curiosity of everyone." Direct questions, the advice books agreed, annoyed many veterans. "Ask him questions about the new lands he has visited," Kupper wrote. Thus, self-help literature suggested that veterans control the subject of war discussion. On the other hand, some veterans returned and were dismayed at the lack of interest in their adventures. "When I got home, the folks . . . didn't ask me any questions, particularly," recalled navy frogman Daniel Turner of Madison, a situation he found "curious." As he later learned, "they were going under the premise that had been publicized in the media, 'Don't irritate the veteran.'" Some veterans found civilians' questions trivial and indifferent. "I could not blame the civilians for showing little real interest in my life in the Marine Corps," wrote Eugene Petersen. "Their questions were perfunctory and my answers lacked much enthusiasm." Marine corps veteran Annette Howards recalled that although her husband—also a veteran—would be asked questions about the war, "there were never any questions asked about what I did or what my experiences were."[53]

Family members were often uneasy about the camaraderie that existed among veterans. Returning veterans frequently sought out the company of other ex-soldiers. Despite the negative feelings many had about the military, veterans often felt most comfortable when meeting with other ex-servicemen and women. In fact, military life often creates a great sense of camaraderie among soldiers. After months and years of military service, the civilian world seemed strange, breeding a sense of isolation in many veterans. "There will be days when you will feel very lonely," Morton Thompson warned his fellow veterans, but he assured them that they were not alone. "All over America there will be literally millions of servicemen and -women who will be going through the same thing you are. . . . You got company, brother." By gathering with others who had shared the experience of wartime military service and returning from it, veterans rekindled the sense of camaraderie they had known in war. Contact with fellow veterans provided them with a forum to discuss the war and their readjustment problems in a comfortable, sympathetic environment.[54]

Because a majority of young American men saw military service in the war, finding fellow veterans was not a difficult task for those returning home. Perhaps the most common meeting place for veterans—at least in Wisconsin—was the local tavern. "The Circle Bar was the homecoming headquarters for veterans," recalled James Underkoffler of his return to Portage. "After I was discharged," recalled Jerome Nelson of Two Rivers, "I made up for lost time by going to bars and getting acquainted with a lot of friends who were now out of the service, just reminiscing." Army veteran Donald May recalled that the taverns in his native Fond du Lac were "loaded six deep. Lots of GIs." Ex-bomber pilot Ralph Jacobsen of Stoughton recalled spending the summer of 1945 "out at the lake, at the bars every night, a lot of the guys coming back. It was a great summer." "The guys were coming back," according to Milwaukee navy veteran Richard Scheller, who returned home in 1946, "and it seemed like every week we were having a reunion with some guys. . . . There were bars we'd hang out in, and they just all showed up."[55]

Taverns were not the only places veterans gathered, of course. As James Underkoffler recalled, he and other veterans formed a basketball team at the local armory after the war, which they called the "Ruptured Ducks"—the nickname the veterans gave the eagle insignia on their discharge pins. Wherever they might meet, it was clear that veterans tended to enjoy the company of other veterans. Family members were assured that a veteran's desire to visit with other veterans was normal. "If for some time to come," Dumas and Keen told their readers, "the husband seems to prefer the company of other ex-soldiers to that of his wife or family, the wife should not allow herself to be jealous. It does not mean that their marriage is going on the rocks." In time, they assured, "he will . . . gradually find the companionship of his family more and more satisfying." Indeed, they suggested that veterans' organizations could become a social outlet for both husband and wife. "Each year they will look forward to district, state, and national meetings," they assured. "The people they meet will become mutual friends, for they will all have interests *and* experiences together."[56]

Veterans' Organizations

In his humorous look at postwar America entitled *Back Home*, Bill Mauldin—creator of the cartoon characters Willie and Joe so beloved by GIs during the war—poked fun at America's veterans' organizations. In one cartoon, Mauldin portrayed a veteran about to leave a military separation center, duffel bag tossed over his shoulder. As he is walking out the gate, he receives a warning. "Two used-car salesmen and three veterans' organization representatives waitin' fer you to come out," read the caption. Sixteen million veterans returning from World War II presented an unprecedented opportunity for veterans' organizations to recruit new members. During the war, GIs expressed a favorable opinion of such groups. In a 1945 army survey of soldiers in Europe, 55 percent indicated that they planned to join a veterans' group; only 11 percent said they would not.[57]

In the 1940s, the American Legion was the largest and most important veterans' association in the United States. Initially open only to World War I veterans, the organization extended its membership to veterans of World War II in 1942. The American Legion was a notoriously powerful political lobby for veterans. During the 1920s and 1930s, the Legion continually pressured federal and state governments for readjustment programs for World War I veterans, but perhaps its greatest legislative accomplishment was the GI Bill of Rights, passed in 1944, for veterans of World War II (see chapter 1). From its inception, the American Legion was known for promoting a nationalistic brand of patriotism, and became infamous for its zealous anticommunism. Patriotism and anticommunism remained hallmarks of the Legion's outlook after World War II as well.

However, the American Legion was more than just a political and patriotic lobby; it was also a social organization. The local American Legion "posts" that dotted the American landscape usually had a bar (at least in Wisconsin), and often a dance hall as well. Legionnaires also formed auxiliary organizations for the wives and children of its members, and were noted for their community work, including baseball and civics programs for young people.[58]

Although the American Legion was the largest veterans' group in the United States, it was only one of many seeking new members after World War II. America's second largest group was the Veterans of Foreign Wars (VFW), which had long accepted veterans from any conflict so long as they had served overseas in wartime. (The American Legion also accepted those who had served within the United States.) The Disabled American Veterans (DAV) also opened its ranks to World War II veterans, provided they had a service-connected disability. World War II veterans created new organizations as well. The American Veterans of World War II (Amvets), formed by student-veterans in December 1944, claimed a national membership of 60,000 by mid-1946. Many World War II veterans joined or formed various unit- or service-specific organizations, such as the Marine Corps League, the 32nd Division Veterans' Association, the Submarine Veterans of World War II, to name just a few active in Wisconsin after World War II. Like the American Legion, most of these groups also formed auxiliary groups and acted as social clubs as well as political advocates for veterans. Returning World War II veterans who wished to join a veterans' organization had no shortage of options.[59]

World War II veterans joined these veterans' groups in large numbers in the years immediately following the war. They did so for a variety of reasons. The political stances of such groups—most notably their positions on veterans' benefits—brought many into the organizations. Ex-infantryman Italo Bensoni of Hurley, Wisconsin, saw the American Legion as "an avenue [to make politicians] keep their promises," and for "protecting what [politicians] promised was going to be given to us." Army veteran John Wozniak of Stevens Point joined both the American Legion and DAV because "alone you can't do much, but collectively there's more power when more people speak at one time." Because of their activities in veterans' welfare, some returning veterans felt obligated to join these organizations. John Gill, seriously wounded in Normandy in 1944, received a letter from the government informing him that he would receive a pension for his war injuries. Gill was puzzled, not having filed a disability claim, but he soon received another letter from a local VFW post telling him that they had filed the claim in his behalf. "I thought they'd done this for me [so] I really ought to join," he stated. Another Madisonian, ex-bomber pilot John Miller, suffered from war-related psychiatric problems and joined the DAV because "they helped me so much." He noted that "they take care of [claims] for me because there are a few times when I'm not able to." In the 1945 army survey, 42 percent of respondents indicated that protecting veterans' rights and providing personal help to veterans and their families were major reasons for their plans to join a veterans' association.[60]

Although only 9 percent of soldiers in the 1945 army survey indicated that "social activities" would be an important reason for joining a veterans' group, significant numbers of ex-soldiers were attracted to the social opportunities such organizations provided. Army veteran Elmer Jaeger of Milwaukee joined an American Legion post because "they had a good pool table and poker games over there." "The VFW in Eau Claire had a pub and an eating place," recalled army veteran John Walters of that city. "My wife and I had been out there a couple of times," he recalled, "and we kind of enjoyed it." Milwaukee army veteran Marvin Moebius joined a local Legion post because he and his wife were in a "dancing mode," and a local post had weekend dances. Navy veteran Dale Bender also recalled that one particular Milwaukee post had "tremendous dances every Saturday night" and was "a nice place to take a date." Army veteran Fred Hochschild joined an American Legion post in Milwaukee for the opportunity to bowl on the same team as a "world-renowned bowler" who was also a Legion member.[61]

The social isolation many veterans experienced upon their return home led many former GIs into veterans' organizations. Veterans often enjoyed the opportunities to congregate with other ex-soldiers that such groups presented. Army air force veteran Joseph Taber joined the VFW in Cuba City, Wisconsin, primarily "so I could talk and swap stories with people who had been through the same experience I had." Middleton army veteran Richard Elver found in his local VFW post "an opportunity to meet people in the same boat you were in." According to Elver, "it's hard to tell somebody what really happened, [and] if you tell them what really happened, do they believe you?" While returning veterans may have been reluctant to discuss the war with family members, veterans' organizations provided many with a chance to talk in the comfortable environment of the local veterans' post. Italo Bensoni described his American Legion post in Hurley as "a place where a veteran can express one's self."[62]

Some veterans found themselves under considerable pressure to join a veterans' group. Many had fathers who had served in World War I, for example, and who strongly encouraged their young sons to join. In other cases, stronger forms of coercion were employed. As a young lawyer in Madison, John Winner often went before a local judge who was a member and strong promoter of the American Legion. "He practically told each veteran . . . who came in there that they would do much better in his court if they joined the American Legion," he recalled. Another army veteran, Leslie Moede of rural Manitowoc County, recalled the circumstances under which he joined the American Legion:

In our village of Reedsville, we had Dr. [E. C.] Carey, who at one time was state [vice] commander of the American Legion. And I was on the farm working, grinding something, and I got a piece of steel in my eye, so I went to Dr. Cary to have this piece of steel removed. I was leaning back in this chair . . .

and he said, "you're a veteran, aren't you?" "Yea." He said, "do you belong to
the Reedsville Legion?" "No." Still fooling around in my eye, he said, "don't
you think you should belong to the Legion?" "Yea, I think I should," and then
he took out the piece of steel that was in my eye. So I joined the American Legion.

Returning World War II veterans swelled the membership ranks of veterans'
organizations. Nationally, membership in the American Legion grew from one
million on the eve of World War II to nearly 3.3 million in 1946. Of all Legionnaires in 1946, nearly 70 percent were veterans of World War II. American Legion membership in Wisconsin more than doubled after the war. In 1940, the
Wisconsin American Legion had a membership of 35,545, all of whom were
veterans of World War I. By 1945, the number rose to more than 49,000, and
peaked in 1947 at 92,347, with one historian estimating that about half of the
organization's members were World War II veterans. The VFW saw an even
more dramatic rise in membership. Nationally, the VFW grew from 201,170 in
1940 to 1.5 million in 1946. In Wisconsin, membership rose from 6,957 in 1940
to 44,760 by 1946.[63]

Despite such impressive increases in membership, veterans' groups enrolled
only a minority of World War II veterans. In fact, World War II veterans showed
less of a propensity to join these associations than did their World War I counterparts. Although approximately 20 percent of America's World War I veterans
were members of the American Legion in 1941, by 1946 only about 14 percent
of World War II veterans belonged to the organization. Even at its peak membership of about 46,000 World War II veterans in 1947, the Wisconsin American Legion figure represented only about 15 percent of the state's roughly
300,000 World War II veterans. After 1947, American Legion and VFW membership declined slightly. Because many veterans joined more than one association, adding together the membership totals of all veterans' groups does not provide an accurate count of overall veterans' group membership. Though the pre-
cise number of veterans who belonged to any veterans' association at any given
time is impossible to obtain, they probably involved no more than 25 percent of
World War II veterans at any one time.

In the immediate postwar years, many veterans were not interested in joining such groups, while others joined briefly and then left. What attracted some
veterans to these organizations drove others away. Many potential members disliked the organized veterans' emphasis on obtaining benefits. Otto Junkermann
of Milwaukee was invited to join a local American Legion post. "I went to the
meeting," he recalled, "and I heard nothing but complaining and whining and
crying about, 'we need this, and we need that.'" Junkermann bravely took the
floor and asked the Legionnaires why they were "whining" so much. "I was
drummed out of there more or less by mutual agreement," as he remembered.
Others disliked the version of "Americanism" espoused by the American Legion,
the VFW, and other such groups. Richard Bates of Baraboo, Wisconsin, who

fought in Burma as part of the famed "Merrill's Marauders," joined both the American Legion and the VFW under pressure from his father, but let his membership lapse after a year. "The leadership in both of them at the time was World War I men who were established reactionaries," he recalled. "They hated Roosevelt, they hated the New Deal, they hated unions, and I couldn't stand going to a meeting of [either group] and listen to those old bastards bitch."[64]

The brand of social activities for which the major veterans' groups were noted also drove many potential recruits away. Such groups had a strong reputation for drinking, which did not appeal to many veterans. Milwaukee army veteran David Brenzel joined a VFW post upon his return to America, but soon dropped out largely due to the perceived emphasis on alcohol. "Meetings always started slowly," he recalled,

> and everyone was full of beer by the time the meeting got started. As senior vice commander, I had to stand and salute every guy who left the meeting. And hell, everyone's full of beer, and everyone's running back and forth. This is a veterans' post? Stand up and salute every guy who's got weak kidneys? That was the last veterans' group I had anything to do with.

"I didn't have time for their kind of recreation," opined Stoughton navy veteran Robert Beckstrand, "just cards and booze." Many new veterans simply wanted to avoid anything associated with the military. Ex-fighter pilot Wesley Todd briefly joined an all-marine American Legion post in Milwaukee, but soon dropped his membership. He recalled entering the post and being greeted by a woman veteran "in a marine uniform [who] said, 'Hi, gyrene. Hang up your gear on the bulkhead' All this salty talk. I just didn't get anything out of that." "Naval service was too fresh in my memory to want to be reinforcing it," claimed Pearl Harbor survivor Dorwin Lamkin of Hudson, Wisconsin. "You couldn't get me to march in a parade unless I had a gun in my ribs," claimed Robert Beckstrand. "I'd had enough." Veterans' groups simply "didn't offer me anything I was looking for," claimed Madison's Raymond Malmquist.[65]

Many World War II veterans were interested in veterans' organizations but were dissatisfied with the existing veterans' milieu. In the 1945 army survey, 20 percent suggested they would join an organization that would "promote improvements . . . for everyone (not just veterans)—promote good government, national prosperity, democracy, [and] social programs." A segment of the World War II veteran population rejected traditional organizations and sought to create a new kind of veterans' group. Such sentiments led to the emergence of the American Veterans' Committee (AVC). The AVC was founded in 1944 by a small group of World War II veterans led by Charles Bolté, an American who joined the British army before Pearl Harbor and was wounded in North Africa. The AVC sought to distance itself from more traditional veterans' groups such as the American Legion and the VFW, replacing the military-like organization of "posts" and "commanders" with more civilian-sounding "chapters" and "chairmen." Its politics also differed from that of the American Legion and kindred groups. Adopting the slogan "citizens first, veterans second," the AVC was the home of political liberals who hoped to make veterans a force for peace and social good in postwar America. The AVC pressured lawmakers for action on veterans' issues, such as increases in GI Bill allowances and housing. However, the AVC was also involved in broader issues, such as support for the United Nations and the postwar struggle for civil rights.[66]

Many Wisconsin veterans found the AVC, with its nontraditional style, and its focus on peace and social issues, refreshing. Sidney Podell of Milwaukee liked the fact that the AVC was an organization for veterans that was "not just merely glorying over the fact that we had been in service," but working toward larger social goals. Madison army veteran Norris Tibbetts recalled that he was proud to associate with "right thinking veterans who disdained the Legion as a bunch of grubby beer drinkers." Roth Schleck, also an army veteran from Madison, gravitated to the AVC because "I didn't believe in the veterans trying to bleed the country." The AVC was strongest on college campuses flooded with veterans on the GI Bill after the war (see chapter 4), and indeed, its membership rolls included many young veterans who would become prominent in government, and academia, and other fields. Wisconsin AVC members who went on to become political notables in the Badger State included Gaylord Nelson (Wisconsin governor and U.S. senator), Horace Wilkie (chief justice of the Wisconsin Supreme Court), and Henry S. Reuss (U.S. congressman from Milwaukee). Despite a promising start, the AVC had declined sharply by 1950. Not only were the veterans leaving the campuses by that time, but the AVC also suffered from accusations of communist sympathies and infiltration, much like other liberal groups of its day. "Behind the scenes" of the AVC's first national convention in Milwaukee in 1946, recalled Henry Reuss, "a slate of candidates backed by the Communist Party USA almost staged a coup but was stopped short without dragging the conflict to center stage." Though hobbled by internal factionalism and the open hostility of traditional veterans' groups, the AVC was a force in the politics of veterans' affairs in Wisconsin during the late 1940s.[67]

Many veterans were simply too busy to join any organizations. Madison army veteran Erin Karp recalled that he was interested in joining a veterans' group, but that he simply did not have the time to do so. "I was working nights," he recalled, "and all these organizations wanted me to join. I can't go to meetings at night, and I don't want to join an organization unless I can participate." Army veteran Vernon Bernhagen of Wisconsin Rapids explained that "there were so many things going on all the time, family raising, (I had four sons) . . . and then I was working a part-time job with my dad, in addition to my full-time job with the electric company. So I just didn't have much time." Others cited the cost of membership as a reason for not joining. Oconto's Charles Smith was interested in joining the Marine Corps League, but recalled that he "didn't have three dollars in his pocket" and felt that he could not afford to join. Madison army veteran Joseph Connors spoke for thousands of veterans in Wisconsin and millions across the nation when he explained simply, "I was never a joiner."[68]

One segment of the veteran population that frequently encountered resistance in joining veterans' groups was women veterans. Most veterans' organizations did not specifically bar women from membership, but female military service was such a rarity before World War II that an all-male membership policy was simply assumed. When women veterans returned home from World War II, many wanted to join veterans' groups as did their male counterparts but often found themselves being discouraged from doing so. Juanita Wilkie returned to Madison from overseas service as a WAC cryptographic officer only to find her membership application to the VFW denied. "The older men blamed the young men, and the young men blamed the older men," she recalled. She was invited to join the women's auxiliary, however, since her husband was also a veteran. Connie Allord recalled that when her veteran-husband was asked to join a local American Legion post, she was invited to join the auxiliary. Mrs. Allord demanded to join the post as a veteran, and after some delay she was finally admitted. "I never got any invitations to join," recalled navy veteran Carol McLeester. "Anything that ever came to the house was addressed to my husband." "I thought about" joining the American Legion, recalled Madison army nurse Elizabeth O'Hara Baehr, "but they really didn't want women. They didn't encourage it." By 1954, only about 500 women had become members of the Wisconsin American Legion. Though some women held offices such as departmental child welfare chairman, state historian, and even one district commander, few held positions of power in the organization in the decades following World War II.[69]

In short, the veterans of World War II were not of one mind on the issue of veterans' organizations. Many believed such groups to be helpful to the readjustment process, as they provided both political advocacy and a veteran-friendly social environment in the years immediately following the war. However, others saw such groups as a hindrance to readjustment—a reminder of the military years they longed to put behind them as they faced the postwar era. The way veterans approached the issue of veterans' organizations depended on the personal readjustment needs of the individual veteran.

Conclusion

Crossing over from the military world back to civilian life raised many confusing issues and questions in the minds of American's World War II veterans. "Because of their uncertainties," Baruch and Travis wrote, "many [veterans] are asking: 'Am I normal?'" Advice writers sought to allay these fears and reassure veterans that they were passing through a turbulent but temporary phase in their lives. "This very wondering about normalcy is normal," wrote Baruch and Travis:

If a person, in the face of all of this, can honestly claim: "It didn't affect me!"—we should look at him with suspicion. A man would have to be hard as nails and altogether impenetrable if he were to let a war go by without being affected. He would be a monster—not a man. No human being could possibly live through such epochal events without feeling uprooted.

Many veterans did indeed find that the war had changed even the most intimate aspects of their lives. Most veterans had not anticipated difficulties, and many were not prepared to confront them. "In some ways we wanted to pick up where we had left off," wrote Eugene Petersen, "but if we gave it some deep thought we knew this was not possible."[70]

Confronting personal issues—like being "nervous out of the service," rekindling relations with family and friends, or joining a veterans' group—were usually the first readjustments to civilian life that veterans had to make. For those who sought assistance, a body of self-help literature existed to provide advice on making the personal transition back into the civilian world. Veterans were urged to take charge of their lives, while family members were asked to play a supportive role. The reestablishment of traditional male-female relationships, advice writers implied, would provide further reassurance and security in the unsettled world that was postwar America. Precisely how faithfully veterans followed such advice cannot be known; there were undoubtedly sixteen million strategies for meeting the challenges of personal readjustment. Most veterans met the personal challenges to readjustment in just a few weeks or months upon returning home. Though veterans were generally fitted back into family and community life, problems of finding a job and a home, or meeting war-related medical problems, remained.

Notes

1. Morton Thompson, *How To Be a Civilian* (Garden City, N.Y.: Doubleday, 1946), 28-41.

2. For discussion of veteran readjustment literature, see Susan Hartmann, "Prescriptions for Penelope: Literature on Women's Obligations to Returning World War II Veterans, *Women's Studies* 5 (1978): 223-229, and Elizabeth Fox-Genovese, "Mixed Messages: Women and the Impact of World War II," *Southern Humanities Review* 27 (1993): 235-250. For more on Hollywood and the veteran, see David A. Gerber, "Heroes and Misfits: The Troubled Social Integration of Disabled Veterans in *The Best Years of Our Lives*," in *Disabled Veterans in History*, ed. David A. Gerber (Ann Arbor: University of Michigan Press, 2000), 70-95; and William F. Fagelson, "From Combat to Conformity: Hollywood Narrative, World War II and the Postwar Gender Crisis," M.A. thesis, University of Texas at Austin, 1997.

3. J. J. Kuhn, *I Was Baker 2: Memoirs of a World War II Platoon Sergeant* (West Bend, Wis.: DeRaimo Publishing, 1994), 223-224; Dunn interview, Wisconsin Veterans'

Oral History Project, Wisconsin Veterans' Museum Research Center, Madison, Wis. (cited hereafter as WVOHP).

4. Dorothy Baruch and Lee Edward Travis, *You're Out of the Service Now* (New York: Appleton-Century, 1946), 1-2; Thompson, *How to Be a Civilian*, 125; Herbert I. Kupper, *Back to Life: The Emotional Adjustment of Our Veterans* (New York: L. B. Fischer, 1945), 122.

5. Kupper, *Back to Life*, 73-74; Irvin L. Child and Marjorie Van de Water, eds., *Psychology for the Returning Serviceman* (Washington, D.C.: Infantry Journal Press, 1945), 3; Thompson, *How to Be a Civilian*, 51; Podell interview, WVOHP; Eckstam interview, WVOHP; Amy Lindgren, ed., *Understanding the Former Prisoner of War: Life after Liberation: Essays by Guy Kelnhofer Jr., Ph.D.* (St. Paul, Minn.: Banfil Street Press, 1992), 45.

6. Jack C. Plano, *Fishhooks, Apples, and Outhouses* (Kalamazoo, Mich.: Personality Press, 1991), 298; Jack Chase interview, Stephen E. Ambrose World War II Interview Collection, Wisconsin Veterans' Museum Research Center, Madison, Wis. (cited hereafter as Ambrose Collection); Meland interview, WVOHP; Mercier interview, WVOHP.

7. Robert Peters, *For You, Lili Marlene: A Memoir of World War II* (Madison: University of Wisconsin Press, 1996), 102-105.

8. Gill interview, WVOHP; Eckstam interview, WVOHP; Fehling interview, WVOHP, Hendersin interview, Wisconsin Women in World War II Oral History Project, State Historical Society of Wisconsin Archives, Madison, Wis. (cited hereafter as WW2OHP); Alexander G. Dumas and Grace Keen, *A Psychiatric Primer for the Veteran's Family and Friends* (Minneapolis: University of Minnesota Press, 1945), 10; Maxwell Droke, *Good-by to GI: How to Be a Successful Civilian* (New York: Abingdon-Cokesbury Press, 1945), 57.

9. Kupper, *Back to Life*, 42-43; Gladys Day interview, WW2OHP; Allord interview, WW2OHP; Botts interview, WVOHP; Dumas and Keen, *Psychiatric Primer*, 8.

10. Droke, *Good-by to GI*, 8-9, 31; Baruch and Travis, *You're Out of the Service Now*, 2; Flaten interview, WVOHP; Eugene T. Petersen, ed., *A Chance for Love: The World War II Letters of Marian Elizabeth Smith and Lt. Eugene T. Petersen, USMCR* (East Lansing: Michigan State University Press, 1998), 407.

11. Hargraves interview, WW2OHP; Howards interview, WVOHP; Allord interview, WW2OHP.

12. Thompson, *How to Be a Civilian*, 62-66, 203; Baruch and Travis, *You're Out of the Service Now*, 21. For more on women veterans in the United States, see June Willenz, *Women Veterans: America's Forgotten Heroines* (New York: Continuum, 1983).

13. Dumas and Keen, 12; Dunn interview, WVOHP; Malmquist interview, WVOHP; Droke, *Good-by to GI*, 40; Petersen, *A Chance for Love*, 407.

14. Dumas and Keen, *Psychiatric Primer*, 19; Samuel Stouffer, et al., *The American Soldier* (Princeton, N.J.: Princeton University Press, 1949), vol. 2, 614, 637-639; Gerald Wilkie interview, WVOHP; Eckstam interview, WVOHP; Petersen, *A Chance for Love*, 407.

15. Dumas and Keen, *Psychiatric Primer*, 12, 19; Thompson, *How to Be a Civilian*, 75, 180; Baruch and Travis, *You're Out of the Service Now*, 22-23; Stouffer, *American Soldier*, vol. 2, 614.

16. Meisner interview, Ambrose Collection; University of Wisconsin-LaCrosse Oral History Project, *Vivid Memories of War: La Crosse Remembers World War II: An Oral History of La Crosse Area Veterans* (La Crosse: LaCrosse Central High School;

University of Wisconsin-LaCrosse Oral History Project, 1996), 67; Doro interview, WVOHP.

17. Charles Bradley, *Aleutian Echoes* (Fairbanks: University of Alaska Press, 1994), 255-256; Stoll interview, WVOHP.

18. Dumas and Keen, *Psychiatric Primer*, 12; Thompson, *How to Be a Civilian*, 122-133; Baruch and Travis, *You're Out of the Service Now*, 29.

19. Kupper, *Back to Life*, 95; Waller, *The Veteran Comes Back*, 10-14, 186-191.

20. Malmquist inverview, WVOHP; Petersen, *A Chance for Love*, 405; Stouffer, *American Soldier*, II, 615.

21. Toki interview, WVOHP; Schleck interview, WVOHP; Doro interview, WVOHP; Pinkerton interview, WVOHP.

22. Van Ells interview, WVOHP; Joseph Taber interview, WVOHP; Boxill interview, WW2OHP.

23. Fergot interview, WVOHP; Owen interview, WVOHP; Pressentin interview, WVOHP; Scovill interview, WVOHP; Stouffer, *American Soldier*, vol. 2, 641.

24. Scheller interview, WVOHP; Bensoni interview, WVOHP; Baruch and Travis, *You're Out of the Service Now*, 187; Dumas and Keen, *Psychiatric Primer*, 16.

25. Joseph Taber interview, WVOHP; Fellows interview, WVOHP; Dunn interview, WVOHP; Baruch and Travis, *You're Out of the Service Now*, 45.

26. Kupper, *Back to Life*, 69; Thompson, *How to Be a Civilian*, 151-175; Baruch and Travis, *You're Out of the Service Now*, 45.

27. Droke, *Good-by to GI*, 52; Grace Sloan Overton, *Marriage in War and Peace: A Book for Parents and Counselors of Youth* (New York: Abingdon-Cokesury Press, 1945), 9-10.

28. Howard Kitching, *Sex Problems of the Returned Veteran* (New York: Emerson Books, 1946), 24, 30, 63, 102; George K. Pratt, *Soldier to Civilian: Problems of Readjustment* (New York: Whittlesey House, 1944), 182; Overton, *Marriage in War and Peace*, 95.

29. Tom Brokaw, *The Greatest Generation* (New York: Random House, 1998), 250-252; Connors interview, WVOHP; Howards interview, WVOHP; Howards interview, WW2OHP.

30. Overton, *Marriage in War and Peace*, 37; Asbury Nix, *Corregidor: Oasis of Hope* (Stevens Point, Wis.: Trade Winds Publications, 1991), 176; Plano, *Fishhooks, Apples, and Outhouses*, 276; Esser interview, WVOHP; Robert D. Grove and Alice M. Hetzel, *Vital Statistics Rates in the United States, 1940-1960* (Washington, D.C.: U.S. National Center for Health Statistics, 1968), 105-106.

31. Dumas and Keen, *Psychiatric Primer*, 25; Kitching, *Sex Problems*, 24; Hendersin interview, WW2OHP; Special Correspondence file, Papers of William F. Lorenz, State Historical Society of Wisconsin Archives, Madison, Wis.

32. Grove and Hetzel, *Vital Statistics Rates*, 110-111; Dumas and Keen, *Psychiatric Primer*, 25.

33. Dumas and Keen, *Psychiatric Primer*, 8, 22; Kupper, *Back to Life*, 183-184.

34. Baruch and Travis, *You're Out of the Service Now*, 47-48; Overton, *Marriage in War and Peace*, 37; Kitching, *Sex Problems*, 15. For more on the impact of World War II on sexuality, see John Costello, *Virtue Under Fire: How World War II Changed Our Social and Sexual Attitudes* (Boston: Little, Brown, 1985).

35. Bradley, *Aleutian Echoes*, 47; Eckstam interview, WVOHP; Baruch and Travis, *You're Out of the Service Now*, 50-51.

36. Thompson, *How to Be a Civilian*, 85-86; Kitching, *Sex Problems*, 49-50; Baruch and Travis, *You're Out of the Service Now*, 47, 50.

37. Kitching, *Sex Problems*, 107-110; Baruch and Travis, *You're Out of the Service Now*, 51-52, 58; Child and Van de Water, *Psychology for the Returning Serviceman*, 87-88.

38. Baruch and Travis, *You're Out of the Service Now*, 53; Kupper, *Back to Life*, 159.

39. Peters, *For You, Lili Marlene*, 105. For more on gays and lesbians and World War II, see Allan Bérubé, *Coming Out under Fire: The History of Gay Men and Women in World War II* (New York: Free Press, 1990); and John D'Emilio, *Sexual Politics, Sexual Communities: The Making of a Homosexual Minority in the United States, 1940-1970* (Chicago: University of Chicago Press, 1983).

40. Thompson, *How to Be a Civilian*, 207; Baruch and Travis, *You're Out of the Service Now*, 58-59; Kitching, *Sex Problems*, 89-97.

41. Thompson, *How to Be a Civilian*, 206-207; Kupper, *Back to Life*, 183.

42. Grove and Hetzel, *Vital Statistics Rates*, 114; Kitching, *Sex Problems*, 27. For more on postwar family formation, see Elaine Tyler May, *Homeward Bound: American Families in the Cold War Era* (New York: Basic Books, 1988).

43. Bradley, *Aleutian Echoes*, 261-262; Giese interview, WVOHP; Pratt, *Soldier to Civilian*, 177.

44. Kupper, *Back to Life*, 93-94; Tauchen interview, WVOHP; Lechnir interview, WW2OHP.

45. Plano, *Fishhooks, Apples, and Outhouses*, 301; Clampitt interview, WVOHP; Petersen, *A Chance for Love*, 407.

46. Baruch and Travis, *You're Out of the Service Now*, 94, 99-100; Kupper, *Back to Life*, 189-190.

47. Benjamin Bowker, *Out of Uniform* (New York: Norton, 1946), 118, 122; John Scocos interview, WVOHP; Scocos interview, WVOHP, Page interview, Ambrose Collection; Wozniak interview, WVOHP; Winner interview, WVOHP.

48. Plano, *Fishhooks, Apples, and Outhouses*, 296; Peters, *For You, Lili Marlene*, 102; Willett interview, WVOHP; Luetke interview, WVOHP.

49. Baruch and Travis, *You're Out of the Service Now*, 208; Juanita Wilkie interview, WVOHP; Coleman interview, WVOHP; Petersen, *A Chance for Love*, 407.

50. Chipman interview, WVOHP; Stoll interview, WVOHP; James Bradley, *Flags of Our Fathers* (New York: Bantam Books, 2000), 258.

51. Bradley, *Flags of Our Fathers*, 259. Descriptions of combat, of varying quality, appear in numerous histories of the war. For two exceptionally thoughtful works on the subject, see Paul Fussell, *Wartime: Understanding and Behavior in the Second World War* (New York: Oxford University Press, 1989) and J. Glenn Gray, *The Warriors: Reflections on Men in Battle* (New York: Harper and Row, 1970). Fussell and Gray each saw combat in World War II and became noted academicians after the war.

52. Underkoffler interview, WVOHP; Bradley, *Flags of Our Fathers*, 256-258.

53. Baruch and Travis, *You're Out of the Service Now*, 215; Kupper, *Back to Life*, 179; Turner interview, WVOHP; Petersen, *A Chance for Love*, 407; Howards interview, WVOHP.

54. Thompson, *How to Be a Civilian*, 32-33.

55. Underkoffler interview, WVOHP; Nelson interview, WVOHP; May interview, WVOHP; Jacobsen interview, WVHOP; Scheller interview, WVOHP.

56. Underkoffler interview, WVOHP; Dumas and Keen, *Psychiatric Primer*, 26.

57. Bill Mauldin, *Back Home* (New York: William Sloane Associates, 1947), 25; Stouffer, *American Veteran*, vol. 2, 622-624.

58. For more on the American Legion after World War II, see Thomas A. Rumer, *The American Legion: An Official History, 1919-1989* (New York: M. Evans, 1990). For a Wisconsin perspective see George E. Sweet, *The Wisconsin American Legion: A History, 1919-1992* (Milwaukee: Wisconsin American Legion Press, 1992). For an interesting essay on the continuing anticommunism of the Legion with a Wisconsin perspective, see Richard M. Fried, "Springtime for Stalin: Mosinee's 'Day Under Communism' As Cold War Pageantry," *Wisconsin Magazine of History* 77 (1993-94): 83-108.

59. For overview of veterans' organizations, see Rodney Minott, *Peerless Patriots: Organized Veterans and the Spirit of Americanism* (Washington, D.C.: Public Affairs Press, 1962). For a Wisconsin perspective, see Richard H. Zeitlin and Mark D. Van Ells, "Politics, Community, Education: A Brief History of Veterans' Organizations in Wisconsin and America," *Wisconsin Academy Review* 40 (1994): 7-8.

60. Bensoni interview, WVOHP; Wozniak interview, WVOHP; Gill interview, WVOHP; Miller interview, WVOHP; Stouffer, *American Soldier*, vol. 2, 623.

61. Stouffer, *American Soldier*, vol. 2, 623; Jaeger interview, WVOHP; Walters interview WVOHP; Moebius interview, WVOHP; Bender interview, WVOHP; Hochschild interview, WVOHP.

62. Elver interview, WVOHP; Bensoni interview, WVOHP.

63. Winner interview, WVOHP; Moede interview, WVOHP; Rumer, *American Legion*, 283; Sweet, *Wisconsin American Legion*, 36, 62-63, 74; Bill Bottoms, *The VFW: An Illustrated History of the Veterans of Foreign Wars of the United States* (Rockville, Md.: Woodbine House, 1991), 104. Wisconsin VFW membership figures are courtesy of Mr. Larry Danielson, quartermaster and departmental adjutant of the organization.

64. Junkermann interview, WVOHP; Bates interview, WVOHP.

65. Brenzel interview, WVOHP; Beckstrand interview, WVOHP; Todd interview, WVOHP; Lamkin interview, WVOHP; Malmquist interview, WVOHP.

66. Stouffer, *American Soldier*, vol. 2, 623. For more on the AVC, see Charles Bolté, *The New Veteran* (New York: Reynal and Hitchcock, 1945) and Robert L. Tyler, "The American Veterans' Committee: Out of a Hot War and into the Cold," *American Quarterly* 18 (1966): 419-436.

67. Podell interview, WVOHP; Tibbetts interview, WVOHP; Schleck interview, WVOHP; Henry S. Reuss, *When Government Was Good: Memories of a Life in Politics* (Madison: University of Wisconsin Press, 1999), 27; Tyler, "American Veterans' Committee," 423-436.

68. Karp interview, WVOHP; Bernhagen interview, WVOHP; Smith interview, WVOHP; Connors interview, WVOHP.

69. Juanita Wilkie interview, WVOHP; Lorraine Allord interview, WVOHP; McLeester interview, WVOHP; Baehr interview, WVOHP; Sweet, *Wisconsin American Legion*, 111.

70. Baruch and Travis, *You're Out of the Service Now*, 5-6; Petersen, *A Chance for Love*, 406.

Chapter Three

"Everyone Will Come Out of Here Wounded or Sick": Medical Readjustments

In *A Psychiatric Primer for the Veteran's Family and Friends*, authors Alexander Dumas and Grace Keen tell the story of five women on a train platform in a midwestern town waiting for loved ones to return home from World War II. Four of the women are expecting men suffering from medical problems. Mary waits for her husband, a telephone lineman before the war who was "always wanting action," but who had been paralyzed by a land mine. Betty is waiting for the arrival of her fiancé, Dick, a navy dentist who lost his "good right arm" when a Japanese torpedo struck his ship. Sarah waits for her son and Edith for her husband, both of whom were being discharged with psychological problems. Each of the women waits nervously for the train to arrive, anticipating what the future will be like with a disabled veteran in their lives. Mary stands on the platform staring thoughtfully at a row of telephone poles, "her hand resting on the shiny wood of the wheelchair" in which her husband would "live the rest of his life." Sarah paces the platform and "clutches her purse and knots and unknots her handkerchief." "What will this mean for the future?" Edith asks herself pointedly—a question in the minds of all of the women portrayed, as well as millions of Americans who awaited the return of loved ones diseased or wounded in World War II.[1]

Millions of American veterans returned from World War II with medical conditions acquired or exacerbated by the war: injuries caused by combat or accidents, diseases of various kinds, and psychiatric disorders. The extent to which veterans with war-related medical conditions could readjust to civilian life varied considerably, depending on the severity of the condition. Those veterans who suffered the loss of a limb faced a lifetime of coping with a wartime disability, for example, while those who had contracted a disease such as malaria usually suffered for a few months or years after the war. To handle the large number of veterans who returned with medical readjustments to make, the federal government, as well as that of Wisconsin, revamped its plans and facilities for caring for veterans diseased or injured by war. Whatever the case, medical conditions often stood in the way of the veteran returning fully to civilian life.

Injuries to the Body

According to a 1973 congressional estimate, 670,846 Americans suffered non-fatal battle wounds in World War II. The army had the highest number of casualties with 565,861, accounting for roughly 5 percent of the army's total wartime strength. The navy had 37,778 nonmortal combat wounds, while the marines suffered 67,207. The marines suffered the highest casualty rate. Roughly one in ten of the nearly 670,000 marines who served in World War II had been injured in battle. Of all Americans who received nonfatal wounds battlefield wounds, 3,567 listed Wisconsin as their preservice state of residence. According to these figures, approximately 4 percent of all Wisconsin World War II veterans suffered nonmortal battle wounds.[2]

Artillery caused the most battlefield injuries. Of all U.S. Army combat casualties during World War II, explosive projectiles, such as artillery shells and mortars, accounted for fully 57.7 percent of all nonfatal wounds, and 51.2 percent of combat deaths. Bullet wounds were a distant second, accounting for just 19.7 percent of nonfatal wounds, though 31.8 percent of all combat deaths. The third leading cause of nonfatal combat injury was land mines, with a distant 3.4 percent. Shrapnel, bullets, and a variety of other agents caused many kinds of wounds. According to army statistics, wounds classified as "lacerating, penetrating, or perforated" topped the list, with 317,004 throughout the war years. Abrasions and nonspecified types of wounds accounted for another 47,111 cases. Bone fractures were the next most common kind of injuries. Simple fractures (in which the break is confined beneath the skin) accounted for 16,144. Compound fractures (in which bone penetrates the skin) were much more common, accounting for 114,590. However, the ways of meeting injury on the battlefield—blasts, burns, crushing, concussions, to name just a few—are horrifying, brutal, and endless.[3]

By the time of World War II, a number of administrative and medical developments gave injured soldiers a better chance of surviving their wounds than at any other point in history up to that time. Military medical officials had developed a highly effective evacuation system for wounded soldiers. The wounded passed through a chain of medical facilities, each becoming more comprehensive the farther behind the lines one went. Surgeons worked close to the front, and the injured could often be evacuated by air. New drugs such as penicillin helped reduce the instances of gangrene and other wound infections that had claimed so many lives in past wars. The development of blood plasma transfusions helped many bleeding patients survive shock. However, a wounded soldier's chances of surviving also depended greatly on the part of the body affected. Wounds to the head and chest had relatively low survival rates. According to army statistics, head wounds accounted for 32.5 percent of all combat deaths, but only 7.4 percent of nonfatal wounds. Wounds to the chest and abdomen fared only slightly better. Wounds to the extremities, by contrast, had significantly higher survival rates. Injuries to the upper extremities accounted for just 8.2 percent of combat deaths, but 26.6 percent of nonfatal wounds. The lower extremities accounted for only 8.3 percent of combat deaths, but fully 41.5 percent of nonfatal injuries.[4]

Depending on their severity, wounds and fractures to the extremities sometimes forced surgeons to amputate limbs. Army doctors recorded 9,434 major amputations as a result of combat action during World War II. Of these, a majority—5,482—involved a lower extremity, while 3,456 involved the upper extremities. Army doctors recorded 60 double amputations of the upper extremities, and 436 of both lower extremities. However, in many cases soldiers suffered what is known as "traumatic amputation," in which parts of the body are shorn away in combat through explosions, land mines, and other causes. Army medical officers recorded 10,912 combat-related traumatic amputations during World War II.[5]

At the same time, some soldiers had shrapnel and other foreign objects lodged so deeply into their bodies that the objects could not be safely removed or found at all. Army doctors documented 2,726 cases in which soldiers retained foreign objects. One such case was that of Col. Herbert M. Smith, a native of Neillsville, Wisconsin, who served in the 32nd Infantry Division. In action against the Japanese on December 7, 1942, Smith and several of his men were showered with shrapnel from a Japanese mortar exploding overhead. Smith's body was littered with shrapnel, including severe damage to one of his kidneys. Although surgeons had removed numerous fragments, some deeply imbedded in his body were left inside. Informed of this while on the operating table, Smith claimed that leaving the shrapnel inside was "O.K. by me!" Milo Flaten of the 29th Infantry Division retained a piece of shrapnel "about the size of a quarter" in the back of his head, a souvenir of a battle in Germany. Many veterans returned to civilian life not knowing that they retained artifacts of combat inside their bodies. John Gill, an army medic from Madison, had been severely wounded in Normandy in 1944 and discharged from the service. Nearly fifty years later, in 1992, surgeons removed from the lining of his heart shrapnel he had not known was there.[6]

Another common form of combat injury, often requiring amputation, was that caused by extreme cold. Though commonly known as "trenchfoot," cold injuries affected other parts of the body, but especially the digits and extremities. In cold weather, the blood vessels in the extremities contract in order to shunt blood flow to vital organs, reducing the oxygen supply to the arms and legs. In severe cases, permanent damage to blood vessels and nerve endings occurs, and gangrene can set in. The army recorded 30,792 cases of cold injury during World War II. Of all army cold injury cases, 27,264 occurred in the European theater, and 98 percent of those occurred in the last two years of the war. The problem was especially acute during the 1944-45 Battle of the Bulge, where an unexpected German counterattack in December led to bitter winter fighting without adequate foot gear. However, soldiers who took part in the Italian and Aleutian campaigns also suffered cold injuries. Though usually associated with ground forces, cold injuries also plagued air crews, due to the extreme cold of high altitudes, which could also freeze exposed tissues.[7]

Even when cold injuries did not result in losing digits or whole extremities, they could still plague the veteran long after the war. Permanent tissue damage caused by cold could affect veterans for years after discharge, and possibly even for the rest of their lives. For at least four years after the war, Battle of the Bulge veteran Raymond Ray of Madison reported that "the feet would swell," but "gradually that went away." Norris Tibbetts, a ski trooper who trained in the high mountains of the American West and first saw action in the Aleutian Islands, also experienced the lingering effects of cold injuries after the war. "My feet have never quite recovered" from the war, he claimed, especially from the Aleutian campaign, where he got "rotten feet." After the war, Tibbetts noted that he had "spots that freeze very quickly," not only on his feet but his "fingers, nose, and ears too."[8]

Many soldiers also became blind or deaf as a result of combat action. In combat, the flash of an explosion could injure a soldier's eyes, as could shrapnel and other foreign objects. Madison native Phillip Stark, a machine gunner in the 84th Infantry Division, caught bullet fragments in his left eye in the Battle of the Bulge, and spent time in a hospital ward in England devoted to soldiers with eye injuries. Stark lost sight in the affected eye, but considered himself lucky: "The guy right across from me caught two pieces of shrapnel, one in each eye." Stark recalled that the man was left completely blind, but that "he didn't have a scratch on the rest of his body." By the end of 1945, the army had discharged 1,706 soldiers for combat-related blindness. Of those, 1,583 suffered a loss of sight in one eye, 45 had been partially blinded in both eyes, and 78 blinded in both eyes. Hearing loss could also result from the loud noises of battle, as well as the constant droning of airplane propellers or other pieces of machinery. Discharges for deafness were somewhat fewer than for blindness. The army recorded 250 soldiers becoming partially deaf in both ears, and 133 completely deaf. Another 597 were discharged for defective hearing.[9]

Wounded soldiers often had to spend months or even years recovering in military hospitals. Long periods of hospitalization often left the bodies of wounded soldiers severely atrophied. Joseph Connors spent nine months in military hospitals after being wounded in action in the Philippines, much of that time with a leg immobilized in a cast. Once the cast was removed, recalled Connors, "my leg was very small" due to a lack of exercise. Connors remembered that "it took awhile" to build up the muscles in his leg, a task aided by his work as a mail carrier after leaving the army. Some veterans spent even longer periods in the hospital, which had even greater effects on their bodies. Milwaukeean Malvin Kachelmeier was wounded on Okinawa on April 9, 1945. Damage to an artery in his leg forced its amputation four inches below the knee. Despondent at the loss of his leg, Kachelmeier refused food and had to be restrained. Though he recovered emotionally, infection forced surgeons to amputate another segment of his leg above the knee. After the second amputation, the stump continued to bleed and drain. During his hospitalization and transport from Okinawa, Kachelmeier's weight fell below 100 pounds. Upon returning to hospitals in the United States, Kachelmeier benefited from various activities and his condition improved. Surgeons performed several exploratory operations without success, until one surgery in April 1946 discovered a silk suture that had been left inside his leg. Kachelmeier ambulated with crutches, learned to walk with a prosthetic leg, and was finally discharged from the hospital on July 3, 1946—nearly fifteen months after being wounded in action.[10]

Soldiers with amputations or other kinds of disfiguring injuries often endured stares, whispers, and social stigmatization from civilians. Ex-infantryman Herman Owen, wounded at Buna, New Guinea, in 1942 and subsequently discharged, returned to his hometown of Rice Lake before the end of 1943. "When I got home, I weighed 115 pounds," he recalled, and he was "using two canes to get around." Like all returning veterans, Owen was required to register with his local Selective Service board. "When I came down to the draft office," he recalled, such a hush fell over the room that "you could hear a pin drop." When he asked someone why everyone had grown so silent, he was told: "'Don't you know you're the first combat veteran to be discharged here?'" While serving as a WAC medical technician in a Missouri army hospital, Mary Ann Renard of Milwaukee worked extensively with amputees and disfigured soldiers. "There were a lot of cases," she recalled, in which visitors would "come down to see their husbands or their boyfriends," but then "were never heard from again, because they just couldn't . . . tolerate what war had done to them." She also noted that the wounded soldiers were reluctant appear in public, but Renard and other WACs at the hospital worked with them to obviate their fears. "We dared these fellas to go out with us," she recalled, "take us out to dinner, take us out dancing, to get them used to going out into the public." Most of the wounded men went out in public with the WACs despite their own concerns and the shocked reactions of civilians. Years later, Renard received a letter from one of her former patients who told her that he was "making a go of it, thanks to some of [the WACs] who dared them to face the public and do what they wanted to do."[11]

Most soldiers wounded in action eventually returned to duty, many to be wounded again. However, others were provided with medical discharges because of their wounds. In all, the U.S. Army discharged 108,114 soldiers for battle injuries during the years 1942 to 1945. Whether given a medical or a standard form of discharge, many of those wounded in action would suffer long-term effects of those injuries years after the end of the war. Self-help books provided veterans and their families with advice on how to cope with war-induced disabilities. Maxwell Droke, for example, told the disabled veteran to "face your handicap squarely—and the forget it. Yes, *forget* it." He explained that "you can let this physical impairment turn and twist your life until you are a morbid, melancholy misfit," or "you can resolve here and now that the real you, the spiritual you, the you that really matters, is bigger than anything—*anything*—that has happened or can happen to your physical form." "How a person reacts to disaster depends pretty much on what kind of person he was before," wrote Dumas and Keen, and asked family members to be supportive of their disabled heroes. "If he can no longer dance, play tennis, dive, and swim with friends," they told their readers, "he must learn to take pleasure in beating them at checkers, or a rousing game of poker, in the vicarious excitement of the armchair sports expert, or perhaps in a totally new interest such as music or reading." They warned that the veteran might become depressed and socially withdrawn, but urged family members to be patient and encouraging no matter how difficult the situation became. "There is no magic that will produce the new life for the handicapped," they wrote, but "the longest journey begins with a single step."[12]

Battle was not the only way soldiers could be injured. Indeed, most injuries during World War II resulted not from combat but from accidents. Whereas army hospital admissions for battle were just over 700,000, those for accidents totaled 1.9 million. Noncombat duties could often be hazardous. Training could be physically rigorous and often involved live fire, which posed countless risks of accidents, as did work with heavy equipment, large vehicles such as tanks, and aircraft. Indeed, during World War II the army suffered 12,594 deaths in vehicle accidents and 26,414 deaths in aircraft accidents. In all, accidents claimed 61,503 army lives. Most victims of accidents survived, but the flesh wounds, broken bones, and other injuries incurred in accidents, like those in battle, could also plague veterans in the postwar years.[13]

Motor vehicle accidents generated the largest toll of accident victims requiring hospitalization, with 230,788. Following closely behind were injuries related to sports and athletics, with 228,032. The third and fourth leading causes of accident injuries usually involved training exercises. Falls and jumps accounted for 226,174 hospital admissions, while firearms and ammunition resulted in 113,605. Injuries related to tools and instruments resulted in 104,472 admissions. Although aircraft accidents were the leading cause of accidental death in the army, they resulted in only 46,153 hospital admissions. Since accidental injuries often involved training for combat, the types of accidental injuries recorded were often similar to those found in combat operations. Wounds of all kinds were the leading type of accidental injury in the army, accounting for 620,332. Fractures of all kinds totaled 398,472. Although sprains accounted for just 15,045 of the army's battle injuries, for accidents they totaled 423,832, second only to wounds. Like combat, accidents also resulted in amputations and loss of sight and hearing. Indeed, the army recorded 4,578 amputations for non-battle-related injuries, and discharged 2,767 for full or partial blindness and 13,751 for hearing problems.[14]

Dwarfing both combat and noncombat injuries was hospitalization due to disease. The army alone recorded more than fourteen million hospital admissions for disease. However, World War II marked a turning point in the medical history of the American military. For the first time in U.S. history, war deaths due to injury and accident surpassed that of disease. By the middle of the twentieth century, doctors understood disease transmission much better than they did just a half century before. A more advanced understanding of medicine allowed for improved methods for the prevention and treatment of diseases, as well as the development of drugs. Vaccines had been developed for many of the diseases that had traditionally bedeviled armies. The vast majority of American military personnel stricken with disease during World War II survived. Indeed, of the army's 306,230 deaths in World War II, only 14,904 resulted from disease.[15] However, many veterans also returned home with the lingering effects of diseases that they had acquired while in service.

Many of the diseases service personnel contracted during the war occurred in everyday life in the United States, such as various strains of cold and influenza. However, many other diseases—and those causing the greatest and most long-term debilitation—were often caused by the peculiar circumstances of military service. Perhaps the most notable disease in this regard was tuberculosis, a communicable lung disease caused by *mycobacterium tuberculosis*, to which troops in crowded barracks or ships were often exposed. Tuberculosis is spread person to person primarily though expectorated respiratory secretions (i.e., coughing, sneezing, and spitting). The disease may lay dormant in the lungs for years, unbeknownst to the host, until an event triggers release of the organism. During World War II, the U.S. Army saw almost 30,000 cases of tuberculosis, while the U.S. Navy had about 8,500. One afflicted sailor was LeRoy Dalton of Lodi, Wisconsin. Dalton contracted tuberculosis while in the Pacific, but it was not until he was attending the University of Wisconsin after the war that doctors diagnosed his condition, and not until May 1948 that Dalton finally "broke down" from the disease. Dalton spent fourteen months in a Madison sanatorium, interrupting his education. After finishing law school, Dalton had a portion of his lung removed as a result of the disease. In addition to suffering from the disease itself, Dalton also recalled the social stigmatization that tuberculosis engendered at the time. "When I was growing up, tuberculosis was a disease that poor families got," he recalled. "When I was in the hospital I felt sort of inferior, but I got over that."[16]

American soldiers not only fought in exotic and unfamiliar lands, but they also contracted exotic and unknown diseases. In particular, soldiers and sailors contracted numerous diseases endemic to tropical regions, but unfamiliar, if not unknown, to Americans. From North Africa and Sicily through the Asian subcontinent to jungles of East Asia and the southwest Pacific, Americans served and fought in areas where diseases such as malaria, dengue fever, and yellow fever were common. Clouds of disease-carrying mosquitoes often plagued U.S. military camps in these areas. The tropical environment was also the home of numerous other kinds of pests, vermin, and fungi, which could cause any number of ailments. Of the tropical diseases that affected American troops overseas, malaria was the most common, and one that had lingering effects on veterans after the war. Malaria is a protozoan infection spread by the mosquito genus *anopheles*, and is endemic to tropical areas around the world. Once bitten by the mosquito, the protozoa breed in the host's liver, then attack the red blood cells. The most notable symptoms of the disease include high fever, chills, nausea, and vomiting. In some cases, malaria might result in the discharge of bloody urine, a complication known by the nickname "blackwater fever." In extreme cases (and depending on the type of malaria contracted), malaria can result in kidney failure, coma, and even death. In all, the U.S. Army recorded 403,689 cases of malaria between 1942 and 1945. During that same period, the U.S. Navy counted 113,744 cases.[17]

The problem was particularly acute early in the war. Precautions to prevent malaria and other mosquito-borne diseases were nonexistent during the early campaigns, most notably those at Guadalcanal, New Guinea, and in Burma. Among the first units sent into combat in the southwest Pacific was the army's 32nd "Red Arrow" Infantry Division, a National Guard unit that originated in Wisconsin and Michigan. By the end of the 1942-43 campaign at Buna, New Guinea, disease had taken a greater toll on the division than had the Japanese. Although the division suffered 1,954 combat casualties in the Buna campaign, 2,952 had been hospitalized for malaria and various other diseases. After the battle, a check of 675 Red Arrow troops revealed that 53 percent of them were running fevers ranging between 99 and 104.6 degrees Fahrenheit. "I expect that almost everyone in the division will come out of here either wounded or sick," reported a medical officer in New Guinea to his superiors. Fully 37 percent of the army's malaria cases occurred in 1943, while that year accounted for more than 49 percent of the navy's cases.[18]

After the disease debacles such as that at New Guinea, the U.S. military began to take malaria prevention seriously. Troops began to drain and oil swampy areas near their camps, for example, or spray breeding areas with poison to kill the mosquitoes. The services also began malaria education programs among the troops. In addition, drugs also proved effective against the disease. Quinine had been used to treat malaria for centuries, but during the 1930s German scientists had devised a more effective drug, Atabrine, which American military doctors began to use to treat and prevent malaria. The troops disliked the Atabrine pills, however. Besides the pill's bitter taste and tendency to turn the soldier's skin yellow, it was also rumored to make men sexually impotent. Because of the drug's effects, real and imagined, GIs generally disliked taking it. Indeed, troops resisted taking the pills so much that their officers and NCOs often had to ensure that the troops actually ingested the pills by watching them place them in their mouths and swallow, and then checking under their tongues to ensure they were not hiding the pill so they could spit it out when the superior was not looking.[19]

Because malaria could remain in the victim's liver and bloodstream for so long, it continued to affect many veterans years after the war when not treated properly. Relapses were common. A change in climate, such as a soldier leaving the jungles of the South Pacific for the cold of a Wisconsin winter, could trigger a relapse, as might any episode that lowered the body's resistance to disease. Richard Bates, a veteran of the Myitkyina battle and other campaigns in Burma, experienced a malaria relapse while on the troop train home. He remembered how "the guys" on the train "piled their coats on top of me" to keep him as comfortable as possible. Joseph Tauchen contracted malaria while in the Philippines, but his symptoms did not appear until after he returned home to Madison. "Christmas day I got sicker than a dog," he recalled. Just before his discharge, Tauchen had stopped taking his Atabrine pills, and he apparently contracted the disease just before he left the Pacific. "You never knew when it was coming," recalled Red Arrow Division veteran Gifford Coleman of his malaria attacks. For army veteran V. G. Rowley of Blue River, who saw action on Cape Gloucester and other areas of the southwest Pacific, malaria relapses became routine. "I'd go to the hospital, walk in, and they knew who I was," he remembered, "they'd give me a bed, a doctor would come in and treat me, I'd rest up a while, and [they'd] let me go."[20]

In the years after World War II, physicians treated malaria with drugs such as Atabrine and quinine, as well as new drugs like plasmoquin and chloroquine which had been developed during the war.[21] Treatment of the disease, combined with the removal of the victim from a malarial environment, led to a gradual subsiding of relapses among veterans back home. "Physically I'm so damn disgustingly healthy that I can get only 10 percent disability on malaria," 32nd Division veteran George Tinkham of Baraboo wrote a fellow veteran in 1947, "which by the way is so disabling that it is necessary to waste thirty seconds ever[y] ten days in order to gulp three Atabrine tablets." Within a year, Tinkham's malaria was gone (as was his disability check). "[I] don't feel quite so much like climbing any coconut trees as I did five years ago," he wrote, "but I think that's [on account of] cold weather." However, some veterans continued to experience relapses into the 1950s. "It took years to shake," claimed Gifford Coleman. Richard Bates remembered having numerous relapses up to 1954, three episodes of which required hospitalization.[22]

Malaria was just one of many diseases borne by mosquitoes and other insect vectors that infected American troops overseas. Dengue fever, another common disease endemic to tropical regions, also infected American troops. A viral infection characterized by high fever, rash, and severe pain in the joints and muscles, dengue was also known to American troops as "breakbone fever." Other exotic diseases American troops acquired included sandfly fever, yellow fever, encephalitis, and various types of typhus. Like malaria, many of these diseases also had long-term effects that plagued veterans in the postwar years. Joseph Taber of Cuba City, who saw service with the army air force in the South Pacific, recalled that upon returning home he would occasionally experience relapses of dengue fever, which would "just lay me down for three or four days," as he remembered.[23]

Unsanitary conditions in military camps and in the field often resulted in troops suffering from a variety of gastrointestinal disorders. One of the most common ailments of the digestive system was dysentery, a disease of the large intestine which can be caused by an amoeba or a bacteria. Dysentery is characterized by frequent watery stools, often containing blood and mucus, and accompanied by severe abdominal cramps. The disease is commonly spread through unsanitary cooking and eating conditions, especially by flies hopping from feces onto food. Ailments of the alimentary canal plagued some veterans long after discharge. Madisonian James O'Dair, whose plane was hit on a raid on Japan but landed in Soviet territory, was interned in the Soviet Union during the war.[24] O'Dair found that food handling and preparation practices in wartime central Asia was not what he was used to in the United States. "A good part of the cooking was done outside," he recalled. "We had just a big old iron pot. I'd go out and see what we were having, and it was the same thing every day: something stewing in there; it was a cow's head with horns, hair, eyeballs, everything on it. . . . We got so hungry, everything tasted good." Sanitation in Soviet central Asia was "just terrible," he remembered; camel dung was strewn about, and people were washing and defecating in the same river. "I still had dysentery for five years after I got out," he recalled. "A lot of people did."[25]

Many veterans returned from war with what might be termed "social diseases." While in the armed services, many young men and women were exposed to sexual activity and alcohol—more so than in civilian life, and many for the first time (see chapter 2). Sex and alcohol may have provided GI Joe and GI Jane with an escape from the realities of war, but when the shooting stopped they had consequences that affected their civilian lives as well. For example, increased sexual activity during the war often led to venereal disease. The army recorded more than one million cases of venereal disease between 1942 and 1945. The most common forms of venereal disease among U.S. troops in World War II were gonorrhea and syphilis. Venereal disease was also a major problem for military officials in occupied Germany and Japan after the war. Indeed, venereal disease rates rose among U.S. troops in Europe *after* the fall of Germany and the onset of occupation, as garrison troops had more opportunities to seek liaisons with German women. If left untreated, gonorrhea can cause sterility in its victims, while syphilis can severely damage the victim's nervous system and even lead to death. The number of veterans who returned home to infect wives or lovers cannot be known, but was probably fairly low. During the war, military doctors found penicillin effective against venereal disease, which military doctors treated in great numbers. To keep treatment for venereal disease off their service records, some were lucky to receive informal treatment from a physician.[26]

Alcohol may have relieved the soldier's wartime stress and boredom, as well as helped them celebrate the end of the war, but it is also an addictive substance and many found themselves alcoholics after the war. Excessive alcohol consumption can affect a wide range of organs, but is most commonly associated with liver problems. Alcoholism seems to be a significant yet poorly understood problem of veteran readjustment. The first important VA study of alcoholism and the veteran, undertaken in the 1970s, revealed that about one out of every four World War II veterans in VA hospitals in the early 1970s was classified either as an alcoholic or a "problem drinker." According to the study, among all veterans (of whom World War II veterans constituted a majority) alcoholism among VA patients in the 1970s was most prevalent among those who were separated or divorced from their spouses. It is not known how many of these veterans became alcoholics as a result of exposure to drinking in the military, or to factors connected with prewar or postwar experiences. However, it seems likely that a good number of alcoholic World War II veterans began drinking in excess while in the service of their country.[27]

Not counted in official wartime statistics were veterans who were used as "guinea pigs" in the testing of nuclear and chemical weapons. The end of World War II marked the dawn of the nuclear age. Soldiers who served in the period between 1945 and 1947 (the year the government officially declared an end to World War II) were sometimes involved in early experiments in atomic warfare. Operation Crossroads, a 1946 atomic test at Bikini Atoll in the South Pacific, involved an estimated 42,000 troops. Among them was David Bradley, an army physician who had entered the University of Wisconsin medical school in 1941, transferred to Harvard, and then joined the armed forces in 1945. A radiological monitor on the operation, Bradley's task was to "grab Geiger counters . . . and go with" troops assigned to "clean up the mess" and assess the possibilities for the decontamination of ships. He later recalled the dangers to which the troops were exposed and the futility of protecting them. "I can still see, as though it were yesterday" he wrote fifty years later,

> young men going forth in their little boats, laughingly, full of ignorance and bravado, to do their duty. They absolutely trusted us "Geiger men" to protect them—and we secretly knew we could not protect them. Too few film badges, too few electroscopes, unreliable Geiger machines. Even at our scientific best, we could measure only one of six kinds of radiation, external gammas.

Bradley found the ships permeated with radiation, "from the hot spots on the decks to the air in the corridors to the grime on hands and clothing." Years later, some of these veterans developed cancers associated with radiation poisoning, such as leukemia and lung cancer. When they approached the government for treatment, they typically found military records closed for reasons of "national security," and a VA that refused to recognize their ailments as being service connected. "A pathetic story," Bradley later wrote, "a shameful, costly panorama of deception" and "a travesty of medicine." Some troops were subjected to experiments other than nuclear. In 1993, the VA acknowledged that as many as 60,000 soldiers had been used in tests involving the use of mustard gas and Lewisite during World War II. Of these, roughly 4,000 were subjected to tests under combatlike conditions. Though resulting in injuries, these soldiers were ordered never to reveal the nature of the experiments in which they participated. Years later many of these veterans developed skin and respiratory conditions, but were afraid to come forward. Not until the 1990s were these veterans' ailments routinely recognized as being service-connected.[28]

Perhaps no group of World War II veterans suffered more medical problems than former prisoners of war. Ex-POWs suffered from physical wounds and diseases, but had also endured the horrors of life in enemy prison camps. Contrary to the belief of some that POWs "sat out the war," many in fact suffered some of the most intense brutality, depravation, and torture of World War II. As conditions in wartime Germany deteriorated, so did those for American war prisoners there. By late in the war, many "Kriegies" (as American POWs in Germany were known) were on the brink of starvation. Those in the stalags of

Eastern Europe were sent on forced marches during the winter of 1944-45 to avoid the oncoming Red Army. During these marches soldiers frequently suffered cold injuries to the feet and other extremities. Conditions for American prisoners in the Pacific theater were even worse. The *bushido* ("way of the warrior") code, which animated Japanese military thinking, viewed surrender as dishonorable and thus war prisoners as disgraced. When they invaded areas of Southeast Asia in 1941 and 1942, the Japanese were unprepared for large numbers of enemy prisoners. Consequently, Allied prisoners of the Japanese suffered dreadfully. Starvation, disease, torture, and murder were everyday facts of life for American prisoners in the Pacific. Whereas only 1 percent of American captives died in German prison camps, more than one-third of U.S. prisoners in Japanese hands perished in captivity.[29]

Life in prison camps only multiplied the already-existing disease problems. Conditions such as tuberculosis, malaria, and dysentery not only went untreated in the camps, but their incidence was often increased and complicated by extremely crowded and unsanitary conditions. Wounds often went untreated and became infected. In addition, war prisoners developed other diseases in camp not seen in other segments of the veteran population, especially for those veterans held captive by the Japanese. Perhaps most notably, malnutrition led to a number of ailments. For example, camp survivors frequently suffered from a condition known as beriberi, caused by a deficiency of vitamin B_1 (thiamine). There are two types of beriberi, both of which affected many POWs: wet beriberi swells and weakens the heart muscles, while dry beriberi damages the nerves and can lead to extreme pain and loss of motor control. Another common problem in POWs was a vitamin D deficiency, which frequently led to diminished vision in the prisoners, and in some cases blindness. Malnourishment, in turn, made POWs even more susceptible to diseases, as it decreased their immune capacities, and also slowed the healing of wounds.[30]

After repatriation, the former POWs were provided with large amounts of food, something about which they dreamed and fantasized while incarcerated. Madison's William Donovan, an army physician held in the Pacific, recalled that on the way home that there was a "special car for POWs" that had "all kinds of food and everything." He had fond memories of food on his train trip home:

> All the way back from San Francisco to Chicago, every time they'd stop, women in the town there would have sandwiches. They'd have pheasant sandwiches—everything you can imagine—a big spread there, all kinds of food, wonderful food. In addition, they had a special WAC there who was supposed to give us anything we wanted. . . . We had all the liquor we wanted too, although we didn't drink much of anything. A drink would really affect you.

Asbury Nix of Stevens Point, also held by the Japanese, recalled eating ice cream for the first time in years. "This was the dream life," he wrote, "as we sat in the galley and filled up on the best tasting ice cream in the world. We had dreamed about all the goodies for so long, that we had almost forgotten what it would taste like." However, binge eating, especially of rich foods, could cause considerable trauma in the veteran's gastrointestinal tract for months after liberation. Patricia Bredenson, whose husband Lou was a POW in Germany, recalled that "when he came home and got the food here he'd throw up an awful lot, until he got used to it."[31]

Upon returning home, many POWs found that with a regular diet they were able to recover their health to a significant degree. "After the war," remembered Milwaukeean David Brenzel, a veteran of the Corregidor battle and four years of Japanese imprisonment, "most of my [physical] problems could be solved with plenty of food, rest, and recreation." However, others never recovered. Organs damaged by beriberi, for example, sometimes never regained complete function. Sight lost to vitamin D deficiency might never come back. Some POWs were so damaged physically by their ordeal that they suffered from poor health for the rest of their lives, and frequently died young. A 1954 study showed that although the mortality of European POWs was not significantly higher than that of the typical American white male of the time, for prisoners of the Japanese the mortality rate was nearly four times higher in the first year after liberation. In the six years following the war, ex-POWs from the Pacific, according to the study, were three times more likely to die of cardiovascular diseases, four times more likely to die of digestive disorders, and nine times more likely to die of tuberculosis than normal.[32]

Injuries to the Mind

Not only did World War II damage the bodies of thousands of American troops, but it also affected the minds of many others. Mental disorders related to war and military service have been observed since the earliest days of recorded history. But with the epidemic of psychiatric casualties resulting from World War I occurring just decades before, and with the development of the psychiatric profession in the early part of the twentieth century, the American military of the 1940s anticipated psychiatric casualties. Indeed, the armed services hoped to minimize such casualties by screening recruits and keeping those with histories of mental problems, or those believed susceptible to them, out of the military. Despite screening for psychiatric problems, the World War II caseload for neuropsychiatric patients, or "NPs," was far greater than for World War I. One historian has estimated that 1.3 million American service personnel suffered from some kind of psychiatric disorder during World War II.[33]

Service personnel might be hospitalized or discharged for a variety of psychiatric reasons. Despite attempts to screen recruits and draftees for mental disorders, many young men and women began to exhibit signs of mental illness after they had entered the service. Many such symptoms may have developed in these individuals even if they had never entered the armed forces, but others were perhaps stimulated by the stresses of military life. For example, in 1943 the *Milwaukee Journal* described the cases of several Sheboygan County recruits who had been discharged for mental problems. In one case, a thirty-three-year-old farmer grew homesick to the point of despondency and "begged to be allowed to go home." In another case, a young man started to have "hallucinations and religious delusions" and was discharged from the service. "In none of these cases," reported a local judge who had committed the veterans to local mental institutions upon their return to Wisconsin, "was there any history of previous mental disorder. It is quite likely that were it not for the shock which each experienced in the change from his established routine, coupled with fears of engaging in combat, none of these [men] would have developed mental trouble necessitating commitment." The services also discharged people with behaviors or personalities the services deemed undesirable. "Among this general group," according to a War Department circular, were:

> homosexuals, grotesque and pathological liars, vagabonds, wanderers, the inadequate and emotionally unstable, petty offenders, swindlers, kleptomaniacs, pyromaniacs, alcoholics, and likewise those highly irritable and arrogant individuals, so-called pseudoquerulents, 'guard-house lawyers,' who are forever critical of organized authority and imbued with feelings of abuse and lack of consideration by their fellow men.

Such men and women might pose a threat to military discipline, officials believed, and could potentially "develop full-fledged psychotic states."[34]

But the psychiatric effects most commonly associated with warfare are those resulting from combat. Feelings of guilt commonly plagued many combat veterans after the war. The source of such guilt varied. For some, traditional cultural and religious injunctions against killing were by necessity violated in combat. "Everything they have learned about morality . . . [has] been violated," advice writers Baruch and Travis told their readers, "all of a sudden, killing— they were told—was a virtue." Psychiatrists have also observed a phenomenon in combat veterans, as well as others who have survived traumatic experiences, known as "survivor guilt." Robert Jay Lifton, the noted psychiatrist who studied psychiatric disorders in Vietnam War veterans, has described survivor guilt this way: "[It is] the soldier-survivor's sense of having betrayed his buddies by letting them die while he stayed alive—at the same time feeling relieved and even joyous that it was *he* who survived, his pleasure in surviving becoming a further source of guilt." After being wounded on Iwo Jima, Clayton Chipman recalled that he "felt guilt that I left my buddies," and asked himself, "Why was I spared? How can you be thankful and guilty at the same time?" "For awhile when I got back there was a guilt feeling," recalled Battle of the Bulge infantryman Raymond Ray, who asked himself, "'Why didn't I get it over there?'" Ray's guilt feelings lingered long after the war. "It's something you don't ever get over," claimed Ray, "because you figure they were a living, breathing human being, and then, wham! That's it."[35]

But the psychological problem most commonly associated with combat is one known today as Post-Traumatic Stress Disorder (PTSD), an anxiety disorder resulting from extreme trauma. Though associated with war veterans, PTSD is also found among victims of other traumatic experiences such as rape, torture, political imprisonment, child abuse, plane crashes, and even automobile accidents. The syndrome did not receive its present name until 1980, when the suffering of Vietnam War combat veterans put the psychiatric toll of battle into the public spotlight. Though the term PTSD was not known in the late 1940s, psychiatrists at the time observed—and veterans experienced—its symptoms in the years after World War II. Thousands of World War II veterans returned home with symptoms of what psychiatrists at the time called "combat fatigue" or "operational fatigue," and what would later be called PTSD.[36]

The root of PTSD in veterans is the emotional numbing a soldier must inflict on himself to endure the extreme trauma of combat or torture. A stark example of emotional numbing is the case of Robert Witzig, a navy veteran from Grant County, Wisconsin. Witzig was a sailor aboard the USS *Indianapolis* when it was sunk by a Japanese submarine in 1945. Suffering from severe facial wounds, Witzig spent five days afloat in shark-infested waters, never sleeping, listening to the agonized moans of dying sailors, and watching "those big sharks twisting around and rubbing on my legs." Despite his desperate situation, Witzig never gave up hope that he would be rescued, and described how he coped psychologically. "You're not going to have any self-survival in you," he said, "if you let your scaredness beat the life out of you." Once the trauma is past, the numbing process continues in many veterans, a process psychiatrists call "psychic numbing" or "emotional anesthesia." However, emotional tensions lay beneath the surface, haunting the subconscious of the victim. Not everyone who experiences a traumatic event acquires PTSD. Its development depends greatly on the length of exposure to trauma, and may be heightened if the trauma is man-made. A family history of mental disorders may also increase the risk of developing the disorder. Because of sustained exposure to the traumas inherent in warfare, combat veterans run a relatively high risk of developing PTSD. In addition, prisoners of war, especially those subject to brutalization and torture, are also highly susceptible.[37]

Those who suffer from PTSD experience symptoms that fall into three basic categories. One category is the persistent reliving of the trauma. Veterans often experienced intrusive thoughts about combat or imprisonment long after the war. "I have memories flood back on me every so often," claimed combat veteran James Underkoffler of Portage, "though I don't weep." John Scocos, a bombardier and ex-POW in Germany, found that he would "daydream" about the war upon his return to Fond du Lac. Unpleasant war memories might affect veterans for decades after the war, and result in unusual behaviors. "One of the things that stuck with me for years," said former navy frogman Daniel Turner of Madison, was "a reflection back to riding troop ships all over the Pacific." Before a landing, the ship chaplains would give services for the troops, with the Catholics usually meeting at the bow. He recalled:

Then, as the day began to break . . . they threw the landing nets over the side of the ship, and when they went over the side they dropped into [the landing craft] and took off for the line of departure. This was immediately after the communion. So . . . now it's starting to break dawn and the boats are taking off, and the Japs are shelling and raising them up, and hitting these boats and blowing them all to heck, lost a lot of men on every landing in that way. . . . It got so routine for me, that they'd have communion and . . . "this is my body broken for you, this is my blood," etc., in the communion service, and at least on board ship . . . they'd have unleavened bread, at least it cracked. You could hear this thing crack and then, "this is my blood shed for you." This I could see as soon as the boats were out in the water, I could see men, dismembered, blood, bodies, oh boy, broken bodies, "this is my body broken for you." Sometimes we had to go ashore, for a pick up job, and there was still blood . . . hanging around in the water. It just so turned my stomach and my head that I just couldn't go to communion. For years and years, I'd go to church, but when they had communion, I just had to get up and leave.

It was not until the 1980s, when a pastor at a new church discussed the memories with him, was Turner able to take communion again. "There are lots of little things [about combat]," observed Madison's Robert Wallace, who saw action with an all-black "Buffalo Soldier" unit in Italy and then later in the Korean War, "and you wonder why?"[38]

Dreams are another common way in which traumatic stress is relived. Many veterans dreamed about the horrors of war for months and even years after discharge. Dead comrades lived on in the dreams of veterans years after the conclusion of hostilities, for example. Eugene Eckstam, a navy physician who survived the ill-fated Exercise Tiger off the coast of England in 1944 (in which German submarines sank U.S. ships practicing amphibious landings), had nightmares about that incident "for at least five to ten years afterward." The memory of hearing sailors trapped behind a door and burning to death came back in his dreams. "I was burning up and trying to get into that tank deck and save those guys. Yea, they were terrifying nightmares." Richard Elver served in a graves registration unit in Europe. Not only was Elver tasked with clearing battlefields of dead bodies, but he also witnessed the execution of American troops who had been convicted of capital crimes such as murder. After the war, the sight of U.S. troops being executed intruded into Elver's dreams. "I dreamt for a long time . . . about the hanging crew," he recalled.[39]

The emotional anxieties of war—those which the soldier must control in order to be an effective fighter—were also relived during sleep. Many veterans had dreams related to combat or other frightful episodes. "I used to have lots of dreams" recalled Jack Chase. "I dreamed that a hand grenade . . . slipped off [my uniform] and was going to blow up. I didn't know when it [fell] off so I didn't know when it was going to blow up." Former paratrooper Jack Dunn dreamed that he was falling out of a plane and his parachute would not open. The surreal nature of combat sometimes came back to veterans in dreams. Combat "was so funny yet so dramatic that it's hard to believe," according to Donald

Pechacek, a veteran of 2nd Ranger Battalion. "Sometimes I wake up at night and I can't believe that really happened—that there even was a war. It's so ridiculous, people killing people for what? It's just so crazy." Dreams related to wartime traumas need not be the result of combat, but any distressing, life-threatening event. Charles Bradley had a recurring nightmare involving a mountain-climbing accident in the Aleutians. "I wake up yelling and grabbing for a disappearing hand-hold," he later wrote, "I lie there sweating and shaking, so loaded with adrenaline there can be no more sleep that night."[40]

The second group of PTSD symptoms involved intensified physical or emotional responses related to combat, which psychiatrists characterize as "increased arousal" or "anxiety reactions." For years after the war, many veterans lived in a state of heightened alert, as survival techniques learned in combat persisted into civilian life. Marine corps veteran Robert Botts described himself as being "really jumpy" and "really tense" upon his return from the Pacific. Patricia Bredenson recalled how her husband Lou, an ex-POW from Madison, was "nervous and different" after the war, and that he "couldn't relax like he could before." Arousal and anxiety among combat veterans often resulted in unusual behaviors such as avoiding crowds or open spaces, trying not to turn one's back to a crowd, or carrying weapons. Wesley Kuhn of Black Creek, Wisconsin, a veteran of the bloody fighting on Iwo Jima, carried a knife with him for years after the war. "When I traveled on business," he later admitted, "I would check into a hotel room, and one of the first things I did was lay my K-Bar knife on the chair next to my bed." Another Iwo Jima survivor, John Bradley of Antigo, kept a knife in his dresser drawer. "He wasn't a hunter," his wife later reflected. "He had no use for that knife other than for protection." Because of such tension, many veterans experienced difficulties sleeping. Clayton Chipman recalled that up until the time he was married in the early 1950s "nobody could move in our house and I was awake." "There'd be a movement at night, and I'd wake up just like that," recalled Pacific combat veteran Douglas Oldenburg. "You could sleep," recalled Robert Botts, "but even in the soundest sleep [if] the slightest thing was there you were wide awake and alert."[41]

Returning veterans also experienced exaggerated startle responses for months and sometimes years after the war. Loud noises, for example, might send a returned combat veteran scurrying for cover long after their return home. "For a long time," recalled 99th Infantry Division veteran Donald Wiberg of Milwaukee, "you heard a loud bang and you were ready to drop to the ground." Wiberg explained that this was a combat survival instinct. "It was the way you were able to preserve yourself," he explained. "If you didn't do it automatically, you were dead." In civilian life, loud noises might rekindle dormant memories of combat. Walking down State Street in Madison, Joseph Connors encountered workmen unloading furniture. "They took one of these planks, and they flipped it," he recalled. "It made this sound and I damn near dove into the street." One common problem for veterans was fireworks. Charles Smith was bedridden in a naval hospital in San Diego when a 1945 Independence Day fireworks display "drove me a little bonkers." Bill Tritz returned home on July 4, 1945. "I remember that so clearly because I woke up in the middle of the night and firecrackers were going off all over and it scared the living hell out of me. I was back in the war."[42]

Other sounds might stimulate similar reactions in combat veterans. Jean Lechnir recalled how whizzing and whistling sounds affected her husband Ray, a veteran of combat in Europe. "If you had the radio on," she described, "and you hear a sound like . . . a bullet coming in, if he was sleeping on the davenport he'd roll off the davenport and try to crawl under it." The sound of an aircraft engine also sent a few veterans running for cover. "When a local airplane would fly over I'd tend to dive into a ditch," recalled Donald Mercier, "because when we were on Morotai we were strafed and bombed every day, three or four times." James Spohn, who had been an infantryman in Europe, had a similar reaction. In combat, Spohn had heard the sound of early German jet fighters screeching overhead. The jets "must have made an impression on me," Spohn later wrote, because when he heard a jet airplane fly over his Madison apartment in 1946 he "dove under the table." Soon after returning to Milwaukee, Milo Flaten was shocked to hear a noise he believed to be the sound of a German V1 rocket. "I came home one night and all of a sudden I heard that engine. I ran and woke up my folks and said, 'There's a V1 coming!'" The next day, Flaten heard the same sound, "about every hour—that 'er er er,' that very distinctive motor." Only later, after reading the newspaper, did Flaten learn that he was indeed hearing a German "buzz bomb." A captured V1 rocket was on display at a Milwaukee lakefront festival.[43]

The intensified emotions and anxieties associated with PTSD often clouded the thoughts of its victims, and resulted in an inability to concentrate or complete specific tasks. Francis Johnston of Kenosha, a tail gunner on a bomber in the Pacific, recalled that his inability to concentrate after the war led to any number of problems in his everyday life, such as counting the correct amount of money to pay for goods and services. "I gave [the cashier] a $5 bill," he recalled of one such incident at a movie theater, "and hoped he'd give me the correct change." The inability to concentrate could be of particular importance for veterans going to college after the war. Ex-POW Henry Renard recalled difficulty in focusing on his college schoolwork. "I got so that I'd read a page, I'd read it ten times, and I couldn't tell you a word that was on it," he recalled. "I was throwing books and I couldn't study," recalled ex-fighter pilot D. C. Pressentin, but "that calmed down" after a few months. An inability to concentrate could affect PTSD sufferers for long periods of time. USS *Indianapolis* survivor Robert Witzig was giving a talk about his war experiences decades after the war when he found that he had suddenly "cut right out" and stopped speaking, which he attributed to his PTSD. "People didn't know any different," he joked of the incident, "or pay a bit of attention."[44]

The third category of PTSD symptoms is avoidance. In an effort to evade stimuli that might trigger intrusive thoughts, dreams, or combat reactions, veterans frequently avoided any kind of activity that might remind them of the war and its horrors. While family members were often curious about the war experiences of their loved ones, many veterans were hesitant to discuss them (see chapter 2). This was particularly true of those traumatized by combat. Robert Esser of Madison, a combat messenger with the 30th Infantry Division in Europe, avoided talking about the war because "it was like I was back in it again." Veterans suffering from PTSD often became socially withdrawn. When Lou Bredenson came home to Madison "everybody wanted to see him," his wife Patricia remembered, "and he didn't want to see anybody. 'Let them come to me rather than me going all over to see them.'" Ex-POW William Donovan feared that upon his arrival back in Madison that he would be subjected to "some kind of ceremony," and "I didn't want that." To avoid that possibility, Donovan and his wife "arrived in Madison . . . a day before we were supposed to." Others become engrossed in their work as a way of avoiding painful memories of war. Milwaukee's David Brenzel, a former prisoner of the Japanese, suffered from nightmares for decades after the war, but commented that "it's a good thing" that his job as an editor at the *Wisconsin Tax News* "kept me pretty busy."[45]

The psychic numbing associated with PTSD often left veterans feeling emotionally dead. "To be filled with joy, to be excitedly happy on graduation, on being married, on achieving a promotion, on the birth of a child, or on celebrating an anniversary—these are not common responses for those afflicted with psychic numbing," according to ex-POW Guy Kelnhofer. "One is more likely to find them standing dry-eyed at the burial of a loved one or reacting with calm equanimity when accidents or serious illnesses threaten the lives of family members." Not only was such numbing necessary in order to survive combat or prison camp, but it also helped some veterans handle suppressed anger and hatred. "Inside each of us is a caged tiger of hate, rage, and outrage," claimed Kelnhofer:

> That tiger thirsts for revenge, for the blood of those who made us suffer so cruelly and for so many years. That ravening beast is securely locked up and there is little chance that he will ever escape to do his bloody work. But now and then, when someone does us an injury or threatens our welfare, the beast stirs and he begins to claw at his restraints, smelling the enemy again.

The suppressed memories and emotions characteristic of PTSD led many veterans to experience a series of other emotional difficulties related to the condition. Depression, survivor guilt, and outbursts of anger are commonly associated with PTSD, for example. Veterans also suffered from the physical manifestations of emotional disturbances, such as ulcers, or addiction to drugs and alcohol, to numb painful memories.[46]

Living in the present but haunted by the past, those suffering from PTSD have been described as existing simultaneously in two different worlds. In her landmark work *Trauma and Recovery*, psychiatrist Judith Herman has equated this dual existence to the concept of "doublethink" in George Orwell's novel *1984*—the ability to hold two contradictory thoughts in one's mind simultaneously. "The experience of the present is often hazy and dulled," wrote Herman, "while the intrusive memories of the past are intense and clear." World War II veterans suffering from PTSD did indeed live in two worlds. On the one hand, they had left the war and returned home. On the other hand, part of their thoughts still lingered in the traumatic wartime past.[47]

Thousands of veterans returned home to experience nightmares, heightened states of anxiety, and other symptoms of PTSD, but did not necessarily have Post-Traumatic Stress Disorder. Nightmares, exaggerated startle responses, and avoidance of war-related stimuli are all normal reactions to the stresses of war. "It has been observed," wrote psychiatrists Samuel Futterman and Eugene Pumpian-Mindlin in 1951, "that mild traumatic states . . . are almost universal among combat troops immediately after battle." For a diagnosis of PTSD to be made, one must exhibit symptoms in all three of the diagnostic categories: reliving the trauma, increased arousal, and avoidance of stimuli. In addition, such symptoms must also significantly impair a veteran's functioning in his or her social or occupational worlds. Even if a diagnosis of PTSD is made, the veteran may suffer from an acute case lasting only several months, after which the symptoms fade and disappear. In fact, most symptoms of PTSD subside about six months after the trauma.[48]

How did veterans suffering from PTSD symptoms cope? Upon returning home, many veterans simply tried to eradicate the memories of war from their minds. Italo Bensoni, who fought in the Battle of the Bulge, attributed his ability to move beyond the memory of war through sheer "determination in [my] own mind to just get it out of [my] system." According to Bensoni, "I got out of my head the things in the past [that] flashed back in my memory sometimes. It wasn't going to drive me off my rocker." "I just tried to erase those thoughts, or those visions of what I had seen," recalled army veteran Vernon Bernhagen of Wisconsin Rapids. "I didn't want to dwell on it." James Spohn recalled that he "learned to block out the tragedy of war," and that he had "shut the door on World War II at the end of the war." The extent to which veterans were successful in avoiding or suppressing the traumatic war memories cannot be known. Former navy corpsman John Bradley "seemed almost to have erased [the war] from his memory," his son James later wrote, but observed that "forgetting had not come easily." As John's wife recalled, "he'd be sleeping, his eyes were closed . . . but his body would shake, and tears would stream out of his eyes, down his face." His nocturnal weeping continued for four years after he returned home.[49]

Advice books also provide guidance in coping with the mentally disturbed veteran. "Modern methods of psychaitric treatment are performing wonders," psychiatrist George Pratt assured his readers, but he also told family members that they would be essential to the veteran's recovery. "The kind of atmosphere we create for him at home," he wrote, "will do more than anything else to expedite his recovery." Self-help authors assured that psychological injuries were just as genuine as physical ones and urged veterans and family members to seek psychiatric care if necessary. "He doesn't need a lawyer, a minister, or a policeman," Dumas and Keen wrote of the troubled veteran, "he needs a doctor." Family support undoubedly helped many veterans cope with the psychological impact of the war, but the ex-soldiers of World War II apparently drew comfort from fellow veterans as well. Because military service cut so deeply into the generation of young men that fought World War II, that war's combat veterans had a built-in support group that helped alleviate the sense of isolation many PTSD sufferers experienced, and perhaps quickened the recovery from PTSD symptoms. Frank Freese of Madison, a combat veteran of the 84th Division in Europe, stated that he would occasionally "wake up kind of shaken," but did not think it unusual. "Everybody had the same thing," he explained. "We just wanted to get the uniform off and forget about it." "We didn't think anything about it," according to Iwo Jima survivor Clayton Chipman. "We thought it was normal."[50]

However, many World War II veterans developed more severe and chronic cases of PTSD. Guy Kelnhofer recalled that after his repatriation and return to Wisconsin that he suffered uncontrollable "nightmares, nervous tremors, para-noia, and crying episodes [which] caused me to seek medical advice." After ob-servation in a naval hospital, Kelnhofer was given an honorable discharge from the marines as "unfit for further duty." PTSD is considered "chronic" if symp-toms persist past six months, and this was the case for many World War II vet-erans. Kelnhofer recalled that he experienced what he termed "problems of ad-justment" for fifteen years after the war, until "I believed that my behavior . . . was normal."[51]

Some World War II veterans experienced a delayed onset of PTSD. In 1951, psychiatrists Futterman and Pumpian-Mindlin commented that "five years after the war, we still encounter fresh cases that have never sought treatment until the present time." Such was the case of Madison's John Miller, a bomber pilot in the European theater, who recalled that "it took several years before things started hitting home." Certain stimuli could cause a delayed onset, or re-vive symptoms, of PTSD in veterans who believed they had put the war behind them. Futterman and Pumpian-Mindlin noted a marked increase in cases after the outbreak of the Korean War in June 1950, for example, both of new patients and of previous ones whose symptoms had returned. Guy Kelnhofer believed he had his PTSD symptoms under control for more than a decade, but in 1974 he met a Japanese man about his age at a professional conference. He remembered:

> Before long, I noticed that I was getting nervous for no reason that I could de-termine. My hands started to tremble and then my whole body began to shake. In embarrassment, I excused myself and left the room. Later it occurred to me that, in the back of my mind, I may have been speculating about the wartime activities of the man who was my age. When I related that incident to my wife and tried to tell her how I felt about the way the Japanese had treated us in cap-tivity, I broke down and wept, unable to continue.[52]

PTSD could seriously affect these veterans' family lives. For example, war-related dreams impacted upon family members as well. Oftentimes such night-mares constituted a fairly minor problem. Portage native Carlyle Van Selus, a

bomber crewman shot down over France but who evaded capture, noted that he
had nightmares for several years after the war, but his wife would "calm me
down, and it would be over." Richard Meland remembered that his wife would
occasionally ask him: "What were you yelling about last night in your dream?"
Other times it could endanger the physical safety of a spouse. Ruth Dresen described a nightmare her husband Dave, an ex-POW, had after the war:

> It was just terrible. I was clinging to the outer edge of the bed, and all of a sud-
> den this arm came out . . . and hit me and it startled me and hurt and so I just
> involuntarily hollered out, "Hey," or "Ow," something like that. And his dad
> heard it and came running into the bedroom. He said, "Ruth, are you all right?"
> I said, "I'm all right, dad. I guess Dave must just have had a nightmare."

"Lots of times, I would wake up in the middle of the night, out of the bed,
reaching for a rifle," recalled V. G. Rowley. "My poor wife, I don't know how
she put up with me, to be honest about it."[53]

Psychic numbing and social withdrawal led to numerous other problems for
veterans readjusting to family life. One common complaint of veterans suffering
PTSD is sexual dysfunction, apparently caused by the veteran's fear of intimacy
and emotional attachment. Emotional withdrawal also impacted upon a veteran's
relationship with his wife and children. "We can love our wives and children,"
wrote Guy Kelnhofer, "We can give them loyalty and devotion. But there is a
part of us that will always remain detached and apart." When veterans exhibited
emotional or violent outbursts, they were often aimed at family members—those
closest to them. "It would be no exaggeration to say that we too are prisoners,"
wrote Guy Kelnhofer's wife, Maria, "shackled by love and duty because we are
so closely bound to these men and have invested so much of our lives in them."
"Put simply," wrote Mrs. Kelnhofer, "these men are hard to live with." Indeed,
one study of former POWs revealed that many had never told their spouses that
they had been prisoners.[54]

Chronic PTSD could also affect the economic well-being of veterans and
their families. Emotional outbursts, inability to concentrate, and failing health
made it difficult for those with chronic PTSD to hold down a job. Though Guy
Kelnhofer earned a Ph.D. in resources planning from the University of Chicago
and buried himself in his work, he also changed jobs frequently. After the war,
Kelnhofer accepted positions in Georgia, Minnesota, Massachusetts, Puerto
Rico, Tennessee, and Venezuela. "Looking back," he recalled, "my work record
reveals a record of conflict avoidance, with new jobs every two or three years. I
always thought I had good, compelling reasons for my moves, but after thirty
years of changes, I know now that I was running away from something." The
physical problems related to PTSD also interfered with the sufferer's economic
livelihood. Madison ex-bomber pilot John Miller lost his job flying commercial
planes for a major airline because of his PTSD-induced stomach ulcers. "I
wasn't able to pass the physical," he stated. Robert Witzig claimed that after the
war he "couldn't work for somebody else because I was constantly in trouble"

with employers. Compounding Witzig's situation were his disfiguring facial injuries. "How are you going to work in public," he asked, "with people poking fun at you?"[55]

During World War II and the years immediately following it, therapy for war-related psychological problems focused on having patients relive the trauma through psychoanalysis, in the hope it would serve as a cathartic experience though which the victim would move beyond the trauma and resume a normal life. In the military, combat stress cases were handled as close to the front as possible, so as not to sever the soldier's connection with his fellow fighters. The afflicted soldiers were provided with psychoanalysis, food and rest, then returned to duty. For more severe cases, doctors used drugs and hypnosis to recover memories of suppressed traumas. In rare instances, doctors used electric shock and insulin shock (in which insulin is driven into the brain through electricity). After discharge from the military, psychiatrists used standard psychoanalysis, drugs, hypnosis, and shock treatments to treat continuing effects of trauma and stress on war veterans, with practitioners reporting mixed results. However, many psychiatrists believed that once the victims were removed from the stresses of combat, their mental problems would naturally abate. As a result, interest in the long-term impact of war on the mind did not develop after World War II. "There was little public or medical interest in the psychological condition of returning soldiers," wrote Judith Herman. "The lasting effects of war trauma were once again forgotten."[56]

While many veterans sought and received treatment for war-related psychological problems, countless others did not. By the time of World War II, psychological casualties were recognized as a normal consequence of war. Most psychiatrists understood that combat-induced mental illness was not something that struck just the weak-willed or immoral—that under the extreme circumstances of prolonged combat exposure, even the best of soldiers could suffer psychological trauma. However, old stereotypes about mental illness died hard, and countless veterans did not seek treatment, fearing social stigmatization. Seeking help was also difficult for socially withdrawn veterans. Still others met death before they could seek treatment. A 1954 study of prisoners of war indicated that Pacific theater ex-POWs (a group that suffered high rates of PTSD) had a suicide rate twice as high as normal white men, and died in automobile accidents at a rate more than four times the expected rate. Scores of veterans suffering from war-related psychiatric problems suffered in silence for years after the war.[57]

Federal Medical Programs

When World War II veterans began coming home, the federal Veterans' Administration had a program of medical readjustment benefits for veterans already in place (see introduction). The VA medical system had been serving the needs of the nation's World War I veterans and Spanish-American War veterans; those of World War II were simply added to this system. The federal program consisted of two primary parts. First, the VA had established medical pensions for veterans based on the rating of specific disabilities. Second, the VA oversaw a nationwide system of hospitals and clinics for veterans. Although this already-existing framework served the returning World War II veterans, the sheer size of the World War II generation—sixteen million in all—prompted significant modifications of the VA medical system.

Determining eligibility for VA medical benefits was a laborious and sometimes confusing affair, as the laws frequently changed. In their book *American Law of Veterans*, legal scholars Robert Kimbrough and Judson Glen attempted to explain benefit eligibility to their readers, but conceded that the myriad of applicable laws was "somewhat bewildering to the uninitiated." Generally speaking, to qualify for medical benefits in the 1940s, injuries or diseases had to be "service connected," that is, incurred in the line of duty. This included not only battlefield injuries, but also medical problems caused by accidents or any other diseases or conditions (including mental disorders) a soldier contracted in the military. Injuries or ailments acquired while in service but due to "misconduct," such as alcohol abuse and venereal diseases, did not normally qualify. Under certain conditions, veterans with non-service-connected medical problems could obtain benefits based on their ability to afford private medical care. A veteran who required hospitalization for a non-service-connected disability could be admitted to a VA hospital only if all service-connected disability patients seeking a bed had obtained one.[58]

Pension ratings were based primarily on the degree to which a disease or injury caused an "impairment of earning capacity" to the veteran in civilian life. In other words, pensions were based on economic concerns, and not necessarily on the severity of the injury or its impact on other areas of his or her life. Doctors would rate the degree of a veteran's disability based on specific VA guidelines. Whereas total blindness would earn a veteran a 100 percent disability rating, for example, the loss of smell or taste merited only a 10 percent rating. The determination of a disability rating was based on physical examination of the veteran, as well as appropriate documentation to support a claim of service connection. Cases then went to a VA disability rating board, which approved or denied the amount of the pension. The veteran would have his or her rating revised periodically, and when the disability rating fell below 10 percent he or she no longer received the pension.[59]

The first disability pensions for World War II veterans came as early as 1942, but the number shot up dramatically after 1944, and surpassed one million in 1946. World War II medical pension payments peaked in 1947. That year, 1,758,667 World War II veterans received service-connected medical pension payments, accounting for 12 percent of all living World War II veterans. Throughout the rest of the decade, the number of World War II veterans drawing a disability pension leveled off, averaging just over 1.6 million annually. The monetary value of service-connected pensions continued to climb into the

1950s. In 1950, service-connected medical disability pensions cost the federal government on average $74,642,488 per month.[60]

But statistics do not capture the full extent to which veterans, in Wisconsin and elsewhere, experienced medical readjustment difficulties. Many veterans who desired medical pensions found difficulty obtaining them. Documentation was key to obtaining VA medical assistance, but paperwork supporting the service connection of a disease or injury was often lacking. The state of military records was often incomplete, particularly in the immediate postwar years, as military records were still scattered around the globe. To help establish documentation of service-connected medical problems, servicemen and women were interviewed about the state of their health as part of the discharge process. Although many veterans noted medical problems and had them placed in their records, the desire of many others to leave the military as quickly as possible led many young troops to forego documenting any injuries or diseases upon their discharge. "So anxious was I to complete the process that I rejected suggestions from the discharge staff to spend an extra day processing a claim for my knee injury received when hit by a tank in 1944," wrote army veteran Jack Plano of Merrill, Wisconsin. "I wanted nothing more than that piece of paper titled 'Honorable Discharge from the Army of the United States of America.'" As ex-marine Clayton Chipman recalled, filing a disability claim would have forced him to stay an extra three days at the separation center. He asked: "What kid is going to stay a couple extra days?" Physical examinations may not have documented all of the veteran's medical problems. Ex-POW J. J. Kuhn of Milwaukee found unsympathetic examiners at his discharge physical exam. "Army medics gave us all physicals," he wrote, "telling us that all of our aches and pains were in our heads." Kuhn demanded another examination, at which the physician called him a "gold brick." The veteran claimed that he then "hauled off and hit him in the chin," and noted proudly that "at least I got all that I told them added to my record."[61]

Many veterans who did suffer disabilities but lacked adequate documentation to establish service connection found they had trouble obtaining a pension after the war. As a former prisoner of the Japanese, David Brenzel acquired various medical conditions while in prison camp, such as tuberculosis, beriberi, and dental problems. When he sought VA medical attention after the war, Brenzel found himself being grilled by skeptical doctors. "They wanted to establish service connection for every tooth in my head," he later recalled angrily. When John Hall of Madison tried to file a claim for wounds that he had received in combat, he learned that the VA had lost his records. "When I told them about gunshot wounds," he recalled, "they'd say, 'Well, we don't have any records,'" and refused to process his claim. With the help of the Red Cross, Hall was able to obtain relevant documents and affidavits from witnesses to file his claim and receive a medical pension.[62]

Hall was not alone in having to track down records and witnesses to verify various medical conditions. As the chaplain of the 135th Medical Regiment in the southwest Pacific, the Reverend Anselm Keefe of DePere received many

letters after the war asking for statements regarding medical conditions that
never been properly documented, but for which veterans now sought treatment.
"Hoping you won't mind too much I'm asking a personal favor," began one
such letter to Keefe in 1947:

> Here's my story. During my stay in New Guinea and the Islands I contracted
> what was so commonly called jungle infection or jungle rash. I was never hos-
> pitalized on that account, but was treated by our Co. A officers as well as others
> of the 135th. Ever since my discharge from the Army I've had trouble with my
> feet and especially soreness and rash of the anal region. Up until 6 mos. ago
> there was an Army Doctor in Amery, Wis and he got me free doctoring also
> free medicine. My veterans Service Officer at Balsam Lake Wisc. advises that I
> write one of the officers that treated me while I was in New Guinea and get a
> signed, notarized statement to that effect.

Keefe continued to receive such letters well into the 1950s. In 1954, the wife of
a veteran diagnosed as being paranoid schizophrenic wrote to Keefe asking for
an affidavit seeking to establish his mental problems as service connected so the
veteran could be admitted to a VA hospital. Keefe not only wrote the affidavit,
but told the veteran's wife that "I'm keeping you all in every mass I say."[63]

Despite the VA's efforts to have a standard disability rating system, the
judgment of the extent to which a disease or injury impaired a veteran's ability
to make a living varied from doctor to doctor. Many veterans claimed that there
were gross inequities in the pension system. According to former bomber pilot
and ex-POW Henry Renard of West Bend, getting a pension—and the amount
of that pension—often depended on the doctor one saw. Renard claimed that
many veterans he knew suffered less from "nervousness" than he did, but received higher pensions. Some physicians were known to judge disability ratings
more harshly than others. Floyd Schmidt, an ex-POW in the European theater,
sought attention for cold injuries to his feet which he believed he had developed
during the war. Instead of finding a sympathetic ear, the doctor he saw scolded
him, stating that "all you guys want is money." He walked out of the doctor's
office without compensation for his condition. Not all veterans who filed for a
disability pension received one. Indeed, as VA administrator Omar Bradley recalled, during his tenure at the VA about half of all claims were rejected.[64]

The focus on economic impairment ignored the ways in which war-related
medical problems affected other aspects of a veteran's life course. While helping
a wounded comrade get to a medic on Iwo Jima, a marine veteran from northern
Wisconsin suffered a gunshot wound to his genitalia, rendering him unable to
father children or have a normal sex life after the war. Poor documentation of
his injury, combined with the judgment that his wounds interfered modestly with
his ability to make a living, led to the combat veteran receiving only a small
disability pension. The nature of his injuries and the perceived parsimony of
Uncle Sam left the ex-marine feeling angry and depressed after the war. "I figure what happened to me was worth a hell of a lot more than they ever gave
me," he claimed.[65]

Many veterans never sought VA compensation for service-connected medical problems from which they continued to suffer after the war. In some cases, the veteran's desire to avoid the military—or anything that reminded them of it—kept them from seeking VA medical attention. Norris Tibbetts of Madison, who suffered frozen feet in the Aleutians and then malaria in the Philippines, avoided the VA despite the lingering health problems caused by service-connected conditions. "I didn't want to get tangled up with veterans at that point," he remembered. "I didn't want to get back into the machine." Other veterans believed that their medical problems were not serious enough to warrant medical attention from the VA. John Scocos of Fond du Lac, a former prisoner of war in Germany, experienced lingering problems with his feet and back after the war, but did not seek VA medical attention. "I felt that some other poor soul who was worse off than I should be benefiting," he claimed, "rather than myself." Although Joseph Taber suffered from relapses of dengue fever after the war, he did not seek treatment from the VA, stating that "I thought [the VA] was for guys who didn't have arms or legs." "I never felt I deserved any special consideration," claimed James Underkoffler, wounded in Holland in 1944. "I didn't ask too much of the VA," recalled Madison combat veteran Akira Toki. "I just let things slide by."[66]

Veterans of World War II were also entitled to hospitalization benefits, both for short-term conditions and long-term "domilicary" care, on the same basis as those of previous wars. In addition, the VA also established outpatient clinics at many of its medical facilities, and made provisions for veterans to receive treatment from approved non-VA physicians, or from state and local hospitals if VA facilities were unavailable in the veteran's area. The VA divided hospital patients into four categories of prioritization, ranging from Category A (veterans with service-connected conditions who required hospitalization or treatment for that condition), to Category D (veterans with non-service-connected disabilities who could not afford hospitalization or treatment in private facilities).[67]

The Veterans' Administration hospital system needed an extensive overhaul if it was to accommodate the needs of returning World War II veterans. On the eve of Pearl Harbor, the VA had ninety-one hospital facilities located in forty-five states and the District of Columbia, with construction underway on fourteen projects to build new hospitals or renovate existing ones. It was the largest hospital system in the United States. During fiscal year 1941, VA hospitals had 187,374 admissions, mostly veterans of World War I. The war hit VA medical services hard. During the war, the agency lost 7,000 employees, including some of its most talented doctors and nurses, as many joined the armed services. In 1942, the War Department agreed not to call to active duty VA physicians who were reservists, and even detailed some of its own doctors to work for the agency. In addition to manpower problems, VA hospitals also suffered from shortages of supplies and equipment due to the war, despite being ranked rather high in federal war priorities.[68]

Shortages of staff and materiel came just as World War II veterans began to arrive in VA hospitals. The first World War II veteran reached a VA hospital in

April 1942, but as casualties mounted so did the stress on VA medical facilities. By 1946, admissions of World War II veterans rose to 349,000, and the following year jumped an additional 53 percent to 533,000. The increasing rate of admissions tells only part of the story. During the late 1940s, nearly every VA hospital had long waiting lists, as veterans of previous wars now had to compete with the growing ranks of World War II veterans for beds. Thousands of veterans eligible for VA medical care were forced to stay in non-VA hospitals, or went without hospitalization altogether. "The most urgent task we faced at the VA," claimed VA administrator Omar Bradley when he took the reins of the agency in 1945, "was that of drastically upgrading the quality of VA medicine."[69]

In response to the growing demand for medical services, the Veterans' Administration undertook several initiatives. One of the first priorities was to construct new hospitals. Between 1940 and 1950, the VA spent more money on hospital construction than it had in all of its previous history. Between 1922 and 1940, the VA (and its predecessor agency, the Veterans' Bureau), had spent more than $115 billion on hospital construction. By 1950, that figure had quadrupled to $437 billion. In 1947 alone, the VA expended $153 billion in the construction of hospitals. The agency built new hospitals, but also made improvements to many existing ones. The VA also condensed space in many existing hospitals to further increase bed capacity. In addition, the VA obtained temporary hospital facilities from other government agencies, most notably hospitals administered by the armed services. By 1950, the VA administered 136 hospitals, which had a total of 577,715 admissions that fiscal year. Another twenty-six hospitals were under construction that year, slated to provide 20,000 additional beds.[70]

Not only did the VA increase the number of hospitals, but it also increased the number of doctors, nurses, and medical professionals in the VA medical system. Staffing the VA hospitals with quality personnel proved to be one of Bradley's greatest challenges as VA chief. Many medical professionals deemed service in the VA hospitals unattractive. In the VA medical system, professional personnel fell under existing civil service regulations, in which promotion was often based more on seniority than on performance or even competence. The pay in the VA was also low as compared to other workplaces in the medical profession. Often VA hospitals were located in remote areas, having been built on existing government lands or in the districts of powerful congressmen. As a result, the Veterans' Administration was not held in very high esteem in the medical profession. Indeed, in 1945 a spate of news magazine articles lambasted the VA medical system, characterizing it as "medieval" and providing "third rate care to first rate men." While such media characterizations may have been exaggerated and sensationalistic in some cases, they were essentially correct. Omar Bradley admitted that when he assumed the helm at the VA in 1945, those physicians applying for VA jobs were the "dregs of the medical profession." Sixty percent of applicants were over the age of sixty, recalled Bradley of his first year at the VA, and a few "had been committed to mental institutions for alcoholism or insanity." Hiring quality doctors, Bradley believed, was the "cornerstone" of improving VA medicine.[71]

To tackle the problem of attracting quality doctors and improving the service (and reputation) of the VA medical system, Bradley turned to Gen. Paul R. Hawley, who had served as the army's chief surgeon in the European theater during World War II. Adopting the slogan "medical care second to none," Hawley formulated a plan to minimize administrative red tape and transform VA hospitals from the nadir to the zenith of the medical profession in the United States. He planned to create a separate medical division within the VA, the Department of Medicine and Surgery, which would focus its power and attention exclusively on the medical affairs of veterans. To attract quality personnel, he proposed hiring doctors and nurses outside the civil service system, where advancement would be based more on training and performance than on seniority, and where salaries would be higher. Hawley also hoped to affiliate VA hospitals with top medical schools. The affiliation plan was the brainchild of respected Chicago-area surgeon Dr. Paul R. Magnuson, whom Hawley brought to the VA as his top deputy. By connecting VA hospitals with medical schools, Hawley and Magnuson believed that veterans would benefit from the most current knowledge and trends in the medical profession. Residents and interns would also increase the numbers of medical personnel working in VA hospitals. The plan would radically transform the way VA hospitals cared for veterans. Congress passed a bill outlining the proposals by the end of 1945.[72]

Hawley's plan encountered stiff opposition, however. Entrenched bureaucrats in the VA opposed any changes in the administration of the agency. VA medical personnel feared demotion and dismissal if the new regulations were enacted. Opposition also came from the Civil Service Commission, which resisted any changes to existing government hiring procedures. Opponents vigorously lobbied President Harry S. Truman to veto the bill. During a contentious meeting at the White House, Bradley threatened to resign if doctors and nurses were not hired outside of civil service. In the end, Truman came down on the side of reform and signed Public Law 293 into law in January 1946. Almost immediately medical residents began working in VA hospitals. The number of physicians in the VA system rose dramatically, from 2,300 in 1945 to more than 4,000 by 1947. "Public Law 293 was our Magna Carta," claimed Magnuson, who noticed an instant improvement in morale among VA medical professionals. "I saw people in the Medical Department throw out their chests and act like men," he later wrote. "They saw for themselves how we cut down on their paperwork . . . so they could spend their time practicing medicine. They saw, above all, how the treatment of their patients improved, and that is all that is really necessary with any doctor who is worth his salt."[73]

The Veterans' Administration undertook other efforts to revamp and revitalize its medical system in preparation for the onslaught of World War II veterans. In 1945, the VA established the Prosthetic Appliances Service, replaced in 1948 with the Prosthetic and Sensory Aids Service, to conduct research on and improve the quality of artificial limbs, hearing aids, and similar devices for vet-

124	Chapter Three

erans. In 1946, General Hawley organized the Board of Consultants to the Medical Service, a special medical advisory group of prominent physicians to oversee VA medical policies. The first chairman of the board was the noted Dr. Charles W. Mayo of the Mayo Clinic in Minnesota, whose presence added a measure of prestige to the VA medical system. To lessen the burden on VA hospitals and clinics, the VA established a "hometown care" program, which essentially expanded the use of approved non-VA physicians to treat veterans in their local communities on a fee-for-service basis. By 1947, more than half of all VA-approved outpatient treatments were performed by non-VA providers. In just two years, the patient load of the Veterans' Administration hospitals increased dramatically, and the quality of medicine practiced at the VA had improved. "Those were exciting days in the Veterans' Administration Medical Department," Magnuson later crowed.[74]

In his memoirs, Omar Bradley identified revamping the VA's medical facilities as "the most difficult task of all" those he tackled in his two-year tenure at the agency. However, it was work that the general found deeply gratifying. Bradley's sense of accomplishment came from more than just a job well done. "By reason of my position in the U.S. Army in World War II," he wrote,

> I had been compelled to send hundreds of thousands of men into battle. I had heard the mournful cries of the wounded on the battlefield. In countless Army field hospitals, I had seen the maimed stoically enduring nearly unbearable pain. Nothing I have done in my life gave me more satisfaction than the knowledge that I had done my utmost to ease their way when they came home.

Unfortunately, many of the improvements were short lived. The departure of Bradley and Hawley in 1947 ended the era of medical reform at the VA. Described by one observer as the "bureaucrat's bureaucrat," Bradley's successor, Carl R. Gray Jr., placed more power over medical matters in the hands of VA administrators at the expense of the Department of Medicine and Surgery. Hawley's successor, Paul Magnuson, fought Gray's handling of medical matters until he was forced from office in 1951. Criticism of the VA's medical system increased over the years. Many charged, for example, that the VA's affiliation with medical schools had turned veterans into "guinea pigs" for untrained residents and interns. After World War II, the quality of VA medicine improved substantially, but Hawley's goal of providing veterans with "medical care second to none" was not achieved.[75]

Wisconsin's Medical Programs for Veterans

With the VA medical system so overstressed in the immediate aftermath of the war, the burden of caring for the sick and wounded veteran often fell upon state and local governments. In devising its programs for World War II veterans, Wisconsin prepared for the medical problems that returning veterans might face.

Wisconsin's medical benefits for veterans consisted of two primary activities. First, the state offered emergency grants to qualified veterans to meet immediate medical needs. The state also revamped its existing health care facilities for veterans, most notably the Wisconsin Veterans' Home at King.

Chapter 443, Laws of 1943—the act that created the Veterans' Recognition Board and the Postwar Rehabilitation Trust Fund (see chapter 1)—allowed the board to disburse trust fund money to veterans and their dependents for "emergency aid or relief as it may deem advisable to prevent want and distress." Various medical emergencies could clearly inhibit or even prevent a veteran's readjustment to civilian life. Burdensome medical bills, for example, could severely hinder a veteran's economic livelihood, and medical conditions left untreated could adversely affect the veteran's long-term health. To qualify for Wisconsin emergency grants, the veteran had to be unable to meet the emergency financially. Unlike for federal benefits, medical conditions did not need to be service connected to qualify for state aid; they only had to hinder the veteran's ability to work or otherwise affect his or her readjustment. Indeed, emergency grants could be used if the medical emergency involved a family member such as a wife of child, provided that the veteran was financially unable to meet the emergency. The inclusion of family members, as the *Blue Book* stated in 1946, "has already helped many Wisconsin veterans make a new start without the handicap of a big hospital bill incurred by a sick wife, child, or dependent parent."[76]

The WDVA dispensed two kinds of grants related to medical matters. The first, which the WDVA classified simply as "medical" grants, were used to defray the cost of medical emergencies. Veterans or their dependents who were beset by illness and who could not pay their doctor bills could apply for an emergency medical grant. The WDVA also provided emergency grants for hospitalization. The long waiting lists at VA hospitals forced many veterans to seek assistance at state, local, or private hospital facilities, often at the veteran's own expense. The WDVA medical hospitalization grants helped alleviate these costs. In 1944, Dr. William F. Lorenz, noted psychiatrist and medical adviser to the Veterans' Recognition Board, outlined a plan under which veterans could be hospitalized in local general hospitals using Postwar Rehabilitation Trust Fund money. Under the Lorenz plan, hospitals would reserve bed space for local veterans with medical emergencies. The recognition board would then reimburse the hospitals with trust fund money under a standard billing procedure. Such a system, Lorenz argued, would entail no new legislation, minimize red tape, and provide veterans with prompt treatment in their own communities. The Wisconsin Hospital Association agreed to the plan, which began operating before World War II ended. With the help of hospitalization grants, veterans could obtain a hospital bed and treatment until a spot in a VA hospital opened up. They could also get attention for non-service-connected ailments not normally covered by the VA, but which hindered their ability to make a living. The WDVA hospitalization grants also assisted many young families in having children. In fact, according to the 1946 *Blue Book*, hospitalization grants "have been used principally for emergency and obstetrical cases."[77]

Both types of medical grants saw their highest usage in 1946 and 1947—in the immediate aftermath of the war. Hospitalization grants outpaced medical grants, both in the number issued and average cash value of the award. Between 1946 and 1950, medical grants averaged $68.55, while hospitalization grants averaged $84.05. As the size of VA medical facilities grew, and as the veterans became better off financially and more settled into civilian life, the number of grants declined. Between 1946 and 1950, the WDVA awarded 9,993 medical and hospitalization grants worth $764,875.[78]

World War II also led to the renovation and expansion of the Wisconsin Veterans' Home in Waupaca County. Still widely known in the 1940s as the "Grand Army Home" because of its Civil War veteran origins, the institution cared for approximately 450 persons when America entered World War II in 1941. The "members," as its residents were called, were mostly Spanish-American War and World War I veterans and their family members. In fact, in 1941 widows and mothers outnumbered male veterans roughly two to one. In 1945, the facility housed one veteran of the Civil War. The home was administered by a board of managers, and before 1945 fell under the state adjutant general's office. In the 1945 consolidation of state veterans' agencies the facility came under the authority of the new Wisconsin Department of Veterans' Affairs, though the board of managers remained.[79]

In 1941, the Wisconsin Veterans' Home had seen little change since the turn of the century. Residents enjoyed an idyllic setting in the Chain-O-Lakes resort region in central Wisconsin, but the home was an antiquated health care facility badly in need of renovation. The home's administrators had called for improvements since the early 1930s. Members lived in numerous wooden cottages and dormitories built in the 1880s, scattered about the campus and in need of repairs. Even before Pearl Harbor, demand for the home's services was on the rise among veterans of World War I. America's entry into the war put further pressure on the home. As federal veterans' hospitals filled up with World War II veterans, the Grand Army Home experienced a rise in applications from those of World War I squeezed out of federal facilities. "Probably at no time since the founding of the Grand Army Home," reported acting commandant Col. Carlton L. Brosius in 1942, "has the urgent need been greater . . . to increase our domilicary capacity for incoming membership."[80]

Governor Goodland set his sights on the ancient facility early. He convened hearings into conditions at the home in December 1942, when he was still lieutenant governor. Grand Army Home administrators told horrifying details of conditions. August Frey, a member of the home's board of trustees, described the facility's status as "most deplorable." According to him, almost all the buildings on the grounds were fire hazards. "In one ramshackle old building there are 154 bedridden patients." he reported, and warned that "if a fire ever got started it would take a terrific toll." The wiring and plumbing in the buildings were "just about gone," according to Colonel Brosius. Upon becoming governor, Goodland authorized planning to make the Wisconsin Veterans' Home "one of the biggest veterans' facilities in the Middlewest." By 1943, home officials envisioned a massive building project to update and expand the facility, including a new hospital, power plant, and dormitories to accommodate 1500 veterans and family members.[81]

Expansion proceeded slowly during the war years because funds and building materials were channeled into the war effort. However, the anticipated renovations and new construction took place rather rapidly after 1945. One of the first priorities was the construction of a new powerhouse for the facility. Construction on new hospital facilities also got underway. In addition to new buildings, older facilities were upgraded, including repainting and the refinishing of furniture, expansion of the home's cemetery, and the installation of new roofs, sidewalks, and lighting around the grounds. In particular, renovation efforts focused on fire prevention, including new fire exits, installation of fire alarms, and upgrading of the facility's fire department. New hospital equipment had also been purchased. By 1953, the Wisconsin Veterans' Home had grown considerably, though not to the extent anticipated in 1943. Operating costs of the facility had risen from $262,549 in 1943 to $823,586 in 1953, and the size of the campus had grown from 95 to 136.25 acres, though the facility still accommodated fewer than 600 residents. The expansion of the facility continued into the 1960s, though the expectation of 1500 members was never reached.[82]

The expansion at the home had little direct impact on World War II veterans in the ten years immediately following the war. During the late 1940s, the number of World War II veterans in the facility fluctuated between one and five—all of whom were over the age of forty. By June 1956—ten years after the cessation of hostilities—only fourteen World War II veterans resided there. However, the number of World War I veterans had increased from 113 in 1946 to 216 in 1956. As World War I veterans grew older, they began to require longer-term hospital care. The Wisconsin Veterans' Home was geared to meet the needs of the ex-doughboys, and in so doing freed up space in federal VA medical facilities for World War II veterans. As World War II veterans reached advanced ages toward the end of the century, the facility would be available to them as well, in large part due to the renovations of the 1950s and 1960s.[83]

Conclusion

The extent to which veterans of World War II had to make medical readjustments to civilian life depended greatly on the type and severity of their injuries. Many veterans returned home and encountered few, if any, medical readjustment problems, and in most cases such problems subsided over time. But for those who lost limbs or other parts of the body due to war, readjustment would be—at least in some ways—always incomplete. In addition to war's impact on the body, many would also be forever tormented by the memories of war, and here, too, the process of readjustment would always be unfinished. Unresolved medical problems not only caused pain and physical hardship for the veteran, but also affected his or her ability to make a living and enjoy a normal social life. To assist veterans in recovering from and coping with war-related medical problems, the federal Veterans' Administration established programs for pensions, hospitalization, and outpatient care. By 1950, disability pensions for World War II veterans had reached a grand total of $4.3 billion. To supplement federal medical benefits, the Wisconsin Department of Veterans' Affairs provided emergency grants to meet hospital bills, which by 1950 had reached nearly $1 million. Such figures, wrote Omar Bradley in his memoirs, "are not usually remembered when adding up the total cost of World War II." Such costs are not lost on the veteran, however, whose long-term health and well-being was sometimes sacrificed for victory.[84]

Notes

1. Alexander G. Dumas and Grace Keen, *A Psychiatric Primer for the Veteran's Family and Friends* (Minneapolis: University of Minnesota Press, 1945), 1, 75-76, 105-106, 158-159.

2. U.S. Congress, Congressional Research Service, *U.S. Military Personnel and Casualties in Principal U.S. Wars* (Washington, D.C.: Congressional Research Service, 1973), 9-11.

3. Frank A. Reister, *Medical Statistics in World War II* (Washington, D.C.: Department of the Army, 1975), 8, 20, table 7.

4. Albert E. Cowdrey, *Fighting for Life: American Military Medicine in World War II* (New York: Free Press, 1994), 153-176; Reister, *Medical Statistics*, 21.

5. Reister, *Medical Statistics*, 23, table 7.

6. Reister, *Medical Statistics*, 23, table 7; Herbert M. Smith, *Four Score and Ten: Happenings in the Life of Herbert M. Smith* (Eau Claire, Wis.: Heins, 1994), 101-105; Flaten interview, Wisconsin Veterans' Oral History Project, Wisconsin Veterans' Museum Research Center, Madison, Wis. (cited hereafter as WVOHP); Gill interview, WVOHP.

7. Reister, *Medical Statistics*, tables 7, 7a-d; Graham Cosmas and Albert E. Cowdrey, *Medical Service in the European Theater of Operations* (Washington, D.C.: U.S. Army Center for Military History, 1992), 488-496. For complete discussion of cold injuries in World War II, see Tom F. Whayne and Michael E. DeBakey, *Cold Injury, Ground Type* (Washington, D.C.: Department of the Army, 1958).

8. Ray interview, WVOHP; Tibbetts interview, WVOHP.

9. Stark interview, WVOHP; Reister, *Medical Statistics*, 23.

10. Connors interview, WVOHP; Malvin Kachelmeier file, World War II Small Collections, Wisconsin Veterans' Museum Research Center, Madison, Wis.

11. Owen interview, WVOHP; Mary Ann Renard interview, WVOHP.

12. Reister, *Medical Statistics*, 23; Maxwell Droke, *Good-by to GI: How to Be a Successful Civilian* (New York: Abingdon-Cokesbury Press, 1945), 105; Dumas and Keen, *Psychiatric Primer*, 45, 50-53.

13. Reister, *Medical Statistics*, 13, 30-31, 46.

14. Reister, *Medical Statistics*, 46, table 27.

15. Reister, *Medical Statistics*, 11.

16. J. Claude Bennett and Fred Plum, eds., *Cecil Textbook of Medicine*, 20th ed. (Philadelphia: W. B. Saunders, 1996), 1683-1689; Ramzi S. Cotran, et al., *Robbins Pathologic Basis of Disease* (Philadelphia: W. B. Saunders, 1994), 324-327; John B. Coates, ed., *Preventive Medicine in World War II*, vol. 5, *Communicable Diseases Transmitted Chiefly through Respiratory and Alimentary Tracts* (Washington, D.C.: Department of the Army, 1958), 259-280; Reister, *Medical Statistics*, table 38; U.S. Navy, Bureau of Medicine and Surgery, *Medical Statistics, United States Navy* (Washington, D.C.: Navy Department, 1945), 53; Dalton interview, WVOHP. For more on the history of tuberculosis, see Mark Caldwell, *The Last Crusade: The War on Consumption, 1862-1954* (New York: Atheneum, 1988) and Georgina D. Feldberg, *Disease and Class: Tuberculosis and the Shaping of Modern North American Society* (New Brunswick, N.J.: Rutgers University Press, 1995).

17. Bennett and Plum, *Cecil Textbook of Medicine*, 1893-1896; Cotran, *Pathologic Basis of Disease*, 362-363; John B. Coates, ed., *Preventive Medicine in World War II*, vol. 6, *Communicable Diseases: Malaria* (Washington, D.C.: Department of the Army, 1963); Cowdrey, *Fighting for Life*, 58-89. For more on the history of malaria, see Gordon Harrison, *Mosquitoes, Malaria, and Man: A History of the Hostilities since 1800* (New York: Dutton, 1978).

18. Samuel V. Milner, *Victory in Papua* (Washington, D.C.: U.S. Army Center for Military History, 1957), 323-324; Reister, *Medical Statistics*, table 27; U.S. Navy, *Medical Statistics*, 65.

19. Coates, *Malaria*, 11-59; Cowdrey, *Fighting for Life*, 58-89.

20. Bates interview, WVHOP; Tauchen interview, WVOHP; Coleman interview, WVOHP; Rowley interview, WVOHP.

21. Russell L. Cecil, ed., *A Textbook of Medicine*, 7th ed. (Philadelphia: W. B. Saunders, 1947), 439-442.

22. Tinkham to Keefe, 1 April 1947 and 4 February 1948, Papers of Father Anselm Keefe, Wisconsin National Guard Materials, Wisconsin Veterans' Museum Research Center, Madison, Wis. (cited hereafter as Keefe Papers); Bates interview, WVOHP.

23. John B. Coates, ed., *Preventive Medicine in World War II*, vol. 7, *Communicable Diseases: Arthropodborne Diseases Other Than Malaria* (Washington, D.C.: Department of the Army, 1964); Joseph Taber interview, WVOHP.

24. The Soviet Union did not enter the war against Japan until August 1945. Prior to that date, American airmen who strayed into Soviet airspace were detained, but not held "prisoner" or turned over to the Japanese.

25. Bennett and Plum, *Cecil Textbook of Medicine*, 689-695, 738-740; Coates, *Respiratory and Alimentary Tracts*, 319-518; O'Dair interview, WVOHP.

26. Cotran, *Pathologic Basis of Disease*, 343-346; Reister, *Medical Statistics*, 38; John Willoughby, "The Sexual Behavior of American GIs during the Early Years of the Occupation of Germany," *Journal of Military History* 62 (1998): 155-174.

27. Cotran, *Pathologic Basis of Disease*, 389-390; Alice P. Carmody, Louis Mesard, and William F. Page, *Alcoholism and Problem Drinking, 1970-1975: A Statistical Analysis of VA Hospital Patients* (Washington, D.C.: Veterans' Administration, 1977). For historical context, see Mark Edward Lender and James Kirby Martin, *Drinking in America: A History*, rev. ed. (New York: Free Press, 1987).

28. David Bradley, "Fallout," *Wisconsin Medical Alumni Magazine* 36 (1996): 20-22; Constance M. Pechura and David P. Rall, eds., *Veterans at Risk: The Health Effects of Mustard Gas and Lewisite* (Washington, D.C.: National Academy Press, 1993); *New York Times*, 7 January 1993. For more on Operation Crossroads, see David Bradley, *No Place to Hide, 1946/1984* (Hanover, N.H.: University Press of New England, 1983). For

more on "atomic veterans" generally, see Jim Lerager, *In the Shadow of the Cloud: Photographs and Histories of America's Atomic Veterans* (Golden, Colo.: Fulcrum, 1988); Howard L. Rosenberg, *Atomic Soldiers: American Victims of Nuclear Experiments* (Boston: Beacon Press, 1980); and Michael Uhl and Tod Ensign, *GI Guinea Pigs* (Chicago: Playboy Press, 1980). In addition to veterans of Operation Crossroads, an estimated 195,000 World War II soldiers who served on occupation duty in Hiroshima and Nagasaki, Japan, in 1945 and 1946 were exposed to residual radiation from the first atomic bombs dropped in combat.

29. For more on the American prisoner of war experience in the Pacific during World War II, see E. Bartlett Kerr, *Surrender and Survival: The Experience of American POWs in the Pacific* (New York: William Morrow, 1985). For an excellent overview of ex-POW narratives in American history, see Robert C. Doyle, *Voices from Captivity: Interpreting the American POW Narrative* (Lawrence: University Press of Kansas, 1994).

30. Bennett and Plum, *Cecil Textbook of Medicine*, 1155-1158; Cotran, *Pathologic Basis of Disease*, 408-425.

31. William N. Donovan, *POW in the Pacific: Memoirs of an American Doctor in World War II* (Wilmington, Del.: SR Books, 1998), 123; Asbury Nix, *Corregidor: Oasis of Hope* (Stevens Point, Wis.: Trade Winds Publications, 1991), 136; Bredenson interview, Wisconsin Women in World War II Oral History Project, State Historical Society of Wisconsin Archives, Madison, Wis. (cited hereafter as WW2OHP).

32. Brenzel interview, WVOHP; Bernard M. Cohen and Maurice Z. Cooper, *A Follow-Up Study of World War II Prisoners of War* (Washington, D.C.: GPO, 1954), 15-25; M. Dean Nefziger, "Follow-Up Studies of World War II and Korean War Prisoners," *American Journal of Epidemiology* 91 (1970): 123-138.

33. Paul Wanke, "American Military Psychiatry and Its Role among Ground Forces in World War II," *Journal of Military History* 63 (1999): 127. For more on the work of military psychiatrists during World War II, see Edwin G. Boring, *Psychology for the Armed Services* (Washington, D.C.: Infantry Journal Press, 1945); Roy R. Grinker and John P. Spiegel, *Men under Stress* (Philadelphia: Blakiston, 1945); and Edwin A. Strecker and Kenneth E. Appel, *Psychiatry in Modern Warfare* (New York: Macmillan, 1945). For historical context, see Kyra Kester, "Shadows of War: The Historical Dimensions and Social Implications of Military Psychology and Veteran Counseling in the United States, 1860-1989," Ph.D. diss., University of Washington, 1992.

34. *Milwaukee Journal, They Can't Eat Medals* (Milwaukee, Wis.: Journal Company, 1943), 25-27; George K. Pratt, *Soldier to Civilian: Problems of Readjustment* (New York: Whittlesey House, 1944), 72-73.

35. Dorothy Baruch and Lee Edward Travis, *You're Out of the Service Now* (New York: Appleton-Century, 1946), 31; Robert Jay Lifton, *Home from the War: Learning from Vietnam Veterans* (Boston: Beacon Press, 1992), 105-106; Chipman interview, WVOHP; Ray interview, WVOHP.

36. For an excellent discussion of the literature on PTSD in World War II veterans, see Paula P. Schnurr, "PTSD and Combat-Related Psychiatric Symptoms in Older Veterans," *PTSD Research Quarterly* 2 (1991): 1-2. Also included in this issue are abstracts of books and articles related to PTSD in World War II veterans.

37. Witzig interview, WVOHP; American Psychiatric Association, *Diagnostic and Statistical Manual of Mental Disorders*, 4th ed. (Washington, D.C.: American Psychiatric Association, 1994), 424-429. For more on the nature of traumatic stress, see Judith Herman, *Trauma and Recovery* (New York: Basic Books, 1997).

38. Underkoffler interview, WVOHP; Scocos interview, WVOHP; Turner interview, WVOHP; Wallace interview, WVOHP.

39. Eckstam interview, WVOHP; Elver interview, WVOHP.

40. Chase interview, Stephen E. Ambrose World War II Interview Collection, Wisconsin Veterans' Museum Research Center, Madison, Wis.; Dunn interview, WVOHP; Pechacek interview, WVOHP; Charles Bradley, *Aleutian Echoes* (Fairbanks: University of Alaska Press, 1994), 85.

41. Botts interview, WVOHP; Bredenson interview, WW2OHP; James Bradley, *Flags of Our Fathers* (New York: Bantam Books, 2000), 306, 318; Oldenburg interview, WVOHP; Chipman interview, WVOHP.

42. Donald Wiberg interview, WVOHP; Connors interview, WVOHP; Smith interview, WVOHP; Tritz interview, WVOHP.

43. Lechnir interview, WW2OHP; Mercier interview, WVOHP; James F. Spohn, "Recollections of the European Theater," paper presented before the Madison Literary Club, 1988, copy in Spohn file, WVOHP; Flaten interview, WHOHP.

44. Francis Johnston interview, WVOHP; Henry Renard interview, WVOHP; Pressentin interview, WVOHP; Witzig interview, WVOHP.

45. Esser interview, WVOHP; Bredenson interview, WW2OHP; Donovan, *POW in the Pacific*, 124; Brenzel interview, WVOHP.

46. Amy Lindgren, ed., *Understanding the Former Prisoner of War: Life after Liberation: Essays by Guy Kelnhofer Jr., Ph.D.* (St. Paul, Minn.: Banfil Street Press, 1992), 15, 21.

47. Herman, *Trauma and Recovery*, 87-90.

48. Samuel Futterman and Eugene Pumpian-Mindlin, "Traumatic War Neuroses Five Years Later," *American Journal of Psychiatry* 108 (1951): 401; *DSM-IV*, 426.

49. Bensoni interview, WVOHP; Bernhagen interview, WVOHP; Spohn, "Recollections of the European Theater"; Spohn interview, WVOHP; Bradley, *Flags of Our Fathers*, 259, 306.

50. Pratt, *Soldier to Civilian*, 112; Dumas and Keen, *Psychiatric Primer*, 137; Freese interview, WVOHP; Chipman interview, WVOHP.

51. Lindgren, *Life after Liberation*, 11.

52. Miller interview, WVOHP; Lindgren, *Life after Liberation*, 11-12; Futterman and Pumpian-Mindlin, "Traumatic War Neuroses," 401.

53. Van Selus interview, WVOHP; Meland interview, WVOHP, Dresen interview, WW2OHP; Rowley interview, WVOHP.

54. Lindgren, *Life after Liberation*, 41, 45-50.

55. Lindgren, *Life after Liberation*, 14, 175; Miller interview, WVHOP; Witzig interview, WVOHP.

56. Wanke, "American Military Psychiatry," 140-141; Gerald N. Grob, *The Mad among Us: A History of the Care of America's Mentally Ill* (New York: Free Press, 1994), 191-222; Kester, "Shadows of War," 121-127; Futterman and Pumpian-Mindlin, "Traumatic War Neuroses," 407-408; Samuel Paster and Saul D. Holtzman, "A Study of One Thousand Psychotic Veterans Treated with Insulin and Electric Shock," *American Journal of Psychiatry* 105 (1949): 811-814; Herman, *Trauma and Recovery*, 24-26.

57. Wanke, "American Military Psychiatry," 142-145; Cohen and Cooper, *Follow-Up Study of World War II Prisoners of War*, 18-20.

58. Robert T. Kimbrough and Judson B. Glen, *American Law of Veterans*, rev. ed. (Rochester, N.Y.: Lawyers Co-operative Publishing Co., 1954), 488.

59. U.S. Veterans' Administration, *Schedule for Rating Disabilities* (Washington, D.C.: GPO, 1945); Kimbrough and Glen, *American Law of Veterans*, 489-497.

60. U.S. Veterans' Administration, *Administrator of Veterans' Affairs Annual Report*, 1950 ed. (Washington, D.C.: GPO, 1951), 198. For World War II veterans, non-service-connected disability pensions were not significant before 1950.

61. Jack C. Plano, *Fishhooks, Apples, and Outhouses* (Kalamazoo, Mich.: Personality Press, 1991), 301; Chipman interview, WVOHP; J. J. Kuhn, *I Was Baker 2: Memoirs of a World War II Platoon Sergeant* (West Bend, Wis.: DeRaimo Publishing, 1994), 230, 244.

62. Brenzel interview, WVOHP; Hall interview, WVOHP.

63. Frederickson to Keefe, 20 December 1947, Keefe Papers; Kudija to Keefe, 30 May 1954, Keefe Papers; Keefe to Kudija, 4 July 1954, Keefe Papers.

64. Henry Renard interview, WVOHP; Schmidt interview, WVOHP; Omar Bradley, *A General's Story* (New York: Simon and Schuster, 1983), 454.

65. Voight interview, WVOHP.

66. Tibbetts interview, WVOHP; Scocos interview, WVOHP; Joseph Taber interview, WVOHP; Underkoffler interview, WVOHP; Toki interview, WVOHP.

67. Kimbrough and Glen, *American Law of Veterans*, 565-571.

68. U.S. Veterans' Administration, *Annual Report*, 1941 ed., 11-13; U.S. House Committee on Veterans' Affairs, *Medical Care of Veterans*, 90th Cong., 1st sess., 1967, Committee Print 4, 166-167.

69. U.S. Veterans' Administration, *Annual Report*, 1942-47 eds.; *Medical Care of Veterans*, 191-192; Bradley, *General's Life*, 457.

70. U.S. Veterans' Administration, *Annual Report*, 1950 ed., 6-10, 239. For more on the VA hospital expansion in the context of the American medical establishment, see Paul Starr, *The Social Transformation of American Medicine* (New York: Basic Books, 1982), 335-363.

71. *Medical Care of Veterans*, 171-173; Bradley, *General's Life*, 457-462; Robert Klein, *Wounded Men, Broken Promises: How the Veterans Administration Betrays Yesterday's Heroes* (New York: Macmillan, 1981), 35-46.

72. *Medical Care of Veterans*, 207-211.

73. Bradley, *General's Life*, 457-459; Paul R. Magnuson, *Ring the Night Bell: An American Surgeon's Story* (Boston: Little, Brown, 1960), 289-305; U.S. Veterans' Administration, *Annual Report*, 1946 ed., 3.

74. Robert S. Stewart and William M. Bernstock, *Veterans' Administration Prosthetic and Sensory Aids Program Since World War II* (Washington, D.C.: GPO, 1977), 1-5; *Medical Care of Veterans*, 215-218; U.S. Veterans' Administration, *Annual Report*, 1947 ed., 12; Magnuson, *Ring the Night Bell*, 298.

75. Bradley, *General's Life*, 457, 462; Klein, *Wounded Men, Broken Promises*, 47-50; Magnuson, *Ring the Night Bell*, 320-350.

76. Wisconsin Legislative Reference Bureau, *Wisconsin Blue Book*, 1946 ed. (Madison: Legislative Reference Bureau, 1946), 146.

77. William F. Lorenz, "Prompt Medical Service to Veterans," *Wisconsin Medical Journal* 44 (1945): 432-434; WDVA Board meeting minutes, 13 April 1945, 8 June 1945, Records of the Wisconsin Department of Veterans' Affairs, State Government Records, State Historical Society of Wisconsin Archives, Madison, Wis. (cited hereafter as WDVA); *Blue Book*, 1946 ed., 146-147.

78. WDVA Board meeting minutes, 1946-50, WDVA.

79. Wisconsin Veterans' Home, *Annual Report for the Grand Army Home for Veterans*, 1941 ed. (Madison: State of Wisconsin, 1941). In addition to the Wisconsin Veterans' Home, Wisconsin also worked with the American Legion to maintain Camp American Legion in the Wisconsin north woods as a rest camp for veterans. In 1924, the state

purchased a lakeside resort using money from the Soldiers' Rehabilitation Trust Fund, then leased the land to the American Legion, originally at the rate of $1 a year. The Wisconsin American Legion then administered the rest camp. For more, see George E. Sweet, *The Wisconsin American Legion: A History, 1919-1992* (Milwaukee: Wisconsin American Legion Press, 1992), 17-18, 76, 93-94.

80. Wisconsin Veterans' Home, *Annual Report*, 1941-42 eds.; *Wisconsin State Journal*, 16 December 1942.

81. *Wisconsin State Journal*, 16 December 1942; *Capital Times*, 16 December 1942; *Green Bay Press-Gazette*, 1 October 1943.

82. Wisconsin Veterans' Home, *Annual Report*, 1940-60 eds.

83. Wisconsin Veterans' Home, *Annual Report*, 1946-56, eds.

84. U.S. Veterans' Administration, *Annual Report*, 1950 ed., 194; Bradley, *General's Story*, 454.

Chapter Four

"My Mind Was Like Virgin Soil": Educational Readjustments

The passage of the 1944 GI Bill of Rights and its generous educational benefits for World War II veterans caused much consternation in the world of American higher education. Though college and university officials welcomed the influx of federal dollars the veterans would bring, they also believed that the government was using higher education in an experiment to ward off unemployment and feared that their institutions would be inundated with unqualified, maladjusted veterans. Some administrators were outspoken about their concerns. Harvard University president James B. Conant, for example, feared that "we may find the least capable among the war generation . . . flooding the facilities for advanced education." University of Chicago president Robert M. Hutchins went even further, claiming that the GI Bill would create "educational hobo jungles" that would train intellectually deficient veterans for nonexistent jobs, and insisted that "education is not a device for coping with mass unemployment." However, when veterans arrived on campus in large numbers after 1945, college and university administrators were pleasantly surprised at the determination and capability of the student-veteran. By the end of the decade, Conant had retracted his earlier statements, and proclaimed World War II veterans "the most mature and promising students Harvard has ever had."[1]

To find a niche in the postwar economy, veterans often saw education as the key to their success, advancement, and security. For many of these veterans, World War II had been an interruption in their education—and thus a threat to their survival in the postwar American economy. Thanks to the GI Bill, as well as other federal and state educational programs, veterans flocked to America's colleges and universities after World War II, an episode that transformed both the veterans and the world of American higher education. Upon entering military service, fewer than half of American military personnel had completed high school. Before the war, colleges and universities were typically the domain of the wealthy and the gifted, and predominantly white and Protestant. Most Americans considered a college education out of reach. Federal veterans' benefits helped to change that. By the time World War II veteran eligibility for education under the GI Bill ended in 1956, 2.2 million ex-servicemen had attended a college or university using federal veterans' benefits, and more than 3.5 million had obtained training at a trade, vocational, or correspondence school. Educational readjustment programs had provided an avenue for millions of World War II veterans for reentry into the civilian economy.

Educational Benefit Programs

It was Title II of Public Law 346, better known as the GI Bill of Rights of 1944, that formed the backbone of federal educational assistance to World War II veterans. However, the federal government had several other programs through which veterans could receive education and training. Wisconsin veterans also enjoyed educational support from the state government. If federal benefits proved insufficient, the Wisconsin Department of Veterans' Affairs stepped in with supplemental money for Badger State veterans pursuing their studies. Thanks to federal and state lawmakers, Wisconsin's World War II veterans had more opportunities to receive an advanced education than did previous generations of veterans.

As originally formulated in 1944, the provisions of the GI Bill far outpaced those of any other federal educational program for veterans in American history. Veterans with more than six months of service and a discharge other than dishonorable were eligible for one year of college or technical school with the government paying tuition and fees. After the first year, veterans were eligible for additional years of education equal to the amount of time they had served in the military. Thus, a veteran who had served two years in the armed forces would be eligible for a total of three years schooling. In no case would a veteran's eligibility extend beyond four years, and benefits had to be used within seven years of the war's termination. Veterans who entered service after age twenty-five were eligible only for one year of training, but could obtain additional years if they could prove that the war had interrupted their education.

In addition to covering a veteran's tuition, the GI Bill also paid for the student-veteran's books and sundry school supplies up to a maximum of $500. Veterans also received a stipend to cover living expenses while studying. Under the original 1944 law, single veterans received $50 per month for room and board, and married veterans $75 per month. Generally speaking, veterans could choose any occupation or profession they wished. They could attend virtually any institution of higher education as long as they could meet whatever admission qualifications the school imposed. In no case was a school required to accept an unqualified student. The only restriction the government imposed on the veteran's selection of a school was that an institution had to be accredited by the state in which it operated. The program allowed veterans to attend both public and private institutions of higher learning, as well as technical and vocational schools. Under the GI Bill, veterans could pursue careers in an incredibly wide range of occupations and professions, from priest to professor, or from administrator to zookeeper.

In subsequent years, the federal government liberalized the terms of the GI Bill. In December 1945, the law was significantly expanded in scope. Congress abolished the twenty-five-year-old age limitation, for example, and extended the time period under which veterans had to complete their studies from seven to nine years, giving veterans until 1956 to complete their education or training. Congress also raised subsistence payments. The VA and members of Congress received numerous complaints from veterans, as well as from the American Legion and other powerful veterans' groups, that subsistence payments did not keep up with the inflationary postwar economy. In December 1945, Congress raised rates from $50 to $65 a month for single veterans and from $75 to $90 for married veterans. By 1948, Congress had raised subsistence allowances to $210 for single veterans, $270 for veterans with one dependent, and $290 with two or more dependents.[2]

Even more generous than the GI Bill—but limited to disabled veterans—was the Veterans' Vocational Rehabilitation Act of 1943, better known as Public Law 16. The purpose of Public Law 16, signed by President Roosevelt on March 23, 1943 (and amended thereafter), was to enhance the employment options of disabled veterans through educational opportunities. To qualify, veterans had to have been honorably discharged, have a medical disability rating of at least 10 percent, and prove that they needed education to overcome their handicap. Public Law 16 was more generous than the GI Bill in several respects. For one, disabled veterans could obtain up to four years of education under Public Law 16 irregardless of the amount of time served in the military, with additional schooling possible in some cases. There was no limit on expenses for books and supplies. To cover living expenses, veterans under Public Law 16 received their medical disability pension, the same level of subsistence payments available to those using the GI Bill, as well as additional amounts. However, veterans utilizing Public Law 16 were required to have their course of study approved by the Veterans' Administration. If the veteran's medical pension fell below 10 percent, he or she was no longer eligible for educational assistance under the law.[3]

A third program that helped put some veterans through school after World War II was Public Law 113, an amendment to the Vocational Rehabilitation Act of 1920. This act provided educational and training benefits for civilians injured in "industry or otherwise" during wartime. Veterans who fell under Public Law 113 included those who served in the merchant marine or in women's auxiliary organizations such as the Women's Army Auxiliary Corps (WAAC) and the Women's Airforce Service Pilots (WASPS), whom the government did not recognize as being veterans for benefit purposes. Like the GI Bill and Public Law 16, Public Law 113 provided its recipients with payments for tuition, books, and other educational expenses. However, Public Law 113 was administered by the federal Office of Vocational Rehabilitation—not the Veterans' Administration. Merchant mariners and members of women's auxiliary organizations who had not been injured in the line of duty were not eligible for federal educational assistance of any kind as a result of their wartime service.[4]

In keeping with its policy of supplementing federal veterans' benefits, Wisconsin's contribution to the education of its veterans consisted of using emergency grants from the Postwar Rehabilitation Trust Fund. For Wisconsin veterans pursuing higher education, the WDVA enhanced federal educational benefits in two primary ways. First, veterans could apply for grants from the trust fund to cover emergency expenses. Student veterans—particularly those married and with children—frequently found that their allowances under the GI Bill or

Public Law 16 might not stretch until the end of the month, particularly if an emergency arose. Veterans also found that subsistence checks from the federal government often arrived late, especially at the beginning of a student-veteran's first semester of school. The WDVA would grant small emergency sums if federal payments were late, or if federal benefits were "not sufficient to maintain a decent standard or would slow their progress in school." The amount of such grants varied, depending "solely by the situation of the applicant," according to WDVA director Leo Levenick, but would enable "the student and his family the normal standard of living . . . [while] pursuing his education."[5]

The WDVA also underwrote registration expenses for veterans who qualified for the GI Bill or Public Law 16 but whose paperwork had not yet cleared the federal system. To receive GI Bill or Public Law 16 benefits, veterans had to have a certificate of eligibility from the VA. Tuition and fee payments for veterans then went directly from the federal government to the educational institutions. However, delays in processing applications and certificates meant that the colleges and universities did not always receive tuition payments from the government at the beginning of a semester. "Having found living quarters and made plans to resume their education," reported the *Blue Book* in 1946, "they found the registration dead line at hand but they were unable to go ahead and enroll." WDVA director Levenick explained what such delays meant to many veterans:

> These were men whose education had already been delayed from two to four years because of time spent in military service. Many were married and were enrolling for five or six year courses. This meant that they would be well over 30 years old before they graduated and could even get started with their plans for a home and a family. Any further delay amounted to disaster in their eyes.

In such cases, the WDVA would work with the registrars of colleges and guaranteed the expenses of GI students until federal benefits finally came through. "Then he could go ahead and get started on opening day," wrote Levenick, "rather than waste any more time waiting." By the end of 1950, the WDVA had provided $178,901.96 in educational grants to Wisconsin veterans.[6]

Despite generous educational benefits, many experts believed that only a select few veterans, perhaps one million, would use them to attend a college or university. Veteran readjustment advice books rarely touched upon the subject of education. Morton Thompson's humorous *How to Be a Civilian*, for example, made no mention of veterans going to college. In retrospect, the omission seems odd. But as historian Keith Olson has pointed out:

> Certainly the idea of an ex-marine wearing a freshman beanie, a thirty-year-old playing college football, or a young coed being simultaneously wooed by a fuzzy-cheeked teenager and a twenty-four-year-old former fighter pilot contained exceptional material to satirize. But satire has no point unless it is associated with widely shared experience or knowledge. When Thompson wrote, Americans apparently lacked a coherent image of the student-veteran.

Self-help books that addressed education betrayed limited expectations for the student-veteran. "Going to college has been the dream of many," wrote Baruch and Travis, "and yet, when some started out seriously on the college or university course, they found that this was not all a bed of roses." One concern of veterans was their older age in relation to that of the typical undergraduate. "Though in actual years you may not be far removed from your classmates," wrote Maxwell Droke, "you feel that you have matured out of proportion to your years." Droke also noted that an "inner restlessness" might make it "difficult, and in some cases impossible, for you to devote yourself wholeheartedly to books, lectures, [and] theories." Writers also suggested that the practically minded veterans might find degree requirements mystifying. Baruch and Travis quoted several student-veterans who complained about having to learn "mumbo jumbo that won't be useful in later life." Droke encouraged students to keep studying nevertheless. "Simply because the curricula of our schools may not be ideally adapted to your present desire," he wrote, "that is no reason why you should fail to take full advantage of the education offered." Veterans also had the same concerns as other students, such as the taking of tests. Baruch and Travis quoted one veteran who described examinations as having "scared me more than flying through flak." Advice writers urged veterans to continue their studies and take advantage of the historic opportunity for a higher education the GI Bill provided. "For the first time in the history of America," wrote Baruch and Travis, "economic and social position do not matter in the opportunity to secure an education. The thing that counts most is an individual's desire for such training or education."[7]

The public may not have had a clear image of the student-veteran, but the veterans themselves were often keenly aware that they were entitled to an education at government expense. The GI Bill was "very thoroughly known" among veterans, according to ex-marine James Bohstedt of Madison. "Everybody knew about it and knew what to do." Milwaukee army veteran Donald Wiberg claimed that his top postwar priority was to "take advantage of the GI Bill" and resume his studies. When discharges from the military services accelerated after 1945, so did enrollments in colleges and universities, as well as technical and vocational schools, in Wisconsin and across the nation. Higher education in the United States would never be the same again.[8]

The Veteran Invasion

The arrival of veterans to campuses following World War II has often been described using military metaphors. "Veterans Storm the Academic Beachhead," was one headline in the *New York Times Magazine* in 1946, for example; "Army of War Veterans Moves on UW As Registration Begins," announced Madison's *Capital Times* that same year. Journalists looking for eye-grabbing headlines found the use of the wartime imagery to describe the arrival of the veterans to campus in the postwar period irresistible. However, the images were also a fairly apt description of the situation. World War II veterans, often still clad in their uniforms, did indeed seem to "invade" campuses after the war. Many individual veterans had long planned their strategies for their entry into, or return to, campus life. Administrators, in turn, devised strategies to cope with the onslaught. But unlike a military operation in which deadly combat ensues, the veterans usually found themselves welcomed with open arms.[9]

For many veterans, returning to school or beginning their studies was their top postwar consideration. Marine corps veteran Charles Smith of Oconto described college as his "number one priority" upon returning to Wisconsin. Ex-bomber pilot Rupert Cornelius of Madison described himself as "anxious" to go to college after the war. James Spohn was so anxious to resume his studies that his first stop when he returned to Madison was the University of Wisconsin. "The first thing I wanted to do was enroll in Law School," he recalled, and he registered for classes even before he had visited his fiancée. "I went in and enrolled and got my registration set up," he remembered, "and who should I meet coming out of Bascom Hall but my [future] wife's sister." He recalled that his fiancée was "a little perturbed that I saw her sister before I saw her," but he also noted that "it worked out well" in the end.[10]

Veterans were anxious to receive an education because many Americans viewed education as the key to economic advancement and security. "There is an inescapable connection between the school bell and the cash register," claimed self-help author Maxwell Droke, who drew on his World War I experiences to encourage the new generation of veterans to obtain as much education as they could. "Education was not, I regret to say, too highly regarded by the rank and file of the armed forces in my day," he told them, resulting in economic dislocation for many ex-doughboys. He warned veterans that failure to obtain education or training would cripple their future earning potential, especially in a time of economic flux and change. "Never has there been an age when formal learning . . . meant as much as now," he told veterans. "Many avenues are already closed to the uneducated," he noted, while "others are narrowing perceptibly." "We cannot too strongly emphasize," wrote Droke,

> the truth that if you are ever going to complete your formal education, *it must be now*. The longer you wait, the greater will be the disparity of age between yourself and your classmates, and the greater will be your own reluctance to take the plunge. . . . If you fail now to accept your Government's liberal offer to provide an education at the taxpayer's expense, you are in all probability sentencing yourself to a life of circumscribed opportunity and limited income. That's putting it pretty bluntly. But it is no more—or no less—than the truth.

Having grown up during the Great Depression, returning veterans understood clearly the meaning and implications of Droke's emphatic words. "The parents of my generation knew that their kids were going to have a better life," recalled Madison navy veteran Sam Onhieber, but they "knew they had to get it through education." Some saw education as essential to survival in a competitive postwar job market. "I was determined that I was going to go [back to college]," recalled James Bohstedt, "because I had come to realize that an education was going to be essential." Even beyond economic concerns, many veterans viewed education as a key step in making the transition from the military to the civilian world. As Madison army veteran Paul Graven characterized his desire to go to college: "I wanted to go back to school and finish, so I could start my life."[11]

However, other veterans had not previously considered going to college and were lured into it by the GI Bill and Public Law 16. Army veteran John Gill returned to Madison and worked for his father in his downtown clothing store. "I hadn't thought too much about going to school," Gill recalled, "but [then] I thought, 'it's all free and they give you $80 a month and they pay for your books.'" Gill majored in economics with the hope that study in that field could be beneficial to his father's clothing business, which he later purchased when his father retired. V. G. Rowley of Blue River, a cheese maker before the war, enrolled at the University of Wisconsin only after considerable urging from his wife and a friend, as well as the dean of the university's agriculture college. Once enrolled, Rowley viewed college as little more than "a reprieve long enough to become healthy" from his recurrent malaria. But while attending college, Rowley "saw that so many people were going to school, and the job market was going to be pretty tight, maybe I'd better stay in and not drop out like I thought I would a few times." Madison's John Hall, an army veteran wounded in Europe, recalled that he could bring in more money by going to school on Public Law 16 than he by could working.[12]

Many veterans have maintained that they would not have been able to receive a college education were it not for the GI Bill or Public Law 16. "If it hadn't been for the GI Bill," former pilot James Edsall of Madison stated quite explicitly, "I wouldn't have been able to go to college." Hudson navy veteran Dorwin Lamkin, who attended the University of Kansas, came from a family background in which attending college was not an expectation. "My mother was a first generation American," he remembered. "She went to business college and was regarded as the most highly educated person in the family." Others have claimed that the GI Bill allowed them to stay in school and complete their education, or receive advanced training or graduate degrees that would not otherwise have been possible. "I had always wanted to go to college," recalled navy veteran LeRoy Dalton. "The GI Bill made it possible to go and stay there" (Dalton went to both college and law school at the University of Wisconsin). Considerable anecdotal evidence suggests that the GI Bill allowed thousands from working class or lower middle class backgrounds to attend school, men and women who would not otherwise have gone to college.[13]

However, extrapolating from such anecdotal information has been difficult. Historians and social scientists—those few who have studied the GI Bill in detail—suggest that the law may have had a more limited effect than is popularly believed. A study undertaken by Norman Fredericksen and William B. Shrader in 1951 concluded that only 20 percent of veterans attending a college or university (about 400,000) would not have been there had it not been for the GI Bill. In a 1976 study, University of Wisconsin demographer Neil Fligstein estimated that veterans using the GI Bill received about 2.7 years of education and training above that which nonveterans received, but cautioned that "the tentative nature of this conclusion should be stressed." Keith Olson, in his 1974 study of the GI Bill, suggested that the additional degrees earned after the war under the GI Bill did not offset those lost through low enrollments during the Great Depression and World War II. Although many veterans claim that the GI Bill provided them with an education they would not otherwise have received, its ultimate effect on the general educational attainment in the United States remains unclear.[14]

Veterans from racial and ethnic minority groups had the same educational benefit rights as those of Euro-Americans, but often faced more obstacles in utilizing them. Many schools had discriminatory admissions policies, for example, either officially or unofficially. Minority veterans typically had more difficulty satisfying a school's academic admission requirements, since they tended to enter the armed services with lower educational attainment than did whites. The extent of minority education under the GI Bill and Public Law 16 is difficult to ascertain. Reliable statistics on minority enrollment at Wisconsin's colleges and universities schools do not exist. The University of Wisconsin did not track minority enrollment until the 1960s, for example. Traditionally black colleges in the South saw burgeoning enrollments after the war, suggesting that many members of minorities who were in a position to gain an education under the GI Bill and Public Law 16 did so. It should be noted, however, that black colleges—already suffering from overcrowding and poor facilities before the war—were forced to turn applicants away in droves during the postwar years. In 1947, African Americans made up only 4 percent of all student-veterans nationwide, though they comprised roughly 8 percent of the wartime military. Of those black veterans in higher education, 70 percent attended predominantly black colleges in the South.[15]

Returning veterans demonstrated a clear preference for America's most prestigious colleges and universities. With the federal government paying tuition, veterans applied to America's most exclusive institutions with little concern about finances. As *Time* magazine asked in 1946: "Why go to Podunk U. when you can go to Yale?" These schools, in turn, welcomed the influx of federal subsidies and accepted large numbers of student-veterans. Many Wisconsin veterans attended some of the nation's most elite schools using the GI Bill. William Brunsell of Evansville, an army French interpreter in Europe, wrote a letter to Harvard law school while in the service. "I said that I was interested in going to your law school and I'm getting out [of service] in the spring," he told Harvard, and asked, "Can I come?" Two weeks later, as he remembered it, Brunsell received a letter informing him that he had been accepted, and to let them know when he planned to begin his studies. Ivy League institutions such as Harvard, Yale, and Princeton, as well as elite public universities such as the Universities of Michigan and California, were flooded with applications from veterans following the war. According to a 1946 VA study, 41 percent of veterans using the GI Bill attended just thirty-eight of the nation's major colleges and universities.[16]

One of those major institutions was the University of Wisconsin in Madison, considered one of the top undergraduate and graduate institutions in the nation. According to one survey, the University of Wisconsin ranked fifth in veteran enrollment nationwide in 1947.[17] Many veterans were thrilled with the opportunity to attend Wisconsin's premier institution of higher learning. In 1947, an Iowan named William Appleman Williams, who had commanded a navy destroyer in the Pacific during the war, applied for graduate study in history at Wisconsin after the war and was accepted. "I was terribly excited to be entering what was unquestionably the best on-campus History Department in the country," he later wrote. "It was, for that matter, probably the best liberal arts faculty in the nation."[18]

Veterans swelled enrollments at the Madison campus. During the war, enrollment figures dropped from 11,416 in the fall of 1938 to just 5,904 by the fall of 1943. Postwar enrollment not only rebounded, but surpassed previous totals. Between the 1945 and 1946 fall semesters, enrollment jumped from 9,028 to 18,598. Much of this rise was due to veterans, whose enrollments rose from 1,347 to 11,076 during that same year. Enrollment at the university peaked in the fall of 1947, when 18,693 registered, more than 10,000 of whom were veterans. Indeed, veterans composed a majority of all students on the University of Wisconsin campus between 1946 and 1948. In addition to the Madison campus, the University of Wisconsin Extension offered courses at branch locations across the Badger State, the largest of which was located in Milwaukee. In fact, the extension provided classes to veterans free of charge, and many ex-servicemen and women signed up. By 1946, an estimated 3,900 veterans were taking courses through the extension, composing 72 percent of enrollment. By 1946, more than half of all student-veterans in Wisconsin attended either the Madison campus or one of the extension branches.[19]

The University of Wisconsin was so flooded with veterans that it limited out-of-state admissions for undergraduates. As enrollments rose between 1945 and 1947, the percentage of nonresident undergraduates declined from 34 percent to just 10 percent. Large public universities in other states, also inundated with veterans, instituted similar policies. Although many Wisconsinites were able to attend large public universities in other states, others found their applications denied. One was Madison navy veteran Sam Onhieber, who had hoped to pursue his studies in Arizona, where his mother had relocated due to health problems. However, when he applied at the University of Arizona in Tucson he was told that that institution was no longer accepting out-of-state students. Madison army veteran John Cumming, an immigrant from Scotland who had lived in New York, Iowa, and Wisconsin, could not obtain state residency for tuition purposes in any state. Though the University of Wisconsin took only a handful of nonresident students, it charged in-state students using the GI Bill the higher nonresident tuition rate. The policy provoked outrage in many quarters. The *Capital Times*, for example, characterized the policy as "just an attempt to grab while the bag is open." The university justified the policy—approved by the VA—by arguing that the influx of federal GI Bill money lessened the financial burden on nonveteran students and on the Wisconsin taxpayer.[20]

Although veterans tended to favor large, prestigious schools such as the University of Wisconsin, many also enrolled at other kinds of institutions. The reasons a veteran chose a particular institution varied. Some simply were not admitted to some of the largest and best schools and had to seek their education elsewhere. In a tight housing market (see chapter 6), many veterans chose to attend school at institutions close to their parents' homes. Some veterans selected schools based on religious considerations. WAC veteran Renate Lucht of LaValle chose to attend Valparaiso University in Indiana because it was a Lutheran school, for example. Wisconsin's second-largest university in the years after World War II was Marquette University, a Jesuit institution in downtown Milwaukee. Not only did Marquette recover from the declining enrollments of the war years, the size of the university's student body doubled, from just over 4,000 in 1940 to a peak enrollment of 8,700 in 1948, with veterans constituting more than half of the student body. Indeed, in 1946 nearly 60 percent of student-veterans in Wisconsin attended either Marquette or the University of Wisconsin's Madison campus.[21]

Many student-veterans were uncomfortable at large institutions such as the University of Wisconsin and Marquette. The crowded conditions and the anonymity of a large campus, the long lines for books and supplies, and the large number of veterans reminded many ex-servicemen too much of the military years they longed to forget. One such veteran was ex-marine Charles Smith, who enrolled at the University of Wisconsin but did not find the environment to his liking. With the large number of veterans around campus, Smith recalled, "I thought I was still in the service." After one semester he left the university and resumed his studies at Milton College, a school with fewer than 200 students located fifty miles south of Madison, where he appreciated the smaller classes and better access to faculty members. James Zeasman of Madison also attended the University of Wisconsin, but "felt like I was still a number." He recalled that "in a year and a half at the university I was never in two classes with the same person." Unhappy in Madison, he transferred to the Stout Institute, a smaller state-run college in Menomonie. Zeasman preferred the atmosphere at Stout. "We used to sit in the student union and play pinochle with the dean of men in the evening," he recalled fondly. Although overcrowding at major universities forced many veterans into smaller schools, many simply felt more comfortable at "Podunk U."[22]

Like the mammoth University of Wisconsin, the state's smaller public colleges also saw enrollments rise after World War II. Enrollment at the Stout Institute, for example, jumped from 276 in 1943 to 967 by 1949. At Central State Teachers College in Stevens Point, the student body grew from 225 to 856 between 1944 and 1946. Platteville State Teachers College saw enrollments rise from a low point of 216 in the 1943-44 academic year to 744 in 1949-50—a new school record. The Wisconsin Institute of Technology, just two blocks away from Platteville State, saw even greater fluctuations. By the 1944-45 academic year, the institute had just twenty-two students—down from ninety-eight at the time of Pearl Harbor. Serious discussion about closing the institution or merging with nearby Platteville State ensued. But after World War II returning veterans boosted enrollment to a record 269 students in 1947-48, and plans to terminate or merge the facility were shelved. "Due in part to the GI Bill," one historian of the institute has written, "the school was saved."[23]

The state's smaller private colleges also saw burgeoning enrollment. Ripon College in Fond du Lac County saw the student body increase from 183 in 1944 to 689 in 1948. Northland College, a Congregationalist school in Ashland in far northern Wisconsin, saw enrollment jump from 106 to 189 between 1944 and 1945, with the number of men rising from 18 to 99 in that same period. Enrollments at Northland continued to rise; by the fall of 1947 enrollment had topped 300—a new school record. In the fall of 1945, Lawrence College in Appleton had 580 students, 471 of whom were women. In two years, enrollments rose precipitously, especially for men. In the fall of 1947, Lawrence reached an all-time high enrollment of 1,059 students (611 men and 450 women), of whom 354 men and four women were using the GI Bill. Beloit College had 635 students in the spring of 1946. The number of students there, especially veterans, continued to rise. By 1949, enrollment had reached 1,095.[24]

Though veterans were not as prevalent at small public and private colleges as they were at larger schools, they nevertheless dominated these institutions as well. "A small college . . . filled the ticket for men like me," wrote one student-veteran at Northland College, "who might need some individual attention to get back in the swing of things." The veteran was chagrined to learn that he was "just one of forty or fifty GIs who had had the same idea. A steady stream of khaki poured through the halls." In 1946, the Wisconsin school with the highest percentage of veterans in its student body was the Wisconsin Institute of Technology in Platteville, with 86 percent. However, the percentage of veterans in the student population was normally smaller at the smaller schools. In 1946, veterans comprised 46 percent of students in Wisconsin's nine state-run teachers colleges—significant but far below the 62 percent at the University of Wisconsin. The Badger State's small private colleges saw similar numbers. In 1946, veterans constituted a majority of students in just three small private colleges: Carroll, Milton, and St. Norbert. Many students at the smaller public and private colleges were nonveterans squeezed out of the larger schools by the rise in veteran enrollment. Nevertheless, veterans were often a significant segment of the student body even at Wisconsin's smallest colleges.[25]

Often forgotten in discussions of the GI Bill and its effects on the nation's educational institutions is the fact that many veterans opted to attend a variety of technical and trade schools. Veterans could use the GI Bill and Public Law 16 to pursue training in many careers. Madison's Raymond Ray pursued a career as a commercial artist, and enrolled at the Colt School of Art in his hometown. A disabled veteran, Ray attended school under Public Law 16, and the government paid for all necessary art supplies, including his watercolors and paints—"you name it." Richard Elver, who served in a graves registration unit during the war, pursued a career as a mortician and attended the Wisconsin Institute of Mortuary Science in Milwaukee on the GI Bill. As at the four-year colleges and universities, veterans also dominated trade and technical schools. Robert Blake of Boscobel, who studied accounting at Madison Business College, recalled that this classmates were "95 percent veterans." Otto Junkermann, who studied industrial design at the Layton School of Art in Milwaukee, remembered that the only classmates of his who were not veterans were women. In 1946, 1,998 veterans were enrolled at Wisconsin's trade and business schools.[26]

Veterans could also attend one of Wisconsin's fifty vocational and technical schools administered by the State Board of Vocational and Adult Education. Wisconsin's vocational and technical schools had much to offer returning veterans. Those who had not completed high school could obtain a high school equivalency certificate from such an institution, for example, before attending a college or university. These schools also offered courses in a wide variety of trades and occupations, including barbering, cosmetology, electronics, firefighting, plumbing, and steamfitting. Navy veteran Harvey Fehling of Beaver Dam was one such veteran, who learned sheet metal working at his local vocational institution using the GI Bill. Army veteran Willard Diefenthaler of Kiel earned several certificates in electronics and related fields from state vocational schools in Manitowoc and Sheboygan using his veterans' benefits. Veteran enrollment at vocational and technical schools, like that at other institutions, rose dramatically during the postwar years, from 877 in October 1945 to a peak of 12,147 in April 1947. By June 1948, Wisconsin's vocational and technical schools had provided training to 30,951 World War II veterans, or nearly 10 percent of the state's World War II veteran population.[27]

Veterans could even use their educational benefits to take approved correspondence courses. Correspondence courses provided veterans with opportunities to learn a trade or improve upon their skills while working and raising a family without having to attend classes. Bill Tritz of Waukesha, a mechanic, used his federal educational benefits to take several work-related correspondence courses. "I knew that I needed more education," he recalled, but, since he was working, "the only time I could get that was at night." Correspondence courses were widely available through colleges and universities, state and local boards of vocational education, and approximately 200 for-profit correspondence schools across the country. To qualify for federal benefits, veterans had to take correspondence courses from institutions certified in the state in which they operated, and the student-veteran could not receive living expenses. The quality of correspondence courses varied. Veterans were frequently warned about "fly-by-night" schools and "quack" correspondence courses, which sprang up to take advantage of the GI Bill and its beneficiaries. Francis Brown of the American Council on Education warned veterans to be wary of courses that made "excessive statements about the values to be received, diplomas and degrees given, and tie-ups with production concerns." Nevertheless, Brown conceded that if courses were chosen carefully, veterans could "wisely enroll" in a correspondence course to further their education. In 1946, 952 Wisconsin World War II veterans were taking correspondence courses.[28]

Although some campuses experienced floods of veterans, others received just a trickle. Veterans could use federal educational benefits to attend religious seminaries, for example, but few actually did. At Concordia College, a Lutheran theological seminary near Milwaukee, only three of the college's fifty-nine students in 1946 were veterans using federal benefits. Women's colleges also saw only modest numbers of veterans. Mount Mary College, a Catholic women's school in Milwaukee, saw enrollments rise due to the fact that women students were being forced from coeducational schools; only twenty of the school's 500 students in 1946 were veterans. Just one mile from the veteran-cramped University of Wisconsin campus was Edgewood College, a Catholic women's institution run by the Sinsinawan Dominican Sisters, which did not record a single student using the GI Bill or Public Law 16 between 1944 and 1956.[29]

Colleges and universities made numerous accommodations for student-veterans. For example, many institutions provided veterans with college credit for a variety of military experiences. As early as 1942, for example, the University of Wisconsin provided student-veterans with ten elective credits to former enlisted men and fifteen to officers (later equalized to fifteen credits irregardless of rank). In 1944, the university adopted a policy of permitting veterans "maximum flexibility in such matters as entrance requirements, attainment examinations, and substitution of courses or the earning of credit by examination, but without lowering standards of quality." Veterans who took part in the Army Specialized Training Program (ASTP) or the navy's V-12 program, which sent selected soldiers and sailors during the war to college campuses for specialized education and training in certain advanced fields, could have their work transferred to the university for credit. In addition, the university would usually accept other advanced military training received from correspondence courses administered by the U.S. Armed Forces Institute. Veterans were also exempt from mandatory physical education and military science classes. Most of Wisconsin's other colleges and universities followed the University of Wisconsin's lead in these areas.[30]

Many schools also provided accelerated and expanded schedules of classes for veterans. Beginning in the fall of 1945, the University of Wisconsin began abbreviated eight-week sessions to allow veterans to enter school at dates other than the beginning of the fall and spring semesters. It also expanded the class schedule, with the earliest classes beginning at 7:45 a.m. and night classes running as late as 9:30 p.m. The University of Wisconsin and other schools operated full-time summer sessions as well. Tiny Northland College began its first summer session ever in 1946. Officials at Northland found the eight-week session rather successful. The session enrolled sixty students, who "meant business," according to one observer. Other small institutions did not establish special sessions, but rather allowed transfer credits from other institutions on a liberal basis. The accelerated curricula allowed student-veterans to complete their schooling before their benefit entitlement expired. By expanding the days and hours of operation, universities and colleges could also reduce demand on class-rooms and other campus facilities.[31]

Colleges and universities offered their student-veterans a variety of counseling services. In 1945, the University of Wisconsin established the Office of Veterans' Affairs (OVA) to counsel veterans about their rights under state and federal benefit laws and to keep them up-to-date on any changes in benefit programs. The OVA established an information center in the heart of the campus and published a monthly newspaper. That year the university also established the Veterans' Business Office, which coordinated the payment of tuition and other benefits to veterans. At Marquette University, each college within the university appointed special guidance counselors for veterans. Many schools established veterans' affairs committees, composed typically of representatives of the registrar's office, administration, faculty, and guidance counselors, to assist veterans in navigating their way through college life and the government benefit programs. In addition, the federal Veterans' Administration had established its own counseling offices on six college campuses in Wisconsin by 1946.[32]

Wisconsin's colleges and universities assisted veterans in still other ways. Some schools provided student-veterans with remedial and refresher courses. The University of Wisconsin, for example, provided veterans with such courses in subjects such as mathematics and English. The university's law and medical schools offered refresher courses not only for students whose training had been interrupted by the war, but also for doctor and lawyer alumni-veterans who had been out of practice during the war years. Some institutions even allowed veterans who had not completed high school to enter. The University of Wisconsin, for example, admitted veterans who had not finished high school if they could "prove to the Registrar and the appropriate Dean" that they were capable of completing college work satisfactorily. Such proof typically included consideration of a veteran's high school record, military training and performance, and aptitude or achievement tests.[33]

The Veterans as Students

The veterans who went to college after the war were anxious to finish their education as quickly as possible. One reason was that veterans had a specific limit on the amount of the time for which they qualified for government assistance. However, the drive for economic security also pushed many veterans through college at a breakneck pace. Some felt that their military service had taken several productive years out of their lives. "We felt like we had three or four years that we had to make up," recalled navy surgery technician Lawrence Landgraf of Hayward, who attended the University of Wisconsin after the war. "There was that desire to get out, go to work, and get married," recalled army veteran Douglas Oldenburg of Madison, who also attended the University of Wisconsin. "I didn't want to take any more time in school than I had to." "I think everybody felt that way," surmised ex-bomber navigator and University of Wisconsin law student Sidney Podell. "Enough of being a school boy."[34]

Indeed, some veterans were so anxious to get to work that they left school or passed up the opportunity to attend college altogether. Army veteran Charles Howe of Monroe enrolled at nearby Platteville State to study agribusiness. "Now I can go to college because I got all this money from Uncle Sam," he recalled thinking. "It will take me all the way through." Howe delved into his studies, but within weeks of matriculating his brother approached him and proposed a business venture. "We were going to buy chickens and eggs and haul them to Chicago and make all kinds of money," Howe recalled. He left school in Platteville, and later his business venture collapsed as well. Howe did not return to school, but rather sought other employment. Navy veteran Mildred Beltmann of Milwaukee noted than in retrospect she and her husband (also a veteran) were "sorry" that they did not use the GI Bill, but remembered that after the war "we both wanted to get on with our lives, get married, settle down, and have a family." Although the drive for economic security drove many veterans to the campuses, in some cases it kept eligible veterans away from them.[35]

Anxious to finish school as quickly as possible, the majority of student-veterans were very serious and diligent students. William Appleman Williams spoke for millions when he described himself as being "highly motivated" in his studies. "I wasn't going to fool around," commented former Marquette University student-veteran David Brenzel. Veterans often viewed their studies as a job, and frequently described it that way. "I made it a job," recalled John Hall, who attended the University of Wisconsin. "It was business," claimed navy veteran LeRoy Dalton, a law student at the University of Wisconsin. Army veteran John Moses, another law student on the Madison campus, described student-veterans as being "deadly serious" about their studies. "There was the occasional dude who thought this was a free ride," recalled Dorwin Lamkin of Hudson, "but for the most part vets were pretty good students." Student-veterans like Kenneth Adrian, an air force veteran from Cassville who attended Platteville State, were in the minority. "Before the war we had to work pretty hard," he recalled, but "after the war the government was paying for it [and] we didn't study as hard."[36]

Whether resuming their studies interrupted by the war or entering college for the first time, student-veterans had usually been out of a classroom setting for several years. Many veterans expressed anxieties about acquiring or redeveloping the study habits necessary to succeed in school. The ability to focus and concentrate proved particularly hard for those veterans suffering from war-related psychological problems (see chapter 3). In a freshman English class at Northland College in 1946, student-veterans were asked to summarize their first year in school. Many noted concern about resuming their studies, but also that they were able to conquer those problems. The following comment was typical:

> After being out of school for approximately eight years—four years of that spent in service—I wasn't very enthusiastic about going to school again. Concentrating on assignments outside of school was very hard. There was always

something more pleasurable than to sit and pore over some dry book, or to try
to work out problems that didn't make any sense anyway. This task of applying
myself was probably the hardest thing to learn.

But once study habits had been developed, many veterans began to enjoy school.
"I soon found to my surprise," wrote another student-veteran in the class, "that I
was enjoying myself. Books and my studies gradually acquired a brighter aspect."[37]

Some veterans needed little acclimation to college life. Indeed, some hun-
gered for their studies and thrived in the academic environment. Stoughton navy
veteran Robert Beckstrand, who pursued a career as a Lutheran minister, described Oberlin College in Ohio as a "grind factory," but he enjoyed the hard
work all the same. "I just found the homework interesting," he recalled. "[I was]
glad to delve into it, just eager." Sidney Podell "jumped into summer school" at
the University of Wisconsin as soon as he returned home, and reveled in his
studies. "My mind was like virgin soil," he remembered. "It was a real pleasure
and I worked very hard." Even veterans who had not been to college before the
war found themselves intellectually stimulated. Army veteran Jack Chase of
Milwaukee claimed that in his studies at the University of Wyoming knowledge
"soaked in pretty quickly" after the war. "There was plenty of room for it," he
claimed. "There was a brain up there, but nothing in it."[38]

The diligence of the student-veteran paid off in terms of grades. Campuses
across the nation noted that veterans had better grades than their nonveteran
counterparts. At the University of Wisconsin, for example, student-veterans consistently had a higher grade point average (GPA) than did nonveterans. During
the spring semester of 1946, for example, male undergraduate veterans had a
grade point average of 1.66, compared to nonveteran undergraduates who compiled a 1.57 average. Married veterans compiled an even higher GPA, averaging
1.80. "One of the reasons for the showing of these veterans with families," according to university adviser Paul L. Trump, was that "they are taking this
education business in dead seriousness because they have responsibilities, in
contrast with Joe College of yesteryear." Veterans consistently outperformed
nonveterans in grades. In the spring of 1947, veterans compiled a 1.673 GPA,
compared with the nonveteran average of 1.582. Women veterans outperformed
non-veteran women. In the spring of 1946, women veterans had a 1.648 GPA,
and non-veteran women 1.613. The trend was evident at other schools as well.
"Most of the men" with perfect 4.0 GPAs at Beloit College in the fall semester
of 1946, the *Beloit College Bulletin* reported, "are GI students."[39]

Veterans who had started college before the war and resumed their education afterward often noted that their classroom performance was much improved. Many ascribed their scholastic success to having matured while in the
military. Ex-fighter pilot and law student D. C. Pressentin believed "that hiatus
in my education really helped me, because I don't think I was mature enough to
go to school" before the war. Many veterans attributed their improved academic
success directly to their war experiences. University of Wisconsin returning stu-

dent Roger Scovill claimed that "the discipline I learned in the Marine Corps had trained me eloquently for being able to assume a study program" he could not have undertaken before the war. "My grades improved through my sophomore, junior, and senior years," he recalled, "and I was able to drag my poor freshman records out of the mud" and graduate in the top one-third of his class. Sidney Podell claimed that the war "settled me down" and provided him with a "therapeutic interlude" in his studies. "Before the war, I didn't really know what I wanted to do and I really wasn't concerned about grades," recalled Podell, "and if something [more interesting came up] I cut class." A study of returning students at the University of Wisconsin indicated that 99 out of 114 of them had higher grades after the war as compared to their prewar scholastic performance.[40]

Numerous observers noted that the student-veteran of the 1940s was career directed. However, the career paths that the veterans chose varied considerably. Many veterans pursued studies in technical fields and other well-paying occupations. At the University of Wisconsin, 27.6 percent of veterans in the class of 1949 were in the College of Engineering, for example, compared to just 16 percent of nonveterans. However, most student-veterans that year, 38.1 percent, studied the liberal arts, pursuing work in a wide variety of disciplines. According to the American Council on Education, liberal arts ranked first among the academic fields that veterans chose most frequently using the GI Bill and Public Law 16. According to the survey, engineering, medicine, and law ranked among the most popular fields of veterans, but so did education, art, and music. World War II student-veterans may have been serious and career-driven, but they pursued careers in a wide variety of professions.[41]

The older, mature, and experienced veterans posed a challenge to the traditional relationships and institutions on campus. For example, student-veterans interacted with the faculty differently than did nonveteran students, both at the undergraduate and graduate levels. Most college and university professors expected to be treated with deference and respect. Young college students in their late teens or early twenties—often awed by these instructors—usually provided it. However, veterans who had commanded troops in the field, administered far-reaching operations, or endured the hardships of combat tended to view their college professors not as gods but as mere mortals. "We didn't want to be treated like children," recalled medical student Gordon Marlow, and student-veterans made that sentiment clear to the faculty. For the most part, the student-veterans listened politely to their instructors and respected their academic expertise. However, many veterans were willing to speak up and challenge their professors if they did not agree with them. William Appleman Williams recalled a graduate seminar in which the professor "got so infernally absurd that I got up and walked out." The professor "made it his business to get a hold of me over the phone and ask me for an explanation," he recalled. Williams replied simply that "I got bored to death with the nonsense." The professor conceded that "I know some of my lectures are pretty routine," and added, "You GIs don't mess around, do you?"[42]

Student-veterans were more than just cranky; they raised the level of intellectual discourse in many classrooms. Madisonian Frank Freese recalled that one of his professors at Syracuse University remarked to him that it was "easier to teach GIs" because they "didn't sit there and take everything, they would question. If they didn't agree with you, they'd start arguing with you." William Appleman Williams, who later became a prominent member of the history faculty at the University of Wisconsin, reflected back on his years as a graduate student there in the years after World War II. "The combination of excellent faculty and alert veterans created an interplay between students and faculty that has been largely forgotten in all the talk about the silent generation of the 1950s and the activism of the 1960s," he wrote. "Many, many GIs were able to harvest the bountiful intellectual crops that grew in Madison between 1946 and 1951."[43]

Faculty members often had great respect for the interested and serious student-veterans. Navy veteran Sterling Schallert attended law school at the University of Wisconsin before the war and completed his studies afterward. Schallert noted a changed attitude by the faculty members toward the students. In particular, he recalled an "old irascible" professor named Herbert Page, who before the war was "very sarcastic to us," but afterward was "very congenial" and even told jokes in class. University of Wisconsin medical resident Anthony Richtsmeier also noted how his mentors treated him and other residents with considerable respect, despite the rigorous training they received. "Even though we had to work in serfdom," he recalled, "they treated us as equals because we were all so much older." "My conception of the professors as dried up old codgers peering over a pile of books proved wrong," admitted former Northland College student-veteran Jerry Patterson. According to him, professors "met us half way" in "solving our problems," and that classes were "presented with enough color to make it interesting one man to another." In class, "everything goes," claimed Patterson. "Even our GI sense of humor (modified form, of course) is allowed."[44]

The veterans also had the respect of the nonveteran students. Army air force pilot Robert Dean of Scandinavia recalled that nonveteran undergraduates at Luther College in Iowa "respected" and "looked up to" the veterans. However, the veterans often looked upon the younger nonveteran students with indifference. With veterans making up a majority of male students on many campuses, the nonveteran male student was often seemingly invisible. Navy veteran Fred Risser of Madison (son the Progressive state senator Fred Risser) recalled that veterans were so common during his time at the University of Oregon that those men who were not veterans seemed somehow "different." Some veterans even looked upon the nonveterans contemptuously. Combat medic John Dunn saw nonveteran students at Marquette University as being "much younger and less mature." He admitted that such an attitude might seem "strange," since the veterans really "weren't that much older," but attributed the difference to military experiences, noting that in combat "you mature very, very fast in some ways." Ex-fighter pilot Wesley Todd of Wauwatosa attended the Citadel military academy in South Carolina before the war, but after the war did not want to return to a military environment. Todd visited the University of Wisconsin and Lawrence College, but was unimpressed. "Everybody looked so childish to me," he recalled, that he opted to go into business rather than return to college.[45]

Having endured months and years of military discipline, student-veterans chafed at the rules and regulations of college life. In the late 1940s, universities and colleges employed a system of *in loco parentis* (in the place of parents), involving rigorous enforcement of curfews, bed checks, and other such procedures. Administrators were sometimes at a loss as to how to treat the older, more mature student-veteran. Veterans disliked being treated like the younger students. For example, army veteran Calvin Hewitt of Kenosha, a survivor of the northern European campaign, was taken aback when Beloit College called his parents when school officials became concerned about his grades. For the most part, colleges and universities suspended the rules of *in loco parentis* for the veterans, and accommodated the wishes of these older students. For example, Platteville State allowed a smoking lounge in the college's main hall "largely as a result of pressure from the veterans." When the veterans left the campuses after 1950, colleges and universities resumed the practice of *in loco parentis*, which was eventually overturned by the student activism of the 1960s.[46]

Veterans were exempt from mandatory Reserve Officer Training Corps (ROTC) training on most campuses. After the war, some veterans enjoyed harassing the nonveterans who were required to participate in the program. Frank Freese recalled that at Syracuse University he and other veterans "used to stand around the quadrangle making fun of the poor kids who were marching around, making fools of themselves." At the University of Wisconsin, D-Day veteran Milo Flaten entered the advanced ROTC program for a little extra money. Flaten and other ROTC cadets marched in a parade in Madison celebrating the centennial of Wisconsin statehood in 1948. As they marched up Madison's State Street from the campus to the capitol, Flaten recalled that his fellow veterans greeted his unit with much derision. "About fifteen guys" according to Flaten—many known to him personally—stood on the roof of a local tavern overlooking the street and "threw eggs at my unit as we went up State Street in this parade."[47]

Veterans typically refused to participate in old college traditions such as the wearing of freshmen beanies and various hazing rituals, and it was the rare nonveteran who was brave enough to confront the student-veteran about such matters. Many veterans also looked with disdain upon fraternities and sororities. "We . . . didn't pay any attention to fraternities [or] sororities," claimed former University of Wisconsin student-veteran Lawrence Landgraf. Army veteran Donald Wiberg of Milwaukee, who attended the University of Minnesota, claimed that the studious, hard-working veterans "didn't have time for fraternities." John Dunn claimed that "fraternities . . . looked like kid stuff" to him. "I think most GIs thought the fraternity system was so childish as to be beneath their time and trouble," wrote William Appleman Williams.[48]

Not all veterans held such opinions. As the enrollment of veterans rose, so did membership in "Greek" organizations. Ex-bomber pilot Rupert Cornelius noted that his fraternity at the University of Wisconsin was "filled with veterans." Even after years of military service, Cornelius claimed that being a member of a fraternity "taught me there's a lot of different kind of guys in the world and you've got to learn how to get along with them." Fraternities grew on other campuses as well. At Lawrence College, each of the college's five fraternities were reported to be "filled to capacity." At Beloit College, the Pi Kappa Alpha fraternity was revived after World War II, with returning veterans providing "the nucleus of the revived chapter." However, as historian Keith Olson has pointed out, many veterans joined Greek houses for different reasons than did traditional undergraduates. Joining a fraternity or sorority could provide the student-veteran with a place to live in a tight housing market, for example. Hazing rituals and other more traditional aspects of Greek campus life were downplayed or suspended during the veteran years. Because so many student-veterans were married, Greek social activities were often fairly subdued events that included the wives and families of members, as opposed to the rowdy drinking parties usually associated with such organizations. "The increased membership" spurred by veterans, Olson claimed, had ironically "helped to undermine the brotherhood theme of fraternities."[49]

Indeed, significant numbers of veterans participated in other traditional college activities. Veterans often dominated such extracurricular activities as sports, musical and drama groups, student government, and the school newspapers on campuses after 1945. Due to the intimacy of smaller schools, veteran involvement in such activities was probably increased at those institutions. Northland College in Ashland was typical of many small colleges in this respect. Northland saw extracurricular activities blossom with the return of the veterans. As the college's alumni magazine, the *Northern Light*, reported in 1946:

> The student paper has taken on new zest. The college annual is tuning to a whole new tempo. Instead of limited material having to submit to basketball drubbings, an impressive squad of men averaging well over six feet in height is running up an impressive number of victories. A men's chorus has been started, football for next year is in the air. Northland is definitely getting on a post war basis.

At Northland—as on other campuses—veterans played a key role in the revitalization of these activities. "Social activities meant little at first," one student-veteran at Northland reported, "but after a month I began taking interest—and I think that some of us are even getting a school spirit." Nevertheless, veterans probably partook in these activities with less zeal than did nonveterans. Officials at Northland noted that as the population of veterans began to decline in the late 1940s, there was "a greater interest in the rah-rah activities of college life" again.[50]

One activity student-veterans made time for was dating. Many veterans who started college unmarried often left school betrothed. The veterans—somewhat older, more mature, and overwhelmingly male—proved popular with female students. "Last year I didn't care how I dressed or what I looked like," one women student at Northland College was quoted as saying in 1946, "but look at me now! Classes are interesting, and it's fun do go down to the commons at mealtime." Robert Dean recalled that at Luther College veterans were "popular with the females," and that the nonveteran males "didn't like us too much for that." Some veterans attributed their popularity with women to generous government benefits. Ex-fighter pilot Clifford Bowers recalled of his days at the University of Wisconsin that "the old characters [veterans] had money, and when you have money you can have girls." A history of Northland College described the situation this way: "The girls, who had been victims of the manless years, found it 'perfectly heavenly'; and the veterans, after their experiences in the far places of the earth, seemed not to disagree!" Whatever the case, veterans often found time in the busy schedules for the opposite sex. The postwar "baby boom" had its origins, to a substantial degree, on the nation's college and university campuses.[51]

The student-veterans' lack of emphasis on social activities was due not only to their studiousness. Many were also married and had children. In 1946, fully 15 percent of Beloit College student-veterans were married. At the University of Wisconsin that same year, the figure was more than 20 percent. Madison army veteran Robert Esser recalled that during his time at the University of Wisconsin his social life generally consisted of "traveling around in married groups." In navy veteran Sterling Schallert's estimation, most of his fellow students in the law school were married, as he was, and many had children. The demographics of the law students changed the way they interacted, according to Schallert. "Smokers," all-male events before the war, "turned out to be family picnics" after the war.[52]

Despite increases in subsistence allowances from the federal government, some veterans using the GI Bill or Public Law 16 still found it difficult to make ends meet financially. Federal subsidies "cover the basic things," one University of Wisconsin student-veteran claimed in 1946, "but for clothes, laundry, dry cleaning, [and] social activities," the allowances fell short. "It covers room and board," reported another, "and nothing else." Student-veterans who were married and with children usually faced the toughest financial problems. "We were mostly eating hamburger that was laced with bread," claimed ex-cargo pilot Kenneth Johnson, who attended the University of Wisconsin. "That would continue on and on until there wasn't much meat in it, but mostly bread." To bring in more money, many student-veterans also held jobs. "About every third semester I had to take off and work," recalled Madison army veteran John Moses, who raised three children while attending the University of Wisconsin law school. Not all veterans experienced such dire economic circumstances, however. "We got by comfortably," claimed army veteran and University of Wisconsin medical student Sigurd Sivertson of La Crosse. But he added: "We didn't require much then. We were happy with the little we had."[53]

Due to a buoyant postwar employment market (see chapter 5), student-veterans were often able to find part-time work to supplement their federal subsistence checks. Student-veterans held a variety of jobs. Former University of

Wisconsin student-veteran Elmer Jaeger worked for a packing company in his
native Milwaukee during summers. Bernard Cook, an air force air traffic controller during the war, worked in a machine shop while attending the University
of Wisconsin extension in his hometown of Milwaukee and "did all my chemis-
try homework on the streetcar." Many students held more than one job. LeRoy
Dalton worked his way through the University of Wisconsin law school doing
janitorial work and selling programs at campus sporting events. Otto Junkermann, a navy veteran studying at the Layton School of Art in Milwaukee,
earned extra money doing freelance drafting and working on the bottling and
canning lines at the Schlitz brewery. "Most of the students would try to get work
like that," Junkermann recalled, because the breweries needed workers "just as
the summer vacation got started." Junkermann worked for Schlitz during the
school year as well, and recalled how he balanced school and work: "At 12 a.m.
I'd wind up at the brewery, then at 7 or 8 I'd get off and rush to school, then
after school I'd spend a couple of hours doing my drafting, and then I'd sleep on
weekends."[54]

Stress on Facilities

The influx of student-veterans after World War II not only changed traditional
relationships in American higher education, but it also changed the physical
structure of the college and university campuses. The flood of veterans over-
taxed existing classroom facilities and housing accommodations. In response,
colleges and universities began building programs. Like the changes to the social and cultural structure of higher education, many of the changes wrought by
the veterans were temporary, but also foreshadowed long-term changes at colleges and universities in Wisconsin and across America.

    The massive number of veterans in the schools crowded existing classroom
space. Former paratrooper Jack Dunn recalled that at Marquette University after
the war many of his classes were "ungodly large," and personal attention from
faculty members was all but impossible. The University of Wisconsin had the
most severe overcrowding problem. "I remember you'd come into some lecture
halls and if you didn't get there early you didn't get a seat," remembered John
Gill of his time there. "People were standing up along the walls." Those attending graduate and professional programs experienced the same crowding. Frank
Remington, former law student and air force veteran, recalled that "almost
never" could he find a seat in one class in Bascom Hall, "except on the stairs."
"I remember in the years after the war having seminars of twenty-five students,"
recalled University of Wisconsin history professor Merle Curti, a state of affairs
he called "ridiculous." Crowded classes could be especially difficult for disabled
veterans. Because of war wounds suffered in the Philippines, former University
of Wisconsin student Joseph Connors recalled that he "wasn't walking real fast,"
and "by the time I got [to class] all the seats would be taken." He eventually left
school.[55]

To expand the number of classrooms on campuses, colleges and universities erected temporary buildings. In Wisconsin, no campus contained as many temporary buildings as that of the University of Wisconsin in Madison. Beginning in 1946, the university obtained temporary structures from the federal government and placed them in various areas around the campus. The first temporary classroom buildings on campus were surplus Quonset huts—corrugated metal structures characterized by their semicircular shape. Most of the Quonsets were located in and around the Library Mall at the east end of campus, where they provided classrooms and library space. The Quonset structures seemed misplaced and unsightly amidst the stately permanent buildings of the mall. Standing before the elegant Greek Revival Wisconsin State Historical Society building was a large Quonset surrounded by several smaller ones, sometimes referred to as the "sow and little pigs." In 1947, the university also obtained surplus military barracks and office buildings from Camp McCoy (an army ninety miles northwest of Madison), disassembled them, and rebuilt them on the campus. Most of the twenty-six temporary buildings were located on the west end of campus, providing classrooms and laboratories for science and engineering students, as well as a cafeteria.[56]

Other Wisconsin schools used temporary buildings to accommodate the influx of student-veterans. Marquette University obtained more than a dozen surplus buildings from the federal government and used them for classrooms. Even some of the state's smallest institutions erected temporary buildings obtained from the federal government. Northland College used a surplus military building to "provide a temporary student union until a permanent one could be built." Beloit College managed to obtain an unused aircraft hangar (measuring 160 by 180 feet, and 43 feet high) and converted it into a permanent field house. The college made modifications to the structure, such as installing a glass façade and erecting brick buildings on the sides, making the structure appear less military. The field house held more than 2,000 people for sporting events and assemblies for the growing college. "The purchase price effected a great saving over the cost of such a building erected on a regular contract basis," the college crowed, and it "became immediately available whereas regular construction at this time would not be possible."[57]

The enlarged student bodies, along with the expanded classroom facilities, necessitated the hiring of more teachers. According to a 1946 study by the *New York Times*, fully 30 percent of 500 colleges and universities surveyed reported shortages of instructors. At the University of Wisconsin, the number of assistant, associate, and full professors rose from 618 in 1940 to 897 by 1948. Increases came mostly in the lower ranks, with the number of assistant professors rising by 54 percent during that period. The ranks of nontenure-track instructors grew even faster, from 418 in 1940 to 870 in 1948. Other colleges and universities also hired many new faculty members in the immediate postwar years. At Lawrence College, the faculty (full-time and part-time) grew from sixty-one in 1946 to eighty by 1948. Between 1946 and 1948, the size of the Beloit College faculty grew from fifty-six to eighty-eight. In the search for new instructors, schools often hired teachers who had not completed their doctoral programs. Of Beloit College's thirteen new assistant professors and instructors in 1948, only two had Ph.D. degrees, and three more were in the process of completing those degrees.[58]

At major universities such as the University of Wisconsin, the influx of World War II veterans greatly increased the use of teaching assistants. The use of graduate assistants in teaching at colleges and universities in the United States dates to the nineteenth century. However, it was the boom in enrollments after World War II that brought the use of teaching assistants, in the words of one scholar, into "full flower." Between 1940 and 1948, the use of graduate assistants to teach classes more than doubled, from 665 to 1,402. Many of the veterans disliked the use of temporary instructors and teaching assistants. "I think I had one class from a full staff member," recalled army veteran James Zeasman of his days at the University of Wisconsin. "Otherwise, they were all teaching assistants, except for lecture sections." Others did not view their teaching assistants so negatively. Ex-bomber navigator Paul Fergot, for example, remembered how both faculty and teaching assistants "took a personal interest" in his work.[59]

Indeed, many of the part-time and unranked instructors and teaching assistants were veterans themselves. While attending graduate school in geology at the University of Wisconsin, navy veteran Daniel Turner received an instructorship, and recalled that many of his colleagues were veterans as well. Before the war, Madison's Gordon Marlow had completed one year of medical school at the University of Wisconsin until he "ran out of money" and joined the navy. Returning to campus in September 1945, he expected that he would have to take his first year over again. Instead, he was told that the medical school was "very short of instructors," and was asked to teach histology and neurology. The following year he joined the medical school class he had been teaching. Indeed, many of the tenure-track faculty hired were World War II veterans as well. Of the thirteen new faculty Beloit College hired in 1948, nine had seen military service in World War II.[60]

The greatest practical problem facing most colleges and universities following World War II—in Wisconsin and across the nation—was that of housing the veterans who flooded the campuses. The 1946 *New York Times* survey of colleges indicated that fully 80 percent of the schools queried experienced housing shortages for students. Traditionally, schools housed students in dormitories. However, existing dormitories, which had been relatively sparsely populated during the Great Depression and World War II, became crowded with the return of the veterans. Schools developed various strategies for coping. The University of Wisconsin, for example, converted single dormitory rooms to double rooms. Before the war, the university's Tripp Hall had a capacity of 250 students, but after the war was reconfigured to house more than 400. Other schools followed suit. At Beloit College, two women's dormitories were converted to cramped facilities for men, and women in the remaining dorms were forced to "double up." Even with such measures, colleges and universities had difficulty housing their students adequately. In particular, there were virtually no facilities for veterans married and with children.[61]

Colleges and universities also assisted veterans in finding apartments or rooms in the community. However, because of a severe postwar housing crunch, student-veterans had difficulty finding off-campus housing. Many veterans lived with their parents and commuted to school. Robert Esser of Madison was one who lived with his parents while attending the University of Wisconsin under Public Law 16, and recalled that he "saved money while . . . in school." Veterans like Esser were fortunate; for others, attending college could often involve traveling significant distances. Ralph Jacobsen attended the University of Wisconsin, but lived with his wife at his parents' home in Stoughton, a small city twenty miles south of Madison. He drove to Madison daily with six other student-veterans, all living in the Stoughton area. Army veteran Richard Eager commuted even farther to Madison, traveling more than twenty-five miles from the village of Evansville. Of the 483 men enrolled at Beloit College in the fall of 1946, 60 commuted to Beloit from another city, and from as far away as Rockford, Illinois—twenty miles to the south.[62]

Once again, surplus government facilities helped colleges and universities house the flood of veterans going to college on the GI Bill and other veterans' programs. By 1947, the University of Wisconsin had created 2,680 temporary housing units for veterans and their families, primarily through surplus government buildings. On many college campuses after the war, so-called "vetsvilles" sprang up to house the student-veterans. Perhaps the first such vetsville in the United States was located at the southwestern corner of the University of Wisconsin campus at Camp Randall Park. During the Civil War, Camp Randall had been the primary training ground for soldiers in Wisconsin. By the time of World War II, the Camp Randall grounds had become the home of the university's athletic facilities and engineering buildings, and was one of the last open spaces in the campus area. Civil War monuments dotted the park, and the university's president, E. B. Fred, sought the blessing of the local Civil War descendants' organization before deploying the trailers in the park. In the aftermath of World War II, Camp Randall would be used to house student-veterans, many of whom lived among the memorials to a previous war.[63]

In August 1945, the university began installing of ninety-one house trailers, obtained from the federal government, on the Camp Randall grounds. The first veterans moved into the trailers the following month. The trailers were arranged in grids on the grassy areas of the park, with boardwalks connecting the units. Because the trailers had no running water, residents of "Randall Park," as the site became known, shared common toilet and laundry units. The facility was open only to married veterans, who were charged $25 a month for smaller units and $32.50 for the larger "expansive" trailers. As the number of student-veterans increased, so did the number of trailers at Camp Randall. By early 1946, an additional 113 trailers were installed on nearby grounds along Monroe Street, in a complex that became known as "Monroe Park." Because of their proximity to campus, the Camp Randall trailer parks were the most popular of the temporary student-veteran housing projects.[64]

As the student population continued to grow in the postwar years, the university opened other housing facilities off campus. Truax Field, an army air force base six miles northeast of the campus on the outskirts of Madison, provided housing for single as well as married student-veterans. The Truax student housing facility opened in January 1946 when the university converted the base hospital into an apartment building. The former hospital housed 562 single male veterans and 100 couples without children. Later that year, the university gained control of other buildings on the base, which housed an additional 960 single men and provided space for a cafeteria, a library, and recreational facilities. Two miles west of the campus, married students lived in a complex of resort cabins, trailers, and Quonset huts known as University Cabin Courts, which the university purchased in 1946 in the midst of the housing crunch. In a wooded area at the far western end of the campus, about 200 students even lived in a tent colony along the shores of Lake Mendota during summer sessions, with the university providing toilet facilities and other basic amenities.[65]

The largest facility for housing student-veterans at the University of Wisconsin was located thirty-five miles from the campus. Badger Village, as the facility was known, adjoined the Badger Ordnance Works between Sauk City and Baraboo, at the foot of the scenic Baraboo Range. During the war, ordnance workers lived in a complex of temporary housing units across the road from the plant, and when the war ended they moved out and the student-veterans moved in. The north end of the complex consisted of row houses, while the south side was composed of military barracks. Badger Village was a self-contained community of 2,700 residents at its peak, complete with its own schools, community center, interdenominational church, fire company, newspaper, and even a federal post office. Rudyard Goodland, grandson of Wisconsin governor Walter S. Goodland, was reputed to have been the Badger Village's "first entrepreneur." In 1946, Goodland and another village resident established the Badger Beer Depot, an enterprise they sold two years later. Badger Village also had its own A&P grocery store, gas station, and barber shop.[66]

The quality of the dwellings at the Badger Village, Truax Field, and other makeshift housing facilities often left much to be desired. Susan Davis, a university counselor who worked with veterans' wives, described the accommodations at Badger Village in this way:

> The apartments themselves consist of a living room, a kitchenette, one or two bedrooms, one or two closets, and a bathroom with a shower. Hot running water and electricity are supplied by the university. Each apartment has a jacket heating stove. Cooking is done with a small coal stove. Both the inside and outside walls are made of plaster board, and are uninsulated.

The common toilet and laundry facilities in many of the complexes were uncomfortable and inconvenient, especially in winter. The standard coal-burning stoves posed numerous safety risks, and also left the interior of the veterans' homes covered in coal dust if not maintained carefully. In fact, the coal stoves were so unpopular that most residents purchased hot plates for cooking instead. As the population of the housing complexes rose, demand for electricity and water often outstripped supplies, resulting in frequent shortages of both. "In North Badger there were from three to five units on one circuit," according to one historian of the village. "Consequently only one person could iron at a time." Ex-cargo pilot Kenneth Johnson of Madison, an engineering student, recalled that he and his wife moved out of Badger Village "when the rats started to get aggressive." "I'd . . . have to kick the wall," as he remembered. "That would shut them up for awhile, but then they'd be back gnawing on the wall again."[67]

The thin walls of the temporary structures posed many problems. Paul Fergot, ex-bomber pilot and engineering student from Oshkosh, described his home in Badger Village as a "paper house." Perhaps the most common recollections of those who lived in the vetsvilles were those surrounding the close quarters and lack of privacy in the complexes. Note, for example, the following story commonly told among residents of the Badger Village:

> During lunch one of the husbands—only recently come to join his small family, rose ceremoniously, went to the storage cupboard, and returned with a catsup bottle, which he handed to his wife. "Thank you, dear, but why the catsup bottle," was the query. "Why," said Friend Husband, "I thought you asked for it." Laughter pealed out. "Oh, my no! That was Janet in the next apartment."

Brutal Wisconsin winters caused additional suffering. "When we had a real blizzard," Paul Fergot recalled, "the snow would blow in between the roof and the wall, and when you'd wake up in the morning there'd be a blanket of snow on the bed." "Living there was not exactly like being a pioneer going across the country," according to Kenneth Johnson, "but it wasn't exactly what you'd call being in the lap of luxury."[68]

The veterans and their spouses were allowed, indeed even encouraged, to "spruce up" their apartments and trailers. Susan Davis described the work of young couples in the converted hospital building at the Truax complex:

> Really the couples worked hard—papering, painting, varnishing. The wives made attractive drapes and bed covers; the men concocted shelves and cupboards, made lamps and hung pictures. Order came out of chaos, coziness, and color supplanted drabness and bareness. Pride and artistic ability made even the prosaic "delivery" room of the hospital an attractive living room.

In Badger Village, one young mother "painted a design of animals on the children's wall," one observer noted, "and when the last snow leaked in she added some large black bees to cover the spots." William Cameron, who had been a student-veteran at the Truax complex, recalled how residents frequently "scrounged" for items to decorate their homes. Residents also spruced up the exteriors of their homes, decorating them with window boxes and vines. At

Badger Village, residents had access to a garden plot, which helped supplement the family diet. "In gardens set down in the heart of Wisconsin's choicest farm lands," Susan Davis noted, "how the vegetables do grow!" In all of the university's housing complexes, veterans and their families made the austere accommodations as livable and attractive as they could.[69]

However, residents also found themselves making more practical alterations to improve upon old or faulty equipment. For example, frozen pipes were a common problem in uninsulated buildings and trailers. Bernard Cook of Milwaukee recalled how Badger Village residents frequently poured salt down the drains to keep them from freezing. "Sometimes it worked," he recalled, "and sometimes it didn't." Ex-cargo pilot and law student Frank Remington (who would later become a distinguished faculty member of the university's law school), lived in a row house in Badger Village. He recalled how "some people, in an attempt to have hot water, would strap oil burners onto the water tank in the bathroom, and on more than one occasion burned a hole through the roof of the row house." Remington described the frequency of such fires as "disconcerting."[70]

For those living at remote sites such as Truax Field or Badger Village, the university ran buses to and from the campus. Those veterans living at Badger Village had an especially arduous journey, having to catch early buses for morning classes and returning home late at night. Army veteran Richard Bates recalled his schedule taking the "old World War I school buses" from Badger Village to the campus in Madison. "I used to catch the 6:15 a.m. bus three days a week," Bates remembered. "I'd come back on the 5:15 bus. The other two days I'd have a night class, both semesters. Then I'd catch the 10:15 bus, and we'd get back—if we were lucky—about 11:30, and then catch the 6:15 bus the next morning." "You did a lot of sleeping on the bus," recalled Badger Village resident Paul Fergot, "and you tried to do homework. It was difficult, but you could read texts." However, the old buses frequently broke down. Paul Fergot recalled that on one ride to campus "the wheel fell off." According to Kenneth Johnson, one winter day the door of the bus was stuck open. "In the middle of winter we were going home with that blast of air," he recalled. "We were sitting there huddled up as close as we could get . . . to keep from freezing to death." The university seriously considered holding classes at Badger Village to help relieve the veterans' transportation woes and spare the ancient buses until the university obtained several newer buses from the federal government in 1947.[71]

If married veterans were unusual at the University of Wisconsin before the war, children were an even more extraordinary sight. Anxious to begin families, student-veterans often began having children while still attending school. Badger Village and the Camp Randall trailer parks, in particular, were inundated with children, mostly infants. Fully 75 percent of couples in the Camp Randall complex had children, for example. As a football player, marine veteran Farnham "Gunner" Johnson lived inside Camp Randall Stadium, which overlooked the Randall Park and Monroe Park trailer complexes. "You'd look down and see the trailers and little kids running around," he recalled, "and it looked like a primitive painting." "So many babies were born at Badger Village," according to one historian of the facility, "that on Halloween some pranksters changed the large Badger Village entrance sign to read, 'Rabbit Village.'"[72]

Raising children amid the makeshift housing facilities of the campus, as well as around the hectic schedules of the student-veteran, could pose more of a parenting challenge than usual. "How does a young mother," asked Susan Davis, "with a tiny baby, manage to do the family washing in a central laundry with no place to 'store' her baby?" Davis noted the solution of one young mother at Randall Park. "Six-fifteen on many a dark wintry morning found her at the laundry and she was back at her trailer," she wrote, "work completed, before her husband left for his seven-forty-five [sic] class on the hill. Stamina, I guess you call it." However, child rearing among so many other young parents also had its advantages. Couples frequently exchanged babysitting, for example. The university not only established schools at Badger Village and Camp Randall, but also provided nurseries for infants and preschoolers. The nursery school provided "proper outlets for [children's] pent-up muscles and minds," according to Susan Davis, as well as time for the parents to study, work, or even enjoy the "infrequent tonic" of relaxation.[73]

In fact, family life in the university's various vetsvilles could often pose a challenge to young, newly married couples. As in any community, domestic disputes sometimes erupted. However, Susan Davis suggested that a kind of community watchfulness and solidarity usually kept such tensions in check. "Late reading aloud and family arguments," she observed, "just don't survive many 'goings over' by Mr. And Mrs. Next Door. Because these young people speak most directly and say what they think, misunderstandings and disagreements are relatively short lived." Perhaps the major problem facing the veterans' wives was a sense of loneliness and isolation—especially at the distant Truax and Badger Village communities. The student-veterans' wives kept busy in numerous ways. Many women worked outside the home to supplement the family income. Others attended school themselves, including many wives who were also war veterans. The Red Cross also sponsored daytime activities for the camp wives, including sewing, knitting, and various arts and crafts. "We can put up with it now," one historian of the village quoted many young wives as saying, "because we know that next year or a year from June it will all be over, and we can move into a conventional home."[74]

Student-veterans from racial and ethnic minorities also required housing at the University of Wisconsin, but housing was an area in which minorities had long faced discrimination. Although no formal policy of racial segregation existed on the campus, race relations were a growing problem on the campus after 1945. Accounts of the racial climate with regard to campus housing vary. In her pamphlet on the student-veteran's wife, Susan Davis told the story of an African American woman named Pauline Coggs, wife of student-veteran Theodore Coggs of Milwaukee, and resident of the Monroe Park trailer complex. The Coggses were prominent and respected members of the Monroe Park community, according to Davis. Both Mr. and Mrs. Coggs were active in the Monroe

Park student government, Mrs. Coggs serving as its secretary-treasurer, and Mr. Coggs as its second mayor. "The Monroe Villagers tell you," Davis wrote, "that living closely as they do, with a unique opportunity to observe each other's capacities and achievements, tends to level completely racial and religious intolerances and prejudices."[75]

However, racial tensions did exist on the campus in the post-World War II years. In a survey of students taken by the student newspaper, the *Daily Cardinal*, in the spring of 1945 (just before the veterans began to overwhelm the campus), only 2 percent of respondents stated that they would object to sitting next to an African American in class. However, blacks and whites living in the same housing facilities proved to be more controversial. According to the survey, 18 percent of students stated that they would move out of their dormitory or apartment if an African American was permitted to move in, and 11 percent believed that landlords would be justified in refusing to rent to black students. Although 66 percent believed that "inter-racial cooperative houses should be encouraged on campus," fully 46 percent of students also stated that that it "would be better for all concerned if Negro students lived by themselves in separate rooming houses." Stemming from an incident in which a black graduate student was forced to move out of the University Club, a student committee in 1949 called for the elimination of all questions relating to race on applications for housing. The university's residence halls director, Lee Burns, denied that black students were in any way segregated in campus housing facilities. Nevertheless, the university eliminated all references to race on housing applications and included an equal rights statement on the applications for good measure.[76]

The housing experiences of Madison's student-veterans and their families were shared by those on other Wisconsin campuses. Like the University of Wisconsin, many of the smaller state-run and private colleges imported trailers. At Platteville State, for example, thirty house trailers deployed near the school's athletic facilities accommodated married veterans on that campus. Smaller schools were also able to obtain surplus buildings from the military. At the Stout Institute in Menomonie, married veterans lived in barracks the college obtained from a military base in Iowa. At Beloit College, veterans were temporarily housed in the gymnasium until its military barracks were ready for occupancy. The college also asked veterans "to have their wives remain at home until the units are completed." Northland College obtained six army barracks for student-veteran housing, three for married veterans and three for single men.[77]

Smaller institutions attempted a variety of other methods to house the veterans. At Whitewater State Teachers College, veterans were housed in the local armory. In addition to housing veterans in barracks and Quonset huts, Lawrence College also housed men "in the east annex of the conservatory of music, basement rooms in Main Hall, and in the Alexander gymnasium." Eau Claire State Teachers College not only received surplus government buildings, but it also purchased homes near the campus for housing purposes. Ripon College purchased a number of homes for both married veterans and faculty members, as well as erected seven temporary barracks obtained from the federal government, including three in a distant section of campus known as "Siberia."[78]

Despite the harsh conditions in the campus housing projects, veterans later looked back fondly at their years in them. It was in these years that reunited couples could once again enjoy each other's company, and for newly married couples it was their very first years together. In addition, having grown up in depression and survived a war, living in "paper houses" under crowded conditions did not seem all that bad to many. Indeed, living with a spouse and children was probably more enjoyable under any conditions than living in an army barracks during morning reveille. The student-veterans also knew such conditions were temporary, and once their education was completed they could look forward to a new life with more economic security and material goods. Bernard Cook of Milwaukee, a survivor of the Badger Village, described his feeling about his days in student housing this way: "It was a great experience, but I wouldn't want to do it again." Paul Fergot summed up his experience at Badger Village this way: "You couldn't really ask for a much better life to come back to, as long as you could see the future."[79]

As the veterans completed their education, the makeshift classrooms and housing facilities began to disappear. Most of the Quonsets and temporary buildings were demolished or removed in the 1950s and 1960s during the campus building boom of those decades. However, the veteran influx following World War II helped to spur building programs at colleges and universities across Wisconsin and the nation. At the University of Wisconsin, construction on faculty housing began in 1947, and apartments for married students were completed in 1955. The university also undertook a massive program of dormitory construction. Smaller campuses also saw expansion too. Though the World War II student-veterans largely disappeared from college campuses by the mid-1950s, enrollments in that decade continued to climb, as prosperity and a variety of government programs put higher education within reach of millions of Americans. The student-veterans of World War II blazed the trail for the great wave of students in the so-called "baby boom" generation—often the children of World War II veterans—who arrived on America's college campuses in the 1960s.[80]

Conclusion

In a May 1950 editorial in the *Green Bay Press-Gazette*, Ira L. Baldwin, vice president of the University of Wisconsin asked: "May I tell you a success story from the vast educational experiment known as the GI Bill of Rights?" Baldwin told the story of a student-veteran named "Jim Jones," an ex-marine from rural Wisconsin who had studied agriculture the University of Wisconsin under the GI Bill. Jim, like other veterans, studied hard, received good grades, worked at an outside job to supplement his benefits, and graduated. Baldwin praised the GI Bill for allowing ordinary young men like Jim to go to college:

It applied to rich and poor, to those who could afford higher education and those who could not have attended colleges and universities without help. Undoubtedly there were a few who misused its benefits. There were hundreds of thousands, however, like Jim, who were given and eagerly accepted an opportunity to serve better their nation in peacetime.

Upward of five million World War II veterans attended a college, university, trade, or technical school at government expense. The veterans, in unexpectedly large numbers, eagerly pursued education in a great variety of occupations and professions, with the hope of finding a secure place in the postwar economy. [81]

After graduation, these men and women had to utilize those skills in the workaday world of postwar America. As originally envisioned and drafted during the 1940s, the GI Bill was largely an effort to forestall unemployment, by keeping veterans in school and out of the bread line, and preparing them for a place in the postwar economy. While the veterans were in school, unemployment remained in check. But what would happen as the student-veterans filtered into the civilian economy?

Notes

1. For more on the origins and development of the GI Bill of Rights, as well as its historiography, see chapter 1.

2. Keith Olson, *The GI Bill, the Veterans, and the Colleges* (Lexington: University Press of Kentucky, 1974), 36-39; U.S. House Committee on Veterans' Affairs, *Laws Relating to Veterans and Their Dependents Enacted on and after September 16, 1940*, 80th Cong., 2d sess., 1948, Committee Print 357, 13, 29.

3. Davis R. B. Ross, *Preparing for Ulysses: Politics and Veterans during World War II* (New York: Columbia University Press, 1969), 38-49; Francis J. Brown, *Educational Opportunities for Veterans* (Washington, D.C.: Public Affairs Press, 1946), 11-18.

4. Brown, *Educational Opportunities for Veterans*, 18-19.

5. Wisconsin Legislative Reference Bureau, *Wisconsin Blue Book*, 1946 ed. (Madison: Legislative Reference Bureau, 1946), 145; *Wisconsin Journal of Education*, September 1944. For more on the development of WDVA policy toward educational grants, see chapter 1.

6. *Blue Book*, 1946 ed., 143-144; WDVA Board meeting minutes, 19 January 1951, Records of the Wisconsin Department of Veterans' Affairs, State Government Records, State Historical Society of Wisconsin Archives, Madison, Wis.

7. Olson, *GI Bill*, 28; Dorothy Baruch and Lee Edward Travis, *You're Out of the Service Now* (New York: Appleton-Century, 1946), 127-131; Maxwell Droke, *Good-by to GI: How to Be a Successful Civilian* (New York: Abingdon-Cokesbury Press, 1945), 78-80.

8. Bohstedt interview, Wisconsin Veterans' Oral History Project, Wisconsin Veterans' Museum Research Center, Madison, Wis. (cited hereafter as WVOHP); Donald Wiberg interview, WVOHP.

9. *New York Times Magazine*, 12 August 1945; *Capital Times*, 21 January 1946.

10. Smith interview, WVOHP; Cornelius interview, WVOHP; Spohn interview, WVOHP.

11. Droke, *Good-by to GI*, 75, 79-80; Onhieber interview, WVOHP; Bohstedt interview, WVOHP; Graven interview, WVOHP.

12. Gill interview, WVOHP; Rowley interview, WVOHP.

13. Edsall interview, WVOHP; Lamkin interview, WVOHP; Dalton interview, WVOHP.

14. Norman Fredericksen and William B. Schrader, *Adjustment to College* (Princeton, N.J.: Educational Testing Service, 1951); Neil Fligstein, *The GI Bill: Its Effects on the Educational and Occupational Attainments of US Males, 1940-1973* (Madison: Center for Demography and Ecology, University of Wisconsin-Madison, 1976); Olson, *GI Bill*, 45-49.

15. Charles Bolté and Louis Harris, *Our Negro Veterans* (New York: Public Affairs Committee, 1947), 10-15, 18-20; David H. Onskt, "'First a Negro . . . Incidentally a Veteran': Black World War II Veterans and the GI Bill of Rights in the Deep South, 1944-1948," *Journal of Social History* 31 (1998): 527-532; Neil A. Wynn, *The Afro-American and the Second World War*, rev. ed. (New York: Holmes and Meier, 1993), 115-116.

16. Brunsell interview, WVOHP; *Wisconsin State Journal*, 12 January 1946.

17. According to the survey, undertaken at the University of Cincinnati, only the University of California at Berkeley, University of Minnesota, University of Illinois, and Ohio State University had higher numbers of veterans. *Capital Times*, 30 December 1947.

18. William Appleman Williams, "My Life in Madison," in Paul Buhle, ed., *History and the New Left: Madison, Wisconsin, 1950-1970* (Philadelphia: Temple University Press, 1992), 266.

19. Olson, *GI Bill*, 85; *University of Wisconsin Press Bulletin*, 9 February 1944; *Milwaukee Journal*, 27 October 1946.

20. Onhieber interview, WVOHP; Cumming interview, WVOHP; Olson, *GI Bill*, 84-85, 87-88; *Capital Times*, 23 May 1945.

21. Lucht interview, WVOHP; Raphael N. Hamilton, *The Story of Marquette University: An Object Lesson in the Development of Catholic Higher Education* (Milwaukee, Wis.: Marquette University Press, 1953), 331, 365; *Capital Times*, 5 December 1945; *Milwaukee Journal*, 27 October 1947.

22. Smith interview, WVOHP; Zeasman interview, WVOHP.

23. Walker D. Wyman, ed., *History of the Wisconsin State Universities* (River Falls, Wis.: River Falls State University Press, 1968), 262-264; Justus F. Paul, *The World Is Ours: A History of the University of Wisconsin-Stevens Point, 1894-1994* (Stevens Point, Wis.: Foundation Press, 1994), 83-84; Richard D. Gamble, *From Academy to University, 1866-1966: A History of Wisconsin State University, Platteville, Wisconsin* (Platteville: Wisconsin State University, 1966), 262-263; Thomas B. Lundeen, *Jubilee! A History of the College of Engineering at the University of Wisconsin-Platteville* (Platteville: University of Wisconsin-Platteville, 1983), 87-88. The Wisconsin Institute of Technology was eventually merged with Platteville State in 1959, and is now known as the University of Wisconsin-Platteville.

24. Robert Ashley and George H. Miller, *Ripon College: A History* (Ripon, Wis.: Ripon College Press, 1990), 172; Nathaniel B. Dexter, *Northland College: A History* (Ashland, Wis.: Northland College, 1968), 182; *Northern Light*, September-October 1947; *Lawrence Alumnus*, October 1947; *Beloit College Bulletin*, April 1946, September 1949.

25. *Northern Light*, April 1946; *Milwaukee Journal*, 27 October 1946.

26. Ray interview, WVOHP; Elver interview, WVOHP; Blake interview, WVOHP; Junkermann interview, WVOHP; *Milwaukee Journal*, 27 October 1946.
27. Fehling interview, WVOHP; Diefenthaler interview, WVOHP; Kathleen A. Paris, *A Political History of Vocational, Technical, and Adult Education in Wisconsin* (Madison: Wisconsin Board of Vocational, Technical, and Adult Education, 1985), 81-100; Robert James Spinti, "The Development of Trade and Industrial Education in Wisconsin" (Ed.D. diss., University of Missouri, 1968), 203-245.
28. Tritz interview, WVOHP; *New York Times*, 20 January 1946; Brown, *Educational Opportunities for Veterans*, 75-76; *Milwaukee Journal*, 27 October 1946.
29. *Milwaukee Journal*, 1 September 1946, 27 October 1946. Sister Jean Richter, keeper of the Edgewood College archives, provided the information on veteran enrollment at Edgewood College to the author.
30. For development of the University of Wisconsin's policy, see Olson, *GI Bill*, 81-82. Specific policies regarding the transfer of credits and aptitude testing at individual institutions may be found in Wisconsin Department of Veterans' Affairs, *Wisconsin Colleges and Universities Approved for Education of Veterans by Governor's Advisory Educational Committee* (Madison: Wisconsin Department of Veterans' Affairs, 1946).
31. Olson, *GI Bill*, 82; Dexter, *Northland College*, 185. Policies for specific schools may be found in *Wisconsin Colleges and Universities Approved for Education*.
32. Olson, *GI Bill*, 82-83; *Wisconsin Colleges and Universities Approved for Education*, 8.
33. Olson, *GI Bill*, 81-82; *Wisconsin Colleges and Universities Approved for Education*, 39. For a history of remedial education at the college level, see Theodore Markus and Arthur Zeitlin, "Remediation in Higher Education: A 'New' Phenomemon?" *Community Review* 16 (2000): 167-177.
34. Landgraf interview, WVOHP; Oldenburg interview, WVOHP; Podell interview, WVOHP.
35. Howe interview, WVOHP; Beltmann interview, WVOHP.
36. Williams, "My Life in Madison," 267; Brenzel interview, WVOHP; Hall interview, WVOHP; Dalton interview, WVOHP; Moses interview, WVOHP; Lamkin interview, WVOHP; Adrian interview, WVOHP.
37. *Northern Light*, May-June 1946.
38. Beckstrand interview, WVOHP; Podell interview, WVOHP; Chase interview, Stephen E. Ambrose World War II Interview Collection, Wisconsin Veterans' Museum Research Center, Madison, Wis.
39. *Wisconsin State Journal*, 29 September 1946, 5 June 1947; Olson, *GI Bill*, 86; *Beloit College Bulletin*, April 1947.
40. Pressentin interview, WVOHP; Scovill interview, WVOHP; Podell interview, WVOHP; Olson, *GI Bill*, 86.
41. Olson, *GI Bill*, 86-87; Brown, *Educational Opportunities for Veterans*, 131.
42. Marlow interview, WVOHP; Williams, "My Life in Madison," 267ff.
43. Freese interview, WVOHP; Williams, "My Life in Madison," 267.
44. Schallert interview, WVOHP; Richtsmeier interview, WVOHP; *Northern Light*, April 1946.
45. Robert Dean interview, WVOHP; Risser interview, WVOHP; Dunn interview, WVOHP; Todd interview, WVOHP.
46. Hewitt interview, WVOHP; Gamble, *From Academy to University*, 129.
47. Freese interview, WVOHP; Flaten interview, WVOHP.
48. Landgraf interview, WVOHP; Dunn interview, WVOHP, Donald Wiberg interview, WVOHP; Williams, "My Life in Madison," 267.

49. Cornelius interview, WVOHP; *Lawrence Alumnus*, October 1947; *Beloit College Bulletin*, April 1947; Olson, *GI Bill*, 91-92.

50. *Northern Light*, February 1946, May-June 1946; Dexter, *Northland College*, 192.

51. *Northern Light*, February 1946; Robert Dean interview, WVOHP; Bowers interview, WVOHP; Dexter, *Northland College*, 185.

52. *Beloit College Bulletin*, October 1946; Esser interview, WVOHP; Schallert interview, WVOHP.

53. *Capital Times*, 1 December 1946; Kenneth Johnson interview, WVOHP; Moses interview, WVOHP; Sivertson interview, WVOHP.

54. Jaeger interview, WVOHP; Cook interview, WVOHP; Dalton interview, WVOHP; Junkermann interview, WVOHP.

55. Dunn interview, WVOHP; Gill interview, WVOHP; Remington interview, WVOHP; Curti interview, University of Wisconsin Oral History Project, Univerity of Wisconsin Archives, Madison, Wis. (cited hereafter as UWOHP); Connors interview, WVOHP.

56. Jim Feldman, *The Buildings of the University of Wisconsin* (Madison: University of Wisconsin Archives, 1997), 251, 256-257; Allan G. Bogue and Robert Taylor, eds., *University of Wisconsin: The One Hundred and Twenty-Five Years* (Madison: University of Wisconsin Press, 1975), 76.

57. Hamilton, *Marquette University*, 300-301; Dexter, *Northland College*, 187-188; *Beloit College Bulletin*, June 1946.

58. *New York Times*, 24 February 1946; Olson, *GI Bill*, 88-89; *Lawrence Alumnus*, January 1946, January 1948; *Beloit College Bulletin*, October 1947, October 1948.

59. John L. Chase, et al., *Graduate Teaching Assistants in American Universities: A Review of Recent Trends and Recommendations* (Washington, D.C.: U.S. Department of Health, Education, and Welfare, 1970), 3-5; Olson, *GI Bill*, 88-89; Zeasman interview, WVOHP; Fergot interview, WVOHP.

60. Turner interview, WVOHP; Marlow interview, WVOHP; *Beloit College Bulletin*, October 1948.

61. *New York Times*, 24 February 1946; Barry Teicher and John W. Jenkins, *Housing at the University of Wisconsin* (Madison: University of Wisconsin History Project, 1987), 51-52; *Beloit College Bulletin*, October 1946.

62. Esser interview, WVOHP; Jacobsen interview, WVOHP; Eager interview, WVOHP; *Beloit College Bulletin*, June 1946.

63. Fred interview, UWOHP; Teicher and Jenkins, *Housing at the University of Wisconsin*, 45.

64. Feldman, *Buildings of the University of Wisconsin*, 248; Teicher and Jenkins, *Housing at the University of Wisconsin*, 49-51.

65. Feldman, *Buildings of the University of Wisconsin*, 290; Teicher and Jenkins, *Housing at the University of Wisconsin*, 49-51. The tent colony predated the war. It began in 1913, and housed mainly graduate students. The colony continued until 1962.

66. Teicher and Jenkins, *Housing at the University of Wisconsin*, 45-47; Erhart Mueller, *Badger Village and Bluffview Courts* (Baraboo, Wis.: Bluffview Acres, Inc., 1982), 58.

67. Susan Davis, *The Student Veteran's Wife* (Madison, Wis.: Privately published, 1947), 31; Mueller, *Badger Village*, 11; Kenneth Johnson interview, WVOHP.

68. Fergot interview, WVOHP; Davis, *Student Veteran's Wife*, 31; Kenneth Johnson interview, WVOHP.

69. Davis, *Student Veteran's Wife*, 13, 20, 31; Mueller, *Badger Village*, 11; William B. Cameron, "The University Truax Project," unpublished paper, Department of Sociology, University of Wisconsin, 1947, in Veterans' Housing subject file, General Files, University of Wisconsin Archives.

70. Cook interview, WVOHP; Remington interview, WVOHP.

71. Bates interview, WVOHP; Fergot interview, WVOHP; Kenneth Johnson interview, WVOHP; Teicher and Jenkins, *Housing at the University of Wisconsin*, 48-49.

72. Farnham Johnson interview, WVOHP; Mueller, *Badger Village*, 18.

73. Davis, *Student Veteran's Wife*, 25, 28-29.

74. Davis, *Student Veteran's Wife*, 17; Mueller, *Badger Village*, 9.

75. Davis, *Student Veteran's Wife*, 28.

76. *Daily Cardinal*, 1 May 1945; Teicher and Jenkins, *Housing at the University of Wisconsin*, 52-54. According to the 1945 *Daily Cardinal* survey, 1 percent of respondents stated that they would move out of their dormitory or apartment if a Catholic student moved in, and 8 percent if a Jewish student moved in.

77. Wyman, *Wisconsin State Universities*, 40, 264-265; Dexter, *Northland College*, 185.

78. Wyman, *Wisconsin State Universities*, 85-86, 312; *Lawrence Alumnus*, May 1946; Ashley and Miller, *Ripon College*, 172-173.

79. Cook interview, WVOHP; Fergot interview, WVOHP.

80. Many of the temporary buildings at the University of Wisconsin remained as permanent structures on the campus until the very end of the twentieth century. In May 2000, several post-World War II temporary buildings on the southwestern part of the campus were demolished to make way for a new engineering building. A Quonset hut in the heart of the campus remained. For more, see Feldman, *Buildings of the University of Wisconsin*; and Teicher and Jenkins, *Housing at the University of Wisconsin*; *Capital Times*, 10 May 2000.

81. *Green Bay Press-Gazette*, 26 May 1950.

Chapter Five

"I Still Had a Little of the Depression in Me": Economic Readjustments

"No previous military force," observed advice writer Benjamin Bowker, "was ever so preoccupied with future job prospects throughout a great war as that of the United States. Nor was any nation more concerned about the economic status of those who would return from fighting a war." Finding a place in the civilian economy after discharge has been a problem that has historically plagued veterans. To Americans in the 1940s, the recent past gave particular cause for concern. Just twenty years before, American troops returning from World War I had faced turbulent economic conditions and widespread unemployment. During the Great Depression, World War I veterans had marched on the nation's capital to gain an early payment of the bonus promised them. The Bonus March of 1932 ended disastrously for all concerned. Congress voted against the early payment, and the army burned down the veterans' encampment, forcibly removing the ex-soldiers from Washington. As World War II came to a close, Americans understood rather keenly that reemployment and prosperity would be crucial to readjusting war veterans to the civilian world. "Adequate employment opportunity," Bowker continued, was "a major factor in healthy readjustment." Another writer, the humorist Morton Thompson, expressed the same sentiment. "Having a job," he wrote, "takes the soldier-on-leave element out of being a Civilian."[1]

The notion of returning to a civilian job was one that gave many veterans considerable anxiety. A July 1945 survey of U.S. Army soldiers returning from overseas revealed that 21 percent of them "worried a lot" about finding work upon returning home, while 49 percent said they "worried a little." In another survey, fully 56 percent of army troops anticipated a depression after the war. Interestingly, veterans were optimistic about their own personal job prospects. According to a 1945 army survey of its soldiers, 79 percent believed that most soldiers would find it "very hard" or "fairly" hard to find a job. However, when asked of their own prospects, only 46 percent believed that to be the case. Nevertheless, more than half of all army personnel polled expressed fears about finding work in the postwar world. Government officials were fearful as well, and as a result lawmakers in the 1940s passed a bewildering array of economic benefits for returning veterans, including reemployment assistance, on-the-job training, civil service preference, and loans and grants. Never before had the nation done so much to ensure that the returning veteran would have a job after the war. When the conflict finally ended in 1945, the nation waited anxiously to see if the array of programs enacted would be effective.[2]

Everyday Economic Concerns

Even before veterans could look for work, they faced several economic challenges. During the war, American industry focused on producing materials for war. After the war, the United States saw a great shortage of consumer goods—everything from shoes to automobiles. Complicating the shortages of such goods was the inflationary nature of the postwar economy. Between 1945 and 1950, the wholesale price index rose from 54.6 to 81.8, or 8.3 percent on an average annual basis—a sharp contrast to the deflation that had been experienced during the depression years.[3] Shortages and inflation were more than just minor inconveniences for veterans; they could also impede further economic readjustment. Newly married couples required various goods to establish their new households, for example. An automobile was often essential to finding and keeping work, as was a proper suit of clothes. However, in the competition for such scarce yet expensive goods in the postwar world, veterans had certain advantages that helped ease these everyday economic difficulties.

One common problem that beset returning veterans was finding adequate clothing. Many had worn nothing but military clothing for years, and getting back into civilian clothes proved a challenge to some veterans. In a few cases, the problem was psychological. "I felt comfortable in a uniform," recalled navy former physician Eugene Eckstam. "Civilian clothes were abnormal." More commonly, however, veterans were anxious to shed their uniforms as quickly as possible. Upon arriving back in Madison, Wisconsin, army veteran Raymond Ray recalled that "getting out of the GI clothing" and finding some "new fancy clothes" was one of his first priorities. "I could finally wear the clothes I wanted," recalled Madison's Paul Graven of his discharge from the army. "It was very easy to become accustomed to that." After obtaining some civilian clothes upon his return to Milwaukee, Eugene Petersen wrote to his fiancée Marian Smith in northern Wisconsin that he finally felt as though he would be able to "convert one of these days" to civilian life. In another letter, Petersen beamed that he had gone "shopping today & got a blue shirt and a pair of $13.50 shoes. I am really going to look sharp!!"[4]

However, for many veterans, shedding their uniforms proved unexpectedly difficult. "I was gone for three and a half years," recalled Milwaukee army veteran Fred Hochschild, "and the clothing I had was outdated and old." The styles had changed, but so had the young men and women. Many veterans had left home as adolescents and had grown to adulthood while in the service. When they finally returned from the war, they often discovered that their old clothes did not fit them anymore. "In a large cardboard box I found my old jeans and a plaid woolen shirt," recalled Robert Peters of his first day home. "I doffed my army wear, and, though the old clothes were short in the legs, they felt good."

To complicate matters, civilian clothes were difficult to find in stores in the immediate aftermath of the war. "When I wanted to get married," recalled army veteran Vernon Bernhagen,

> I wanted to buy a white shirt. I went into a store in Stevens Point, and you couldn't buy a white shirt. This one retailer there did have white shirts underneath the counter, but only for his favorite customers. I had been in there earlier trying to buy a white shirt (they wouldn't sell me one), and they told me they didn't have any. But my [future] brother-in-law went over there. He was a favorite customer there, before he went in the service too, and he talked to the guy [and bought one]."[5]

While GIs often fantasized about the day they could wear civilian clothes again, veterans' advice writer Morton Thompson warned them not to dispense with their military apparel too hastily. "Clothing was no longer free," he reminded fellow veterans. "Even if your stuff wears out legitimately, they don't *give* you new." New civilian clothing, he warned, was both expensive and of low quality. The military clothing with which the veteran left the service, by contrast, was of excellent quality. "Even in peacetime," wrote Thompson, "you couldn't buy better material." He urged veterans to reuse military clothing as much as possible. Thompson described various ways to make military clothing look civilian. For example, khaki shirts could be dyed a darker color for fewer than $5. Overcoats could be dyed and tailored for less than $50 and "you'd have an overcoat you couldn't touch right now for a hundred and ten dollars [sic]."[6]

Veterans also tried to alter their prewar civilian clothes to fit postwar styles and bodies. In La Crosse, WAC veteran Delores Hendersin recalled that while she was looking for a teaching job she and her mother were "busy remodeling clothes, trying to make them more in style." Marian Smith sewed a new white shirt for her fiancé Eugene Petersen. "If all the love that goes into this labor shows," she wrote him, "it will surely be beautiful." She also managed to locate used clothes for her husband-to-be, including some owned by a relative killed in the war. "We looked through some of Franklin's things too," she wrote. "He has two white shirts & three colored ones, but I don't think you could wear them. They're 14-½. I'll iron one of the white ones and bring it down for you to try anyway. He has about a dozen pair of shorts & shirts which you can have, also." In preparing to head off to the University of Wisconsin in Madison, Robert Peters had difficulty finding a new suit. He went to the only men's store in his hometown of Eagle River, which had just one suit in stock, a "heavy, brown worsted affair" that the proprietor offered to alter for the veteran. The store owner "pinned the sleeves back, took tucks in the waist and seat, and promised that I'd be in 'style.'" The result, Peters later recalled, was a "severely reshaped suit," a "wretched thing" that Peters wore "a few times in Madison, then burned it in the trash."[7]

In addition to clothes, many other consumer goods were hard to procure. Veterans trying to establish themselves in civilian life found obtaining many ordinary household goods difficult. "People were coming out of the service and setting up housekeeping," recalled ex-marine Annette Howards, "but there was a shortage of just about everything." She found that in order to acquire simple household items such as linens and sheets, she had to put her name on waiting lists at retail stores around Milwaukee. She also learned that some of her relatives, more savvy to civilian ways, had placed her name on waiting lists as well. In La Crosse, Delores Hendersin also remembered that locating ordinary items such as towels, sheets, and pillowcases was a problem after the war. "By that time," she recalled, "they were just about out of everything here in the states." Once located, the quality of household goods often left much to be desired. Annette Howards received a phone call from her mother-in-law with the good news that she had located a rug. "I didn't ask what color it was," Howards remembered, "and it turned out to be an awful maroon, but I had a rug on my floor." Lou Bredenson and his wife Patricia could not find a refrigerator. "We went to Goodwill," Mrs. Bredenson recalled, "and bought an old fashioned ice box with ice." Ex-pilot Kenneth Johnson of Madison and his wife managed to find a refrigerator while living in Badger Village, but discovered that it caused unexpected headaches. "As soon as the neighbors found out," remembered Johnson, "they were all knocking on the door [and] bringing the peas, corn, beans, and frozen stuff over. Pretty soon our refrigerator was filled with other people's stuff."[8]

Automobiles were also difficult to come by in postwar America. "Because I had saved my money assiduously for over three years," wrote army veteran Jack Plano, "I decided to visit my local Ford dealer and consider purchasing a new car now that the auto companies were retooling for the civilian market." Plano had not expected what transpired:

> Remembering the cute car prices from the Depression era, I asked what kind of a deal I could get on one of the new Fords that would soon be rolling off the production lines. After much study and contemplation, the salesman proudly quoted me a price of $1,100, plus taxes of course. Eleven hundred dollars for a car? I told him that price was crazy, [and] that I would bide my time until the inflated wartime economy cooled and car prices became reasonable. He gave me a "you'll be sorry" look and the wheeling and dealing was over for me. Later, I found out that all of the car sales people in Merrill had long lists of buyers, and that I had had the chance of being near the top of those lists.

Those veterans who were able to put their cars into storage during the war had a great advantage in transportation capabilities afterward. Before the war, Madisonian Joseph Tauchen drove a 1934 Ford coupe, which his father-in-law stored while he was in the service. Tauchen found that he still depended on that 1934 Ford for transportation for years after the war. Veterans were sometimes shocked at the physical condition of their prewar vehicles. "A lot of people had driven my car," remembered J. J. Kuhn of Milwaukee. "The horn didn't work," he wrote, "and the paint was peeling." Those veterans who were able to purchase or otherwise find automobiles after the war often had to settle for considerably older models. Eugene Petersen obtained from his grandfather a 1931

Pontiac that he used to get to work and school, as well as to make occasional trips to northern Wisconsin to visit his fiancée Marian. "Can't have a gal without transportation, can you?" he asked her. Robert Peters recalled that his father "found an old Model T [Ford] for seventy-five dollars which he repaired and taught me to drive." Despite its age, the Model T successfully transported Peters to Madison so that he could enroll at the University of Wisconsin.[9]

In the years immediately following World War II, America's streets and highways were filled with older model cars. However, keeping these aging vehicles on the road often proved both a challenge and a financial drain. Madison army veteran Robert Clampitt recalled that driving around a ten-year-old car took a lot of money. In fact, he felt compelled to leave school rather than give up his automobile. Joseph Tauchen's 1934 Ford coupe ran well, but he had difficulty finding tires for it. Tauchen was fortunate to have worked at a gas station, where he was usually able to locate the hard-to-find tires because his boss "usually gave me first crack" at the needed tires when they came in. "My grandfather's 1931 Pontiac, despite over 95,000 [miles] on the odometer, was usually reliable," remembered Eugene Petersen. However, on his wedding day in February 1946—on which the temperature had plunged to –20 degrees Fahrenheit— the old automobile finally gave out. "As we prepared to make our getaway," he wrote of the incident, "I could not start it. My new father-in-law was accommodating, however, and he pushed us with [his vehicle] until the motor turned over." Donald Mercier had great difficulties with his car, not the least of which was the fact that "you couldn't get the darn thing started." Mercier took the car to a local garage, where he was told it would cost $250 to repair. Unable to afford that amount, he "drove it into a used car lot and left it running." The car dealer, according to his recollection, paid him $250 for his car.[10]

Automobile manufacturers and dealers sometimes gave veterans preference over other customers. Malvin Kachelmeier of Milwaukee recalled that while he was in a military hospital in Michigan a representative from the Ford Motor Company came into his ward with an offer to sell automobiles with a vacuum clutch specially equipped for amputees. Kachelmeier "gave this party my name without a second thought" and "before long had a new 1946 Mercury." Although Kachelmeier appreciated Ford's concern for the disabled veteran, he nevertheless suspected that the vacuum clutch was "introduced before it was perfected" since it often worked poorly. As Kachelmeier later wrote, "Most of the time [I] drove mine with the system switched off." Even with preference, veterans still had to put their names on waiting lists for new cars. Army veteran Anthony Richtsmeier recalled that a Madison car dealer gave preference to veterans for new cars, but actually getting behind the wheel of an automobile took some time. "I'd go down there every night," he recalled, "waiting to see whether a trailer had come in with new cars." After more than six weeks, Richtsmeier finally received a car. Not all veterans were so lucky. Lucille and Chick Rabidieux of Hayward, both veterans, put their names on a waiting list for a car under a veterans' preference program while working in Chicago but were never able to receive one.[11]

The federal government established a program whereby certain disabled veterans would receive automobiles at government expense. Public Law 663, approved in August 1946, appropriated $30 million to provide World War II veterans who had lost the function of one or both legs, or a leg amputated above the ankle with an automobile "or other conveyance," including any special devices or attachments the veteran required, at a cost not to exceed $1,600. By June 1947, more than 14,000 World War II veterans had received cars through the VA program nationwide, at a cost of $22.4 million. In subsequent years, Congress continued the program and appropriated the requisite funds. By June 1950, the VA had provided 25,014 automobiles, 163 trucks, 93 tractors, 22 station wagons, and 21 jeeps to disabled World War II veterans, at a cost of more than $40 million.[12]

Beginning in 1944, veterans left the service with $300 in "mustering out pay," a cash sum to see them home and sustain them until they found work, and upon discharge veterans were given any back pay owed them. In addition, many veterans returned home with considerable savings. In service, the troops were paid regularly but often had nowhere to spend the money, especially those in combat zones and remote areas or those who were prisoners of war. John Gerlach of Madison saved a significant sum of money while serving as a fighter pilot in the southwestern Pacific. In addition, Gerlach claimed to have "won some money over in New Guinea playing poker," further enhancing his savings. Elizabeth O'Hara Baehr, a former combat nurse in Europe, recalled how she believed herself to be "wealthy when I got home," and therefore she "spent a lot of money on my wedding because I had so much in the bank." "My father's reluctance to pay my . . . tuition [at Marquette before the war] was such an embarrassing and painful memory," wrote Milwaukee's Eugene Petersen,

> that I had determined to be financially independent. Before I left home, my grandfather and I had established a savings account at a suburban bank with the money I had saved with my part time janitorial job and there was $750 on the bottom line. He periodically deposited the money orders I sent him and twice a year drove the six miles to have the interest entered in my passbook. By [1946] it had grown to nearly $3000, a respectable sum considering in the first eighteen months of service life I made less than $60 a month and the last two years never earned more than $200. I did not spend much in the United States Marine Corps.

Madison army veteran John Hall remembered how, while boarding the troop train to take him from Madison, his mother urged him to save money while in the service. As Hall remembered the scene, his mother spoke of the Great Depression, as well as the plight of World War I veterans ("they had those khaki pants on them until 1922," she told him) in urging her son to save. The young serviceman had indeed saved some money while in the military, and purchased war bonds for good measure. As a result, Hall "had some money when I came home from the service."[13]

Indeed, in a few instances veterans returned home to an embarrassment of riches, especially if they came from a background of poverty. Robert Peters had grown up poor in the Wisconsin north woods near Eagle River. He had saved money during the war, and intended to use those savings on his family. First, he wanted to purchase a new home for his parents. "When I first proposed to Dad that we use my army savings to buy Mom a place in town where she would have running water, electricity, and plumbing," Peters later wrote, "he demurred, and, in fact, seemed hurt. I had threatened his virility; he was the provider. Neither of us put it into words, and it was indeed a great step to sell the forty acres he had bought through Roosevelt's Home Owners Loan Corporation. 'I'm going to do it, Dad,' I insisted." Peters purchased a home in the village of Eagle River, complete with insulation, an oil furnace, and electricity. "One other gift remained to be made," Peters wrote: a cemetery plot for his parents. "My mother worried that they were too poor to buy a cemetery plot for her and Dad," he recalled. "I would tease her, saying that we'd carry her into the woods, dig a hole, and drop her in. She was not amused." For $120, Peters bought a plot "large enough for two coffins and my ashes." The great number of returning veterans flush with cash did not go unnoticed by criminal elements. The Wisconsin Department of Veterans' Affairs warned veterans about several scams designed to part the veterans and their money. In one scam, veterans received a letter from a newspaper clipping service informing the ex-soldier that they possessed a "very interesting article" about them, and for 25 cents the service would send a copy. Once the article arrived, the veteran was "chagrined to find it is an old two or three line item from the society locals which he has seen months ago in his home town newspaper." In another, a few "unscrupulous" insurance agents offered to assist veterans in converting their government life insurance policies to private policies. In fact, so-called "GI insurance" was not convertible; veterans were tricked into dropping their less costly government insurance for more expensive private policies. Morvin Duel, the Wisconsin state insurance commissioner, threatened Badger State insurance agents with a three-year revocation of their licenses "where it can be shown that the best interests of the veteran have been jeopardized."[14]

In fact, government life insurance at rates below those of most private insurance companies was an important postwar benefit for many veterans. Public Law 801, passed by Congress in October 1940, provided five-year term life insurance for active-duty military personnel. While in service, soldiers had a small sum deducted from their pay, and in case of death the policy's beneficiary— normally required to be a spouse or parent of the policyholder—would receive compensation. Upon discharge, the veteran had the option of converting his or her term insurance into an ordinary, twenty- or thirty-year payment government life insurance policy. Though the veteran had to continue paying monthly premiums at rates higher than those paid during military service, such payments were still below market insurance rates and did not require the veteran to undergo a physical examination. In addition, the insurance had no travel, occupational, or residential restrictions. The equity could be borrowed against as well.

If veterans did not convert their term insurance by the end of the five-year term they could still keep their insurance, but they would have to undergo a medical examination. Life insurance was one everyday economic concern that veterans—at least those who maintained their government policies—did not have to worry about after the war.[15]

Thus, veterans had access to relatively inexpensive life insurance, providing them with another economic advantage in the postwar world. Discharged veterans were strongly urged to keep up their insurance. "Many of us are uninsurable permanently," stated the Prentice-Hall *Veteran's Guide*, "some at least for a few years. This may be the only insurance you have or the *last* you can get."[16] However, to keep up their GI insurance veterans had to make monthly premium payments. But to pay the premiums the veteran would need to have a job, and it was finding a good job that concerned both veteran and lawmaker the most.

Going Back to Work

According to federal VA administrator Omar Bradley, of all the readjustment challenges a veteran faced, the "most fundamental of all is the job problem." Writing in the magazine *State Government* in 1946, Bradley claimed that "unless a veteran's job problem is settled, nothing is settled."[17] It was the problem of veteran unemployment that concerned lawmakers most as they planned for the return of World War II veterans. Between 1940 and 1945, the federal government passed numerous programs designed to get veterans onto the employment rolls. Barring that, the government hoped to ensure that unemployed veterans did not roam the streets peddling apples, as was sometimes the case after World War I. Indeed, with the Great Depression so recent, the problem of mass unemployment was one with which Americans in the 1940s were intimately familiar. The nation was willing to pay a considerable price to ensure that its former soldiers would be able to find work after the war.

The federal program for veteran reemployment began with the veteran's local draft board. Each Selective Service board was tasked with designating a Reemployment Committee to assist veterans in making the appropriate contacts with employers or other government agencies. Because discharged servicemen were required to register with their local draft boards within ten days of returning home, Selective Service officials would theoretically make contact with every returning male veteran. Local reemployment committeemen could refer veterans to any number of agencies, the most important of which was the United States Employment Service (USES), which maintained twenty-five local offices in Wisconsin during the late 1940s. USES offices maintained lists of jobs and attempted to match up job seekers with those positions. Though the federal plan for coordinating local Selective Service and USES offices into veterans' "information centers" ultimately failed (see chapter 1), veterans nevertheless had federal officials in their own communities to help them find work. In addition, Wisconsin's County Veterans' Service Officers also stood ready to guide veterans to the proper places to find suitable employment.

Guidance would be important in helping veterans get back to work, since the federal government established numerous programs to reintegrate veterans back into the economy. One of the first federal efforts to alleviate potential unemployment problems for World War II veterans was the Selective Service Act of 1940, which required employers to reinstate veterans to their prewar jobs under certain conditions. Under the act, veterans had ninety days from the date of their discharge to reclaim their jobs. Upon returning to work, veterans were entitled to have no loss in rank or seniority—they would be considered having been on a "leave of absence." In fact, a returning veteran would have what was called "superseniority," meaning that the person who replaced the veteran would be let go even if the replacement had more seniority. There were circumstances under which veterans could not reclaim prewar jobs. For example, the job the person left had to have been a permanent one, and not a temporary wartime position. The veteran still had to be able to perform the job tasks. A company could refuse to rehire a veteran if the company's circumstances had changed so much that the job the veteran had held was obsolete or had been eliminated altogether. Veterans could not be fired—except for cause—for one year after being rehired. Should an employer fail to rehire a veteran, the veterans would have the services of a U.S. attorney free of charge.

Overall, veterans reported few problems in obtaining their old jobs. Between July 1944 and August 1946, only sixty-two Wisconsin veterans sought the services of a federal attorney to win their jobs back, resulting in just one lawsuit. Ex-bombardier John Scocos returned to his job as a manager at a Sears store in Fond du Lac. "In fact, they were glad to see us," he remembered. "They were having trouble getting help at that time." Returning veterans often received new jobs with their previous employers. Fred Hochschild returned to the Wisconsin Electric Company in Milwaukee to find that during the war his boss—who had also been drafted into service—had been replaced by "a girl" who would be his new boss after the war. Not wishing to work for a woman, Hochschild "applied for, and got, a different job with the same company." Indeed, some veterans were not only welcomed back with open arms but also returned to promotions. Juanita Wilkie returned to her job with the Unemployment Compensation Department of the Wisconsin Industrial Commission. As she recalled, her military service helped her in terms of workplace advancement. She went back to her office "in my uniform looking pretty snappy, with captain's bars on my shoulders. Everybody took a second look, including the boss." She soon found that she "went up pretty fast" in the agency's chain of command, where she was "equal to, on par with, the men." "I think that maybe they found that I could do something," she surmised. Wilkie was not alone in returning to better positions in the same workplace. The Allis-Chalmers Manufacturing Company in West Allis, for example, pledged to "carry out the spirit as well as the letter of the [veterans' reemployment] law," and interviewed all returning veterans about their previous work in the company as well as their military training. "Some veterans, because of their skills acquired in the service," the company noted, "will qualify for placement in better jobs than they had before."[18]

Though veterans were generally able to return to their previous workplace, many nevertheless did not consider their Selective Service reemployment rights among their most important benefits. While returning veterans did not lose seniority while they were away at war, they also did not receive the promotions and raises in pay that those who stayed behind had. Joseph Tauchen returned to his factory job at Gisholt Manufacturing in Madison, only to find that he now made less money than coworkers who stayed at work during the war. "I bitched," he recalled, "but it didn't do no good." Roth Schleck was offered his job back as an accountant at the First Wisconsin National Bank in Milwaukee, but was told that he would have to return at his prewar salary. Because of this, Schleck considered staying in the army where, as a lieutenant colonel, he would have made more money. Ultimately, Schleck opted for the bank and civilian life. "I couldn't face getting up that early in the morning," he remembered. "[In the army] they're up at the crack of dawn and that seemed so horrible I just couldn't do it."[19]

Many veterans returned to find their jobs waiting for them, but did not always want them back. In fact, a 1944 survey of veterans at army separation centers indicated that at least 40 percent of those leaving the service hoped to find a different job after the war. Gisholt Manufacturing offered Gerald Wilkie his prewar job back, but he declined it because "it wasn't much of a job." "I decided I'd get out and go back to the electric company," recalled WAC veteran Gladys Day of Racine. She worked there for about six months, but then reassessed her future job prospects. "I sat down one day and had a talk with myself," she remembered, and she asked: "Do I want to work here the rest of my life?" The answer she received was "no." In the depression years before the war, Americans had accepted almost any job they could find. However, after the war many veterans hoped for better positions. "There is no particular benefit to the combat major in guaranteeing him the right to go back to the shipping clerk's job he had before the war," claimed veterans' activists Charles Hurd and Charles Bolté. However, some advice writers cautioned veterans against changing jobs too hastily. "How can you go about getting a better job?" Maxwell Droke asked veterans. "The only honest answer," he declared, "is that in all probability you can't. . . . Even with your advantage as a veteran, you may be doomed to disappointment." Scores of veterans ignored Droke's advice. Optimistic about the future and armed with a plethora of government programs, World War II veterans struck out in numerous new career directions.[20]

For veterans who sought a career change after the war, as well as those who had not yet entered the workforce prior to military service, the federal government provided several options to pursue different lines of work. One, of course, was to attend a college or university using Public Law 16 or the educational provisions of the GI Bill of Rights, whereby a veteran could pursue education and training in a great variety of fields (see chapter 4). However, "some veterans may not want to go to school," reported the Wisconsin *Blue Book* in 1946.

"Some may have [already] graduated from college. Many want to go to work at once, or at least learn a useful occupation in order to become self-supporting as soon as possible." Public Law 16 and the GI Bill not only sent veterans to campuses to learn a trade or profession, but they also contained provisions for "on-the-job training" (OJT) with employers. Under the OJT provisions of these laws, veterans would receive both a regular paycheck and a government living allowance while learning a particular trade and gaining valuable skills in the workplace. Employers who participated in the program paid the veteran a training wage, which would rise as the trainee advanced in his or her job skills. In addition to their wages, participating veterans would receive a subsistence allowance equal to that of veterans attending a college or vocational school under the GI Bill or Public Law 16. Veterans who had served more than ninety days and were not dishonorably discharged could receive at least twelve months of training, with an additional month for each month they had served in the military, up to a maximum of forty-eight. Under the program, veterans could seek work in any field and with any employer. The OJT program expanded even further the incredibly wide range of vocational options that World War II veterans could pursue under the GI Bill or Public Law 16. The program also helped the employers, allowing them to hire more workers at less cost until a worker was fully trained in his or her position.[21]

Certification and supervision of the OJT program was the responsibility of the "appropriate agency" in the veteran's state of residence, so the program worked somewhat differently in each of the forty-eight states and the various territories. In Wisconsin, the agency designated with responsibility for supervising the OJT program was the Wisconsin Industrial Commission. Wisconsin employers wishing to hire veterans under the OJT program had to file with the commission, stating the training terms and objectives, and outlining any classes the trainee would need to attend. In addition, employers were required to submit planned training schedules, as well as proposed training wages and wages paid to fully trained workers in the same position. Industrial Commission officials then inspected the place of employment, and if found acceptable, it then notified the Veterans' Administration of its approval so that the veteran could receive the subsistence allowance. In December 1945, the WDVA approved a request from the commission to receive more than $17,000 in trust fund money to hire eight supervisors for the program, as well as travel funds and clerical support for those supervisors.[22]

In Wisconsin, the OJT program worked exceedingly well in many cases. Veterans worked in a fantastic variety of jobs under the program. The types of work a veteran in training did often varied depending on the economy of a particular area. Of nineteen applications filed from the city of Rhinelander in the Wisconsin north woods, for example, more than 25 percent came from businesses catering to tourists, such as retail establishments and resorts. Applications from the rural village of Soldier's Grove in western Wisconsin included jobs at a feed mill, a farm equipment store, a fur farm, and two cheese factories. The Verifine Dairy Company of Sheboygan trained at least two foremen, a refrigeration mechanic, a vacuum pan operator, a butter maker, and two ice cream makers using the OJT program. Kayser Motors in Madison hired fifteen veterans under the program by January 1946. The proprietor, F. C. Doring (himself a combat veteran of World War II) was impressed with the workers and claimed that without them "we'd be right back of the eight ball again" in terms of finding quality workers. Even government agencies hired workers under OJT. In March 1946, the State of Wisconsin announced that it hoped to hire at least 100 veterans on the OJT program in various civil service positions. Many county governments used the OJT provisions of the GI Bill and Public Law 16 to hire assistant veterans' service officers to handle the growing workload in the CVSO offices.[23]

However, some veterans and businesses misused the OJT program. By 1946, "horror stories" of OJT abuses began to circulate. Many applications for GI Bill or Public Law 16 training funds were of dubious merit. In one southern state, for example, a minor league baseball team attempted to hire ballplayer-veterans at a reduced rate arguing that they were "apprentices." In one western retail firm, several well-paid executives applied for OJT benefits on the grounds that they were training for positions such as "vice president." "Even bowling alleys and pool halls are seeking to be approved to train veterans to be pin boys and to rack pool balls!" claimed Francis Brown of the American Council on Education. Authorities in those states refused those applications, but in many cases approved programs turned out to be little more than economic exploitation of worker-veterans. Veterans frequently did not receive the training promised, and were instead used as inexpensive labor. In one southern state, for example, veterans being trained as "refrigerator repairmen" were tasked simply with removing motors from refrigerators so that they could be sent to a factory for repair. After an insurance company in the Pacific Northwest learned that a woman employee was a navy veteran, the company reduced her pay and told her to apply for GI Bill benefits to make up the difference. "It is a pity," opined the *Milwaukee Journal*, "that America cannot carry out even so laudable a purpose as this without being beset by chiselers." Omar Bradley declared quite frankly in 1946 that the OJT program was the "source of more trouble than any other provision of the GI Bill of Rights."[24]

Abuses certainly occurred in the Badger State, as in the case of a veteran hired to train as a meat cutter who found that his work in reality consisted of nothing more than waiting on butcher shop customers. The veteran complained to the VA, and subsequent investigation revealed that although the veteran was paid the reduced training wage, the employer had never even filed for the OJT program. However, such abuses were apparently less common in Wisconsin, thanks in large part to the careful supervision of the Industrial Commission. The commission carefully screened requests for OJT money, and frequently denied training. For example, the Montello Granite Company applied to hire a machinist trainee under the GI Bill. Under the company's proposal, the veteran would be supervised by "an old machinist who worked for us [for] over fifty years," and although now retired "does come over occasionally" to assist the trainee-veteran "when he gets stuck on some particular piece of work, which is not a very great many times." Although the request seemed sincere, the commission denied the application, arguing the supervisor needed to be a full-time employee of the company and that "if this veteran has to perform the duties . . . with only occasional guidance . . . it must be considered that he is in fact [already] competent to do most of the work assigned to him." Because of Wisconsin's careful administration of the OJT program, VA field representative Valentine Hoffman told Governor Goodland in 1946 that VA officials in Washington rated Wisconsin as "the No. 1 state in matters of veterans' rehabilitation."[25]

The GI Bill also made provisions for veterans returning to the farm. Veterans could receive farm training under the GI Bill and Public Law 16 OJT programs. To qualify, the veteran would farm under the supervision of a VA-approved farm agent. In such cases, the agent would visit the veteran's farm on a regular basis and supervise the veteran's farming techniques. Veterans could also enroll in any of the numerous farm training classes that existed in most agricultural states. In Wisconsin, the state's Board of Vocational and Adult Education offered farming courses to veterans, typically held in local high schools. In addition, veterans could also enroll in one of the various agricultural programs administered by the University of Wisconsin or one of the state's teachers colleges. For veterans attending such courses, the VA paid for tuition and books. Farmer-veterans attending classes or farming under VA supervision received the same subsistence allowances as those on nonfarm OJT programs and those veterans enrolled in college.[26]

In addition to the GI Bill's OJT program, farmers and other self-employed veterans could also obtain government loans. Under Title III of the GI Bill, the VA would guarantee up to 50 percent of loans that veterans could receive from both public and private lending agencies up to a limit of $2,000 at 4 percent interest. In other words, veterans could borrow up to $4,000 and have the VA guarantee one-half that amount. In order for the VA to approve a loan, the project for which the veteran sought the loan had to pass an inspection from the VA as to its feasibility and soundness. Although the loan program was most commonly used to purchase homes (see chapter 6), veterans could use the so-called "GI loans" for a variety of other purposes, including the purchase of a farm, livestock, and farm machinery, and the erection, maintenance, and repair of farm buildings. Title III loans could also be used to purchase a business or business property, or to establish working capital for an enterprise, as well as to pay delinquent debts and taxes. Because the loan money came from the lending institution and not the federal government, the veteran applicant still had to meet whatever loan qualifications the lending institution required in terms of income, collateral, or financial solvency. Nevertheless, the federal guarantee of the 50 percent of the loan was intended to encourage banks and other lending institutions to loosen restrictions and put money into the hands of veterans. By 1950, the VA had insured $10,600,821 in farm loans and $10,836,601 in business loans in Wisconsin. Nationally, the figures were $215 million and $369 million, respectively.[27]

Another employment aid for veterans was preference for federal jobs, a practice that dates to the post-Civil War era. In the years after World War I, a series of legislative acts and executive orders formally established a veteran preference system, which was then codified by Public Law 379, the Veterans' Preference Act of 1944. In competitive civil service examinations, disabled veterans were awarded an additional ten points to their total scores, while nondisabled veterans received five additional points. In nonclassified positions filled without competitive examinations, veterans were also to receive special consideration. The law applied to virtually all civilian federal positions, with the exception of judicial and executive branch appointments requiring consent of the Senate.[28]

Having served their country in the military, many veterans opted to serve in the federal civil service as well. Joseph Connors of Madison, an infantryman wounded in the Philippines, left the University of Wisconsin to take a job with the U.S. post office in Madison. Connors was glad to have his position as a letter carrier. "When I was growing up in the depression," he recalled, "the mail man always had a good job. He always had a home. I still had a little of the depression in me." Many other veterans entered government employment regardless of the advantages they received as veterans. As navy veteran Sam Onhieber recalled, he took a job with the Internal Revenue Service in Madison because he was trained as an accountant, not because of any employment advantage. Madison's Frank Freese was a trained forester and worked for the U.S. Forest Service, though he did concede that veterans' preference points might have given him a "slight advantage" over his nonveteran colleagues. Indeed, with so many veterans in society after World War II, veteran preference may not have been all that helpful to many job seekers in the late 1940s. As Joseph Connors recalled, "Seven disabled guys were hired the day I was hired" at the Madison post office. By 1950, veterans constituted 48 percent of all federal employees, and in 1953 that total reached 50 percent.[29]

By the time of World War II, the armed forces had grown more technical and specialized. Military service provided many soldiers with job skills valuable in civilian life. Indeed, there are indications that when entering the military, soldiers frequently sought military specialties that would provide them with useful job skills after the war. Cognizant of the potential for military specialties in the civilian economy, the armed services interviewed departing soldiers and sailors about any specialized training they had received in the service, and listed the veteran's relevant job skills on their discharge papers. Not all military occupations had civilian applications, of course. Milwaukee-area veteran Milo Flaten, who had been an infantryman in the 29th Division, recalled that at his separation interview he was informed that his military specialization qualified him to be a walrus hunter. "I thought that was silly," he later reflected.[30]

However, thousands of other Wisconsin veterans were able to utilize their military experiences in the civilian job market. Floyd Schmidt translated his army truck driving job into a civilian career as a driver. Lester Doro found that his military experiences in a heavy weapons unit in Europe gave him a brief career in demolition, until headaches forced him to leave that line of work. Charles Howe of Monroe found that his experiences as a military policeman in the Persian Gulf during the war led to a career in law enforcement afterward. After the sheriff of Green County (in which Monroe is located) was forced from office, local Republicans—aware of Howe's work as a military policemen—submitted his name to the governor to fill the vacated position until the next election. Howe accepted the job, and continued as an assistant to the new sheriff. He later ran for the position himself and won two terms. Albert Giese's work with diesel engines in the navy landed him a job as a diesel mechanic after the war, a career the veteran greatly enjoyed. In terms of providing vocational training, "the navy . . . was the best thing that ever happened to me," Giese explained.[31]

Armed with the generous educational provisions of the GI Bill, many veterans pursued careers in professions to which they had been exposed during the war. After a stint as a medic in the 82nd Airborne Division, Jack Dunn sought a career as a chiropractor. Mae Kobishop of Stevens Point served in the navy, working as a corpsman at the U.S. Naval Academy. After the war she returned home and worked in her parents' grocery store, but soon grew restless. "I just had to get back in the hospital," she recalled. She sought work as a nurse's aid in a local hospital, and then later obtained her registered nursing degree. Charles Bradley had received a bachelor's degree in geology from the University of Wisconsin before the war, but after graduation opened up a photography shop in Madison. However, his experiences with the North Pacific Combat School in Alaska's Aleutian Islands—where he studied that region's environment in preparation for possible combat operations there—rekindled his interest in geology. Bradley went on to gain his M.S. and Ph.D. degrees in the subject, and later became a respected scholar in that field.[32]

Even veterans who did not obtain specific skills from military service nevertheless believed that they had learned some general skills that helped them in their subsequent careers. For example, Farnham "Gunner" Johnson of Appleton found that the administrative skills he learned as a marine corps officer gave him an edge in the world of business. Kendall Niebuhr believed that the military's emphasis on physical fitness helped him land a job as a Madison fireman. "Military guys were in a lot better shape than most," he recalled. Indeed, wartime military experience sent some veterans into unexpected vocational directions. Bruce Willett of Chippewa Falls found that his combat training during the war led him into careers in the ministry and in social work. The war, he recalled, "my participation in it, and what I was trained to do, made me rethink my whole approach to human life and the sanctity of life." His wartime experiences led him to believe that "violence may not be the way to handle things." Recognizing this, Willett "sought out [areas] where I could express myself in more positive ways." In numerous and disparate ways, wartime service itself provided many World War II veterans with vocational advantages and direction in the postwar years.[33]

Indeed, some World War II veterans found their vocation in the military. At the end of World War II, surveys of army soldiers indicated only about 3 percent expressed a desire to make the army their career, while another 3 percent said they might consider an army career if they experienced difficulty in finding civilian employment. Although relatively few veterans had trouble finding work, many grew unhappy with their civilian jobs and returned to the military. For example, ex-pilot Robert Dean of Scandinavia became "fed up" with the teaching career he sought after the war, and he returned to the air force. Mello Stapleton of Madison left the military briefly between V-E Day and V-J Day, but by the end of 1945 found himself back in the army air force. "[It's] not bad to be a master sergeant with full flying pay," he recalled. Frederick Wald of Marinette took a printing apprenticeship after the war, but found the work unsatisfying. After work one day, Wald entered the air force recruiting office. After being offered his previous military rank back, Wald decided to reenlist. William Crabb went back into the air force after briefly entering the restaurant business in Green Lake County with his brother-in-law. "I didn't like to cook, I didn't like being in the kitchen, I didn't like to wash dishes, scrub floors, I didn't like any part of it," he remembered.[34]

Other factors led many veterans back into the military. Otto Junkermann—who had entered the navy after V-J Day but who qualified for the GI Bill—felt an obligation to rejoin the military during the Korean War out of what he called a "guilty conscience." In his view, "I had all these benefits" but felt that he had "done nothing to earn them," and so he entered the U.S. Marine Corps. Madison's Robert Wallace remembered that he "had a lot of opportunities for school" in the service. In addition, the army promised him that he could remain in an armored unit, a proposition he also found attractive. Others found that they missed the sense of community and camaraderie inherent in military life. The army provided Madison's Robert Clampitt with what he called a "sense of belonging." He recalled that he "tried out civilian life for awhile" after the war, but stated that he "always planned on going back in the army someday. Some people hated it. I really liked it." WAC medical technician Mary Ann Renard took what she called a "short discharge," meaning that she returned to civilian life only briefly after the war. "I just didn't like it," she recalled. "Civilian life just wasn't for me."[35]

For veterans who were unable to find work immediately after discharge, the GI Bill also contained a provision for unemployment compensation. Title V of the law entitled World War II veterans to unemployment benefits of $20 per month for a maximum of fifty-two weeks. Veterans could apply for the benefit either two years after discharge or two years after the official end of the war, whichever occurred later. Like the OJT program, unemployment compensation under the GI Bill was administered by the appropriate agency in a particular state, which in Wisconsin was the Unemployment Compensation Department of the Industrial Commission. To receive benefits, veterans reported to the local USES office, where they were interviewed about their work skills and job preferences. Veterans were then provided with a list of local jobs that matched their skills. Applicants were required to contact the employers on the list, and appear at the USES office each week to report on the status of their job search. If the veteran made more than $20 in one week, the unemployment benefits were terminated. If the veteran made lesser amounts, he or she would receive a reduced allowance that would bring his or her weekly earnings up to $20. Veterans fired for misconduct, or who quit a job without good cause, were barred from further benefits. Title V also contained a "self-employment" allowance, whereby a veteran who earned less than $100 a week in his or her own business or farm would receive an allowance to bring their weekly earnings up to $100.[36]

Many veterans found the unemployment compensation provisions of the GI Bill helpful in reintegrating themselves back into the civilian economy. Rural areas without manufacturing enterprises often had few job opportunities for returning veterans, for example. Navy veteran Robert Blake recalled that "there just weren't all that many jobs" in his hometown of Boscobel in rural southwestern Wisconsin. As he remembered, he was not the only veteran in his area to receive unemployment compensation; "There would be a big line of people" to receive payments, he claimed. Others signed up but found work soon afterward. Army veteran Jerome Nelson of Two Rivers drew unemployment money for only a few weeks until he found steady work with the post office. James Zeasman recalled that he signed up for GI Bill unemployment compensation soon after returning to Madison, but found work at the Oscar Mayer meat packing plant just two days later, so he never had to collect a payment. "I've been fortunate to be in a position," he remembered proudly, "where I have never drawn a penny of unemployment of any sort, any place." In cases such as these, Title V worked exactly as it was supposed to—it provided temporary financial assistance to veterans until they found suitable employment in the turbulent postwar economy.[37]

However, many veterans abused the GI Bill's unemployment provisions. Title V gained an unfavorable reputation as a harbor for veterans supposedly too lazy to work. Veterans receiving the allotment sometimes joked that they were members of the "52-20 Club." As one-time "club" member Jack Dunn remembered, "some [veterans] weren't looking too hard" for work, and that one "could buy a lot of beer for $20 a week." Although veterans receiving unemployment compensation were required to look actively for employment, abusers of Title V learned to obfuscate in order to receive money without working. In September 1946, the *Milwaukee Journal* exposed several ways in which veterans tried *not* to find work. One technique was to appear at a job interview dressed "in a slovenly way and do their best not to impress the employer." Sometimes veterans would demand jobs that could not easily be found. "One chap would take nothing but a job as a deep sea diver and it had to be in Milwaukee," the *Journal* claimed. Many veterans applying for unemployment benefits declared that they were headed for college in the fall, and would take only take temporary work. Veterans would "talk back and forth and pretty soon you learn all the shortcuts," according to Madison army veteran John Hall, who even claimed that "lots of weeks I was too lazy to go up there . . . and get the twenty bucks." Not all abusers of Title V were unwilling to work. Wisconsin Industrial Commission investigators found several cases in which veterans receiving unemployment allowances had failed to disclose that they in fact held jobs, so that they received both a paycheck and an unemployment check.[38]

Precisely how many veterans legitimately needed the readjustment allowance and how many simply wanted to (as the *Milwaukee Journal* phrased it) ride the "gravy train" cannot be known with precision. Willett S. Main, a USES director in Wisconsin, claimed that only an "insignificant" number of Badger State veterans receiving Title V compensation were cheating the system. By contrast, some Wisconsin unemployment compensation officials maintained that "the majority" of veterans on the program were probably "trying to avoid work." By the time eligibility ended for most veterans in 1949, the VA had paid out $3.8 billion in unemployment allowances to veterans nationwide. In all, 59 percent of America's World War II veterans used the program at some point. Program usage in Wisconsin was somewhat lower than the national average, thanks largely to a healthy economy. In all, 52 percent of Wisconsin veterans used the program for a total of $40 million. Of the more than 150,000 Wisconsin veterans who received benefits, officials identified only 200 as fraudulent, with twelve taken to court and only six convicted.[39]

Despite some initial economic turbulence, unemployment was not much of a problem for veterans of World War II. Though after the war unemployment rose from the unnaturally low wartime rates, it did not climb to the extent that many had feared. From a low point of 1.2 percent in 1942, the unemployment rate rose to 3.9 percent in 1946, and then to 5.3 percent in 1950. During the 1950s, unemployment ranged from a low point of 3.0 percent in 1952 to 6.8 percent in 1958. Such rates were far below the double-digit unemployment of the depression years, and even well below the 11.7 percent rate experienced in 1921 after World War I. Along with relatively low unemployment, worker earnings also rose—from an annual national average of $1,299 in 1940 to $2,190 by 1945. Upon the war's conclusion, earnings continued to rise, reaching $3,000 in 1951 and surpassing $4,000 in 1956. Americans' disposable personal income rose from $75.7 billion in 1940 to $206.9 billion in 1950. By 1960, the figure had reached $350 billion. The generation of Americans that had been raised during the Great Depression and had come of age amid the hardships of war was by the 1950s the most economically prosperous the country had yet seen.[40]

Indeed, millions of veterans returned home to find numerous employment opportunities in the expanding postwar economy. At his separation interview, Ralph Lazar of Madison, a lawyer with a background in accounting, was told simply: "I can put you anywhere you want to go." He recalled that "some of the CPA firms that wouldn't even look at me after graduation now had openings," and he quickly found a position with a prestigious Chicago accounting firm. Lazar also found his salary greatly increased. "They were now paying $300 a month," he recalled, "compared to $125 before I went into the army. Several years later, he was able to find work in his hometown of Madison. Some veterans resumed civilian work even before discharge. Army air force veteran John Auby spent his last few months of military service at Truax Field in his hometown of Madison, and resumed his work at a local bakery even before he was discharged. "They begged me to come back," Auby recalled. In fact, many other GIs at Truax worked at the bakery. "They were so short of help," Auby remembered, "that they were using anybody they could get."[41]

The fears of an angry, unemployed mass of veterans selling apples and roaming the streets of America after the war had clearly not materialized. However, the economic reintegration of veterans after World War II was did not occur without some problems. Inevitably, there were some veterans who experienced difficulty in fitting themselves back into the economy. Veterans in certain professions, for example, sometimes found that the war had severely interrupted their practices and eroded their professional skills. Madison attorney Jack DeWitt encountered problems getting his law practice back on track. "I'd forgotten a lot of what I knew about the law," he recalled, "and, of course, I had no clients." Compounding his frustration with his law practice was lingering resentment of colleagues who had not served. "I had some bitterness," he remarked, "about seeing guys who were behind me in law school ahead of me in the profession." Fred Domer, a Milwaukee-area dentist, returned home from the war to find his practice severely interrupted. During the war, he had to give up the office he had rented, and keep his chair and other dental equipment in the garage of a relative. After the war, Domer had trouble finding an office in which to resume his practice. He shared office space with another dentist—also a veteran—until he could locate his own office some months later.[42]

Due in part to the GI Bill, some professions experienced a glut of workers. Engineering was a popular field of study for veterans under the GI Bill (see chapter 4), but many recent graduates claimed to have had difficulty landing a job after leaving school. Stanley McDowell recalled that he "could not find any engineering jobs" for awhile after graduating from the University of Michigan. Through a friend he was finally able to land a position at the Evenrude outboard motor plant in Fond du Lac, and then later at Allis-Chalmers in West Allis. "Those were tough years for engineers," recalled Paul Fergot of Oshkosh, a sentiment echoed by another engineer-veteran, Milwaukeean Donald Wiberg, who claimed that "nobody was begging me to work." Many other professions popular with students under the GI Bill experienced an overabundance of qualified workers. Richard Bates had difficulty finding work as a teacher. "There weren't a lot of teaching jobs opened up yet," he recalled, "because the baby boomers weren't [yet] coming through." While living in Badger Village, Bates serendipitously found work in nearby Baraboo only after a teacher there had left his position suddenly.[43]

Some veterans also found the transition from military to civilian employment emotionally taxing. "The transition restlessness that is complicating all phases of his life . . . may plague him here too," claimed advice writers Dumas and Keen:

> He may feel more or less that the man whose service in the navy has taken him all over the seven seas but whose civilian job as a responsible executive keeps

him in an office all day long. He is upset because he feels he just can't sit at a
desk all day; he can't concentrate on his work. He feels he will simply blow up,
sitting within the same four walls all the time.

Herbert Kupper echoed this theme. "Their impatience and irritability become
readily apparent" on the job, he wrote, but "the difference is he cannot gripe or
become sullen in civilian life. . . . He must fit in with the others" or lose his job.
Morton Thompson warned veterans that the social climate of work would be
very different than it was the military. Unlike the camaraderie military service
often inspires, in civilian life "you may work next to a guy all your life and
never know a thing about him."[44]
    Indeed, some veterans returned to find their civilian jobs uninspiring and
meaningless. Jack DeWitt served as a combat officer in Europe and returned to
his prewar occupation as a lawyer. "It was hard for me to sit down and examine
an abstract," he recalled, "and be concerned about whether the lady that took a
deed in 1890 as Mary Jane Smith was the same Mary Smith that deeded it ten
years later." DeWitt attributed this difficulty to his military experiences.
"You've been in charge of a company of 256 men whose lives are depending on
what you do," he recalled. "All of a sudden you have to worry about . . . petty
things." Spending time confined to an office was also difficult for the former
officer who had commanded troops in the field. As DeWitt confessed, "I spent a
lot of time pacing around that office." Roth Schleck experienced similar emotions upon returning to his job as an accountant. "Even once I got back into the
swing of things," Schleck recalled, "I certainly was a kind of lost soul for
awhile. . . . It was just not that meaningful."[45]
    Other veterans had deep emotional wounds that inhibited their abilities in
the workplace. For veterans returning to factory work, the sounds of machinery
reminded some of combat. Willard Diefenthaler returned to his prewar job in a
woodworking factory in the village of Kiel. He worked there several weeks, but
found the sounds of the workshop too disturbing to continue. "The nailer was
automatic," he recalled. "It sounded like an automatic machine gun. I just got so
goofy that I took off." Using his GI Bill benefits, Diefenthaler pursued a career
in electronics instead. Advice writers assured the veterans and their families that
workplace restlessness was a normal phase of readjustment and would soon
pass. "If he gives it a chance, and gives himself time to readjust," wrote Dumas
and Keen, "he will work into it all right." If the pressure proved too great, they
told their readers, a veteran could occasionally "take a day off and go fishing,
golfing, or hiking in the open air."[46]
    However, many veterans found that war-related disabilities affected their
career choices and performances. Some suffered only minor inconveniences that
inhibited their performance in the workplace to moderate or slight degrees. Bill
Tritz of Waukesha returned from the war with several lingering injuries—shrapnel in his ankle, a chronically sore back, and a "useless" right arm. However, he
claimed that his war injuries affected his work as a mechanic only slightly. "The
only time I had problems was when I had to crawl under a car," he recalled.

"Anything that I could do on top was no problem." Madison's Donald Fellows injured his shoulder while serving in the merchant marine, preventing him from straightening it fully. Fellows pursued a career in acting after the war, and his injury affected his body movements on stage. "I'm a little conscious of it when I see me in a movie," he confessed. "I suddenly see my arm being held oddly," he claimed, and also noted that he frequently kept his hands in his pockets. An incident with an understudy highlighted the slight yet perceptible impact of his injury on his career. "I was in a Broadway show," he recalled, "and . . . my understudy kept carrying his briefcase [in an odd way], and finally the director says, 'Why are you doing that?' and he said, 'Well, that's what Don does.' He says, 'Don does it because he's crippled!'" Joseph Tauchen suffered from recurring bouts of malaria after returning to work at Gisholt Manufacturing in Madison, but downplayed their significance. "Whenever I'd feel it coming on," he recalled, "I'd go down [to the nurse's office] and take a pill. Of course, I'd have to go home, because I was really out." He experienced such attacks for about two years until they eventually subsided.[47]

However, veterans with more serious injuries and medical problems found making a living more difficult. Soon after returning from New Guinea with wounds to his legs in 1943, Herman Owen of Rice Lake found work tending bar, but found the job was "too much on my feet," forcing him leave it. Gifford Coleman, another Pacific war combat veteran from Rice Lake, had attacks of malaria "periodically" while at work. In fact, Coleman remembered that he had to leave several jobs because of his recurrent malaria. Joseph Connors insisted on becoming a letter carrier with the post office despite his war injuries. He carried mail for two years until his war wounds finally forced him to stop. He recalled the day in 1948 that he decided he could not continue:

All these steps go up, and in those days you made two trips. You had two deliveries a day. And we had oodles of magazines—*Liberty, Colliers, Saturday Evening Post*—and on Fridays they'd always go out, and this was on a Friday. And I had all these magazines. Oh, God, and after that first trip I came in and I told the superintendent, "I can't do it anymore." He said, "look, just take out the first class [and] see me when you get back in." While I was back out there he called up the superintendent of mails and explained the situation. Well, he knew that I had a bad leg. And so he said to . . . the superintendent, "tell him we're going to open a [new] parcel post route. . . . Tell him to bid on that."

Connors won the job, which he held for another fifteen years. Indeed, many employers made accommodations for disabled veterans. Allis-Chalmers stated its intention to "make every effort to reinstate veterans incapacitated for their old jobs by placing them in the highest skilled job they can handle." Company foremen were reminded that "handicapped employees are almost always good workers." Disabled veterans unable to maintain a job because of war-related conditions could apply for a government medical pension (see chapter 3).[48]

Some classes of veterans experienced discrimination in the workplace. When the largely male veteran population began returning home from World

War II, women who had entered the workforce often left their jobs—some by choice, but many forced from their jobs to make room for returning men. Women veterans often found themselves unwelcome in the working world as well. In the marines, Connie Allord had served as an air traffic controller at the Cherry Point base in North Carolina. After the war she returned to Madison and hoped to land a similar job at the Madison airport, but was disappointed. "I had a civilian air traffic control license," she recalled, but in seeking civilian employment in the field she was "told flat out that they didn't hire women." Veterans of racial and ethnic minority groups also faced discrimination in many places. In Milwaukee, an African American veteran, who was an experienced auto mechanic before the war and who had served as an army diesel mechanic, went to his local USES office seeking a job in his field. Provided with a list of about fifteen prospective employers, the veteran approached every one but was turned down each time due to what he termed "color restrictions." "I went scouting around," the frustrated man recalled. "I went to every place I know of. I have my own tools. I got all the tools for a garage, but I'm just colored."[49]

As Wisconsin's population of African Americans and other racial and ethnic minorities grew in the 1940s, Wisconsin undertook efforts to eliminate such discrimination. In 1945, the state legislature passed the Fair Employment Act, which declared that it was the policy of the state to "encourage and foster to the fullest extent of the law the employment of all properly qualified persons regardless of race, creed, color, national origin, or ancestry." The law also created the Fair Employment Division within the Industrial Commission, which was tasked with the study and investigation of discrimination in employment. The division found many instances of race-based employment discrimination in the Badger State. A 1947 survey of 123 employers revealed that of 3,943 black workers, only 359 were classified as skilled workers, 21 as clerical, and none in professional positions, leading the agency to conclude that African Americans suffered from severe "underemployment" in Wisconsin. Of the fifty-three complaints of racial discrimination that the division received in the 1950-52 biennium, it found some form of documented race bias in thirty-three of them. Racial discrimination in employment did not end with the creation of the Fair Employment Division; indeed, the agency had no effective enforcement mechanisms until 1957. Nevertheless, the state government machinery for tackling the problem of workplace discrimination had been established in Wisconsin following World War II.[50]

The same cannot be said for the treatment of women in the workplace, however. The Fair Employment Division did not concern itself with sex discrimination at all in the 1940s and 1950s. "It is apparent," claimed the division, that "the serious question of equality and opportunity for all *men* [italics mine] . . . demands the serious consideration of every thoughtful citizen." The popular culture messages to women in the late 1940s suggested strongly to women that they were supposed to give up their wartime jobs and return to domestic life. Veterans' advice writers frequently urged women who had worked during the war years to leave their jobs, in order to assist the readjustment of returning male veterans. Dumas and Keen, for example, reminded married women who wanted to keep working that through marriage they had "taken on the job of making a home," and that a wife's "personal problem must be solved with full consideration for this obligation to the comfort and happiness" of her family. When women veterans such as Connie Allord encountered workplace discrimination, they typically had no recourse.[51]

Wisconsin's Economic Programs for Veterans

Like federal lawmakers, those in Wisconsin worried about the economic situation of returning veterans. Through the Postwar Rehabilitation Trust Fund administered by the Wisconsin Department of Veterans' Affairs, the Badger State offered its veterans economic grants and loans to supplement federal benefits. However, the state's major veterans' organizations also pressed for a cash bonus—just as Wisconsin had provided to its veterans after World War I. But since the buoyant realities of the postwar economy did not correspond to the gloomy prewar predictions, the campaign for a bonus in Wisconsin ultimately failed. The demise of the bonus campaign in Wisconsin suggested the limits to which lawmakers—and taxpayers—were willing to go in the creation of veterans' readjustment benefits in the years after World War II.

In addition to the medical and educational grants discussed in previous chapters, the WDVA also provided veterans with emergency grants that were economic in nature. Economic grants of trust fund money came for a variety of reasons. During the war, emergency grants to the dependents of veterans were common, particularly for family members of disabled veterans whose household income was lowered as a result of the veteran's inability to work. Returning veterans could apply for economic grants to help pay for food, rent, insurance, and other items during temporary emergencies. In particular, such grants assisted veterans who were short on cash as a result of federal benefits being paid late. Grants also covered matters related to employment, including the costs of relocating to another city in search of work. In addition, veterans could obtain grants to assist them in their businesses and farms. In May 1944, for example, the board approved the request of a veteran for a grant to obtain baby chickens, feed, and poultry equipment for his farm. By the end of 1945, the Veterans' Recognition Board and its successor agency, the WDVA, had granted money to veterans and their families in 431 cases classified as dependency, agricultural, or business in nature, amounting to $38,208. The dollar total represented slightly more than a quarter of all grant money dispensed up to that point.[52]

Like medical and educational grants, economic grants from the trust fund continued after 1945, and like the other types of grants, the number rose precipitously as more and more veterans returned home. Economic grants in 1946 were more than double the total of the two previous years. In that year, the WDVA dispensed 1,083 economic grants totaling more than $73,000. Like medical and educational grants, economic grants declined in subsequent years, as the veterans became better established in the civilian world. However, the rate of decline for economic grants was slower than that of other types. In 1950, the WDVA issued 664 economic grants from the trust fund—a 39 percent decrease from the peak 1946 total. By contrast, hospitalization grants dropped 54 percent, medical grants dropped 66 percent, and educational grants a striking 96 percent from their postwar peaks. Of the four basic categories of emergency grants, economic grants ranked fourth in 1946, but in 1950 they ranked first, slightly outpacing hospitalization grants.[53]

In addition to emergency grants, Wisconsin also began a program of economic loans to veterans of World War II. Chapter 409, Laws of 1945, established the Economic Assistance Loan Program. By 1945, the WDVA had ironed out the legal difficulties surrounding loans from the trust fund, and the department was able to have loan repayments returned to that fund. As initially implemented, World War II veterans could borrow up to $750 at 2 percent interest, for a period no longer than three years. In 1947, the loan ceiling was raised to $1,000. To apply for a loan, the veteran had to visit his or her local County Veterans' Service Officer. A local loan committee, usually consisting of the CVSO, a banker, a businessman, and an agriculturist, would investigate the application and send its recommendation to the WDVA's loan advisory committee in Madison, which made the ultimate decision.[54]

The original statute stipulated that veterans could take economic loans "for the purposes of their rehabilitation, education, or for the purpose of aiding and assisting them in the purchase of a property or business." Over subsequent months the Wisconsin Department of Veterans' Affairs expanded its definition of rehabilitation to include a wide range of economic concerns. The WDVA allowed, for example, loans to cover such items as furniture and automobiles, if the department deemed these materials necessary for the veteran's readjustment. Economic loans could be used to consolidate debts the veteran may have incurred while in the service. Veterans could also borrow funds from the WDVA to purchase merchandise stocks for small businesses, and livestock for farmer-veterans. Finally, WDVA economic loans covered circumstances such as making repairs to homes or businesses, the purchase of a mobile home, a down payment for a home, or "other purchases deemed absolutely necessary by the veteran."[55]

The WDVA processed its first economic assistance loan in September 1945, and by the end of the year the agency had distributed 124 loans worth $67,239—nearly as much money as the Veterans' Recognition Board had distributed in grants in its first two years of existence. Not only was state readjustment assistance flowing to the veterans in more significant amounts, but veterans were repaying the loans in a timely and complete fashion. "There are very few delinquencies thus far," reported the chairman of the WDVA's loan advisory committee in February 1946. "In fact," he continued, "the lack of delinquencies is worthy of very favorable comment on the general manner in which this entire matter is being handled." Loans from—and repayments back to—the trust fund continued to soar in 1946. By the end of that year, the WDVA had awarded 2,954 economic assistance loans worth $1.3 million.[56]

But continued fears of depleting the Postwar Rehabilitation Trust Fund haunted officials at Wisconsin's veterans' affairs agency. As a result, the WDVA took as conservative a policy on loans as it did with grants. Indicative of this sentiment was the comment of one WDVA loan counselor who reported that he advised veterans to repay their loans as quickly as possible, "for the reason that there are 310,000 veterans who are potential users of this fund and if loans are repaid each month their 'buddies' will also derive benefits." While agreeing to provide loans for a wide range of economic matters, the WDVA nevertheless dispensed economic loans as sparingly as possible.[57]

As early as 1945, the WDVA loan advisory committee recommended that three particular types of loan applications be "very carefully considered" in order to conserve trust fund money. First, loan officers were told to guard against loans for items that "bordered on luxuries," such as home repairs and automobiles. Second, officials were advised to be wary of applications from veterans seeking loan consolidation for debts not incurred as a result of military service, since their postwar financial difficulties suggested an increased risk of loan default. Finally, officials were to scrutinize "bankable loans"—meaning veterans who could obtain loans through banks and other lending institutions. Guarding against loans to veterans with good credit came not only from the desire to conserve trust fund money, but also to reassure the banking community that, as the WDVA told the Wisconsin Bankers Association, the department was "in no sense going into the loaning business." Indeed, the WDVA went on to tell the bankers to "please remember that one of the first requisites a veteran's eligibility for a [WDVA loan] is that he cannot obtain credit from your bank." Thus, not only did the WDVA deny loans to many veterans with poor credit, but it also denied them to many with good credit.[58]

During the late 1940s, WDVA loan officials continued to screen loan applications extremely closely. In 1950, for example, the committee denied an automobile loan to a veteran who was 30 percent disabled from a gunshot wound to the leg. The veteran argued that having a car to get to work at the post office was a necessity, since walking to and from work aggravated his condition and made him less effective at his job. Noting that the veteran had a steady income and lived within two blocks of a bus stop, the committee denied the loan, stating that "any walking he may do after working hours should not be considered in his rehabilitation program." In many cases, the committee seemed to pass moral judgments as well as financial judgments about loan applications. In 1949, the committee denied a loan to a veteran in the tavern business because "taverns are to be closely watched." By 1950, the committee also recommended against loans to "female Wisconsin veterans who have married and have no independent income for loan repayment." Undoubtedly, the committee received numerous applications from veterans who had histories of bankruptcy and other financial difficulties, and was wise to look at such applications skeptically. However, the committee also denied loans to veterans whose readjustment might have been materially and legitimately aided by an economic assistance loan.[59]

The number of economic assistance loans peaked in 1947, with 4,482 approved loans worth nearly $2.7 million. Like the emergency grants from the trust fund, the number of loans and their cash value declined toward the end of the decade. In 1950, the WDVA approved 2,597 loans worth nearly $1.8 million.[60] How much the decline in both loan and grant awards had to do with the relative economic well-being of veterans, and how much with the conservative loan policies of the WDVA, is unclear. The debate over a bonus for veterans that erupted in the late 1940s, and the ultimate outcome of that debate, suggested that Wisconsin veterans by and large were doing well economically.

The bonus as a method of readjustment assistance came to prominence after World War I. The rationale of a bonus was to compensate veterans for economic opportunities lost while in service. Bonus payments put cash in the veterans' pockets and helped them smooth over temporary economic difficulties. Many veterans also viewed a bonus as a token of gratitude from the state to its veterans for their war services. In 1919, Wisconsin provided its ex-doughboys with a choice of two bonuses, one of which was to be used for educational purposes. At the federal level, agitation for a national bonus led to the Adjusted Compensation Act of 1924, which led ultimately to the 1932 Bonus March and its eventual payment in 1936 (see introduction). Given the scope of the benefit program already enacted for World War II veterans, Americans generally took a dim view of bonus payments to these veterans. According to a 1943 survey, 58 percent of Americans believed that a bonus would be unwarranted if the veterans found "steady" jobs. Nevertheless, as plans for World War II veterans were discussed, bonus proposals reemerged, largely through pressure from veterans' organizations. During the late 1940s and early 1950s, state governments across the nation authorized bonuses for veterans in their states. By 1952, twenty-one states had enacted bonus measures for World War II veterans. Two of Wisconsin's neighbors, Illinois and Michigan, had done so as early as 1946.[61]

Proposals for a Wisconsin bonus emerged as early as 1943, just as serious discussion of Wisconsin's plan for veteran readjustment began to take shape. One assemblyman's plan was simply to use the World War I bonus plan for World War II veterans. Bonus proposals cropped up continually in 1943 and 1944, but in the political fight over consolidating the state's veterans' agencies into the WDVA (see chapter 1), the bonus proposals were defeated, and the issue delayed until federal and state plans for veteran readjustment had taken shape. During 1944 and 1945, Congress passed the GI Bill of Rights, Wisconsin created the WDVA, and World War II came to an end. With the cessation of hostilities and the return of the servicemen and women, pressure increased for the enactment of a bonus measure in the Badger State.

Serious discussion of a state bonus revived in the summer of 1946. The driving force behind the movement was the state's major veterans' associations. Declaring itself "unalterably opposed to . . . any general expansion of taxes or sales taxes," the Wisconsin department of the Veterans or Foreign Wars (VFW) at its annual convention called for the repeal of the state's anti-gambling laws to help pay for a veterans' bonus. The Wisconsin department of the American Legion joined the VFW later that summer. However, divisions over a bonus emerged within the Legion, a portent of the divisive debate to come. An advisory panel at the convention recommended against a bonus. However, the recommendation angered many Legionnaires who favored such a measure. In the end, the Wisconsin American Legion disregarded the panel and a passed resolution favoring a state bonus for World War II veterans.[62]

Proposals for a Wisconsin bonus met immediate opposition from a variety of sources—including prominent veterans—and for a variety of reasons. Some argued that the state was already doing enough for the veterans. One of the first to speak out against a bonus was Leo Levenick, director of the WDVA. Levenick argued that a bonus would be shortsighted and hamper efforts to assist World War II veterans in the future. He argued that once a state authorizes a bonus payment to its veterans, it "clamps together the pages of the statutes and forever afterwards says, 'You've had it.'" He argued that "when a veteran and his wife are lying in a hospital . . . and the bills are mounting to thousands of dollars, he begins to see some merit in having a few dollars left in their state veterans trust fund." Wisconsin's best course of action, Levenick suggested, was to increase the trust fund and continue the grant and loan programs already administered by his agency. Levenick's statement found support in many quarters. Noting that over 12,000 World War II veterans had already received loans or grants from the WDVA, the *Waukesha Freeman* claimed that "Wisconsin is [already] doing a splendid job" with its veterans. "The time may come when veterans will require special treatment from the state beyond what is already being provided," the *Freeman* contended, "but now is not the time."[63]

Another important factor in the development of antibonus sentiment was the potential cost of the program. Estimating the state's World War II veteran population at 350,000, the *Milwaukee Journal* surmised that if the average bonus payment were $200, it would cost the state $70 million; an average bonus of $1,000 would cost the state $350 million. Because the state constitution forbade the state from going into debt, the money for a bonus would have to be raised through taxes. "If tax returns must be diverted to pay for a bonus," the *Journal* warned, "the veterans and their families will share the penalty of poorer public services and facilities. Wisconsin will not have as good schools, hospitals, roads, parks, etc., as it would have, and should have, for the veterans, their children, their friends, and everyone else." The *Waukesha Freeman* echoed the *Journal*'s remarks. "Inasmuch as 30 percent of those who pay taxes next year in Wisconsin will be veterans," the *Freeman* opined, "a good share of the money received in a bonus would have to be paid by the veteran himself." The Wisconsin chapter of the American Veterans' Committee (AVC) called a bonus "a raid on the treasury" that would create "new and burdensome taxes" on Wisconsin's citizens. Some politicians—including prominent World War II veterans—agreed. For example, state senator Warren P. Knowles of New Richmond, a veteran of the navy and a rising star in the state's Republican Party, declared proposals for a state bonus "absurd."[64]

Many feared that politicians pandering for veterans' votes would be drawn to calls for a bonus. Bonuses, claimed the *Janesville Gazette*, are the "pap of irresponsible politicians and others who jingle this bait for their own selfish interests." "When other states pay their veterans a bonus," claimed the *Marshfield News-Herald*, "it will hardly be possible for Wisconsin to avoid it." "Passage of bonus legislation is just as inevitable as history repeating itself," the Marshfield paper stated in another editorial, and warned Wisconsin residents to "get ready to pay." Political columnist John Wyngaard, who specialized in behind-the-scenes reporting at the state capitol, claimed that in his view most legislators did not favor bonus legislation, but felt political pressure to vote for it nonetheless.[65]

By March 1947, a flurry of bonus bills had been introduced to the state legislature. The Democrats—the minority party in search of an issue—were the first to present their proposals. State senator Clement J. Zablocki of Milwaukee introduced a bill, which others signed on to, that would raise $80 million for bonuses. Funds would come from a 60 percent surtax on individual and corporate incomes, and be paid to veterans in installments beginning in 1956. The Republican-dominated taxation committee in the assembly issued its own plan, which proposed to siphon money from the state's highway fund, as well as institute a 50 percent surtax on incomes and inheritances, and deposit these revenues into a special bonus fund to pay veterans at an unspecified future date. The assembly's committee on military and veterans' affairs outlined yet another proposal. Its plan called for an immediate bonus payment of $10 per month for stateside service and $15 per month for overseas service, with a maximum total $500 payment. To raise the funds for it, their bill called for a 60 percent income surtax, as well as additional taxes on items such as beer, wine, cigarettes, cosmetics, jewelry, luggage, hotel bills, juke boxes, and even "customer's bills in cabarets." The military and veterans' affairs committee bill also called for abolishing the existing trust fund and replacing it with a new "veterans' compensation fund" that the WDVA would administer.[66]

The assembly military and veterans' affairs committee held hearings on the bonus issue in April 1947. The majority of those who spoke before the legislature did not favor a bonus. Representatives of hotels, nightclubs, and other businesses singled out in the veterans' affairs committee bill called the proposed taxes "discriminatory," and claimed that many of them would be driven out of business. Some of the harshest rhetoric against the bonus came from the World War II veterans who also addressed the committee. Madison coast guard veteran Horace Wilkie, representing the AVC, called bonus proposals "ill-advised and unsound devices for expressing gratitude to returning servicemen," and suggested the best way to address the needs of veterans was to "knuckle down and lick the problems of housing, loans, education, and our state institutions." Jack DeWitt, a former combat officer and lawyer from Madison, told the committee flatly, "You don't owe us a thing," and stated pointedly that he did not "want some of those jokers I saw enjoying themselves in Paris on $15 a day to get money I'm helping to pay for." Benoni O. Reynolds of Lake Geneva, a student-veteran at the University of Wisconsin, told the committee that he was "against the idea of everybody lining up at the trough," and believed that "a program of aid tailored to meet the veterans needs is much better."[67]

The bonus measures had some powerful supporters, however. Walter Rose, state commander of the American Legion in Wisconsin, appeared before the committee to support a bonus. He told the committee that, in addition to supporting the bonus, the American Legion also proposed to make veterans exempt from any taxes raised to pay for it. Harold S. Clarke, chairman of the Wisconsin VFW's legislative committee, spoke passionately in favor of a bonus. "I'm talking for the veteran who is not here today," he told the assemblymen. Clarke assured the committee that most veterans in Wisconsin favored a bonus, and claimed that if the speakers before the committee were representative of the state's World War II veteran population, "the applause would be ringing in your ears." He went on to claim that his organization represented the common veteran, the "'dirt' veteran, as we speak of the 'dirt' farmer." Despite criticism of the bonus proposals, some legislators continued their support. Assemblyman Richard J. Steffens, Republican of Menasha, an ardent supporter of the bonus, lashed out at the AVC speakers in particular and sounded a note of class antagonism similar to that of Clarke, telling them that "they've got a lot of guts coming up here from college." He went on to assert that the AVC speakers were "all taking their subsistence allowance, I notice," and warned them: "Wait until the depression hits in ten years."[68]

The war of words between veterans over the merits of the bonus spilled over into the newspapers. Although few veterans favoring a bonus spoke before the assembly, scores wrote letters to their local newspapers. "I wonder," wrote Harry F. Mueller of Port Washington,

> if people who are so bitterly opposed to a bonus ever walked so long and far that when they stopped it took only a few seconds to fall fast asleep in the mud and water. Or have you ever gone without sleep for so long that you wanted to tear your eyes out? Have you slept in a foot of snow cold and shivering? Did you ever lie there while planes dove in, churning up the field with machine gun fire? Or listen to the dreaded robot bombs wondering if the engines would shut off over you and in a few seconds explode, blowing you into eternity?

Mueller claimed that "it was then that we dreamed of a new car or our nice soft bed at home." But once back home, Mueller argued, veterans were unable to afford such items in the inflationary postwar economy, and a bonus payment would help them purchase such coveted goods. Sergeant E. T. Kuchta of West Allis, a soldier home on leave from occupation duty that summer, was more blunt. "We were good enough to go overseas and fight," he claimed, but "now we are just bums who would rather live off the 52-20 Club." He believed that "people who sat on their chairs during the war do owe me something." He and other veterans "were willing to give their lives," he argued. "You should be willing to give your dollars."[69]

Veterans who opposed the bonus also wrote letters. Bob Zorn of Milwaukee, an infantryman in the Pacific during the war, believed that a bonus would be "wonderful" but feared it would increase prices and taxes. "I'd like $500," he wrote. "I could use it. But there are two sides to every question, and I believe if we can 'sweat it out' a bit longer the situation will right itself." He urged his fellow veterans to "try not to be selfish" and to "be honest" with themselves and their fellow citizens. Nonveterans also wrote in with their opinions on the bonus issue. "Politicians must think our veterans have the mentality of 2 year olds," claimed "Alice S. V." of Milwaukee. "Do some people honestly believe that all GI brains have ceased to look into the future?" She called a bonus "an insult to the intelligence of our veterans to offer them a certain sum and then ask that they pay it back in pennies over a 10 year period." In a letter to Madison's *Capital Times*, an unidentified citizen from Manitowoc who signed the letter "Taxpayer," argued that veterans and America's corporations—which the writer claimed received numerous tax breaks—"seem to constitute our leisure class." "Taxpayer" argued that instead of giving veterans a bonus, the state should "give the salaried individual a chance and not destroy his initiative with burdensome taxes. Some of us in addition to providing the wherewithal for handouts have to provide for our own old age."[70]

Faced with political pressure from influential veterans' organizations, a voting public hotly divided on the issue, and a tight state budget, lawmakers in Madison decided to place the proposal for a bonus—and the increased taxes needed to fund it—on the ballot in a nonbinding referendum. Action came in the Wisconsin state senate, but the question the senators devised was controversial. In late June 1947, senate Republicans devised a referendum question that read simply: "Shall the legislature enact a 3 percent retail sales tax to raise a total sum not to exceed $200,000,000 to be used to finance a bonus for the veterans of World War II?" Senate Democrats claimed that linking the bonus with the tax would spell certain doom for the bonus measure, and argued that voters should be able to pick from a variety of tax options. But Republicans held firm, and argued that the only kind of tax that could realistically raise the funds needed for a bonus was a sales tax. "Let's not give the people a sugar-coated pill," argued Senator Rudolph Schlabach, Republican of La Crosse. "If people want a bonus, they should know that it's going to cost them money." Senator Fred Risser of Madison—the last Progressive in the state senate—sided with the Republicans, arguing that "it is political cowardice not to include the tax-raising method in the referendum." The senate passed the referendum question, 25-5, with only Democrats voting against it. The measure then passed the Republican-dominated assembly. The referendum question would be put to the voters in the November 1948 general election.[71]

The referendum, as it was worded, pleased no one. Veterans' groups that had backed a bonus came out against this particular referendum question. At its state convention in the summer of 1948, the Wisconsin American Legion passed a resolution favoring the bonus but opposing the tax, since it would force veterans to pay for their own bonus, and urged its members to vote against the referendum question. Wisconsin's VFW expressed similar sentiments. That organization asked its members, and indeed all voters, to "refrain from marking their ballots in the usual manner," but instead write in "Bonus—Yes, Sales Tax—No." In a poll of Wisconsin's VFW posts in early 1948, all responding posts favored a bonus but objected to the sales tax. In a similar poll taken in October 1948, fully 88 percent of responding VFW posts in Wisconsin objected to the sales tax, and not one post went on record as being against the bonus.[72]

The proposed sales tax raised the ire of other groups. Taxpayer organizations objected strenuously to the measure. The bonus measure and the 3 percent sales tax, argued one local taxpayer group, "would saddle the people of this state with a new tax at a time when the tax burden has reached the highest point in history, and would open the way for making this tax permanent." If the 3 percent sales tax were collected, the Wisconsin Citizens Public Expenditure Survey pointed out, it would amount to the equivalent of the entire state budget for fiscal year 1946-47. Others spoke out against the bonus and the proposed tax to pay for it. A poll of farmers taken by the *Wisconsin Agriculturist and Farmer* magazine in October 1948 indicated that 65 percent of Wisconsin farmers planned to vote against the measure. "The boys should get a bonus," claimed a Wood County farmer, "but not by a sales tax." The Wisconsin League of Women Voters came out against the sales tax as well, arguing that a sales tax "ran directly counter to ability to pay," and would especially burden the poor—including low-income veterans.[73]

Indeed, as the election drew near, the bonus referendum had no active political support. "As far as political circles here have learned," wrote John Wyngaard, "there has been no effort anywhere to form a campaign in support of an affirmative vote for the referendum." Meeting with disapproval from veterans' organizations, taxpayer groups, and a variety of other sources, the bonus referendum was doomed to failure. When the election finally came in November 1948, the bonus measure lost, 825,990 to 258,497. Wisconsin was one of four states to reject a veterans' bonus on that election day, while six states approved bonus measures.[74]

After the 1948 defeat, bonus proposals were revived, but again went nowhere. By May 1949 three new bonus measures—supported by the American Legion and the VFW—had been suggested in the state legislature, but remained bottled up in committee. Proposals for World War II bonus payments reappeared in the legislature repeatedly, and involved a variety of funding mechanisms—including income surtaxes, the diversion of funds from the state's veterans' housing trust fund (see chapter 6), and taxes on items such as inheritances, cigarettes, oleomargarine, and property transfers. Indeed, between 1947 and 1967 more than twenty bonus proposals had appeared, but none met with success. As the American economy continued to grow in the 1960s, the economic pressure on most veterans was even less. "It . . . is doubtful," predicted the *Blue Book* in 1962, "that the state will commit itself to a $200,000,000 one-shot payment for which there is at best only a moral obligation." The last bonus attempt, in 1967, proposed a 50 percent increase in proposed a 50 percent increase in liquor taxes to pay for a bonus for World War II and Korean War veterans.[75]

Despite agitation by the state's major veterans' groups, a widespread demand for a World War II veteran bonus did not emerge in the Badger State. In Wisconsin, the bonus failed for several reasons. First, the state's voters did not seem to believe a bonus was warranted. Never before had federal and state governments done so much for veterans. Bonus advocates had difficulty justifying a bonus given the array of economic assistance programs for veterans already in existence. Nonveteran taxpayers also lived in the inflationary, shortage-wracked economy, and the potential for further tax increases to pay for yet another veterans' program apparently made many voters think of their own survival in the postwar economy and led to their decision to reject it. The healthy and improving nature of the postwar economy also influenced opinions on the bonus. Most veterans were apparently doing well economically. The World War II veterans' programs appeared to be having the desired effect of alleviating the problems associated with readjustment to civilian life. A bonus for veterans did not seem to be an economic necessity.

Second, advocates of the bonus probably overestimated the extent of their political influence. Clearly, veterans represented a significant voting constituency, and organizations such as the American Legion and the VFW commanded the attention of lawmakers. However, their strident nature and unwillingness to compromise was unpopular with voters. Probonus veterans also attempted to invoke society's "moral obligation" to the defenders of the nation, but with the existing system of veterans' benefits the public apparently believed that obligation had been met. Opposition to the bonus on the part of many fellow veterans further weakened the case of those favoring the bonus. Given the improving state of the economy and the success of existing veterans' programs, the bonus seemed more like a grab for power and money than an economic necessity. Americans after World War II were willing to pay a high price to integrate veterans back into the civilian world and head off potential veteran unrest. However, they were unwilling to give veterans a blank check. Once it became clear that existing benefits were working, public support for additional programs evaporated.

Conclusion

The ultimate impact of war service and vocational benefits for World War II veterans is unclear. Some studies have indicated that World War II veterans generally had higher incomes than did nonveterans of the same age group, though the reasons for the "veterans advantage" are uncertain. Educational and vocational assistance programs, some have argued, provided World War II veterans with economic opportunities beyond those available to their nonveteran peers. Some scholars also point to the broad mobilization of America's youth during the war. Unlike the Vietnam War period, during which working-class men composed a majority of soldiers while middle- and upper-class youth frequently received exemptions from military service, World War II brought an entire generation of Americans into the armed forces—rich and poor, college graduate and grammar school dropout. Many of those who did not enter the service were classified as unfit for military service. Studies have indeed shown that though World War II veterans earned more than did their nonveteran cohorts, Vietnam veterans earned only as much or even less than did nonveterans. Others have painted a less positive portrait of World War II veterans in the civilian economy. Several studies have indicated the World War II veterans held no particular economic advantage over nonveterans, and some have even suggested that veterans earned less than they might have expected as a result of military service.[76]

What is clear is that the economic readjustment of World War II veterans went much more smoothly than had been anticipated. World War II did not significantly hinder the long-term economic status of most of its veterans, and may well have enhanced the earning potential of some ex-soldiers. As Americans during World War II looked to the postwar period, the primary concern of most with regard to the readjustment of veterans to civilian life was employment. Haunted by memories of the Great Depression and the widespread unemployment following World War I, lawmakers crafted a far-reaching plan to carry veterans from the military to the civilian economy as quickly and as smoothly as possible. The volume of job-related legislation for veterans was unprecedented: retention of prewar jobs, on-the-job training, civil service preference for veterans, and unemployment compensation, to name just a few of the most important programs. Because of the booming postwar economy, widespread veteran unemployment did not develop. As the Wisconsin bonus controversy suggests, most veterans and nonveteran citizens were satisfied with the existing economic assistance programs for veterans. The ease with which the World War II veteran returned to work helped exorcise the ghosts of the Bonus March. Also, if Morton Thompson was indeed correct that "having a job takes the soldier-on-leave element out of being a Civilian," then World War II veterans were indeed able to leave their military service and salary behind them with relative ease.

Notes

1. Benjamin Bowker, *Out of Uniform* (New York: Norton, 1946), 177; Morton Thompson, *How to Be a Civilian* (Garden City, N.Y.: Doubleday, 1946), 91.

2. Samuel Stouffer et al., *The American Soldier* (Princeton, N.J.: Princeton University Press, 1949), vol. 2, 598-599.

3. U.S. Department of Commerce, *Historical Statistics of the United States: Colonial Times to 1970* (Washington, D.C.: GPO, 1975), 199.

4. Eckstam interview, Wisconsin Veterans' Oral History Project, Wisconsin Veterans' Museum Research Center, Madison, Wis. (cited hereafter as WVOHP); Ray interview, WVOHP; Graven interview, WVOHP; Eugene T. Petersen, ed., *A Chance for*

Love: The World War II Letters of Marian Elizabeth Smith and Lt. Eugene T. Petersen, USMCR (East Lansing: Michigan State University Press, 1998), 419, 430.

5. Hochschild interview, WVOHP; Robert Peters, *For You, Lili Marlene: A Memoir of World War II* (Madison: University of Wisconsin Press, 1996), 104; Bernhagen interview, WVOHP.

6. Thompson, *How to Be a Civilian*, 55-56.

7. Hendersin, Wisconsin Women in World War II Oral History Project, State Historical Society of Wisconsin Archives, Madison, Wis. (cited hereafter as WW2OHP); Petersen, *A Chance for Love*, 434; Peters, *For You, Lili Marlene*, 106.

8. Howards interview, WVOHP; Hendersin interview, WW2OHP; Bredenson interview, WW2OHP; Kenneth Johnson interview, WVOHP.

9. Jack C. Plano, *Fishhooks, Apples, and Outhouses* (Kalamazoo, Mich.: Personality Press, 1991), 130; Tauchen interview, WVOHP; J. J. Kuhn, *I Was Baker 2: Memoirs of a World War II Platoon Sergeant* (West Bend, Wis.: DeRaimo Publishing, 1994), 224; Petersen, *A Chance for Love*, 414, 448; Peters, *For You, Lili Marlene*, 106.

10. Clampitt interview, WVOHP; Tauchen interview, WVOHP; Petersen, *A Chance for Love*, 448; Mercier interview, WVOHP.

11. Kachelmeier file, World War II Small Collections, Wisconsin Veterans' Museum Research Center, Madison, Wis.; Richtsmeier interview, WVOHP; Rabidieux interview, WW2OHP.

12. U.S. Veterans' Administration, *Administrator of Veterans' Affairs Annual Report*, 1947 ed. (Washington, D.C.: GPO, 1948), 33-34; U.S. Veterans' Administration, *Annual Report*, 1950 ed., 75.

13. Gerlach interview, WVOHP; Baehr interview, WW2OHP; Petersen, *A Chance for Love*, 406; Hall interview, WVOHP.

14. Peters, *For You, Lili Marlene*, 105-106; *Wisconsin State Journal*, 7 May 1946; *Fond du Lac Commonwealth Reporter*, 21 February 1946.

15. The details of the National Service Life Insurance program as it developed are chronicled in the VA *Annual Report*, 1940-50 eds.

16. Prentice-Hall, *Veteran's Guide* (New York: Prentice-Hall, 1945), 24.

17. *State Government*, March 1946.

18. *Chicago Sun*, 22 September 1946; Scocos interview, WVOHP; Hochschild interview, WVOHP; Juanita Wilkie interview, WVOHP; Allis-Chalmers Manufacturing Co., *You and the Returning Veteran: A Guide for Foremen* (West Allis, Wis.: Allis-Chalmers Manufacturing Co., 1945), 2-4.

19. Tauchen interview, WVOHP; Schleck interview, WVOHP.

20. *New York Times*, 3 June 1944; Gerald Wilkie interview, WVOHP; Day interview, WW2OHP; Charles Hurd and Charles Bolté, "How We Planned for the Veterans' Return," in *While You Were Gone: A Report on Wartime Life in the United States*, ed. Jack Goodman (New York: Simon and Schuster, 1946), 538; Maxwell Droke, *Good-by to GI: How to Be a Successful Civilian* (New York: Abingdon-Cokesbury Press, 1945), 87.

21. Wisconsin Legislative Reference Bureau, *Wisconsin Blue Book*, 1946 ed. (Madison: Legislative Reference Bureau, 1946), 161.

22. *Blue Book*, 1946 ed., 162-163; *Capital Times*, 9 November 1945.

23. Rhinelander files, GI Training Files, Records of the Wisconsin Industrial Commission, Division of Apprenticeship and Training, State Government Records, State Historical Society of Wisconsin Archives, Madison, Wis. (cited hereafter as GI Training Files); Soldier's Grove files, GI Training Files; Verifine Dairy files (Sheboygan), GI Training files; *Wisconsin State Journal*, 20 January 1946, 3 March 1946.

24. *Capital Times*, 16 June 1946; *Milwaukee Journal*, 7 August 1946; Francis J. Brown, *Educational Opportunities for Veterans* (Washington, D.C.: Public Affairs Press, 1946), 82; *Chicago Sun*, 29 May 1946.

25. Montello Granite Company file, GI Training Files; *Capital Times*, 16 June 1946; *Milwaukee Journal*, 7 August 1946.

26. Wisconsin Department of Veterans' Affairs, *Farming in Wisconsin: Information for Veterans* (Madison: Wisconsin Department of Veterans' Affairs, 1946), 20-32.

27. U.S. Veterans' Administration, *Annual Report*, 1950 ed., 365-366.

28. U.S. Civil Service Commission, *History of Veteran Preference in Federal Employment 1865-1955* (Washington, D.C.: GPO, 1955).

29. Connors interview, WVOHP; Onhieber interview, WVOHP; Freese interview, WVOHP; *History of Veteran Preference*, 39.

30. Stouffer, *American Soldier*, vol. 1, 312-329; Flaten interview, WVOHP.

31. Schmidt interview, WVOHP; Doro interview, WVOHP; Howe interview, WVOHP; Giese interview, WVOHP.

32. Dunn interview, WVOHP; Kobishop interview, WW2OHP; Charles Bradley, *Aleutian Echoes* (Fairbanks: University of Alaska Press, 1994).

33. Farnham Johnson interview, WVOHP; Niebuhr interview, WVOHP; Willett interview, WVOHP.

34. Stouffer, *American Soldier*, vol. 2, 598; Robert Dean interview, WVOHP; Stapleton interview, WVOHP; Wald interview, WVOHP; Crabb interview, WVOHP.

35. Junkermann interview, WVOHP; Wallace interview, WVOHP; Clampitt interview, WVOHP; Mary Ann Renard interview, WVOHP.

36. Wisconsin Industrial Commission, *Readjustment Allowances for Veterans* (Madison: Wisconsin Industrial Commission, 1946).

37. Blake interview, WVOHP; Nelson interview, WVOHP; Zeasman interview, WVOHP.

38. Dunn interview, WVOHP; *Milwaukee Journal*, 15 September 1946; Hall interview, WVOHP; Unemployment Compensation Department, Transcripts of Hearings (Veterans' Appeals), State Government Records, State Historical Society of Wisconsin Archives, Madison, Wis. (cited hereafter as UC Veterans' Appeals). For examples, see cases V-528 and V-773.

39. *Milwaukee Journal*, 15 September 1946, 9 March 1947, 13 July 1949.

40. *Historical Statistics*, 135, 164, 224.

41. Lazar interview, Stephen E. Ambrose World War II Interview Collection, Wisconsin Veterans' Museum Research Center, Madison, Wis. (cited hereafter as Ambrose Collection); Auby interview, WVOHP.

42. DeWitt interview, WVOHP; Domer interview, Ambrose Collection.

43. McDowell interview, WVOHP; Donald Wiberg interview, WVOHP, Bates interview, WVOHP.

44. Dorothy Baruch and Lee Edward Travis, *You're Out of the Service Now* (New York: Appleton-Century, 1946), 143; Alexander G. Dumas and Grace Keen, *A Psychiatric Primer for the Veteran's Family and Friends* (Minneapolis: University of Minnesota Press, 1945), 32; Thompson, *How to Be a Civilian*, 89.

45. DeWitt interview, WVOHP; Schleck interview, WVOHP.

46. Diefenthaler interview, WVOHP; Dumas and Keen, *Psychiatric Primer*, 32.

47. Tritz interview, WVOHP; Fellows interview, WVOHP; Tauchen interview, WVOHP.

48. Owen interview, WVOHP; Coleman interview, WVOHP; Connors interview, WVOHP; Allis-Chalmers, *You and the Returning Veteran*, 2-7.

49. Lorraine Allord interview, WVOHP; Hearing No. V-1238, UC Veterans' Appeals.

50. Wisconsin Industrial Commission, *Fair Employment* (Madison: Wisconsin Industrial Commission, 1948); Wisconsin Industrial Commission, Fair Employment Division, *Report, 1950-1952* (Madison: Wisconsin Industrial Commission, 1952); Thompson, *Continuity and Change*, 329-331. For historical context of African Americans in the Wisconsin work force, see Joe William Trotter Jr., *Black Milwaukee: The Making of an Industrial Proletariat, 1915-45* (Chicago: University of Illinois Press, 1985).

51. Dumas and Keen, *Psychiatric Primer*, 8.

52. *Milwaukee Journal*, 4 May 1944; Veterans' Recognition Board minutes, 26 May 1944, Records of the Wisconsin Department of Veterans' Affairs, State Government Records, State Historical Society of Wisconsin Archives, Madison, Wis. (cited hereafter as WDVA); WDVA Board minutes, 15 February 1946, WDVA.

53. WDVA Board minutes, 1946-51, WDVA (data extracted by author).

54. *Blue Book*, 1946 ed., 147-149; Wisconsin Legislative Reference Bureau, *A Thumbnail History of Wisconsin Veterans' Legislation* (Madison: Legislative Reference Bureau, 1988), 7-8; Veterans' Recognition Board minutes, 9 March 1945, WDVA.

55. *Blue Book*, 1946 ed., 147-148.

56. WDVA Board minutes, 15 February 1946, WDVA.

57. WDVA Board minutes, 14 December 1945, WDVA.

58. WDVA Board minutes, 14 December 1945, WDVA.

59. WDVA Board minutes, 23 November 1949, 21 April 1950, 8 August 1950, WDVA.

60. WDVA Board minutes, 1946-50, WDVA (data extracted by author).

61. Jerome S. Bruner, *Public Thinking on Post-War Problems* (Washington, D.C.: National Planning Association, 1943), 27; W. Brooke Graves, *American State Government*, 4th ed. (Boston: D. C. Heath, 1953), 414-416.

62. Veterans of Foreign Wars, Department of Wisconsin, *Proceedings of the Twenty-Fifth Annual Encampment of the Veterans of Foreign Wars Department of Wisconsin* (Madison: Veterans of Foreign Wars, Department of Wisconsin, 1946), 29 June 1946; *Wisconsin State Journal*, 27 June 1946; *Milwaukee Journal*, 8 August 1946.

63. *Beloit News*, 19 June 1946; *Wisconsin State Journal*, 27 June 1946; *Waukesha Freeman*, 12 November 1946.

64. *Milwaukee Journal*, 8 August 1946; *Waukesha Freeman*, 12 November 1946; *Janesville Gazette*, 15 November 1946.

65. *Janesville Gazette*, 5 November 1946; *Green Bay Press-Gazette*, 6 January 1947; *Marshfield News-Herald*, 28 January 1947, 25 April 1947.

66. *Milwaukee Journal*, 19 March 1947; *Capital Times*, 20 March 1947, 21 March 1947; *Wisconsin State Journal*, 20 March 1947.

67. *Milwaukee Journal*, 1 May 1947; *Wisconsin State Journal*, 1 May 1947.

68. *Milwaukee Journal*, 1 May 1947; *Wisconsin State Journal*, 1 May 1947.

69. *Milwaukee Journal*, 27 March 1947, 6 April 1947.

70. *Milwaukee Journal*, 9 April 1947; *Capital Times*, 30 April 1947.

71. *Wisconsin State Journal*, 26 June 1947, 1 July 1947; *Milwaukee Journal*, 27 June 1947.

72. *Milwaukee Journal*, 16 February 1948; *Milwaukee Sentinel*, 29 October 1948; Veterans of Foreign Wars, Department of Wisconsin, *Proceedings of the Twenty-Seventh Annual Encampment, Veterans of Foreign Wars Department of Wisconsin* (Madison: Veterans of Foreign Wars, Department of Wisconsin, 1948), 25 June 1948.

73. *Wisconsin Tax News*, 25 October 1948; *Green Bay Press-Gazette*, 11 October 1948; *Wisconsin Agriculturist and Farmer*, 16 October 1948; *Milwaukee Journal*, 16 October 1948.

74. *Green Bay Press-Gazette*, 11 October 1948; *Blue Book*, 1950 ed., 777.

75. *Green Bay Press-Gazette*, 13 May 1949; *Milwaukee Journal*, 2 June 1949; *Thumbnail History*, 5; *Blue Book*, 1962 ed., 238.

76. For discussion of World War II veterans and their long-term economic status, see Joshua Angrist and Alan B. Krueger, "Why Do World War II Veterans Earn More than Nonveterans?" *Journal of Labor Economics* 12 (1994): 74-97; Robert J. Havinghurst et al., *The American Veterans Back Home: A Study in Veteran Readjustment* (New York: Longmans, Green, 1951); and Jerry Maynard Trott, "A Veterans' Advantage? World War II and Vietnam Compared," Ph.D. diss., Duke University, 1989.

Chapter Six

"A Safe, Quiet, and Peaceful Place": Housing Readjustments

In the predawn hours of April 13, 1945, the U.S. Army's 96th Infantry Division found itself under Japanese attack on the island of Okinawa. One soldier in that unit, TSgt. Beaufort T. Anderson of Soldier's Grove, Wisconsin, faced scores of oncoming Japanese soldiers alone. Armed only with a carbine, he managed to hold off the attackers. After "emptying one magazine at point-blank range into the screaming attackers," Anderson "seized an enemy mortar dud and threw it back among the charging Japs," killing several enemy soldiers. He then found a box of American mortars, which he was able to arm by "banging the bases upon a rock." He then "proceeded alternately to hurl shells and fire his piece among the fanatical foe." Wounded and bleeding, Anderson single-handedly killed twenty-five Japanese soldiers and forced the remainder to withdraw. For his extraordinary efforts on the field of battle, Anderson received the Congressional Medal of Honor, the nation's highest military decoration. But Anderson's battle-field bravery did not help him find a place to live after the war. In 1947, Anderson landed a job with the VA regional office in Milwaukee. However, due to the lack of suitable housing in that city, his wife and two-year-old son had to stay behind in his wife's hometown of Beloit—seventy-three miles away. Anderson was not alone in having trouble finding a place to live. Millions of veterans returned from war to find America in the grip of a severe housing shortage.[1]

For Americans, home ownership had long symbolized independence and individual liberty, exemplified by the adage, "a man's home is his castle." But in the years immediately following World War II, such castles were difficult to attain. After fifteen years of depression and war, home construction had drastically declined, and after the war the nation faced a shortage of adequate dwellings. In the competition for scarce living space, the returning veteran was in a rather poor position. Not only had most veterans been out of the civilian housing market for years, but as young men and women at the beginning of their adult lives, they were also at the bottom of prevailing wage and salary scales and thus faced financial limitations on what they could pay for housing. The propensity of young veterans to marry and have children only complicated matters further. Adequate housing was crucial for the returning veteran to make a successful readjustment to civilian life. To meet this final veteran readjustment need, government—at the federal, state, and local levels—devised housing programs which, though controversial, set the stage for a postwar housing boom.[2]

The Postwar Housing Shortage

The Great Depression that began in 1929 hit the American housing industry particularly hard. The prosperity of the 1920s had launched a boom in home construction. In 1925, housing starts in the United States peaked at 937,000. From there, housing starts declined to 753,000 in 1928, and after 1929 plummeted precipitously. By 1933, housing starts had dropped to only 93,000—down from nearly a million eight years before. The decline in home building meant that Americans had fewer and fewer places to live, but it had other effects as well. Some economists theorized, for example, that the sagging housing industry—which employed thousands nationwide—was acting as a drag on the economy, helping to further the downward spiral of the depression. Not only was America's housing stock in short supply, but also many existing dwellings had become dilapidated. When the Great Depression struck, the mean age of residential structures in the United States was 26.8 years. As housing starts declined, the mean age of housing went up. By the time World War II ended in 1945, the average age of residences in the United States had reached 34.2 years.[3]

To help stimulate the housing industry, the federal government took its first significant steps into the American housing market. In 1932, President Herbert Hoover signed the Federal Home Loan Bank Act and the Emergency Relief and Construction Act, both of which provided federal money to the mortgage and construction industries to stimulate home construction. The parsimonious nature of the plans and the imminent demise of the Hoover administration doomed the projects, however. Hoover's successor, Franklin D. Roosevelt, enacted a more aggressive program. To arrest the rate of foreclosures (which occurred at the rate of 1,000 per day when Roosevelt took office), Congress created the Home Owners Loan Corporation in 1933, which essentially refinanced endangered home loans.

A particularly important part of Roosevelt's programs was the National Housing Act of 1934. He hoped to stimulate private housing industry, which (it was hoped) would restart the housing industry, provide new homes, and help alleviate unemployment. To stimulate home construction, the housing act sought to liberalize credit terms for home purchases. The 1934 law created the Federal Housing Administration (FHA), which insured the loans that private lending institutions made to homebuyers. Prior to the creation of the FHA, the credit terms for the purchase of a home required more money than most Americans could afford. Before 1934, Americans generally needed a down payment of at least 30 percent of the home's purchase price. With FHA loan insurance, lenders were able to allow home purchases with as little as 10 percent down. Federal insurance, and its promise that lenders would recoup a good portion of their money if a loan went bad, also helped to lower interest rates. By extending the typical repayment period to twenty-five years, the FHA also lowered a borrower's monthly payments and thus decreased the chances of foreclosure. In addition, the FHA set minimum standards for construction and home quality that became industry standards. By insuring private home loans, liberalizing credit terms, and setting quality standards, the Housing Act of 1934 and the FHA revolutionized the way Americans purchased homes.

The FHA loan program had a significant impact upon the housing industry. Despite depression conditions, new home starts rose dramatically during the 1930s. From the 1933 low point of 93,000 starts, housing starts by 1941 had reached to 620,000. Home starts using FHA loans jumped from 14,000 in 1935 to more than 220,000 in 1941. Housing starts plummeted again after 1942, this time because building materials were channeled into the war effort. Nevertheless, the FHA showed that the federal government could successfully stimulate the housing industry. "No agency of the United States government," wrote historian Kenneth Jackson, "has had a more pervasive and powerful impact on the American people over the past half century" than the FHA.[4]

Not only were methods of financing homes revolutionized during the years of depression and war, but so were methods of constructing new homes. War production brought jobs back to America, but it also stimulated mass migrations of people. To obtain war jobs, people frequently had to move hundreds or even thousands of miles from their homes. Though jobs often became plentiful, they were concentrated in specific cities and regions with defense-related industries, causing acute housing shortages in those areas. To meet the emergency need for war worker housing, the federal government passed the Lanham Act in 1940, providing $150 million for defense worker housing, a figure later increased to $1.3 billion.

In meeting the wartime needs, the American housing industry developed a number of innovations that also revolutionized the way Americans lived and the number of Americans able to own their own homes. One innovation was the development of mass-produced housing. By the twentieth century, home construction had been combined with the modern industrial assembly line to create the potential for the mass production of dwellings. By the 1930s, builders began to explore ways to construct entire sections of homes in factories and then assemble them on site. During the war, many of the housing units were built to be "demountable." Such housing, architects believed, could be assembled and then disassembled quickly and easily. Housing could be moved to different locations depending on space needs and could then be removed at the end of the war, leaving no abandoned or dilapidated neighborhoods behind. Many builders gained experience in producing large numbers of homes in a short time. The construction company of Levitt and Sons in New York, which up to the 1940s had specialized in upscale homes on Long Island, received a navy contract to build tract housing for defense workers near Norfolk, Virginia, during the war. The Norfolk homes were unspectacular: simple wooden structures on concrete slabs. One of those sons, William J. Levitt, then served during the war in a navy construction battalion, where he helped build airstrips and military camps in the Pacific and gained further insight into mass production of homes and other structures. The wartime experiences of the Levitts and others would lead to a revolution in home building after the war.[5]

World War II also gave rise to the house trailer, or mobile home, as a mode of affordable housing. Trailers for camping and vacationing emerged in the 1920s with the rise of the automobile. In the housing crunch of the 1930s, some began to see the travel trailer as another form of mass-produced affordable housing. Indeed, some Americans began living in trailers during the Great Depression out of necessity. Local governments often disliked trailer dwellers, because they paid no local taxes yet consumed public services such as water and electricity. Many localities passed ordinances discouraging the use of trailers as permanent housing within their boundaries. However, World War II showed the usefulness of the trailer as an affordable permanent dwelling. Trailers could be quickly mass-produced and easily transported to locations where the housing needs were critical. As their utility as homes became evident, the design of trailer homes improved (though in the rush to produce trailers for workers, quality sometimes suffered). During World War II, about 200,000 trailers were used as housing in the United States. According to one estimate, fully one in eight war workers had been housed in a trailer at some point during the war. Mobile homes and prefabricated housing made great strides during World War II, and allowed for significant growth in the housing supply following the war.[6]

When Wisconsin's veterans began returning home in large numbers after 1945, they often had difficulty finding a place to live. The housing problem was most acute in the state's major cities. "Most of the returning veterans are having an extremely difficult time finding living accommodations," wrote Madison coast guard veteran Horace Wilkie to a friend in 1946. Though the most severe shortages occurred in Madison and Milwaukee, housing problems were not limited to the state's larger cities. Veterans returning to smaller cities, villages, and even rural areas also had trouble finding places to live. Jerome Nelson remembered that when he returned from the army, "apartments were hard to come by" in his hometown of Two Rivers, a small city with a population of 10,302 in 1940.[7]

Lack of housing forced some veterans and their families into difficult personal situations. Although army veteran Vernon Bernhagen found a job in Wisconsin Rapids, he "couldn't find anywhere . . . to live" in that city. He eventually found an apartment for his wife and himself in Stevens Point, twenty-one miles to the north. Bernhagen was not the only person who could not find a home in Wisconsin Rapids. He commuted to Wisconsin Rapids with "five other guys," as he remembered. Finding a place to live, Bernhagen later claimed, was "the hardest part" of his own postwar readjustment. Many married couples were forced to live apart. Army veteran Henry Lashway of Sheboygan took a job as a physical education teacher at a junior high school in Des Plaines, Illinois, but due to a lack of housing there his wife was forced to remain in Wisconsin. "I lived in a room and commuted to Sheboygan on weekends," he later wrote, "leaving after school on Friday and returning on Sunday." Lucille Rabidieux, an army nurse in Australia during the war, found work at the Hayward Indian Hospital in northern Wisconsin and was able to live in a women's dormitory at the facility. Her husband, Francis M. "Chick" Rabidieux, also an army veteran and hospital employee, lived in the hospital's men's dormitory, but the couple could not live together. The arrangement became even less desirable when Lucille became pregnant. She finally found a nursing job at a veterans' hospital in Chicago.[8]

Finding a place to live often took personal connections. Horace Wilkie of Madison considered himself fortunate to find "a small house in the suburbs" for his family. He obtained the house, he wrote a friend, only because "my older brother, the doctor, was successful in locating a more expensive and larger house." Another Madisonian, Kermit Bliss, found an apartment through a relative. His brother-in-law lived in a complex known jokingly as "Taylor's Tenements" in downtown Madison. Bliss talked to the complex's owner, and learned of an impending vacancy. "Rather than putting it on the market," Bliss recalled, "he let us rent it." The apartments were "pretty run down," he remembered, but the owner allowed the veteran and his wife to paint and furnish the place as they saw fit. Bliss hoped to live in "Taylor's Tenements" only a short time, but it took them two years to find a better place to live.[9]

Places such as "Taylor's Tenements" were not at all unusual in postwar Wisconsin. Many veterans who were able to find places to live found them less than acceptable. Among the first veterans to return to Wisconsin was Eau Claire native Aleron Larson, a bomber pilot wounded in the Pacific in 1943. He enrolled at the University of Wisconsin in Madison, but was forced to move more than six times before the end of 1944 because of poor accommodations. One basement apartment, for example, proved to be too damp and aggravated Larson's wounded arm. Milwaukeean Robert Reule, who had served on a navy destroyer during the war, claimed that his apartment, which had "no heat, no gas, no nothing," was "not fit for rats." Donald Mercier purchased a trailer and lived in it with his wife in a complex near the village of Oregon in Dane County. The trailers were so close together, Mercier recalled, that "when you opened your window it would hit the next trailer's window." Because the complex had no toilet facilities, Mercier and his wife were forced to use those of a nearby gas station. Jack Miller, his wife Elaine, and their baby lived for a summer in a chicken coop on the outskirts of Madison. "We had to carry diaper water down every day," Elaine recalled, and "Jack would take his bath after dark in the washtub in the back yard."[10]

One reason the Millers ended up living in a chicken coop was that they had an infant. "Most landlords refuse to admit couples with children," reported the *Milwaukee Sentinel* in 1944, "making it even tougher for the veteran who has a baby." Upon returning to Madison, the Millers initially lived with Jack's parents. But when the landlord learned of the presence of a child, the young family was forced to leave. The experience of the Millers was not at all unusual. While attending law school at the University of Wisconsin in Madison, army veteran John Moses sought "a flat where they would accept children, and a place where we could have a dog." According to him, "the nearest [apartment] to the campus I could find" was in Stoughton, a city twenty miles to the south. Though Lucille Rabidieux found a nursing job in Chicago, she and her husband Chick could not find an apartment in Chicago that would take children. Unable to find adequate housing in northern Wisconsin or Chicago, Chick reenlisted in the army and Lucille followed him. Veterans with children who managed to find apartments sometimes found hostile neighbors. Lawrence Landgraf lived with his wife and baby in a small Madison apartment. Sometimes the baby suffered bouts of colic, much to the consternation of their neighbors. "There were times when we could hear the broom handle on the floor," he remembered.[11]

Indeed, many veterans complained about the practices of landlords. "They jacked the price up" on many apartments, claimed Vernon Bernhagen. Lawrence Landgraf recalled that to secure an apartment in Madison he was forced to "pay a year's rent in advance," forcing him to take out a small loan from a bank in his native Hayward. Veterans also complained that they could be evicted on the slightest and most arbitrary grounds. As John Moses recalled of his hard-to-find apartment in Stoughton, as soon as the landlord's daughter and husband returned to town, "we were out." For veterans looking to purchase homes, real estate agents fared little better in the eyes of many veterans than did landlords. Veterans found home prices skyrocketing in the inflationary postwar economy. Henry Lashway—separated from his wife due to the housing crunch—claimed that he "finally had to buy a house, since it was the only way to find a place to live" together. Lashway found the price of housing almost prohibitive:

> About the only things available were duplexes built for Douglas Aircraft employees during the war. In 1946 they were selling for about $6,000 a unit, and everybody thought that it was too much for half a house. The next year they were up to about $9,000, so in desperation we bought an unfinished unit for $8,500.

Whether landlords and real estate agents were "taking advantage" or simply responding to the dynamics of the marketplace, it was clear that in postwar Wisconsin more and more money seemed to buy less and less living space.[12]

With housing in short supply, home prices and rents high, and restrictions on children, many veterans were forced to live with parents and other family members. Ralph Jacobsen and his wife lived in his parents' home in Stoughton for the eight years following the war. "Our living room was the room I was born in," Jacobsen recalled, "so I hadn't moved very much." Mildred Beltmann, navy veteran from Milwaukee, moved back into her parents' home with her new husband, and paid her parents "board" while living there. Such living arrangements were often crowded. In Watertown, army veteran Oscar Hackbarth and his wife occupied a single room in a house that also included his in-laws and several of his wife's younger siblings. Some veterans found such intimate conditions amicable. After marriage, Madison's Roger Scovill and his new bride moved in with his wife's parents until they had saved enough for their own home. The ex-marine remembered living with his in-laws fondly:

> Her mother and I painted a spare bedroom to become our own private living room. New rose floral carpeting was ordered along with a nice studio couch

having pretty complementary colors. Table lamps we had received as gifts would be placed on end tables to enhance our second floor heaven. Happiness together now awaited eagerly.

However, adult couples living in crowded conditions with friends of relatives led to tensions in many other cases. "We stayed with my folks," recalled navy veteran Daniel Turner of Madison, but "after awhile we decided it wasn't going to work out," largely because "my new wife didn't get along with my mother." They soon moved in with a widowed male neighbor, and paid their way there by doing the elderly gentleman's household chores.[13]

Indeed, veterans "doubling up" with family and friends were rather common in the years immediately following the war. In early 1946, an estimated 1.5 million World War II veterans nationwide were living with friends or relatives. As discharges increased and as the marriage and birth rates continued to climb, the situation became even more drastic. Census Bureau surveys of Madison and Milwaukee, taken in mid-1946, painted a bleak picture of the housing situation for veterans. The surveys showed that about one-third of all married veterans in each city lived with a friend or relative. The chances of these families finding their own apartments were slim. The survey revealed that only 0.7 percent of Madison apartments were vacant; in Milwaukee, 0.4 percent. In Madison, fully 18 percent of veterans lived in facilities without one or more "standard facilities" such as central heat, running water, or electric lights; and fully 10 percent lived in rented rooms or hotels. In Milwaukee, those figures were 13 percent and 6 percent, respectively. For veterans hoping to buy or build a home, the prospects seemed even more limited. New housing starts were slow, due largely to a shortage of building materials. Given the housing shortage, only 11 percent of Madison veterans in 1946 anticipated purchasing a home, and in Milwaukee, 17 percent, with an additional 10 percent claiming that they would be in the market for a home if prices were not so high.[14]

Some Americans foresaw trouble if returning veterans could not find suitable homes. In November 1945, the National Housing Agency predicted that more than one million veterans would be "homeless" in 1946. If the veterans' housing situation was not addressed properly, warned Representative Andrew Biemiller, Democrat of Wisconsin, "we will have a real eruption from our veterans that will make the bonus marches look tame in comparison." By late 1946, many veterans had yet to find suitable living quarters. On occasion, veteran anger over the housing shortage resulted in protest action. In October 1946, seventy-five veterans marched into the New York state senate chamber and staged a "sit-down" to protest the lack of housing for veterans. The protester-veterans organized a "veterans' senate" and demanded that the governor, Thomas E. Dewey, call a special legislative session to address the housing crunch. The veterans occupied the chamber overnight and met with Dewey the next day. The governor refused to call the special session, leading the veterans to refer to him as "Do-Nothing Dewey." But while the New York veterans were staging their sit-down strike, the federal government, as well as many state and local governments, were already devising ways to alleviate the nation's housing shortage, especially as it related to the nation's veterans. [15]

Federal Veterans' Housing Legislation

When veterans began returning from the war, federal programs already existed to help them purchase homes. Like other Americans, veterans had access to FHA loans, which had stimulated the housing market during the Great Depression. Title III of the 1944 GI Bill of Rights provided veterans with loan guarantees of up to $2,000 at an interest rate of no greater than 4 percent. Although veterans could use these "GI loans" for their farms and businesses (see chapter 5), they used the program primarily for the purchase of homes. However, veterans often found using the FHA and GI Bill loans difficult in the immediate postwar years. Many were still in college under Title II of the GI Bill and had not yet entered the workforce. Veterans in the working world were still young and at the lower ends of the wage and salary scales. In short, many veterans did not have enough ready cash to buy homes. For veterans who had the funds to purchase a home, there simply were not many homes for sale. With little money and few available places to buy or rent, it seemed that veterans would be consigned to substandard housing for the foreseeable future unless housing production occurred on a massive scale.

By the end of 1945, President Truman was seeking ways of alleviating the housing crisis—particularly for veterans. The president authorized the Federal Public Housing Authority to provide localities with unused military and wartime industrial housing, such as barracks, Quonset huts, demountable units, and house trailers, that could be converted into emergency housing for veterans. By May 1946, Wisconsin communities had been awarded 1,250 housing units from the federal government (not including those going to educational institutions to house student-veterans). More than half of those units went to Milwaukee, but municipalities with smaller populations, such as Fennimore (with a population of 1,592), Waterloo (1,472), and La Farge (921), also received federal units. Life in the community emergency housing units was as austere as that on the college campuses (see chapter 4), but veterans were usually glad just to have a place to live. "It's our first home," remarked navy veteran Palmer Miles as he moved into a trailer in Milwaukee's Sheridan Park in early 1947. "I think we're going to like it." "I hope the floor will be warm enough for the baby's play pen," his wife added. However, by the end of the year residents of Milwaukee's trailer communities began to complain that their homes were little more than "junk." "The trailers are wet, cold, and drafty," reported the *Milwaukee Journal* in December 1947; residents had to "set pails to catch dripping water, and tie shut the doors whose locks are broken with ropes."[16]

Such emergency measures could not hope to solve the nation's severe housing crunch, and President Truman sought more substantive solutions. But in doing so, the chief executive encountered numerous obstacles. In the immediate postwar years, wartime economic controls were still in place and could be utilized to channel funds and resources into home production. However, once the war was over political pressure grew to end such economic controls. In addition, the political fortunes of the Republicans were on the rise. The resurgent Republican Party was hostile to the New Deal and to the continuation of liberal programs under Truman, and vowed to stop them. With regard to housing, the nation's real estate interests vigorously opposed government involvement in their industry. At the same time, liberal Democrats who favored government housing programs saw the advantages of associating their cause with the plight of veterans. Debate over housing policy in the postwar years—for veterans and for all other Americans—would be caught in the crosswinds of a severe housing shortage and the political pressure to relax economic controls and roll back New Deal-style social programs.

In December 1945, Truman appointed Wilson Wyatt, the forty-year-old outgoing mayor of Louisville, Kentucky as "housing expediter" (Truman also appointed Wyatt to the post of National Housing Agency administrator). The Office of Housing Expediter fell under the Office of War Mobilization and Reconversion (OWMR). In early 1946 the OWMR still had wartime emergency powers, leading to Wyatt being dubbed the "housing czar." Wyatt planned to use wartime economic powers to control prices and supplies of building materials. His task was to channel building supplies into the production of houses and to keep those new homes within a price range that ordinary Americans could afford. As Truman explained in January 1946, Wyatt would "be empowered to use every agency of the government and every resource of the government to break the bottlenecks and produce the materials for housing." Truman was careful to point out that the appointment of Wyatt did not signal government intrusion into the private housing industry. The production of housing was "primarily a job for private enterprise to do," the president noted, but "where private enterprise is unable to provide the necessary housing, it becomes the responsibility of the government to do so."[17]

Truman proclaimed that his only instructions to Wyatt were to "make no little plans" to solve the housing crisis, orders which the housing czar followed with great vigor. He met with housing experts in government and more than thirty nongovernment organizations, including architects, business leaders, labor unions, real estate agents, and veterans organizations. Wyatt saw returning veterans as the key to the housing problem. Despite the attempts to stagger military discharges, veterans were returning by the millions in late 1945 and early 1946, and these men and women had difficulty finding decent places to live. The veteran population was also marrying and having children at higher rates that before the war (see chapter 2). For veterans to raise their new families, they would require suitable housing. In February 1946, Wyatt issued a report on his findings, and proposed the creation of the Veterans' Emergency Housing Program (VEHP). He understood the political advantages of a housing program for veterans. The name of the program, Wyatt admitted later, was calculated for political effect. "It contained three persuasive words: veterans, emergency, and housing," he wrote in his memoirs. "In the language of lawyers the name of the program amounted to a *res ipsa loquitor*" (that which speaks for itself).[18]

The goals of the Veterans' Emergency Housing Program were ambitious. Wyatt proposed to build 2.7 million homes within two years, most of which would be reserved for World War II veterans. To accomplish this formidable task, Wyatt planned to keep strong federal controls on prices and building materials. Building materials, for example, would be rationed. The price of new homes was not to exceed $10,000, and wartime rent controls would be maintained. Such actions, Wyatt believed, would channel scarce resources into the production of housing rather than other construction projects, and keep the price of new housing affordable. To stimulate production of building materials, Wyatt's plan proposed spending $600 million dollars in subsidies, or "premium payments," to product manufacturers. Finally, the VEHP called for loans from the Reconstruction Finance Corporation (RFC) to the developing factory-built "prefabricated" housing industry. Indeed, Wyatt anticipated that of the 2.7 million new homes the program would produce, 850,000 would be "prefabs."[19]

President Truman expressed his support for the plan, calling it "bold, vigorous, and eminently practical," and he directed all government agencies to "use every resource at their command to fulfill this program." Public reaction to the plan was also positive, despite its great size, cost, and reliance on continuing wartime economic controls. Many labor leaders, for example, spoke in favor of the measure. The American Federation of Labor, harkening back to the recently won war victory, pledged its support. "Please be assured," the AFL wrote Truman, "that we will do what seems to be impossible again in order to meet the gravest emergency of peace." Several Wisconsin newspapers also registered their support for the bill. The *Oshkosh Daily Northwestern*, for example, called Wyatt's proposals "bold and challenging," but also questioned whether his lofty goals were realistic. "There ought to be cooperation by everybody to achieve it," the newspaper asserted, but "it remains to be seen whether or not it can be done."[20]

Wyatt's plan did not meet with universal approval. When Representative Wright Patman, Democrat of Texas, introduced Wyatt's proposals in the House, it was greeted with withering criticism from a coalition of Republicans and conservative Democrats. Debate over the bill was sometimes tense and mean-spirited. Representative Jessie Sumner, Republican of Illinois, called Wyatt's emergency powers "Hitlerish," and claimed that the bill would "communize the American home and the American home builder." The plan's dependence on price controls came under attack. Opponents argued that limits on the prices of housing would actually hurt veterans, since they—like other Americans—would be unable to sell their homes at a profit, prompting Representative Carl Hinshaw, Republican of California, to ridicule price controls on home sales "idiotic." Opponents argued that price controls were inhibiting the production of building materials. However, they also objected to Wyatt's subsidy plan to stimulate production of such commodities, arguing that it would lead to favoritism toward certain companies. Several opponents complained that the real estate community was being unfairly demonized as "profiteers." Representative Louis Rabaut, Republican of Michigan, called such criticism "a crime," since real estate developers were "the ones who built America." Rabaut argued that "rather than being criticized," developers "should be praised." In fact, many of the bill's opponents had close ties to the real estate industry, particularly Representative Jesse Wolcott of Michigan, ranking Republican on the banking and currency committee, which handled housing affairs. Indeed, real estate interests lobbied hard against the Wyatt plan. "Veterans who prefer home ownership," claimed a representative of one real estate organization, "may be forced into undesired tenancy by self-styled experts who are using the word 'housing' as though they meant human warehousing." Instead, the real estate lobby favored an alternative House bill giving veterans cash grants ranging from $500 to $2,500 toward the purchase of a home.[21]

Pro-VEHP forces counterattacked. "Greedy, vicious propaganda is being used," claimed Representative Patman, "to deny war veterans a chance for decent housing after being absent from home for several years." Claims that price controls were inhibiting home building and the production of building materials, the bill's proponents argued, were disingenuous. Representative William J. Gallagher, Democrat of Minnesota, claimed to have spoken with several builders and lumbermen and the congressman had yet to find one "who is not making money." Representative Lyndon B. Johnson, Democrat of Texas, defended Wyatt's subsidy plan. "Congress has provided [subsidies] for meat and bread and milk and oil and copper and ships," claimed the future president. "Now we quibble about premium payments for homes—veterans' homes," he lamented, "homes they fought to preserve but returned unable to find." Delays in the implementation of the program, Wyatt claimed, resulted in the loss of 3,000 new housing units daily. The House severely gutted the original Patman bill, eliminating both the premium payments and price ceilings, and sent it to the Senate.[22]

However, the Senate was much friendlier to the outlines of Wyatt's original bill. In that body, the Republican leader, Robert Taft of Ohio, had long been an advocate of federal housing programs. Taft had looked favorably upon Wyatt's plan from the outset, blunting the opposition from conservatives in the Senate. As a result, the Senate restored most of what the House had taken out of Wyatt's proposals. Giving in to pressure from the Truman administration, as well as the nation's major veterans' organizations, the House passed the Senate version of the bill. President Truman signed the Veterans' Emergency Housing Act into law on May 22. The subsidy proposal was reduced from $600 million to $400 million, but otherwise the VEHP became law much as Wyatt had originally proposed.[23]

Once in effect, the VEHP encountered numerous difficulties. For one, political opposition to federal housing programs remained strong. Invoking the veteran helped get the VEHP passed over concerted opposition in Congress. Other housing programs were not so lucky. The Wagner-Ellender-Taft bill, which contained provisions for public housing and slum clearance, languished in Congress throughout 1946 and beyond. Representative Wolcott, backed by the real estate lobby, managed to keep the housing bill from reaching a vote in the House. Wartime economic controls were also growing increasingly unpopular with the public. The November 1946 elections, which saw the Republicans take control of Congress, spelled doom for many economic controls on which Wyatt's program depended. Just days after the election, Truman announced that he was lifting all price controls except those on sugar, rice, and rent. Without price controls on building materials, Wyatt's plan was seriously impaired.

Wyatt's goal of eliminating "bottlenecks" and coordinating home building also proved elusive. Several problems emerged. For one, various postwar strikes, including those in the railroad, steel, and lumber industries, inhibited production and delayed shipments of badly needed construction materials. Another problem was the structure of the American housing industry itself. The industry was dominated not by large national corporations, but by thousands of local builders and contractors working under construction codes and union work rules that varied from community to community. Despite such obstacles, many homes were started under the VEHP. Wyatt once boasted, for example, that he expected more than one million housing starts in 1946. However, the problems in the housing industry kept many of these starts from reaching completion. By the end of 1946, partially completed houses dotted the landscape around American cities—including in Wisconsin. In Madison, for example, the *Capital Times* reported that at the end of 1946 many homes stood half-constructed because of a lack of construction materials, especially plumbing supplies.[24]

The VEHP's emphasis on prefabricated housing also proved a major stumbling block. In particular, Wyatt's support for the fledgling and unproven prefabricated housing industry forced conflicts with several other Truman administration officials. When the War Assets Administration (WAA) refused Wyatt the use of a Chicago war plant by the Lustron Company (the WAA had already agreed to turn the plant over to an automobile company), Wyatt invoked his emergency powers and forced the WAA to allow Lustron to use half the plant. The RFC refusal to loan $90 million to the fledgling prefabricated housing industry led to a sharp confrontation between Wyatt and RFC director George E. Allen. Wyatt and Allen argued their cases before the president, and Truman eventually decided against the loan. As guarantees of government money and markets seemed less sure, and as the 1946 election seemed to doom the economic controls on which Wyatt's program relied, many companies that had gotten into the prefabricated housing industry opted to leave the field. Wyatt later characterized the effort to stimulate the prefabricated housing industry as a "great risk," and one that ultimately failed. Wyatt later wrote that his support of the industry was his "one disappointment" with the VEHP, since it was "the only part of the program that was not achieved."[25]

By late 1946, Wyatt's bold plan to house the nation's veterans was no longer politically feasible, and in December he resigned. Further housing measures, Truman conceded, "must now be faced within the framework of the government's announced policy of relaxing controls." Wyatt later looked back on his year as housing czar with considerable satisfaction. "The Veterans' Emergency Housing Program," he wrote,

> had launched the greatest housing boom in the history of the nation. The momentum was well underway. Homebuilding had been force-fed into a strong postwar beginning. Production of all materials was proceeding at record levels. Many new building materials had been successfully introduced—plastics, wall panel boards, flooring made of waste products, core-type sandwich panels, lightweight concrete, and many metals.

Indeed, 1946 saw a sharp rise in housing starts. In that year, housing starts nationally totaled 1,015,000. Although there had been fewer home starts than Wyatt had hoped, 1946 was the first year in American history that home starts had surpassed one million. Despite the sharp rise in housing starts, many Americans—veterans and nonveterans alike—could still not find suitable housing.[26]

Congress continued to wrestle with housing policy throughout the late 1940s. Now in the majority, the Republicans were able to block or modify federal housing initiatives, despite Senator Taft's support of housing programs. One Republican senator elected in 1946, Joseph R. McCarthy of Wisconsin, used the contentious housing issue in an effort to gain publicity for himself. In hearings held across the nation, McCarthy railed against public housing. Not until 1949—after Truman had been reelected and the Democrats had regained control of Congress—was a comprehensive housing law passed, one which included provisions for slum clearance and for public housing projects. But after the demise of the VEHP, housing programs for veterans disappeared from the national debate over housing.[27]

Veterans' Housing Legislation in Wisconsin

"It is in pointed recognition of the fact," observed the Madison *Capital Times* in early 1947, "that tory Democratic and Republican elements in the national congress have emasculated the federal program for veterans' housing and that this crucial issue must now be met by the states." Indeed, state and local governments across the country enacted a variety of veterans' housing bills after World War II. Programs varied from state to state, and included plans for both temporary and permanent housing for veterans using loans, grants, and a variety of other methods. Wisconsin, with its long history of aid to veterans, also tackled the problem of veterans' housing. Though a program eventually emerged, the battle over housing was one of the roughest in Wisconsin politics in the immediate postwar years.[28]

The debate in Wisconsin generally followed the lines of the national debate. Realtors, builders, lumbermen, and others involved in the housing industry fought any government involvement in their field. Fearing high costs, taxpayer groups opposed housing programs as well. However, a housing program for veterans found support in many quarters. Wisconsin's Democrats—like their cohorts on the national level—advocated housing programs not only for veterans but also for other segments of society. By and large, Wisconsin's veterans' organizations also called for veterans' housing legislation. Though several key leaders of the Wisconsin American Legion initially stated their belief that housing was a matter for "private enterprise," the Legion eventually put its weight behind a veteran's housing program. Politicians in both parties, mindful of the potential "veteran vote," also supported veterans' housing.[29]

State officials were not alone in their concern over housing for veterans; local governments also took action. An October 1947 *Milwaukee Journal* poll indicated that the city's residents believed that housing was the top problem facing the city. As early as 1945, county and municipal governments had created local housing authorities around the state, including in the state's largest cities: Milwaukee, Madison, and Racine. Local housing authorities administered the barracks, trailers, and other facilities obtained from the federal government for housing veterans, and also planned to construct other kinds of housing for veterans in their communities, including rental properties, cooperatives, and homes that veterans could eventually purchase. However, local governments found it difficult to raise enough money for veterans' housing developments, and looked to the state government for aid.[30]

Concrete plans for state action on veterans' housing legislation took shape in the spring of 1947 with a series of proposals by state senator Robert Tehan, Democrat of Milwaukee. The main features of Tehan's plan called for the creation of a state housing authority and $10 million in state money to distribute to localities for housing purposes. The legislature held a series of hearings on the housing proposals from April through June 1947, and much of the discussion centered on the problem of housing for returning veterans. The stories legislators heard painted a still-grim picture of the housing situation for veterans in Wisconsin. Martha Lewis of Madison, wife of World War II veteran Robert Lewis and mother of two, choked back tears as she told the senate judiciary committee how over the past few years her family had been forced to live apart due to the housing shortage. In addition, many of the places in which her family was forced to live did not have electricity, running water, or a telephone. "We didn't worry about the source of money when we went to war," Lewis told legislators, "so why can't we find funds to give us homes?" Several veterans told personal stories of family separation and unacceptable living conditions. Robert Hulder of Madison told lawmakers that he had been "looking since last August" for an apartment for himself and his wife. Unsuccessful, they moved in with his in-laws—seven people sharing a five-room apartment.[31]

Although most of those speaking before the committee favored a state veterans' housing bill, several people voiced opposition. "Since the start of the war," E. Tom McGovern of the Wisconsin Home Builders Association told legislators, "we have been bound in red tape at every turn. Instead of loosening that tape it has been getting tighter and tighter." It was "the constant threat of legislation hanging over his head," McGovern complained, that was inhibiting the homebuilder from producing more houses. "Private enterprise, without controls, can lick this situation," assured Arthur Marcus of the American Legion. "If you subsidize, you subsidize high costs." W. F. Hintzman, a Madison real estate agent, told the committee that in his view there was simply "too much sentiment among the youth that we owe them a living." Arguments against Tehan's proposals resonated with many legislators. "I'm a great believer in time," commented state senator George Hipke, Republican of Eau Claire, chairman of the legislature's joint finance committee, and stated his belief that the housing crisis would "work itself out" in the end.[32]

Despite the opposition, legislators were inundated with horror stories about the human suffering caused by the housing shortage for veterans. Ann Burton-Sime of the Blue Star Mothers told lawmakers that the housing shortage was eroding America's sense of morality. She speculated that the rising divorce rate and incidents of juvenile delinquency were due in part to family stress caused by the housing shortage. "If we could find the money to send [veterans] out to die," she reasoned, "we ought to be able to find the money to put a roof over their heads." Walter Cappel of the state's Congress of Industrial Organizations had perhaps the most dramatic evidence that the housing shortage was having a detrimental effect on life in America—at least in the context of postwar American politics. He claimed that in Milwaukee's sixth ward the Communist Party had recruited seventy-five members, arguing that the housing shortage showed the failure of the private enterprise system. William Frazier of the Madison Housing Authority told legislators they had two alternatives to the housing shortage. "Either stop all births at once and shoot the extra population," he said, "or provide housing."[33]

During the 1947 session, legislators passed no fewer than nine housing-related bills, including rent controls, investment incentives for private enterprise to build new housing, and bills strengthening the powers of local housing authorities, including expanded authority to raise funds and invoke eminent domain. The most important of these new laws was Chapter 412, Laws of 1947, which dealt specifically with the returning war veteran. This bill created the Wisconsin Veterans' Housing Trust Fund, and established a new agency to administer it, the Wisconsin Veterans' Housing Authority (WVHA). A five-person board would oversee the WVHA, which would be administered by a director. The governor would appoint both the board members and the director. Money for the trust fund was to be raised by doubling the state's whiskey and wine taxes, an act that would generate an estimated $8 million. The WVHA would dispense trust fund money in the form of grants to local housing authorities that applied for the funds. State money was not to exceed 10 percent of a local housing project's costs. The new housing authority was also charged with drafting housing policies for veterans, conducting research and surveys of veterans' housing needs, and working with federal and local officials on the housing problems of Wisconsin's veterans.[34]

WVHA board members were to serve five-year staggered terms and receive no compensation for their service. Chapter 412 specified that at least three board members be from specific fields: one member from the state's Board of Veterans' Affairs, an architect, and a homebuilder. To fill these slots, Governor Rennebohm appointed WDVA board member James F. Burns, Milwaukee architect A. I. Seidenschwarz, and Green Bay builder Fabian Redmond. For the remaining two positions, the governor appointed Richard U. Radcliff, a professor of land economics at the University of Wisconsin, and Arno V. Dix, chairman of the local housing authority in Port Washington. Rennebohm received some criticism for his choices. The *Capital Times* of Madison, for example, complained that "most of these men are doubtlessly tied up with the real estate interests, who have carried on a relentless fight against decent veterans' housing." Such misgivings were not widespread, and the state senate approved the governor's selections. Rennebohm delayed the selection of a director, however.[35]

The new board held its first meeting on October 6, 1947. One of its first actions was to draft a tentative statement of policy. The board planned to distribute housing trust fund money as widely as possible, so as to avoid the appearance that some communities were benefiting more than others. However, the board also made it clear that the initiative for veterans' housing projects lay with local authorities, and that it would not subsidize projects it deemed overly expensive. The board also expressed a desire to assist the most needy veterans and the most needy communities.[36]

But just as the WVHA swang into action, it faced a legal challenge from the state's tavern owners, whose businesses were most affected by the whiskey and wine taxes from which the housing fund was raised. Soon after the tax was enacted, the tavern keepers argued that the law was overly ambiguous and sued the state for the return of the money they had paid under protest. In addition, they also publicly raised the possibility that the housing program itself was unconstitutional. Providing state government money for housing, they argued, violated Article VIII, Section 10, of the Wisconsin Constitution, which stated that "the State shall never contract any debt for works of internal improvement, or be a party in carrying on such works." A legacy of the nineteenth-century debate over government involvement in building infrastructure on the frontier, the ban on state involvement in internal improvements prohibited the state from engaging in the construction of roads, canals, or other such works. For the state to fund highway and airport construction, constitutional amendments had been passed. While the veterans' housing bill was before the state senate, some in that body questioned whether housing constituted an internal improvement, but as the *Wisconsin State Journal* noted, "public pressure for its [the WVHA] passage forced lawmakers to vote for it despite many doubts as to its legality." The veterans' housing project seemed in jeopardy even before it had distributed a dime for veterans' housing.[37]

Asked for a legal opinion, state attorney general John Martin conceded that the constitutionality of public funds for veterans' housing was a "good question," and expressed doubts about the program's constitutionality. "Any attempts to render specific aid and counsel to a specific local agency," wrote Martin, "run counter to the proposition that state funds must be spent for state purposes, and not for matters of private and local concern, and such activities cannot be carried on." However, he also explored possible grounds on which the veterans' housing program might be held as constitutional. Cash grants and bonuses to veterans, he pointed out, had long been upheld as constitutional on the grounds that such an expenditure of funds was for a "public purpose" to reward veterans for services rendered and "ensure the defense of the republic." "It logically follows," he continued, "that if these purposes may be fulfilled by the provision of housing for veterans, the expenditure of funds for such housing may be held to be for a public purpose."[38]

Although the attorney general may have doubted the constitutionality of the veterans' housing program, he did not question its wisdom. "I certainly don't want to encourage any attack on this law," he told reporters, "because we want to get started and get some houses built." In a speech before a group of tavern owners in West Bend, Martin scolded them for "disrupting" the veterans' housing program. He urged the tavern keepers to "consider the picture from the front of the bar instead of behind the bar." He noted that "you have had pretty good sledding for the past four or five years," and claimed that "as a class of people you are probably better off financially than any other class in the state." He warned the gathering that opposing the veterans' housing bill would be a "mistake" in terms of "public relations," and also noted that recent investigations into the income tax returns of taverns "do not speak well for the tavernkeepers." "But still, with all this," Martin continued, "court action is brought to test the constitutionality of the veterans' housing act in order that you may save yourself from taxes. You may be assured that if the act is found unconstitutional, another will be enacted and the tax will fall in the same place." Liquor, Martin scolded, "is a business that one operates not as a right, but as a privilege granted by the government."[39]

Martin's harsh comments generated a firestorm of denunciations. His speech was a "furious attack" on the tavern owners, according to the *Milwaukee Journal*. While the editorial pointed out that the newspaper "holds no brief for tavern keepers," the threats made by the attorney general were "off base." Tavern owners, they declared, "are citizens just like everybody else. . . . They are not second class citizens." "It is in very bad taste," stated Wisconsin's leading newspaper, "for an attorney general to try to deprive citizens of [their] rights by intimidation." The *Sheboygan Press* argued that the attorney general "must recognize that every citizen has the right to contest any law and the supreme court of the state of Wisconsin is the last resort through which to proceed." When the attorney general "goes outside of his office and threatens the tavern keepers and liquor dealers . . . we feel it is our duty to comment publicly." Others reacted favorably to Martin's comments. "Bully for John Martin!" wrote the *Wisconsin State Journal*, "if anything can shame the stupid and selfish comments of the industry, Mr. Martin's talk ought to have done it."[40]

Questions surrounding the constitutionality of the WVHA had an immediate impact upon its effectiveness. By early November, board members grew impatient with Rennebohm's failure to appoint a director. Professor Ratcliff, acting secretary of the board, claimed to have spoken with the governor's secretary and to have written the governor to urge the appointment of a director, but had yet to receive a reply. "I am convinced there is less attention being paid to this issue than it deserves," an annoyed Ratcliff stated. He conceded that "running the state is a complicated business" and affirmed his belief that "the governor is a good guy," but he nevertheless demanded that Rennebohm appoint a director soon. "We don't have time to do the work the director is supposed to do," claimed Ratcliff. Without a director, the board would be "handicapped" and could not serve the state and the veterans properly. The governor responded that the constitutional challenge to the veterans' housing program was inhibiting the appointment of a director. "While we have contacted six men as prospects for director," the governor claimed, "we found great hesitancy on their part to leave their present work and take over a position that might develop into a very short time job." But by the end of the month, Governor Rennebohm had appointed twenty-eight-year-old Arthur G. Field—lawyer, part-time faculty member at the University of Wisconsin, and World War II veteran—as the director of the housing authority.[41]

As long as the program faced a legal threat, the Wisconsin program for veterans' housing was incapacitated. "It has become evident," wrote *Green Bay Press-Gazette* columnist and political insider John Wyngaard, "that the state's veterans' housing program—if it is ever to make a substantial contribution to the relief of the housing crisis—will do so very slowly." He called the Wisconsin Veterans' Housing Authority a "paper organization" that "holds regular meetings, and [has] long and earnest and diligent discussions about the housing problem," but gets very little done. "With the recent legal complications," Wyngaard surmised, "it appears that nothing is going to get done for some time." The columnist judged the stalled veterans' housing program a tragic missed opportunity. "There is much good will in the capitol toward the housing authority," he believed. "Everybody wants it to succeed . . . but there remains the strongest doubt in informed quarters that the state housing authority will ever get any significant numbers of houses built."[42]

In December 1947, the Wisconsin Supreme Court ruled that the liquor tax that funded the housing trust fund was indeed constitutional, but doubt remained over the constitutionality of providing state money for veterans' housing projects. The crisis came to a head when the board tried to disburse its first payment to a local housing authority. Port Washington was one of several localities to apply for housing trust fund money. To test the constitutionality of the grants, the veterans' housing authority board approved a "token" amount of $1,000 to the Port Washington Housing Authority. The state's budget director, E. C. Giessel, withheld the release of the state money due to the "uncertainty" over the constitutionality. Attorney general Martin then petitioned the Wisconsin Supreme Court for a writ of mandamus to compel Giessel to make the payment. Hearings on the case, *State ex. rel. Martin v. Giessel*, began on February 20, 1948.[43]

In a unanimous decision, the Wisconsin Supreme Court declared that the construction of housing was indeed an "internal improvement" under the state constitution. The attorney general argued before the court that veterans' housing was not an internal improvement but rather a reward from the state to veterans for wartime service, which courts had long upheld as a "public purpose" and thus constitutional. The court rejected such reasoning, arguing that "when discharged the veteran becomes a private citizen," and that when state funds are "used in the construction of houses for a certain class of citizens it is certainly engaging in works of internal improvement." The court also rejected Martin's claim that veterans' housing was akin to the construction of schools and government buildings, arguing that there was a "valid distinction between providing structures necessary for the state's functions and providing structures for the housing of private individuals." Martin argued that the housing emergency was so severe that the ban against internal improvements should be "treated as more elastic, or ignored altogether," but the court refused to be stampeded into a decision favorable to the WVHA, declaring that "emergency does not constitute power." In the end, the court ruled that "the appropriation [of state funds] for the construction of houses for private occupancy, either as a renter or an owner, is certainly carrying on a work of internal improvement," and maintained that "the state must provide for the veteran in some way other than carrying on an internal improvement."[44]

The supreme court's ruling did not invalidate the existence of the WVHA or the trust fund raised for veterans' housing, only the provision for disbursing state money to veterans' housing projects. But the ruling essentially made the WVHA an agency without a purpose. The WVHA continued its operations into 1948. For example, that year it conducted a survey of veterans' housing needs in Wisconsin and found that while the housing conditions of veterans were improving, Badger State veterans in 1948 still suffered in the housing market. The survey found, for example, that fully 13 percent of married veterans statewide were still "doubled up" with family and friends, nearly 10 percent lived in units in need of major repairs, and 5 percent still lived in rented rooms or resort cabins. Only 3.5 percent of Wisconsin veterans lived in publicly financed temporary housing. The survey concluded that one in five Wisconsin veterans still lived in substandard housing three years after the end of the war, with conditions most egregious in the southeastern part of the state. The WVHA also sponsored a conference on veterans' housing that year, in which representatives from the state's building, banking, and veteran communities discussed the housing situation of veterans and ways to meet the problem. Tax money continued to flow into the veterans' housing trust fund, but the WVHA was prohibited from spending it as originally anticipated. None of this money was being spent to house the state's veterans.[45]

Governor Rennebohm received considerable pressure from veterans' groups, public housing authorities, and private citizens to call a special session of the legislature to pass a constitutional amendment to make state involvement in veterans' housing legally acceptable. Further delay in the implementation of a

housing program, one woman wrote the governor, would sow "the seeds of de-
linquency, poor health, [and] fire hazards from bad housing." However, many
Republican leaders urged caution. State senator Gustave Buchen, Republican of
Sheboygan, warned the governor that:

> The special session will be nothing but a field day for the Democrats and Pro-
> gressives to introduce wild and visionary measures, with no hope of passage,
> but will simply try to put the Republicans in a hole. The movement of a special
> session, in my opinion, is purely political, and the Republicans will be the vic-
> tims.

Another Republican senator, Warren P. Knowles of New Richmond, also
warned Rennebohm that a special session would be a "disastrous mistake," both
for the state's Republicans generally and the political fortunes of the governor
personally.[46]

Despite the opposition of many Republicans, Governor Rennebohm apparently saw some political advantages in calling a special session on veterans'
housing. As columnist John Wyngaard noted, the Republicans had done little for
veterans in recent years except for the unconstitutional housing law. Having
something for veterans going into an election, Wyngaard speculated, might be of
benefit to Republican candidates in 1948. If Rennebohm wanted to address veterans' housing before the 1948 elections, he would need to act quickly. Under
the Wisconsin constitution, an amendment had to be passed by the legislature in
two different sessions and then approved by the voters in a statewide referendum. If the governor called a special session in the summer of 1948, the measure
could be passed again when the legislature reconvened in January 1949 and then
be put on the ballot in April 1949. At best, state funds for veterans' housing
projects would not be forthcoming until the middle or end of 1949 at the earliest.
If he did not call a special session, the amendment would have to pass the legislature in 1949 and in 1950, and possibly delay the veterans' housing program
until 1951.[47]

Despite the advice of fellow Republicans, Rennebohm decided to call a
special session of the legislature to deal exclusively with the issue of a constitutional amendment for veterans' housing. As predicted, fierce debate erupted
over the issue of public housing generally. Democrats and ex-Progressives in the
Republican Party wanted to broaden the wording of any constitutional amendment so that it would also encompass nonveteran public housing programs as
well. Senator Tehan argued that a housing amendment limited only to veterans
was "stupidly short-sighted." Local housing authorities told the legislators that if
state housing projects were open only to veterans it might discourage potential
investors due to the limited market. But stalwart Republicans resisted any expansion of the amendment beyond veterans. State senator Rudolph Schlabach,
Republican of LaCrosse, accused public housing advocates of attempting to
"sneak in the back door and trying to steal this money away from the veterans."
Despite the spirited debate, on final passage the state senate approved the "vet-

erans only" amendment without a dissenting vote. The measure then went to the assembly, where efforts to broaden the bill were also defeated. In the assembly, the proposed amendment passed, 93-2, on July 20.[48]

The debate over public housing left a bitter taste in the mouths of many. "Stubborn and blind to reality," insisted Madison's liberal newspaper, the *Capital Times*, "the Republican majority stuck by the Acting Governor, putting party loyalty and loyalty to the big contributors before the public welfare." Madison's other newspaper, the conservative *Wisconsin State Journal* saw the matter differently. "Wisconsin's Republican legislature," they opined, "had staggered through two days of the rankest minority political gas attack on record, and beat off one of the brashest attempts in history to slip a fast trick past the people of Wisconsin." After their attempt to "frighten" the legislature into public housing had failed, Democrats and progressive Republicans "scrambled over to the other side" and "wanted to be known as the friend of the veteran . . . after trying to grab off with his funds for everyone else." Government housing proved to be as controversial on the state level as it had at the national level.[49]

In the wake of the heated debate over public housing, momentum began to build for a program of loans to help individual veterans to meet their housing needs. During the fall of 1948, loan program proposals came from several sources. State senator Rudolph Schlabach, a vociferous opponent of public housing, developed a plan for a loan program for veterans to build or buy homes using money in the veterans' housing trust fund. The WVHA also began to develop a loan program for veterans. In December 1948, the WVHA announced a three-pronged "full-scale attack" on the problem of veterans' housing. One part of that plan called for loans to individual veterans ranging from $1,000 to $2,500 at an interest rate of about 2 percent. The remainder of the plan called for loans to veterans' housing cooperatives and to local housing authorities. As the 1949 legislative session drew near, it was clear that movement toward some kind of veterans home loan program was underway. "There's no doubt," said the *Wisconsin State Journal*, "that the 1949 legislature is going to do something to put the state's weight—and money—behind veterans' housing."[50]

The plan that gained the most momentum came from two Republicans on the senate veterans' affairs committee, Melvin R. Laird of Marshfield and Arthur A. Lenroot of Superior. Laird and Lenroot called for designating 70 percent of the veterans' housing trust fund for veterans' home loans. They proposed a secondary mortgage loan program for individual veterans of up to $2,000 at 2 percent interest for homes under $9,000. To qualify for the loans, veterans had to be able make a 10 percent down payment. The remaining 30 percent of the trust fund would be used to fund local housing authorities, though the state would only pay up to 15 percent of a local housing project's costs. The Laird-Lenroot proposal also called for continuation of the whiskey and wine taxes to fund veterans' programs, and for folding the Wisconsin Veterans' Housing Authority into the Wisconsin Department of Veterans' Affairs. Such a program, the authors argued, would help veterans in all areas of the state—not just those where housing authorities had been created—and would also stimulate to the construction industry. "The purpose of the program," claimed Laird, was "to build houses—and we will have homes for veterans if this bill becomes law."[51]

The spring of 1949 saw stormy debate in Madison on the question of veterans' housing. The loan proposals encountered opposition largely from local government officials and veterans' groups. Rental housing for low- and medium-income veterans, opponents agreed, would best meet the immediate needs of veterans for housing. Horace Wilkie, representing the Madison Housing Authority, told the legislature that a loan program would "benefit only those veterans who can now afford to finance a home," and not aid the ordinary veteran. The state's largest veterans' groups, in a rare show of unity, teamed up to oppose the loan measures. Jack DeWitt of the VFW, speaking for the coalition of veterans' groups, claimed that under the Laird-Lenroot bill, only 5,600 veterans out of the state's 350,000 World War II veterans could benefit from the measure. "Don't bait the veteran to buy when he can't afford it," he told the legislators. "The average veteran only makes $3,000 a year, that's not enough to pay the $900 down on a $9,000 house, let alone keep up with the payments." DeWitt also feared what would happen to veterans lured into spending beyond their means in the event of an economic downturn. "Under the loan program the veteran will be left holding the bag when a depression comes," he warned.[52]

Backing the loan proposals were the real estate lobby and taxpayer groups. "The veteran would rather have the security of owning his own home," declared James J. Arnold of the Wisconsin Association of Real Estate Brokers. "GIs can't purchase homes because they don't have down payments," William F. Double of the Wisconsin Savings and Loan League told legislators, and added that "we shouldn't be interested in erecting large housing units, but should aim at individual ownership." Taxpayer groups also spoke out in favor of the Laird-Lenroot bill. Their support focused largely on the fear of increased government involvement in housing beyond that for the veteran. Once state and local governments become involved in housing, claimed the *Wisconsin Tax News*, "it is probable the result will be active state and local agencies constantly seeking to perpetuate themselves and extend their jurisdiction."[53]

All plans were on hold until the April 1949 referendum on the constitutional amendment. In February 1949, the legislature approved for the second time the constitutional amendment allowing state financial aid to veterans' housing. The second vote on the amendment was less contentious, though the measure did find opposition. Republican state senator (and former WDVA board member) Theodore Jones of Lake Mills voted against the measure, arguing once again that aid to local housing authorities would favor large municipalities over small towns and rural areas, and complained that lawmakers were "trying to do something for the veterans, but they don't know what to do." In April 1949, voters approved the amendment 311,576 to 290,736.[54]

After the passage of the constitutional amendment, Governor Rennebohm further muddied the waters and introduced his own veterans' housing proposal. The governor's plan called for each county to receive a portion of the veterans' housing trust fund (which by mid-1949 had reached $16 million) to spend on veterans' housing as it saw fit. Such a proposal, the governor argued, would treat all areas of the state equitably and would be tailored to meet local conditions. Rennebohm also proposed merging the WVHA into the WDVA. Leaders of the state's veterans' groups backed the governor's plan, but the state legislature gave it a cool reception. State senator Samuel Porter, Republican of Blooming-ton, lashed out at proponents of yet another proposal to aid local housing authorities. "I think you're for public housing, not veterans," he told one backer of the measure. "That's my reaction to every one of you fellows. You fellows have sold the governor a bill of goods." Real estate interests kept up the pressure against aid to local housing authorities. Lewis A. Stocking of the Milwaukee Builders Association told legislators that "low cost housing is here," and that "we don't need housing authorities anymore." Stories of veterans not being able to find homes was "poppycock," in his view, and claimed that "if [a veteran] can't pay for a home, then this is a relief program."[55]

On June 1, the state senate approved the Laird-Lenroot bill, 22-8, and de-feated the governor's proposal by the same margin. In the senate, "the governor was backed only by Democrats and Republican irregulars," reported the *Mil-waukee Journal*. However, the senate bill faced stiff opposition in the assembly. Rather, the lower body passed the governor's plan, 47-39. With the legislature deadlocked, attention focused on a plan by Assemblyman Mark Catlin Republi-can of Appleton. The "Catlin compromise" plan called for a housing program consisting entirely of loans—to both individuals and local housing authorities. Catlin's bill drew considerable fire. Horace Wilkie called the Catlin proposal a "fraud," because it would undercut efforts to build affordable rental housing, and called loans to individuals "a complete repudiation of the 1947 law and a complete disregard to the true nature of the housing problem as it exists throughout the state." Democrats accused Republican stalwarts of playing poli-tics with the veterans. The governor's bill was being opposed, argued assem-blyman William Duffy, Democrat of Greenleaf, "because there are certain inter-ests in the state that don't like the idea of public housing." But with Republicans in the majority, the Catlin plan carried the day. On June 22, the Assembly passed the Catlin compromise bill, 59-36.[56]

An assembly-senate conference hammered out the final details of the bill, which Governor Rennebohm signed reluctantly on August 5. Chapter 627, Laws of 1949, created the Veterans' Housing Loan Program. Eighty percent of the housing trust fund would be allotted to provide secondary mortgage loans to individual veterans. Such loans could not exceed 20 percent of the property's value, the veterans had to have at least 5 percent of the total cost, and properties could not exceed $10,000 in value. The remaining 20 percent of the fund was reserved to provide grants to local housing authorities for veterans' housing, which could not exceed 10 percent of the project's cost. The 1949 Wisconsin housing law for veterans also abolished the Wisconsin Veterans' Housing Authority, and transferred responsibility for veterans' housing to the Wisconsin Department of Veterans' Affairs.[57]

In Wisconsin politics, the issue of housing—either for veterans or for other groups of citizens—was a contentious issue. After years of political battles, Wisconsin enacted a housing program similar to that of the federal government, namely, loans for the purchase of homes. Public housing, even in the guise of helping the returning serviceman, was controversial at the state level as well as the national. The Wisconsin home loan program, according to the *Green Bay Press-Gazette*, was passed "by a conservative legislature [and] designed to emphasize private enterprise in alleviating the housing problem." The program provided veterans with money for homes, but favored those with some economic wherewithal. Home loans meant little to those veterans who could not afford down payments.[58]

End of the Postwar Housing Shortage

Despite the failure to create a mass housing program for veterans, both on the federal level and in Wisconsin, the postwar housing shortage abated after 1950. Housing starts rose steadily during the late 1940s and into the 1950s. After reaching one million for the first time in 1946, housing starts nationally continued to soar. In 1950, housing starts peaked at 1,908,000. Throughout the 1950s, national housing starts averaged about 1.5 million per year. As more homes were being built, the mean age of homes went down. From the peak of 34.2 years in 1945, by 1960 the average age of a dwelling had declined to 28.7 years. Vacancy rates also increased. In 1940, 6.6 percent of housing units were vacant nationally, but by 1960 that figure had risen to 10.1 percent, indicating that more housing was available for sale and rent. The rate of home ownership also rose after World War II. In the 1940 census, 43.6 percent of Americans lived in owner-occupied dwellings. Despite the slowed home production during the war years, the ownership rate had shot up to 55 percent in 1950. For the first time in American history, more Americans owned their own homes than rented. By 1960, the rate of ownership had jumped to 61.9 percent.[59]

   Though it was not clear at the time, the late 1940s marked the beginning of a great housing boom. Growth in the housing supply in the late 1940s and 1950s occurred for several reasons. The primary explanation was the booming nature of the postwar economy. As the economy grew, so did wages and savings, and thus so did the ability of more and more Americans to purchase homes. Government programs also helped fuel the housing boom, and in this regard veterans' benefits played an important role. Not only were veterans gainfully employed and earning money to spend on housing by the 1950s, but they also had access to credit, thanks to VA loan guarantees under the GI Bill of Rights. Between 1945 and 1949, the VA guaranteed the mortgages of more than 1.6 million homes (new and existing) in the United States. During those same years, housing starts under VA inspection totaled 422,800 nationally—accounting for nearly 8 percent of all home starts in the United States. VA home loans became even more important in the 1950s. Between 1950 and 1959, the VA guaranteed nearly 3.8 million home loans. During those years VA-inspected housing starts totaled 1,947,300, accounting for 13.3 percent of all new homes constructed during that decade. The use of VA home loans peaked in the middle to late 1950s, as veterans finished their education or training and became established economically. The number of VA home loans peaked in 1955 at 392,900, accounting for 17 percent of all home starts that year. In 1956, VA home loans financed nearly 20 percent of all home starts in the United States. By 1960 the number of VA home loans had declined, falling below 100,000 that year for the first time since 1949.[60]

The use of VA loans does not tell the complete story of just how much veterans fueled the postwar housing boom. Veterans could also use standard FHA loans to purchase homes. Between 1945 and 1949, the FHA insured nearly one million mortgages. Housing starts under FHA financing during those years totaled 997,100, or 18.5 percent of all new homes. During the 1950s, the FHA insured the mortgages of 3.5 million homes. In the 1950s, FHA programs helped finance 2.8 million home starts, accounting for nearly 20 percent of all new homes constructed in the United States in that decade. Veterans could also combine VA and FHA loans to further increase their buying power. Coast guard veteran John Bach of Madison recalled that when he went to the bank to inquire about a home loan, they worked up a plan by which 15 percent of the loan would be financed by the FHA and 85 percent by the VA. "I should have built a hotel right then," Bach later joked. "Instead I built a little two bedroom home."[61]

Veterans such as Bach often found banks and other lending institutions helpful in using government loan programs to purchase homes. John Wozniak, an army veteran and a loan officer in a Stevens Point bank, recalled that his bank turned down very few GI Bill loans. "If there were any turn downs," recalled Wozniak, "it would be by the VA. . . . If the VA would guarantee, we'd go along." However, some veterans still found lending institutions and real estate agents decidedly unhelpful. In 1946, Sheboygan native Henry Lashway went to a saving and loan institution in Des Plaines, Illinois (where he had taken a job as a teacher), to inquire about a home loan. A loan officer told him he did not qualify for an FHA loan because he did not make enough money. As for a VA loan, Lashway was under the impression that "they didn't seem to want to handle them," and was told that pointedly that "the government had no right to interfere with interest rates." As a young teacher and new resident in what was then a small town, Lashway was "cautious about antagonizing anyone" and did not press the matter further. Not all institutions looked askance at the veteran homebuyer. Marine corps veteran William Luetke purchased a house while in his medical residency at the University of Wisconsin. Despite Luetke's being a physician and a veteran eligible for a GI Bill loan, the first bank he approached refused to loan him money. The bank told the young doctor that he was a "bad risk" because he "wasn't making any money." Undeterred, Luetke "walked across the street" to another bank and "walked out with a GI loan" for a $10,000 home.[62]

As prosperity spread in the 1950s, many other veterans were able to purchase homes without the assistance of government programs at all. Private banks were willing to loan money to veterans who qualified regardless of their military status. Navy veteran Mildred Beltmann, a bank employee, remembered that she and her husband were able to get a bank loan at interest rates lower than those offered by the federal government. Donald and Ella Wiberg of Milwaukee, both veterans, claimed that regular bank loans were "a lot faster and a lot cheaper" than federal loans. Some veterans had managed to save enough money to buy homes without financial assistance from the government or lending institutions. Roger Scovill built his home in the Madison suburb of Monona with his own savings—up to a point. "We never bought anything of value until we could fully pay in cash," he wrote. Scovill hired contractors in the off-season to build the foundation and install the heating, plumbing, and wiring, but he and his wife also did much of the work themselves. But by the time Scovill was ready to finishing the interior he had run out of money, and was forced to borrow money from his wife's parents to finish his home.[63]

Like Scovill, many veterans received financial assistance from family members to purchase homes. Although the savings and loan institution in Des Plaines had rejected Henry Lashway's request for a home loan, his father did not. Lashway's father loaned his veteran son more than $5,000 for a down payment, at an interest rate of 2 percent. Lashway's father loaned his other son a similar sum for a down payment, "and he always told people that he 'bought' us each a house." Kermit Bliss recalled that when housing became available and he could move out of "Taylor's Tenements" he did not have to use federal assistance or a bank loan since he had an "elderly aunt down in Iowa who had a boat load of money in federal bonds." Bliss's aunt loaned him money at an interest rate lower than that of private banks and government programs. When his aunt died a few years later, the loan was forgiven. Army veteran Oscar Hackbarth of Watertown bought a home on money he borrowed from a cousin. "After that," he recalled proudly, "I was on my own."[64]

Wisconsin's Veterans' Housing Loan Program initially affected home building in Wisconsin in a limited fashion. Restrictions on obtaining state home loans were so severe that only a few thousand veterans ever applied for them. Not only was qualifying for a loan difficult, but WDVA officials stated publicly that to conserve funds they could provide only "a small percentage" of Wisconsin veterans with loans, and announced their intention to dispense housing loan money parsimoniously. Unlike federal veterans' housing programs, which guaranteed money loaned by private banks, Wisconsin's home loan money came directly from the housing trust fund for veterans, which WDVA officials feared could be easily depleted. "In order to spread available funds," the WDVA said in a statement, "it is imperative that the individual veteran receive only amounts sufficient to enable him to acquire a home through purchase or construction." The board also stated that it would "exercise strict control" over home loans "in an effort to ensure that further inflation in existing prices for homes shall not result." The small number of WDVA home loans did not significantly influence the inflation of home values in Wisconsin, nor did it add significantly to the state's housing stock.[65]

State veterans' groups lobbied the WDVA to liberalize its home loan policies. In February 1950, the County Veterans' Service Officers Association, for example, met with Governor Rennebohm to discuss changes in the law. The CVSOs told the governor that the $10,000 limit on the price of a home did not take local conditions into consideration. Wesley Schwoegler, Dane County service officer, claimed that in the Madison area $10,000 did not provide a "livable" home. The requirement that a veteran be able to put 5 percent down also kept many low-income veterans from qualifying for home loans, the CVSOs complained. "It is very evident to us in the field," the service officers told the governor, "that the veteran who can qualify for a loan under the law as it now stands, could receive adequate financing from already established lending agencies," but that "the Veteran who really needs the help is the man in the lower income bracket." By early 1951, the CVSO association called for the repeal of the housing program altogether. Housing trust fund money, it argued, could be better spent on a bonus for World War II veterans.[66]

In Chapters 9 and 59, Laws of 1951, the state legislature liberalized the terms of the home loan program by raising the limit on the price of a home to $15,000 and raising the cap on the amount of loans from 20 percent of the price to $3,500. In addition, the program also included Korean War veterans, and the WDVA dropped a requirement that all other funding options be exhausted before a veteran could receive a state housing loan. However, with liberalization came a surge of applications. In fiscal year 1951-52, the WDVA loaned more the $20 million under the housing program, as compared to the $4.5 million in the previous two years of its existence. Concern grew again that the housing trust fund would soon be depleted, and the WDVA began to seek new ways to limit disbursements. Throughout the 1950s, Wisconsin veterans found the WDVA home loan program cumbersome and difficult to use. Robert Blake of Boscobel used the state loan in conjunction with a regular bank loan and money from his family. The WDVA put him through "a lot of hassle about what the house was worth, and whether I could afford it." Nevertheless, some veterans found the state loan program helpful. Milwaukee army veteran Fred Hochschild noted that the state loan helped him buy a home and move out of his mother's house. Robert Blake recalled that, despite his problems with the WDVA, he would not have been able to purchase a home without state loan assistance. By the end of fiscal year 1960, the WDVA had disbursed more than $60 million in home loans to World War II and Korean War veterans.[67]

Much of the building boom of the 1940s and 1950s did not occur in central cities, but rather in suburban areas on the outskirts of them. Techniques for mass-producing homes developed during the war were applied to civilian home production afterward. In New York, the Levitts used their wartime building techniques to build tremendous numbers of suburban homes. Their Levittown development on Long Island, initially open only to World War II veterans, consisted of rows and rows of homes almost exactly alike. Mass production brought down costs, while VA and FHA loan programs increased the buying power of ordinary Americans. Cheap land on the outskirts of major cities made such homes even more affordable. Automobile ownership increased with economic prosperity, and government highway projects—in particular, the development of controlled-access expressways—provided convenient avenues from suburb to central city. Zoning requirements in suburban municipalities typically favored larger lots, creating a sense of space and openness. Home designs, especially the popular ranch style, also suggested space as well as safety—even if on a modest budget. "The dream of a detached quiet house in a safe, quiet, and peaceful place," wrote historian Kenneth Jackson, "has long been an important part of the Anglo-American past and a potent force in the development of suburbs." For American veterans returning home from the most deadly and destructive war in human history, the idyllic environment of the suburbs seemed to have a particular allure.[68]

As in most other states, Wisconsin witnessed great suburban growth during the 1940s and 1950s, especially in the Milwaukee and Madison metropolitan areas. Specific suburban municipalities saw fantastic increases in population, most of which occurred after 1950. Between 1940 and 1950, the village of Menomonee Falls just northwest of Milwaukee grew from 1,469 to 2,469 (a 68 percent increase), then skyrocketed to 18,276 by 1960 (a 640 percent increase). New cities and villages were formed. Rural Brookfield township in Waukesha County west of Milwaukee contained 4,196 persons in 1940 and 7,425 in 1950. By 1960, most of the town had been incorporated as the city of Brookfield, in which 19,812 people lived. In Milwaukee County, seven new cities or villages emerged out of unincorporated lands during the 1950s, three of which had populations of more than 10,000 residents in the 1960 census. The population of central cities also grew, but such growth was vastly outpaced by that which occurred in the suburbs. While the population of the city of Milwaukee grew from 637,392 in 1950 to 741,324 in 1960 (a 12 percent increase), suburban areas outside the city grew from 192,103 to 408,673 between those same years (a 113 percent increase). The city of Madison saw a 32 percent increase in population during that same period, but surrounding suburbs grew by 121 percent.[69]

The men and women who served in World War II had grown up in the Great Depression, endured military camps and barracks, and then, crammed into substandard apartments after the war. Those who could afford a house often reveled in finding that "safe, quiet, and peaceful place" in the suburbs. The sameness of the communities did not seem to bother most suburban veterans. Former sailor Lawrence Landgraf settled in the Madison suburb of Middleton. "It was a project area," he recalled of his new neighborhood, "the same floor plan, only a little different exterior, and it was a great area." Horace Wilkie described his suburban home in Madison this way:

> It is a modern structure with all of the house located on one floor. There are three bedrooms, [a] large living room, and the usual accommodations. The feature of the new house that leaves me somewhat unconvinced is the fact that

there is a tremendous yard, that must be mowed, large numbers of rock gardens that must be maintained and a huge vegetable garden that must be cultivated. My heart skips a beat at the very thought of all this.

In the new suburban areas that sprang up after World War II, veterans often made up significant segments of the population. Lawrence Landgraf recalled that his neighbors in Middleton were "people like ourselves, former vets, all young and [with] young kids." After landing a job in Milwaukee, army veteran and lawyer William Brunsell "bought a lot way out on the edge of Milwaukee County," where he found that that many of his new neighbors were veterans like himself. "The guy across the street was in the army," he recalled, "and I got to know him very well." Brunsell worked at a law firm in downtown Milwaukee, and car-pooled with other young lawyers to and from the city. "Almost all" of those in his car pool were veterans as well, he remembered, but added, "by that time, you didn't ask whether or not a person was a vet." [70]

However, not all veterans were able to enjoy the fruits of suburbia. Veterans from ethnic and racial minority groups—African Americans, in particular— were often barred through legal and extralegal means from joining the movement to suburban communities, or, for that matter, from any area outside of strictly delineated urban zones. The government policies that helped millions of Americans afford their own homes actively discriminated against minorities. The FHA, in the words of historian Kenneth Jackson, "openly exhorted [racial] segregation throughout the first thirty years of its existence." The FHA typically "red-lined" areas where blacks and minority groups lived and refused to insure mortgages in or near those areas. Such policies simply pushed potential home-buyers farther out into the suburbs and kept minorities from obtaining loans at all. Banks and other lending institutions typically refused to loan money to minorities, VA or FHA loan guarantees or not. In any case, poverty and job discrimination often kept many minorities from being in the financial position to obtain a bank loan at all. For African Americans and other minority veterans, housing programs were often a hollow postwar benefit. [71]

Even those minority veterans who had the economic means to afford a home in the suburbs usually could not obtain one. Many housing deeds contained "restrictive covenants," barring the sale of those homes to blacks and other minorities. The 1948 U.S. Supreme Court case *Shelley v. Kramer* declared such covenants unconstitutional, but in practice such discrimination continued well into the 1950s. Wisconsin did not specifically repeal its law permitting such covenants until three years after the landmark Supreme Court case. Realtors also frequently refused to sell homes to African Americans and other minorities. The fair employment division of the Wisconsin Industrial Commission documented several instances in which real estate agents discriminated against minorities, particularly African Americans. In Madison, for example, the division noted that "usually in a real estate deal a conspiracy of some sort governs" to keep blacks from buying homes in particular neighborhoods. Some real estate agents, it claimed, "have been honest enough to admit that they would be 'committing suicide' if they sold to Negroes, since . . . they have a 'gentleman's agreement' never to sell to individuals who might depreciate the property."[72]

Many Euro-Americans made it well known that they did not welcome a minority presence in their neighborhoods. The fair employment division also documented several instances in which blacks were discriminated against in housing. In 1947, for example, an African American woman in Madison placed an offer on a home and the owner was willing to sell, but the real estate agent involved told the owner that his neighbors would "blow his head off" if he sold to the woman. He did not. In another case in Madison, an African American student at the University of Wisconsin (veteran status not noted) "secured lodging with a white family residing in a suburb," but later the "housewife, in a frenzy, contacted the student and indicated that she would be unable to abide by their agreement." An investigation by the fair employment division revealed that "strong opposition from the neighbors forced the action." In 1949, an African American navy veteran named Albert Sanders, attending the Milwaukee School of Engineering, moved into one of Milwaukee's emergency housing trailer camps for veterans. The presence of Sanders and his family created a mob of white camp residents, who signed a petition against blacks in a "white camp" and threatened his family with physical injury. Sanders moved out of the camp, but shocked and shamed camp residents joined with a wide coalition of community leaders to urge Sanders to move back in—which he did. Despite police protection for Sanders and his family, some camp residents remained defiant, one asking, if "we had segregation in the armed forces, why not here?"[73]

As a result, minority veterans were usually forced to live in certain segregated areas of Wisconsin's cities, despite the fast growth of the minority population in the state. In Milwaukee, African Americans spread into the old north side German American neighborhood, as these Euro-Americans fled to the suburbs. Madison's black community remained confined to the Greenbush neighborhood south of the university campus, or to the near east side of the city. Conditions in these areas were less than ideal. Black neighborhoods were typically overcrowded and consisted of older, dilapidated homes. "Negro houses are definitely inferior," claimed the fair employment division of the situation in Madison in 1947. "Approximately 90 percent live in houses which are over 25 years of age," they reckoned, "houses which have been discarded by the more fortunate citizens." African Americans also paid more for housing. In Milwaukee, city investigators estimated that blacks paid 15 percent to 35 percent higher rents than whites of the same income levels. The same investigators also estimated that 10,000 African Americans in that city in 1950 (nearly one-half the total black population at that time) lived in "dwellings considered substandard by census definition." Home ownership rates for blacks were much lower than for whites. In Milwaukee in 1950, nearly one-half of that city's white residents owned their own homes, but only one-quarter of blacks did. Even African American homeowners were forced to stay in traditionally black areas. Judging from the condition of homes in black neighborhoods, claimed one observer, "you can almost pick out the houses which Negroes are renting and those which they have bought."[74]

The emerging suburbs, by contrast, were almost exclusively white. By the 1960 census, the population of African Americans in the Milwaukee metropolitan area had grown to 63,170. However, 62,458 of them (98.8 percent) lived in the city of Milwaukee itself. Suburban municipalities registered negligble black populations. Out of 19,812 residents in Brookfield in 1960, only 8 were African American (0.0004 percent). In Menomonee Falls, blacks made up only 13 of the city's 18,276 residents (0.0007 percent). The new cities of New Berlin (population 15,788) and St. Francis (population 10,065) had no black residents at all. Figures for other minority groups show a similar pattern. Of 1,999 Native Americans in the Milwaukee metropolitan area in 1960, 1,779 lived in the city itself (88.9 percent). Of 1,899 Japanese Americans, Chinese Americans, Filipino Americans, and all others classified as "nonwhite" in the metropolitan area in 1960, 1,515 lived within the city limits of Milwaukee (79.7 percent).[75]

Conclusion

Housing was often the last obstacle veterans faced in their readjustment to civilian life. Though the nation faced a severe housing shortage following the war, Americans could not agree on how to remedy the situation. In the end, the booming postwar economy put money in the pockets of veterans and other Americans, which enabled many to buy new homes. However, government programs—including many aimed specifically at housing veterans—also played a crucial role in making homes affordable to millions of Americans. The housing boom of the postwar years occurred mainly in suburban areas, where veterans could find a "safe, quiet, and peaceful place" after the trauma and travails of war. Not unlike the veterans of ancient Rome who had been colonized on the frontiers of the empire, American veterans of World War II were settled on the fringes of America's cities. However, suburbia was open only to veterans with economic means, and discrimination usually kept veterans from minority groups—whatever their financial situation—out of the new suburbs.

Army veteran William Brunsell's remark that by the 1950s "you didn't ask whether or not a person was a vet," perhaps reveals the way that many veterans viewed their new lives in suburban communities. By the time these veterans had settled in the suburbs, they had usually made their personal adjustments to civilian life, had gained an education or job training, and had found gainful employment. Army veteran Vernon Bernhagen, who claimed that housing was his most troublesome postwar readjustment, admitted that after being able to purchase a home with a government loan that he "started to feel good about being in the service." With the acquisition of adequate housing, the transition from military to civilian life seemed complete. Many veterans could finally say that they were home.[76]

Notes

1. *Milwaukee Journal*, 21 May 1947.

2. For historical works on housing in the United States, particularly as they relate to the middle of the twentieth century, see Glenn H. Beyer, *Housing and Society* (New York: Macmillan, 1965); Richard O. Davies, *Housing Reform and the Truman Administration* (Columbia: University of Missouri Press, 1966); Kenneth T. Jackson, *Crabgrass Frontier: The Suburbanization of the United States* (New York: Oxford University Press, 1985); Nathan S. Keith, *Politics and the Housing Crisis Since 1930* (New York: Universe, 1973); Joseph B. Mason, *History of Housing in America, 1930-1980* (Houston: Gulf, 1982); Irving Welfeld, *Where We Live: A Social History of American Housing, from Slums to Suburbs* (New York: Simon and Schuster, 1988); Gwendolyn Wright, *Building the Dream: A Social History of Housing in America* (Cambridge, Mass.: MIT Press, 1981). Unless otherwise noted, discussion of federal housing policies and programs is based on these works.

3. David M. Blank, *The Volume of Residential Construction, 1889-1950* (New York: National Bureau of Economic Research, 1954), 67; U.S. Department of Commerce, *Historical Statistics of the United States: Colonial Times to 1970* (Washington, D.C.: GPO, 1975), 644-645.

4. Blank, *Volume of Residential Construction*, 67; *Historical Statistics*, 641; Jackson, *Crabgrass Frontier*, 203.

5. Peter S. Reed, "Enlisting Modernism," in Donald Albrecht, ed., *World War II and the American Dream: How Wartime Building Changed a Nation* (Cambridge, Mass.: MIT Press, 1995), 2-41.

6. Allan D. Wallis, *Wheel Estate: The Rise and Decline of Mobile Homes* (New York: Oxford University Press, 1991), 83-124.

7. Wilkie to Short, 14 January 1946, Papers of Horace W. Wilkie, State Historical Society of Wisconsin Archives, Madison, Wis. (cited hereafter as Wilkie Papers); Nelson interview, Wisconsin Veterans' Oral History Project, Wisconsin Veterans' Museum Research Center, Madison, Wis. (cited hereafter as WVOHP).

8. Bernhagen interview, WVOHP; Dave Lashway, ed., *The Memoirs of Henry C. Lashway, First Lieutenant, U.S. Army, World War II*, vol. 1, *Letters and Memoirs* (Privately published, 1996), 283; Rabidieux interview, Wisconsin Women in World War II Oral History Project, State Historical Society of Wisconsin Archives, Madison, Wis. (cited hereafter as WW2OHP).

9. Wilkie to Short, 14 January 1946, Wilkie Papers; Wilkie to Pois, 24 January 1946, Wilkie Papers; Bliss interview, WVOHP.

10. *Milwaukee Sentinel*, 8 December 1944; *Milwaukee Journal*, 30 July 1946; Mercier interview, WVOHP; Miller interview, WW2OHP.

11. *Milwaukee Sentinel*, 8 December 1944; Miller interview, WW2OHP; Moses interview, WVOHP; Rabidieux interview, WW2OHP; Landgraf interview, WVOHP.

12. Bernhagen interview, WVHOP; Landgraf interview, WVOHP; Moses interview, WVOHP; Lashway, *Memoirs*, 283.

13. Jacobsen interview, WVOHP; Beltmann interview, WVOHP; Hackbarth interview, WVOHP; Roger P. Scovill, *What Did You Do, Grandpa? The United States Marine Corps: An Artillery Enlisted Man's Memoir of World War II* (Madison, Wis.: Straus, 1994), 195-196; Turner interview, WVOHP.

14. U.S. Bureau of the Census, *Housing Characteristics in 108 Selected Areas, 1946 Veterans' Housing Surveys and the 1940 Census of Housing* (Washington, D.C.: GPO,

1946); *Capital Times*, 23 July 1946; *Wisconsin State Journal*, 1 August 1946; *Milwaukee Journal*, 24 October 1946.

15. *Wisconsin State Journal*, 30 November 1945; Capital *Times*, 20 October 1946; *Milwaukee Journal*, 21 October 1946.

16. *Milwaukee Journal*, 31 January 1946, 2 May 1946, 5 January 1947, 1 December 1947, 3 December 1947.

17. Harry S. Truman, "The Reconversion Crisis and the Need for Congressional Action," 3 January 1946, in *Public Papers of the Presidents of the United States: Harry S. Truman*, vol. 1946 (Washington, D.C.: GPO, 1962), 7.

18. Wilson Wyatt, *Whistle Stops: Adventures in Public Life* (Lexington: University Press of Kentucky, 1985), 61-67.

19. Harry S. Truman, "Statement by the President on the Veterans' Emergency Housing Program," 8 February 1946, in *Public Papers of Harry S. Truman*, vol. 1946, 114; Wyatt, *Whistle Stops*, 61-67.

20. Harry S. Truman, "Veterans' Emergency Housing Program," 8 February 1946, in *Public Papers of Harry S. Truman*, vol. 1946, 114; New *York Times*, 10 February 1946; *Oshkosh Daily Northwestern*, 12 February 1946.

21. Wyatt, *Whistle Stops*, 67-69; *Christian Science Monitor*, 27 February 1946; *Chicago Sun*, 3 March 1946; *New York Times*, 29 March 1946; *Congressional Record*, 79th Cong., 2d Sess., 1946, 92, pt. 13:1829-1848, 1863-1891, 1440-1964, 1974-1995.

22. *Christian Science Monitor*, 27 February 1946; *Congressional Record*, 79th Cong., 2d Sess., 1946, 92, pt. 13:1829-1848, 1863-1891; *New York Times*, 29 March 1946, 11 April 1946.

23. Wyatt, *Whistle Stops*, 65-66, 70-71.

24. *Capital Times*, 1 December 1946.

25. Wyatt, *Whistle Stops*, 72.

26. Harry S. Truman, "Statement by the President on the Veterans' Emergency Housing Program," 4 December 1946, in *Public Papers of Harry S. Truman*, vol. 1946, 489; Wyatt, *Whistle Stops*, 85.

27. David M. Oshinsky, *A Conspiracy So Immense: The World of Joe McCarthy* (New York: Free Press, 1983), 66-71.

28. *Capital Times*, 1 April 1947. For an overview of veterans' housing programs in other states, see Harold Robinson and John I. Robinson, "State Spending for Veterans' Housing," *Wisconsin Law Review*, 1949: 10-25; and Wisconsin Veterans' Housing Authority, *Summary of Housing Legislation and Notes on Programs* (Madison: Wisconsin Veterans' Housing Authority, 1948).

29. U.S. Congress, Joint Committee on Housing, *Hearings before the Joint Committee on Housing*, 80th Cong., 1st sess., 1948, vol. 1; *Wisconsin State Journal*, 13 February 1947.

30. *Milwaukee Journal*, 12 October 1947.

31. *Capital Times*, 24 April 1947; *Wisconsin State Journal*, 24 April 1947, 5 June 1947.

32. *Capital Times*, 24 April 1947; *Wisconsin State Journal*, 24 April 1947; *Milwaukee Journal*, 14 May 1947, 5 June 1947.

33. *Capital Times*, 5 June 1947; *Milwaukee Journal*, 5 June 1947; *Wisconsin State Journal*, 5 June 1947.

34. *Milwaukee Journal*, 21 May 1947, 26 June 1947; *Wisconsin State Journal*, 26 June 1947; *Capital Times*, 11 June 1947; *Wisconsin Counties*, August 1947.

35. *Capital Times*, 20 August 1947, 8 September 1947, 10 September 1947; *Milwaukee Journal*, 8 September 1947.

36. Minutes of the Board of the Wisconsin Veterans' Housing Authority Meeting, 13 October 1947, Wisconsin Veterans' Housing Authority records, State Government Records, State Historical Society of Wisconsin Archives, Madison, Wis. (cited hereafter as WVHA); *Green Bay Press-Gazette*, 14 October 1947; *Milwaukee Journal*, 14 October 1947; *Wisconsin State Journal*, 13 October 1947, 14 October 1947.

37. *Wisconsin State Journal*, 30 October 1947.

38. *Wisconsin State Journal*, 30 October 1947, 31 October 1947.

39. *Wisconsin State Journal*, 4 November 1947, 5 November 1947.

40. *Milwaukee Journal*, 8 November 1947; *Wisconsin State Journal*, 8 November 1947; *Sheboygan Press*, 12 November 1947.

41. *Capital Times*, 3 November 1947, 4 November 1947; *Wisconsin State Journal*, 4 November 1947, 26 November 1947.

42. *Green Bay Press-Gazette*, 7 November 1947.

43. *Sheboygan Press*, 18 December 1947; *Wisconsin State Journal*, 18 December 1947.

44. Case reports and amicus curie briefs on file at the Wisconsin Law Library, Madison, Wis.

45. *Green Bay Press-Gazette*, 4 May 1948; *Wisconsin State Journal*, 10 December 1948; Wisconsin Veterans' Housing Authority, *Survey of the Housing Accommodations of World War II Married Veterans* (Madison: Wisconsin Veterans' Housing Authority, 1948); Wisconsin Veterans' Housing Authority, *Conference on Veterans' Housing* (Madison: Wisconsin Veterans' Housing Authority, 1948).

46. Pamela H. Rice to Rennebohm, 26 May 1948, Records of the Governor: Oscar Rennebohm, State Government Records, State Historical Society of Wisconsin Archives, Madison, Wis. (cited hereafter as Rennebohm Papers); Buchen to Rennebohm, 25 May 1948, Rennebohm Papers; Knowles to Rennebohm, 28 June 1948, Rennebohm Papers.

47. *Green Bay Press-Gazette*, 15 May 1948.

48. *Wisconsin State Journal*, 19 July 1948, 20 July 1948, 21 July 1948.

49. *Capital Times*, 21 July 1948; *Wisconsin State Journal*, 21 July 1948.

50. *Milwaukee Journal*, 20 October 1948; *Capital Times*, 11 December 1948, 11 January 1949; *Wisconsin State Journal*, 30 December 1948; WVHA Board minutes, 30 December 1948, WVHA.

51. *Capital Times*, 5 February 1949; *Wisconsin State Journal*, 13 April 1949.

52. *Wisconsin State Journal*, 17 February 1949; *Milwaukee Journal*, 13 April 1949.

53. *Milwaukee Journal*, 13 April 1949; *Wisconsin Tax News*, 28 February 1949.

54. *Capital Times*, 1 February 1949; Wisconsin Legislative Reference Bureau, *Wisconsin Blue Book*, 1950 ed. (Madison: Legislative Reference Bureau, 1950), 776.

55. *Capital Times*, 29 April 1949; *Milwaukee Journal*, 29 April 1949, 12 May 1949.

56. *Milwaukee Journal*, 16 June 1949; *Capital Times*, 21 June 1949, 22 June 1949.

57. *Milwaukee Journal*, 6 August 1949; *Wisconsin State Journal*, 6 August 1949; *Green Bay Press-Gazette*, 18 August 1949; *Capital Times*, 14 September 1949; *Thumbnail History*, 6; Wisconsin Legislative Reference Bureau, *Veterans' Housing Legislation in Wisconsin* (Madison: Wisconsin Legislative Reference Bureau, 1953), 2.

58. *Green Bay Press-Gazette*, 18 August 1949.

59. *Historical Statistics*, 639; F. John Devaney, *Tracking the American Dream: 50 Years of Housing History from the Census Bureau, 1940 to 1990* (Washington, D.C.: U.S. Department of Commerce, 1994), 21.

60. *Historical Statistics*, 641.

61. *Historical Statistics*, 641; Bach interview, WVOHP.

62. Bach interview, WVOHP; Wozniak interview, WVOHP; Lashway, *Memoirs*, 283; Luetke interview, WVOHP.

63. Beltmann interview, WVOHP; Ella Wiberg interview, WVOHP; Scovill, *What Did You Do, Grandpa?*, 106, 211-212.

64. Lashway, *Memoirs*, 284; Bliss interview, WVOHP; Hackbarth interview, WVOHP.

65. WDVA Board minutes, 7 October 1949, Records of the Wisconsin Department of Veterans' Affairs, State Government Records, State Historical Society of Wisconsin Archives, Madison, Wis. (cited hereafter as WDVA); *Green Bay Press-Gazette*, 8 October 1949; *Milwaukee Journal*, 16 October 1949; *Wisconsin State Journal*, 22 February 1950.

66. *Wisconsin State Journal*, 22 February 1950; R. B. Lewis to Rennebohm, 21 February 1950, Rennebohm Papers; CVSO Association minutes, 21 February 1950, 17 January 1951, Minute Book I, Records of the County Veterans' Service Officers' Association of Wisconsin, Wisconsin Veterans' Museum Research Center, Madison, Wis.

67. WDVA Board minutes, 26 October 1951, WDVA; *Blue Book*, 1962 ed., 657; Blake interview, WVHOP; Hochschild interview, WVOHP.

68. For more on the postwar suburban milieu, see Jackson, *Crabgrass Frontier*, 231-245, 288; and Wright, *Building the Dream*, 240-261. Michael J. Bennett, *When Dreams Come True: The GI Bill and the Making of Modern America* (Washington, D.C.: Brassey's, 1996), also contains a chapter on the housing provisions of the GI Bill.

69. U.S. Bureau of the Census, *Eighteenth Census of the United States: Population*, vol. 1, part 51 (Washington, D.C.: GPO, 1960), 17, 20-21; William F. Thompson, *The History of Wisconsin*, vol. 4, *Continuity and Change, 1940-1965* (Madison: State Historical Society of Wisconsin, 1988), 229-234.

70. Wilkie to Pois, 24 January 1946, Wilkie Papers; Landgraf interview, WVOHP; Brunsell interview, WVOHP.

71. For more on this issue, see Jackson, *Crabgrass Frontier*, 198-214.

72. Thompson, *Continuity and Change*, 330; Untitled Fair Employment Division statement of purpose, 1947, Records of the Wisconsin Equal Rights Division, State Government Records, State Historical Society of Wisconsin, Madison, Wis. (cited hereafter as WERD).

73. Untitled statement of purpose, WERD; Thompson, *Continuity and Change*, 334-336.

74. Wisconsin Governor's Commission on Human Rights, *Nonwhite Housing in Wisconsin* (Madison: State of Wisconsin, 1954); National Association for the Advancement of Colored People, Madison Branch, *Negro Housing in Madison* (Madison, Wis.: National Association for the Advancement of Colored People, Madison Branch, 1959).

75. *Eighteenth Census of the United States*, 63-66.

76. Brunsell interview, WVOHP; Bernhagen interview, WVOHP.

Conclusion

Readjustment programs for World War II veterans were the most sweeping and far-reaching in American history, but did they work? In short, the answer is yes. Because the size of the World War II veteran population was so large, the "veteran problem" probably concerned a majority of Americans in a direct and personal way. Great public interest in veterans' affairs translated into widespread political support for a broad program of benefits for returning soldiers. The result was the smoothest transition of any generation of veterans to civilian life in American history—a particularly momentous achievement given the unprecedented number of the World War II veterans.

Clearly, World War II veterans—like ex-soldiers for thousands of years before them—experienced difficulties in readjusting to civilian life. However, the comprehensive and generous program of veterans' benefits developed following the war eased that transition to a remarkable degree. World War II veterans appear to have attained more education and earned more money than their non-veteran counterparts. Most veterans owned the homes in which they lived. Because the World War II veteran population was so large, the readjustment programs reached more American households than ever before. Not only did benefit programs lessen the postwar problems of World War II veterans, they also helped to propel an entire generation of Americans into an era of unprecedented prosperity. The effectiveness of the World War II veterans' programs lessened the threat of social and political unrest among ex-soldiers. Unlike the aftermath of other major wars in American history, the post-World War II period saw no important outbreak of veteran agitation. No equivalent to Shays' Rebellion or the Bonus March took place in the 1940s or 1950s; no Hitler or Mussolini arose to prey on the disillusion of jobless veterans who believed that the nation for which they fought had abandoned them. These had been the fears of Americans as they devised a program for those who served in World War II, and they did not come to pass.

One of the lessons of the World War II veteran readjustment experience is that a comprehensive program of benefits is necessary to properly fit the veteran back into civilian life. As this book has tried to stress, readjustment to civilian life was an individual process; not all veterans had the same postwar needs. Perhaps the most significant characteristic of World War II veterans' programs is that they covered nearly all facets of the readjustment problem. The vast array of state, federal, and local programs provided flexibility, so that veterans could find assistance in the areas in which they personally needed it most. Title II of the GI

Bill, for example, helped train veterans for jobs in a great variety of ways, such as providing access to a college education, a technical degree, or on-the-job training. It aided the eighteen-year-old veteran just out of high school as well as the thirty-six-year-old returning to his prewar occupation. Unlike the aftermath of previous wars, the World War II programs also addressed the needs of non-disabled veterans in a far-reaching fashion. Since colonial times, those disabled by war have generally been recognized as having a claim to aid from the government. However, it was the nondisabled veteran, facing readjustment difficulties but receiving little in the way of assistance, who was typically responsible for social and political unrest. After World War II, Americans recognized that all veterans faced readjustment problems as a result of military service, and lawmakers at the federal, state, and local levels took steps to alleviate them.

The cost of these programs was astronomical, however. By 1970, federal benefits to World War II veterans had reached an estimated $87 billion dollars.[1] The conservative fiscal nature of Wisconsin's veterans' programs stands in contrast to that of the federal government. True, the Wisconsin plan aided disabled and nondisabled veterans in a wide range of areas not previously covered in any systematic way, such as education and home loans. Wisconsin even provided benefits for non-service-connected medical conditions, and expanded its medical programs to cover veterans' dependents as well. Nevertheless, tight fiscal policies hindered the effectiveness of this extensive and magnanimous program. The state's home loan program built few houses. Economic loans were denied to many veterans whose readjustment process might have been materially aided by them. Fiscal conservatism prevented a far-reaching veterans' program from not reaching as many veterans as it could have. Another lesson from the World War II veteran experience is that effective readjustment programs can be very expensive.

The debate over veterans' affairs in the late 1940s revealed some of the ideological cleavages in American politics at midcentury. America was at a political crossroads in the late 1940s. After more than a decade of liberal reform under Democratic President Franklin D. Roosevelt and his New Deal, liberalism remained popular with many Americans. However, after World War II liberals began to face a serious challenge from a resurgent conservatism spearheaded by the Republican Party. After World War II, liberals and conservatives continued to debate the size and scope of government, and its proper role in the daily lives of ordinary Americans. In the immediate aftermath of the war, that debate was often conducted in the arena of veterans' affairs. Both camps recognized the obligation of government to assist veterans in readjusting to civilian life, as well as the potential political payoff in doing so. But each espoused different strategies of coping with the problem. The veterans' program that emerged was an amalgam of both liberal and conservative ideas.

Although veterans' programs after World War II had greater public support than did similar programs at any time in American history, there were also limits on how far America was willing to go to support them. Americans were prepared to pay a high price for programs that helped veterans become reestablished in the civilian world as peacefully as possible, but they did not give their ex-soldiers a blank check. Once the readjustment benefit package appeared to be working, support for expanding veterans' programs decreased. Indeed, veterans' programs were so comprehensive, and veterans seemed to be readjusting so well, that veterans sometimes lobbied *against* additional benefits for themselves. In addition, abuses of the benefit programs outraged many Americans. Clearly, not every dollar spent on veteran readjustment in the 1940s and 1950s was one spent well. The existence of the 52-20 Club and violations of the GI Bill's on-the-job training provisions, for example, provoked great anger among veteran and nonveteran alike. Veterans' programs also met stiff opposition when they involved areas where powerful vested interests were concerned, or when government activity—even in the name of the veteran—went beyond traditional practices and relationships. Housing interests stoutly resisted further government activity in their field, for example. Although they were the most comprehensive in American history, veterans' programs following World War II clearly had their limitations.

It should also be noted that not all veterans benefited equally from the readjustment programs. For veterans who sustained amputations or debilitating medical problems as a result of the war, complete readjustment would prove to be elusive. Disabled veterans would forever face challenges fitting into the workplace, for example, as well as the social stigmatization that the physically and psychologically disabled often endure. The social and racial prejudices of the day also impacted upon the effectiveness of readjustment programs. Veterans from minority groups appear to have gained less from the veterans' programs than did whites, as discrimination often blocked access to the benefit rights they had earned through military service. Home loans meant little to the African American veteran shut out of suburban communities by restrictive covenants, for example. Women also tended to benefit from readjustment programs less than did men. In trying to utilize their hard-won benefits, women experienced blatant discrimination. The popular culture messages of the period—that women should return to hearth and home after the war—further inhibited the impact of readjustment benefits for women veterans.

Despite its shortcomings, the readjustment package for World War II veterans was unquestionably successful in fitting most veterans back into American society. In fact, the process of veteran readjustment after World War II went so smoothly that many Americans came to believe that a nontraumatic postwar period was normal. In the aftermath of subsequent wars, the lessons of World War II veteran readjustment would be largely forgotten. Hitler and the Bonus Marchers no longer haunted the minds of lawmakers, but the abusers of the 52-20 Club did. The later wars in Korea and Vietnam did not enjoy the same level of public support as did World War II. They also involved far fewer numbers of soldiers; about five million Americans served in the Korean War, and about eight million during more than a decade of conflict in Vietnam. The creation of comprehensive veterans' benefits after World War II was due in part to the fact that veteran readjustment affected so many American households. The conflicts in Korea and Vietnam did not make nearly the same impression on society that World War II had.

Veterans' programs after the wars in Korea and Vietnam were not nearly as effective as those enacted after World War II. In 1952, an act popularly known as the Korean GI Bill provided Korean War veterans with unemployment, education, and loan benefits, but at significantly lower rates than for their World War II counterparts. The Korean GI Bill, for example, provided veterans with only twenty-six weeks of unemployment benefits, at $26 a week (World War II vets received $20 a week for fifty-two weeks). Similarly, education benefits were limited to one and a half days of education or training for each day of service, not to exceed thirty-six months. Congress passed two GI Bill-type acts for Vietnam veterans, one in 1966 (amended in 1970) and the other in 1972, providing Vietnam-era veterans with educational and housing assistance, but at levels that failed to keep pace with the economic realities of the 1960s and 1970s.[2]

As a result, Korean War and Vietnam War veterans did not readjust to civilian life as well as the men and women who returned from World War II. Unlike those of World War II, veterans of these later wars typically earned less money than did their nonveteran counterparts. So pervasive was the notion that veteran readjustment was a smooth and simple process that when Vietnam veterans returned with PTSD and other psychological problems, the American public tended to view their claims with disbelief and suspicion, forgetting that war has always affected the minds of soldiers. Many Americans perceived the veterans' activism for more comprehensive and effective benefits—a phenomenon in the United States that dated to the Revolutionary War—as little more than "whining" and the veterans themselves as "bums" and "freeloaders." Public support for these veterans did not materialize, and the assistance they received in their return to civilian life suffered as a result. During the 1940s, Americans had learned the lessons of past wars and devised a vast system of readjustment benefits for returning veterans. However, just decades later Americans were unable or unwilling to recall those lessons and apply them to later generations of ex-soldiers.[3]

In his book *The Veteran Comes Back*, Willard Waller told Americans that "the art of rehabilitation" was one that the nation had to "perfect if we are ever to solve the problem of the veteran in our society." With memories of the turbulent World War I years fresh in their memories and sixteen million new veterans about to return home, Americans heeded Waller's advice and created the most effective system of veterans' benefits in American history. The "art of rehabilitation" of which Waller wrote could hardly be called perfected after World War II, but never before had a generation of American veterans received such thorough assistance in making the transition from the military to the civilian worlds.

Notes

1. U.S. Department of Commerce, *Historical Statistics of the United States: Colonial Times to 1970* (Washington, D.C.: GPO, 1975), 1140.

2. For more on benefits available to Korean and Vietnam War veterans, see Theodore R. Mosch, *The GI Bill: A Breakthrough in Educational and Social Policy in the United States* (Hicksville, N.Y.: Exposition Press, 1975), 46-87; Sar A. Levitan and Karen A. Cleary, *Old Wars Remain Unfinished: The Veteran Benefits System* (Baltimore: Johns Hopkins University Press, 1973); and Sar A. Levitan and Joyce K. Zickler, *Swords into Plowshares: Our GI Bill* (Salt Lake City: Olympus, 1973).

3. The volume of literature on Vietnam War veterans is larger than that on World War II veterans. For an introduction to the subject, see Christian G. Appy, *Working Class War: American Combat Soldiers and Vietnam* (Chapel Hill: University of North Carolina Press, 1993); John Helmer, *Bringing the War Home: The American Soldier in Vietnam and After* (New York: Free Press, 1974); Robert Jay Lifton, *Home from the War: Learning from Vietnam Veterans* (Boston: Beacon Press, 1992); Richard Moser, *The New Winter Soldiers: GI and Veteran Dissent during the Vietnam Era* (New Brunswick, N.J.: Rutgers University Press, 1996), and Richard Severo and Lewis Milford, *The Wages of War: When American Soldiers Came Home—From Valley Forge to Vietnam* (New York: Simon and Schuster, 1989), 345-318; and Jonathan Shay, *Achilles in Vietnam: Combat Trauma and the Undoing of Character* (New York: Scribner, 1994). By contrast, very little literature exists on Korean War veterans. For an introduction, see Severo and Milford, *Wages of War*, 315-344.

Bibliography

Manuscripts

National Archives, Washington, D.C.
    Retraining and Reemployment Administration
State Historical Society of Wisconsin Archives, Madison, Wis.
    American Legion. Department of Wisconsin
    Knowles, Warren P.
    Lorenz, William F., Sr.
    Wilkie, Horace
    Wisconsin State Government Records
        Department of Veterans' Affairs
        Division of Apprenticeship and Training
        Governor: Goodland, Walter S.
        Governor: Rennebohm, Oscar
        Unemployment Compensation Department
        Wisconsin Equal Rights Division
        Wisconsin Veterans' Housing Authority
    Wisconsin Women during World War II Oral History Project
University of Wisconsin Archives, Madison, Wis.
    General Files
    University of Wisconsin Oral History Project
Wisconsin Veterans' Museum Research Center, Madison, Wis.
    Ambrose, Stephen E., World War II Interview Collection
    County Veterans' Service Officers Association of Wisconsin
    Wisconsin National Guard Materials
    Wisconsin Veterans' Oral History Project
    World War II Small Collections

Newspapers and Periodicals

Appleton Post-Crescent
Badger Legionnaire
Beloit College Bulletin
Beloit News
Capital Times
Chicago Sun
Chicago Tribune

Milwaukee Journal
Milwaukee Sentinel
New York Times
New York Times Magazine
Northern Light
Oshkosh Northwestern
Sheboygan Press

Christian Science Monitor
Daily Cardinal
Dunn County News
Fond du Lac Commonwealth-Reporter
Green Bay Press-Gazette
Janesville Gazette
La Crosse Tribune and Leader Press
Lawrence Alumnus
Manitowoc Herald-Times
Marshfield News-Herald
Memomonee Falls News

State Government
Superior Telegram
University of Wisconsin Press
  Bulletin
Watertown Times
Waukesha Freeman
Wisconsin Agriculturist and Farmer
Wisconsin Counties
Wisconsin Journal of Education
Wisconsin State Journal
Wisconsin Tax News

Published Works

Albrecht, Donald, ed. *World War II and the American Dream: How Wartime Building Changed a Nation.* Cambridge, Mass.: MIT Press, 1995.

Allis-Chalmers Manufacturing Co. *You and the Returning Veteran: A Guide for Foremen.* West Allis, Wis.: Allis-Chalmers Manufacturing Co., 1945.

Ambrose, Stephen E. *Citizen Soldiers: The U.S. Army from the Normandy Beaches to the Bulge to the Surrender of Germany, June 7, 1944–May 7, 1945.* New York: Simon and Schuster, 1997.

American Psychiatric Association. *Diagnostic and Statistical Manual of Mental Disorders.* 4th ed. Washington, D.C.: American Psychiatric Association, 1994.

Angrist, Joshua, and Alan B. Krueger. "Why Do World War II Veterans Earn More than Nonveterans?" *Journal of Labor Economics* 12 (1994): 74-97.

Appy, Christian G. *Working Class War: The American Combat Soldier in Vietnam.* Chapel Hill: University of North Carolina Press, 1993.

Ashley, Robert, and George H. Miller. *Ripon College: A History.* Ripon, Wis.: Ripon College Press, 1990.

Ayres, Leonard P. *The War with Germany: A Statistical Summary.* Washington, D.C.: GPO, 1919.

Ballard, Jack Stokes. *The Shock of Peace: Economic and Military Demobilization after World War II.* Washington, D.C.: University Press of America, 1983.

Barron County, Wisconsin, Board of Supervisors. *Proceedings.* Barron, Wisconsin, 1940-50.

Baruch, Dorothy W., and Lee Edward Travis. *You're Out of the Service Now.* New York: Appleton-Century, 1946.

Bennett, J. Claude, and Fred Plum, eds. *Cecil Textbook of Medicine,* 20th ed. Philadelphia: W. B. Saunders, 1996.

Bennett, Michael J. *When Dreams Came True: The GI Bill and the Making of Modern America.* Washington, D.C.: Brassey's, 1996.

Bergerud, Eric. *Touched with Fire: The Land War in the South Pacific.* New York: Viking, 1996.

Bernstein, Alison R. *American Indians and World War II: Toward a New Era in Indian Affairs*. Norman: University of Oklahoma Press, 1991.

Berry, Henry. *Semper Fi, Mac: Living Memories of the U.S. Marines in World War II*. New York: Arbor House, 1982.

Bérubé, Allan. *Coming Out under Fire: The History of Gay Men and Women in World War Two*. New York: Free Press, 1990.

Bessel, Richard, and David Englander. "Up from the Trenches: Some Recent Writing on the Soldiers of the Great War." *European Studies Review* 11 (1981): 387-395.

Beyer, Glenn H. *Housing and Society*. New York: Macmillan, 1965.

Blank, David M. *The Volume of Residential Construction, 1889-1950*. New York: National Bureau of Economic Research, 1954.

Bogacz, Ted. "War Neurosis and Cultural Change in England, 1914-1922: The Work of the War Office Committee of Enquiry into 'Shell Shock.'" *Journal of Contemporary History* 24 (1989): 227-256.

Bogue, Allan G., and Robert Taylor, eds. *The University of Wisconsin: One Hundred and Twenty Five Years*. Madison: University of Wisconsin Press, 1975.

Bois, Jean-Pierre. *Les anciens soldats dans la societe française au XVIIIe siecle*. Paris: Economica, 1990.

Bolté, Charles. *The New Veteran*. New York: Reynal and Hitchcock, 1945.

Bolté, Charles, and Louis Harris. *Our Negro Veterans*. New York: Public Affairs Committee, 1947.

Boring, Edwin G., ed. *Psychology for the Armed Services*. Washington, D.C.: Infantry Journal Press, 1945.

Bottoms, Bill. *The VFW: An Illustrated History of the Veterans of Foreign Wars of the United States*. Rockville, Md.: Woodbine House, 1991.

Bowker, Benjamin. *Out of Uniform*. New York: Norton, 1946.

Bradley, Charles. *Aleutian Echoes*. Fairbanks: University of Alaska Press, 1994.

Bradley, David. "Fallout." *Wisconsin Medical Alumni Magazine* 36:1 (1996): 19-22.

―――. *No Place to Hide, 1946/1984*. Hanover, N.H.: University Press of New England, 1983.

Bradley, James. *Flags of Our Fathers*. New York: Bantam Books, 2000.

Bradley, Omar. *A General's Story*. New York: Simon and Schuster, 1983.

Brokaw, Tom. *The Greatest Generation*. New York: Random House, 1998.

Brown, Francis J. *Educational Opportunities for Veterans*. Washington, D.C.: Public Affairs Press, 1946.

Bruner, Jerome S. *Public Thinking on Post-War Problems*. Washington, D.C.: National Planning Association, 1943.

Buhle, Paul, ed. *History and the New Left: Madison, Wisconsin, 1950-1970*. Philadelphia: Temple University Press, 1990.

Caldwell, Mark. *The Last Crusade: The War on Consumption, 1862-1954*. New York: Atheneum, 1988.

Campbell, D'Ann. *Women at War with America: Private Lives in a Patriotic Era.* Cambridge, Mass.: Harvard University Press, 1984.

Carmody, Alice P., Louis Mesard, and William F. Page. *Alcoholism and Problem Drinking, 1970-1975: A Statistical Analysis of VA Hospital Patients.* Washington, D.C.: Veterans' Administration, 1977.

Cecil, Russell L., ed. *Textbook of Medicine,* 7th ed. Philadelphia: W. B. Saunders, 1947.

Chase, John L., et al. *Graduate Teaching Assistants in American Universities: A Review of Recent Trends and Recommendations.* Washington, D.C.: U.S. Department of Health, Education, and Welfare, 1970.

Child, Irvin L., and Marjorie Van de Water, eds. *Psychology for the Returning Serviceman.* Washington, D.C.: Infantry Journal Press, 1945.

Coates, John B., ed. *Preventive Medicine in World War II.* 9 vols. Washington, D.C.: Department of the Army, 1955-69.

Coffman, Edward M. *The War to End All Wars: The American Military Experience in World War I.* New York: Oxford University Press, 1968.

Cohen, Bernard C., and Maurice Z. Cooper. *Follow-Up Study of World War II Prisoners of War.* Washington, D.C.: GPO, 1954.

Congressional Record. Washington, D.C., 1940-60.

Corvisier, André. *Armies and Societies in Europe, 1494-1789.* Bloomington: University of Indiana Press, 1979.

Cosmas, Graham, and Albert E. Cowdrey. *Medical Service in the European Theater of Operations.* Washington, D.C.: U.S. Army Center for Military History, 1992.

Costello, John. *Virtue under Fire: How World War II Changed Our Social and Sexual Attitudes.* Boston: Little, Brown and Company, 1985.

Cotran, Ramzi S., et al. *Robbins Pathologic Basis of Disease.* Philadelphia: W. B. Saunders, 1994.

Cowdrey, Albert E. *Fighting for Life: American Military Medicine in World War II.* New York: Free Press, 1994.

Daniels, Roger. *The Bonus March: An Episode of the Great Depression.* Westport, Conn.: Greenwood Press, 1971.

Davies, Richard O. *Housing Reform and the Truman Administration.* Columbia: University of Missouri Press, 1966.

Davis, Susan. *The Student Veteran's Wife.* Madison, Wis.: Privately published, 1947.

Dean, C. G. T. *The Royal Chelsea Hospital.* London: Hutchinson, 1950.

Dean, Eric T., Jr. *Shook over Hell: Post-Traumatic Stress, Vietnam, and the Civil War.* Cambridge, Mass.: Harvard University Press, 1997.

Dearing, Mary R. *Veterans in Politics: The Story of the GAR.* Westport, Conn.: Greenwood Press, 1974.

D'Emilio, John. *Sexual Politics, Sexual Communities: The Making of a Homosexual Minority in the United States, 1940-1970.* Chicago: University of Chicago Press, 1983.

Devaney, F. John. *Tracking the American Dream: 50 Years of Housing History from the Census Bureau: 1940 to 1990.* Washington, D.C.: U.S. Department of Commerce, 1994.

Dexter, Nathaniel B. *Northland College: A History.* Ashland, Wis.: Northland College, 1968.

Diehl, James M. *Thanks of the Fatherland: German Veterans after the Second World War.* Chapel Hill: University of North Carolina Press, 1993.

Dillingham, William Pyrle. *Federal Aid to Veterans, 1917-1941.* Gainesville: University of Florida Press, 1952.

Donovan, William N. *POW in the Pacific: Memoirs of an American Doctor in World War II.* Wilmington, Del.: SR Books, 1998.

Doyle, Robert C. *Voices from Captivity: Interpreting the American POW Narrative.* Lawrence: University Press of Kansas, 1994.

Droke, Maxwell. *Good-by to GI: How to Be a Successful Civilian.* New York: Abington-Cokesbury Press, 1945.

Duffy, Christopher. *The Army of Frederick the Great.* London: David and Charles, 1974.

Dumas, Alexander G., and Grace Keen. *A Psychiatric Primer for the Veteran's Family and Friends.* Minneapolis: University of Minnesota Press, 1945.

Dunn County, Wisconsin, Board of Supervisors. *Proceedings.* Menomonie, Wisconsin, 1940-50.

Ebel, Charles. "Southern Gaul in the Triumviral Period: A Critical Stage of Romanization." *American Journal of Philology* 109 (1988): 572-590.

Ehlers, Joachim. *Die Wehrverfassung der Stadt Hamburg im 17. und 18. Jahrhundert.* Boppard am Rhein: Harald Boldt Verlag, 1966.

Ellis, John. *The Sharp End: The Fighting Man in World War II.* New York: Scribner, 1980.

Feldberg, Georgina D. *Disease and Class: Tuberculosis and the Shaping of Modern North American Society.* New Brunswick, N.J.: Rutgers University Press, 1995.

Feldman, Jim. *The Buildings of the University of Wisconsin.* Madison: University of Wisconsin Archives, 1997.

Fligstein, Neil. *The GI Bill: Its Effects on the Educational and Occupational Attainments of U.S. Males, 1940-1973.* Madison: Center for Demography and Ecology, University of Wisconsin-Madison, 1976.

Fox-Genovese, Elizabeth. "Mixed Messages: Women and the Impact of World War II." *Southern Humanities Review* 27 (1993): 235-250.

Fredericksen, Norman, and William B. Schrader. *Adjustment to College.* Princeton, N.J.: Educational Testing Service, 1951.

Fried, Richard M. "Springtime for Stalin: Mosinee's 'Day under Communism' as Cold War Pageantry." *Wisconsin Magazine of History* 77 (1992-93): 83-108.

Fussell, Paul. *Wartime: Understanding and Behavior in the Second World War.* New York: Oxford University Press, 1989.

Futterman, Samuel, and Eugene Pumpian-Mindlin. "Traumatic War Neuroses Five Years Later." *American Journal of Psychiatry* 108 (1951): 401-407.

Gamble, Richard D. *From Academy to University, 1866-1966: A History of Wisconsin State University, Platteville, Wisconsin.* Platteville: Wisconsin State University, 1966.

Gerber, David A., ed. *Disabled Veterans in History.* Ann Arbor: University of Michigan Press, 2000.

Glasson, William H. *Federal Military Pensions in the United States.* New York: Oxford University Press, 1918.

————. *History of Military Pension Legislation in the United States.* New York: Arno Press, 1968.

Goodland, Walter S., acting governor of Wisconsin. *Executive Report on State Finances and Messages of Acting Governor Walter S. Goodland.* Madison: State of Wisconsin, 1943.

Goodman, Jack, ed. *While You Were Gone: A Report on Wartime Life in the United States.* New York: Simon and Schuster, 1946.

Graham, Otis L., Jr. *Toward a Planned Society: From Roosevelt to Nixon.* New York: Oxford University Press, 1976.

Graves, W. Brooke. *American State Government.* 4th ed. Boston: D. C. Heath, 1953.

Gray, J. Glenn. *The Warriors: Reflections on Men in Battle.* New York: Harper & Row, 1970.

Greenberg, Milton. *The GI Bill: The Law That Changed America.* New York: Lickle, 1997.

Grinker, Roy R., and John P. Spiegel. *Men under Stress.* Philadelphia: Blakiston, 1945.

Grob, Gerald N. *The Mad among Us: A History of the Care of America's Mentally Ill.* New York: Free Press, 1994.

Gross, Robert A., ed. *In Debt to Shays: The Bicentennial of an Agrarian Rebellion.* Charlottesville, Va.: University of Virginia Press, 1993.

Grove, Robert D., and Alice M. Hetzel. *Vital Statistics Rates in the United States, 1940-1940.* Washington, D.C.: U.S. National Center for Health Statistics, 1968.

Hamilton, Raphael N. *The Story of Marquette University: An Object Lesson in the Development of Catholic Higher Education.* Milwaukee, Wis.: Marquette University Press, 1953.

Harrison, Gordon. *Mosquitoes, Malaria, and Man: A History of the Hostilities since 1800.* New York: Dutton, 1978.

Hartmann, Susan. "Prescriptions for Penelope: Literature of Women's Obligations to Returning World War II Veterans." *Women's Studies* 5 (1978): 223-229.

————. *The Home Front and Beyond: American Women in the 1940s.* Boston: Twayne, 1982.

Havinghurst, Robert J., et al. *The American Veterans Back Home: A Study in Veteran Readjustment.* New York: Longmans, Green, 1951.

Helmer, John. *Bringing the War Home: The American Soldier in Vietnam and After.* New York: Free Press, 1974.

Herman, Judith. *Trauma and Recovery.* New York: Basic Books, 1997.

Hoyt, Edwin P. *The GI's War: The Story of American Soldiers in Europe in World War II.* New York: McGraw-Hill, 1988.

Jackson, Kenneth T. *Crabgrass Frontier: The Suburbanization of the United States.* New York: Oxford University Press, 1985.

Keegan, John. *A History of Warfare.* New York: Knopf, 1994.

Keith, Nathaniel S. *Politics and the Housing Crisis since 1930.* New York: Universe, 1973.

Kelly, Patrick J. *Creating a National Home: Building the Veterans' Welfare State, 1860-1900.* Cambridge, Mass.: Harvard University Press, 1997.

Kennett, Lee. *GI: The American Fighting Man in World War II.* New York: Warner Books, 1987.

Kenosha County, Wisconsin, Board of Supervisors. *Proceedings.* Kenosha, Wisconsin, 1940-50.

Kerr, E. Bartlett. *Surrender and Survival: The Experience of American POWs in the Pacific.* New York: William Morrow, 1985.

Kimbrough, Robert T., and Judson B. Glen. *American Law of Veterans.* Rev. ed. Rochester, N.Y.: Lawyers Co-operative, 1954.

Kitching, Howard. *Sex Problems of the Returned Veteran.* New York: Emerson Books, 1946.

Klein, Robert. *Wounded Men, Broken Promises: How the Veterans Administration Betrays Yesterday's Heroes.* New York: Macmillan, 1981.

Kopperman, Paul A. "'The Cheapest Pay': Alcohol Abuse in the Eighteenth-Century British Army." *Journal of Military History* 60 (1996): 445-470.

Kuhn, J. J. *I Was Baker 2: Memoirs of a World War II Platoon Sergeant.* West Bend, Wis., DeRaimo, 1994.

Kupper, Herbert I. *Back to Life: The Emotional Adjustment of Our Veterans.* New York: L. B. Fischer, 1945.

Lashway, Dave, ed. *The Memoirs of Henry C. Lashway, First Lieutenant, U.S. Army, World War II.* Vol. 1, *Letters and Memoirs.* Privately published, 1996.

Le Bohec, Yann. *The Imperial Roman Army.* New York: Hippocrene, 1994.

Lender, Mark Edward, and James Kirby Martin. *Drinking in America: A History.* Rev. ed. New York: Free Press, 1987.

Lerager, Jim. *In the Shadow of the Cloud: Photographs and Histories of America's Atomic Veterans.* Golden, Colo.: Fulcrum, 1988.

Levitan, Sar A., and Joyce K. Zickler. *Swords into Plowshares: Our GI Bill.* Salt Lake City: Olympus, 1973.

Levitan, Sar A., and Karen A. Cleary. *Old Wars Remain Unfinished: The Veteran Benefits System.* Baltimore: Johns Hopkins University Press, 1973.

Lifton, Robert Jay. *Home from the War: Learning from Vietnam Veterans.* Boston: Beacon Press, 1992.

Linderman, Gerald F. *The World within War: America's Combat Experience in World War II.* New York: Free Press, 1997.

Lindgren Amy, ed. *Understanding the Former Prisoner of War: Life After Liberation: Essays by Guy Kelnhofer Jr., Ph.D.* St. Paul, Minn.: Banfil Street Press, 1992.

Lorenz, William F. "Prompt Medical Service to Veterans." *Wisconsin Medical Journal* 44 (1945): 432-434.

Lundeen, Thomas B. *Jubilee! A History of the College of Engineering at the University of Wisconsin-Platteville, 1908-1983.* Platteville: University of Wisconsin-Platteville, 1983.

Magnuson, Paul R. *Ring the Night Bell: An American Surgeon's Story.* Boston: Little, Brown, 1960.

Manitowoc County, Wisconsin, Board of Supervisors. *Proceedings.* Manitowoc, Wisconsin, 1940-50.

Markus, Theodore, and Arthur Zeitlin. "Remediation in Higher Education: A 'New' Phenomemon?" *Community Review* 16 (2000): 167-177.

Mason, Joseph B. *History of Housing in America, 1930-1980.* Houston: Gulf, 1982.

Mauldin, Bill. *Back Home.* New York: William Sloane Associates, 1947.

May, Elaine Tyler. *Homeward Bound: American Families in the Cold War Era.* New York: Basic Books, 1988.

McConnell, Stuart. *Glorious Contentment: The Grand Army of the Republic, 1865-1900.* Chapel Hill: University of North Carolina Press, 1992.

Milner, Samuel. *Victory in Papua.* Washington, D.C.: U.S. Army Center for Military History, 1957.

Milwaukee Journal. They Can't Eat Medals. Milwaukee, Wis.: Journal Company, 1943.

Minott, Rodney G. *Peerless Patriots: Organized Veterans and the Spirit of Americanism.* Washington, D.C.: Public Affairs Press, 1962.

Morgan, Philip. *Italian Fascism, 1919-1945.* New York: St. Martin's Press, 1996.

Mosch, Theodore R. *The GI Bill: A Breakthrough in Educational and Social Policy in the United States.* Hicksville, N.Y.: Exposition Press, 1975.

Moser, Richard. *The New Winter Soldiers: GI and Veteran Dissent during the Vietnam Era.* New Brunswick, N.J.: Rutgers University Press, 1996.

Mueller, Erhart. *Badger Village and Bluffview Courts.* Baraboo, Wis.: Bluffview Acres, Inc., 1982.

Myers, Minor, Jr. *Liberty without Anarchy: A History of the Society of the Cincinnati.* Charlottesville: University of Virginia Press, 1983.

Nalty, Bernard C. *Strength for the Fight: A History of Black Americans in the Military.* New York: Free Press, 1986.

National Association for the Advancement of Colored People. Madison Branch. *Negro Housing in Madison.* Madison, Wis.: National Association for the Advancement of Colored People Madison Branch, 1959.

Nefziger, M. Dean. "Follow-Up Studies of World War II and Korean War Prisoners." *American Journal of Epidemiology* 91 (1970): 123-138.

Nicholls, A. J. *Weimar and the Rise of Hitler*, 3rd ed. New York: St. Martin's Press, 1991.

Nix, Asbury. *Corregidor: Oasis of Hope*. Stevens Point, Wis.: Trade Winds Publications, 1991.

Oberly, James W. *Sixty Million Acres: American Veterans and Public Lands before the Civil War*. Kent, Ohio: Kent State University Press, 1990.

Ohm, Howard F., ed. *Summary of Action of the Regular Session of the Wisconsin Legislature on Some of the More Important Questions Coming before It*. Madison: Wisconsin Legislative Reference Library, 1941-49.

Olson, Keith W. *The GI Bill, the Veterans, and the Colleges*. Lexington: University of Kentucky Press, 1974.

Onskt, David H. "'First a Negro . . . Incidentally a Veteran': Black World War II Veterans and the GI Bill of Rights in the Deep South, 1944-1948." *Journal of Social History* 31 (1998): 517-543.

Oshinsky, David M. *A Conspiracy So Immense: The World of Joe McCarthy*. New York: Free Press, 1983.

Overton, Grace Sloan. *Marriage in War and Peace: A Book for Parents and Counselors of Youth*. New York: Abingdon-Cokesbury Press, 1945.

Paris, Kathleen A. *A Political History of Vocational, Technical, and Adult Education in Wisconsin*. Madison: Wisconsin Board of Vocational, Technical, and Adult Education, 1985.

Parker, Geoffrey. *The Army of Flanders and the Spanish Road, 1567-1659: The Logistics of Spanish Victory and Defeat in the Low Countries' Wars*. London: Cambridge University Press, 1972.

Paster, Samuel, and Saul D. Holtzman. "A Study of One Thousand Psychotic Veterans Treated with Insulin and Electric Shock." *American Journal of Psychiatry* 105 (1949): 811-814.

Paul, Justus F. *The World Is Ours: A History of the University of Wisconsin-Stevens Point, 1894-1994*. Stevens Point: Foundation Press, 1994.

Payne, Stanley. *Fascism: Definition and Comparison*. Madison: University of Wisconsin Press, 1980.

Pechura, Constance M., and David P. Rall, eds., *Veterans at Risk: The Health Effects of Mustard Gas and Lewisite*. Washington, D.C.: National Academy Press, 1993.

Pencak, William. *For God and Country: The American Legion, 1919-1941*. Boston: Northeastern University Press, 1989.

Peters, Robert. *For You, Lili Marlene: A Memoir of World War II*. Madison: University of Wisconsin Press, 1996.

Petersen, Eugene T., ed. *A Chance for Love: The World War II Letters of Marian Elizabeth Smith and Lt. Eugene T. Petersen, USMCR*. East Lansing: Michigan State University Press, 1998.

Pitkin, R. B. *How the First GI Bill Was Written*. Indianapolis: American Legion Press, 1969.

Plano. Jack C. *Fishhooks, Apples, and Outhouses*. Kalamazoo, Mich.: Personality Press, 1991.

Prentice-Hall. *Veteran's Guide*. New York: Prentice-Hall, 1945.

Prost, Antoine. *In the Wake of War: "Les Ancien Combattants" and French Society*. New York: Berg, 1992.

————. *Les anciens combattants et la société française, 1914-1939*. 3 vols. Paris: Fondation Nationale des Sciences Politiques, 1977.

Pyle, Ernie. *Brave Men*. New York: Henry Holt, 1944.

Reister, Frank A., ed. *Medical Statistics in World War II*. Washington, D.C.: Department of the Army, 1975.

Remand, René. "Les Anciens Combattant et la Politique." *Revue française de science politique* 5 (1955): 267-290.

Resch, John P. *Suffering Soldiers: Revolutionary War Veterans, Moral Sentiment, and Political Culture in the Early Republic*. Amherst: University of Massachusetts Press, 1999.

Reuss, Henry S. *When Government Was Good: Memories of a Life in Politics*. Madison: University of Wisconsin Press, 1999.

Robinson, Harold, and John I. Robinson "State Spending for Veterans' Housing." *Wisconsin Law Review* 1949: 10-25.

Rood, Hosea W. *History of the Wisconsin Veterans' Home, 1886-1926*. Madison, Wis.: Democrat Press, 1926.

Rosenberg, Howard L. *Atomic Soldiers: American Victims of Nuclear Experiments*. Boston: Beacon Press, 1980.

Rosenburg, R. B. *Living Monuments: Confederate Soldiers' Homes in the New South*. Chapel Hill: University of North Carolina Press, 1993.

Ross, Davis R. B. *Preparing for Ulysses: Politics and Veterans during World War II*. New York: Columbia University Press, 1969.

Royster, Charles. *A Revolutionary People at War: The Continental Army and American Character, 1775-1783*. New York: Norton, 1979.

Rumer, Thomas A. *The American Legion: An Official History, 1919-1989*. New York: M. Evans, 1990.

Sauk County, Wisconsin, Board of Supervisors. *Proceedings*. Baraboo, Wisconsin, 1940-50.

Schnurr, Paula. "PTSD and Combat-Related Psychiatric Symptoms in Older Veterans." *PTSD Research Quarterly* 2 (1991): 1-2.

Scouller, R. E. *The Armies of Queen Anne*. London: Oxford University Press, 1966.

Scovill, Roger P. *What Did You Do, Grampa? The United States Marine Corps: An Artillery Enlisted Man's Memoir of World War II*. Madison, Wis.: Straus, 1994.

Severo, Richard, and Lewis Milford. *The Wages of War: When America's Soldiers Came Home—From Valley Forge to Vietnam.* New York: Simon and Schuster, 1989.

Shanahan, William O. *Prussian Military Reforms, 1786-1813.* New York: Columbia University Press, 1945.

Shay, Jonathan. *Achilles in Vietnam: Combat Trauma and the Undoing of Character.* New York: Scribner, 1994.

Sisson, A. F. *History of Veterans' Pensions and Related Benefits.* Washington, D.C.: American University, 1946.

Sivan, Hagith. "On *Foederati, Hospitalitas,* and the Settlement of the Goths in A.D. 418." *American Journal of Philology* 108 (1987): 759-772.

Skelley, Allan Ramsay. *The Victorian Army at Home: The Recruitment and Terms and Conditions of the British Regular, 1859-1899.* Montreal: McGill-Queen's University Press, 1977.

Skopcol, Theda. *Protecting Soldiers and Mothers: The Political Origins of Social Policy in the United States.* Cambridge, Mass.: Harvard University Press, 1992.

Smith, Herbert M. *Four Score and Ten: Happenings in the Life of Herbert M. Smith.* Eau Claire, Wis.: Heins, 1995.

Starr, Paul. *The Social Transformation of American Medicine.* New York: Basic Books, 1982.

Stewart, Robert E., and William M. Bernstock. *Veterans' Administration Prosthetic and Sensory Aids Program Since World War II.* Washington, D.C.: GPO, 1978.

Stouffer, Samuel, et al. *The American Soldier.* 2 vols. Princeton, N.J.: Princeton University Press, 1949.

Strecker, Edward A., and Kenneth E. Appel. *Psychiatry in Modern Warfare.* New York: Macmillan, 1945.

Sweet, George E. *The Wisconsin American Legion: A History, 1919-1992.* Milwaukee: Wisconsin American Legion Press, 1992.

Teicher, Barry, and John W. Jenkins. *A History of Housing at the University of Wisconsin.* Madison: University of Wisconsin History Project, 1987.

Thompson, Morton. *How to Be a Civilian.* Garden City, N.Y.: Doubleday, 1946.

Thompson, William F. *The History of Wisconsin.* Vol. 6, *Continuity and Change, 1940-1965.* Madison: State Historical Society of Wisconsin, 1988.

Trajkov, V., and S. Papadopolous. "La société Thraco-Bulgare en Grèce durant les années 40 du XIXe siècle." *Balkan Studies* 25 (1984): 573-582.

Trotter, Joe William, Jr. *Black Milwaukee: The Making of an Industrial Proletariat, 1915-45.* Chicago: University of Illinois Press, 1985.

Truman, Harry S. *Public Papers of the Presidents of the United States: Harry S. Truman.* 8 vols. Washington, D.C.: GPO, 1961-66.

Tyler, Robert L. "The American Veterans Committee: Out of a Hot War and into the Cold." *American Quarterly* 18 (1966): 419-436.

Uhl, Michael, and Tod Ensign. *GI Guinea Pigs.* Chicago: Playboy Press, 1980.

U.S. Bureau of the Census. *Eighteenth Census of the United States: Population.* Vol. 1, pt. 51. Washington, D.C.: GPO, 1960.

————. *Housing Characteristics in 108 Selected Areas: 1946 Veterans' Housing Surveys and the 1940 Census of Housing.* Washington, D.C.: GPO, 1946.

U.S. Civil Service Commission. *History of Veteran Civil Service Preference in Federal Employment, 1865-1955.* Washington, D.C.: GPO, 1955.

U.S. Congress. Congressional Research Service. *U.S. Military Personnel and Casualties in Principal Wars.* Washington, D.C.: Congressional Research Service, 1973.

U.S. Congress. House. Committee on Veterans' Affairs. *Laws Relating to Veterans and their Dependents Enacted on and after September 16, 1940.* 80th Cong., 2d sess., 1948. Committee Print 357.

————. *Medical Care of Veterans.* 90th Cong., 1st sess., 1967. Committee Print 4.

U.S. Congress. Joint Committee on Housing. *Hearings before the Joint Committee on Housing.* 80th Cong., 1st Sess., 1948. Vol. 1.

U.S. Department of Commerce. *Historical Statistics of the United States: Colonial Times to 1970.* Washington, D.C., GPO, 1975.

U.S. Navy. Bureau of Medicine and Surgery. *Medical Statistics, United States Navy.* Washington, D.C.: Navy Department, 1945.

U.S. Veterans' Administration. *Administrator of Veterans' Affairs Annual Report.* Washington, D.C.: GPO, 1940-60.

————. *Schedule for Rating Disabilities,* Washington, D.C.: GPO, 1945.

————. *Veterans in the State of Wisconsin.* Washington, D.C.: GPO, 1963.

University of Wisconsin-LaCrosse Oral History Project. *Vivid Memories of War: La Crosse Remembers World War II: An Oral History of La Crosse Area Veterans.* La Crosse: La Crosse Central High School; University of Wisconsin-La Crosse Oral History Project, 1996.

Urlanis, Boris. *Bilanz der Krieges: Menchenverluste Europas vom 17. Jahrhundert bis zur Gegenwart.* Berlin: Deutscher Verlag der Wissenschaft, 1965.

Van Ells, Mark D. *Serving Those Who Served: A History of Wisconsin's County Veterans' Service Officers.* Manitowoc, Wis.: County Veterans' Service Officers Association of Wisconsin, 1995.

Van Meerbeeck, Lucienne. "L'Hôpital Royale de l'Armée espagnole à Malines en l'an 1637." *Handelingen van de Koninklijke Kring voor Oudheidkunde, Lettern en Kunst van Mechelen* 54 (1950): 81-125.

Veterans of Foreign Wars, Department of Wisconsin. *Proceedings of the Annual Encampment, Veterans of Foreign Wars Department of Wisconsin.* Madison: Veterans for Foreign Wars, Department of Wisconsin, 1940-50.

Vinovskis, Maris, ed. *Toward A Social History of the Civil War: Exploratory Essays.* New York: Cambridge University Press, 1990.

Wade, Wyn Craig. *The Fiery Cross: The Ku Klux Klan in America.* London: Simon and Schuster, 1987.

Walch, Timothy. *Our Family, Our Town: Essays on Family and Local History Resources in the National Archives.* Washington, D.C.: National Archives, 1987.

Waller, Willard. *The Veteran Comes Back*. New York: Dryden Press, 1944.

Wallis, Allan D. *Wheel Estate: The Rise and Decline of Mobile Homes*. New York: Oxford University Press, 1991.

Wanke, Paul. "American Military Psychiatry and Its Role among Ground Forces in World War II." *Journal of Military History* 63 (1999): 127-146.

Ward, Stephen R., ed. *The War Generation: Veterans of the First World War*. Port Washington, N.Y.: Kennikat Press, 1975.

Watson, G. R. *The Roman Soldier*. London: Thames & Hudson, 1969.

Webb, Henry J. *Elizabethan Military Science: The Books and the Practice*. Madison: University of Wisconsin Press, 1965.

Wecter, Dixon. *When Johnny Comes Marching Home*. New York: Houghton Mifflin, 1944.

Weinberg, Gerhart. "World War II Scholarship: Now and in the Future." *Journal of Military History* 61 (1997): 335-346.

Welfeld, Irving. *Where We Live: The American Home and the Social, Economic, and Political Landscape, from Slums to Suburbs*. New York: Simon and Schuster, 1988.

Whalen, Robert Weldon. *Bitter Wounds: German Victims of the Great War, 1914-1939*. Ithaca, N.Y.: Cornell University Press, 1984.

Whayne, Tom F., and Michael E. DeBakey. *Cold Injury, Ground Type*. Washington, D.C.: Department of the Army, 1958.

Willenz, June A. *Women Veterans: America's Forgotten Heroines*. New York: Continuum, 1983.

Willoughby, John. "The Sexual Behavior of American GIs during the Early Years of Occupation in Germany. *Journal of Military History* 62 (1998): 155-174.

Wirtschafter, Elise Kimerling. "Social Misfits: Veterans and Soldiers' Families in Servile Russia." *Journal of Military History* 59 (1995): 215-236.

Wisconsin Department of Veterans' Affairs. *Farming in Wisconsin: Information for Veterans*. Madison: Wisconsin Department of Veterans' Affairs, 1945.

———. *Wisconsin Colleges and Universities Approved for Education of Veterans by Governor's Advisory Educational Committee*. Madison: Wisconsin Department of Veterans' Affairs, 1946.

Wisconsin Governor's Commission on Human Rights. *Nonwhite Housing in Wisconsin*. Madison: State of Wisconsin, 1954.

Wisconsin Industrial Commission. *Fair Employment*. Madison: Wisconsin Industrial Commission, 1948.

———. *Readjustment Allowances for Veterans*. Madison: Wisconsin Industrial Commission, 1945.

Wisconsin Industrial Commission. Fair Employment Division. *Report*, 1950-52. Madison, Wis.: Wisconsin Industrial Commission, 1952.

Wisconsin Legislative Reference Bureau. *A Thumbnail History of Wisconsin Veterans' Legislation*. Madison: Legislative Reference Bureau, 1988.

———. *Veterans' Housing Legislation in Wisconsin*. Madison, Wis.: Legislative Reference Bureau, 1953.

————. *Wisconsin Blue Book*. Madison: Legislative Reference Bureau, 1940-62.

Wisconsin Veterans' Home. *Annual Report for the Grand Army Home for Veterans*. Madison: State of Wisconsin, 1940-60.

Wisconsin Veterans' Housing Authority. *Conference on Veterans' Housing*. Madison: Wisconsin Veterans' Housing Authority, 1948.

————. *Summary of Housing Legislation and Notes on Programs*. Madison: Wisconsin Veterans' Housing Authority, 1948.

————. *Survey of Housing Accommodations of World War II Married Veterans*. Madison: Wisconsin Veterans' Housing Authority, 1948.

Wisconsin Veterans' Recognition Board. *Attention Returning Veterans (and Families of Veterans)*. Madison: Veterans' Recognition Board, 1943.

Woloch, Isser. *The French Veteran from the Revolution to the Restoration*. Chapel Hill: University of North Carolina Press, 1979.

Wootton, Graham. *The Politics of Influence: British Ex-Servicemen, Cabinet Decisions, and Cultural Change, 1917-1957*. London: Routledge & Kegan Paul, 1963.

Wright, Gwendolyn. *Building the Dream: A Social History of Housing in America*. Cambridge, Mass.: MIT Press, 1981.

Wyatt, Wilson. *Whistle Stops: Adventures in Public Life*. Lexington: University of Kentucky Press, 1985.

Wyman, Walker D., ed. *History of the Wisconsin State Universities, 1866-1968*. River Falls, Wis.: River Falls State University Press, 1968.

Wynn, Neil A. *The Afro-American and the Second World War*. Rev. ed. New York: Holmes & Meier, 1993.

Zeitlin, Richard H., and Mark D. Van Ells. "Politics, Community, Education: A Brief History of Veterans' Organizations in Wisconsin and America." *Wisconsin Academy Review* 40 (1994): 4-9.

Theses and Dissertations

William F. Fagelson. "From Combat to Conformity: Hollywood Narrative, World War II, and the Postwar Gender Crisis." M.A. thesis, University of Texas at Austin, 1997.

Kester, Kyra. "Shadows of War: The Historical Dimensions and Social Implications of Military Psychology and Veteran Counseling in the United States, 1860-1989." Ph.D. diss., University of Washington, 1992.

Spinti, Robert James. "The Development of Trade and Industrial Education in Wisconsin." Ed.D. diss., University of Missouri, 1968.

Trott, Jerry Maynard. "A Veterans' Advantage? World War II and Vietnam Compared." Ph.D., Duke University, 1989.

Index

About the Author

Mark D. Van Ells is assistant professor of history at Queensborough Community College of the City University of New York. He received his B.A., M.A., and Ph.D. degrees from the University of Wisconsin-Madison and is a native of the Badger State. Before assuming his present position with CUNY, he taught at Mt. Senario College and the University of Wisconsin-Platteville. He has also served as archivist/historian at the Wisconsin Veterans Museum in Madison. He presently lives in Westchester County, New York, with his wife and two daughters.